THE PATH OF LIGHT

Also by Anthony Seldon

Churchill's Indian Summer: The Conservative Government 1951–55
By Word of Mouth: Elite Oral History
Ruling Performance: Governments since 1945 (ed. with Peter Hennessy)
Political Parties Since 1945 (ed.)
The Thatcher Effect (ed. with Dennis Kavanagh)
Politics UK (joint author)
Conservative Century (ed. with Stuart Ball)
The Major Effect (ed. with Dennis Kavanagh)
The Heath Government 1970–1974 (ed. with Stuart Ball)
The Contemporary History Handbook (ed. with Brian Brivati et al.)
The Ideas That Shaped Post-War Britain (ed. with David Marquand)
How Tory Governments Fall (ed.)
Major: A Political Life
10 Downing Street: An Illustrated History
The Powers Behind the Prime Minister (with Dennis Kavanagh)
Britain under Thatcher (with Daniel Collings)
The Foreign Office: An Illustrated History
A New Conservative Century (with Peter Snowdon)
The Blair Effect 1997–2001 (ed.)
Public and Private Education: The Divide Must End
Partnership not Paternalism
Brave New City: Brighton & Hove, Past, Present, Future
The Conservative Party: An Illustrated History (with Peter Snowdon)
New Labour, Old Labour: The Wilson and Callaghan Governments, 1974–79
Blair
The Blair Effect 2001–5 (ed. with Dennis Kavanagh)
Recovering Power: The Conservatives in Opposition since 1867 (ed. with Stuart Ball)
Blair Unbound (with Peter Snowdon and Daniel Collings)
Blair's Britain 1997–2007 (ed.)
Trust: How We Lost it and How to Get It Back
An End to Factory Schools
Why Schools, Why Universities?
Brown at 10 (with Guy Lodge)
Public Schools and the Great War (with David Walsh)
Schools United
The Architecture of Diplomacy (with Daniel Collings)
Beyond Happiness: The Trap of Happiness and How to Find Deeper Meaning and Joy
The Coalition Effect, 2010–2015 (ed. with Mike Finn)
Cameron at 10 (with Peter Snowdon)
Teaching and Learning at British Universities
The Cabinet Office 1916–2016 – The Birth of Modern British Government (with Jonathan Meakin)
The Positive and Mindful University (with Alan Martin)
The Fourth Education Revolution (with Oladimeji Abidoye)
May at 10 (with Raymond Newell)
Public Schools and the Second World War (with David Walsh)
Fourth Education Revolution Reconsidered (with Oladimeji Abidoye and Timothy Metcalf)
The Impossible Office? The History of the British Prime Minister (with Jonathan Meakin and Illias Thoms)
The Path of Peace: Walking the Western Front Way
Johnson at 10 (with Raymond Newell)
Truss at 10 (with Jonathan Meakin)

THE PATH OF LIGHT

WALKING TO AUSCHWITZ

ANTHONY SELDON

Atlantic Books
London

First published in hardback in Great Britain in 2025 by Atlantic Books, an imprint of Atlantic Books Ltd.

Copyright © Anthony Seldon, 2025

The moral right of Anthony Seldon to be identified as the author of this work has been asserted by him in accordance with the Copyright, Designs and Patents Act of 1988.

All rights reserved. No part of this publication may be reproduced, stored in a retrieval system, or transmitted in any form or by any means, electronic, mechanical, photocopying, recording, or otherwise, without the prior permission of both the copyright owner and the above publisher of this book.

No part of this book may be used in any manner in the learning, training or development of generative artificial intelligence technologies (including but not limited to machine learning models and large language models (LLMs)), whether by data scraping, data mining or use in any way to create or form a part of data sets or in any other way.

The picture acknowledgements on p. 357 constitute an extension of this copyright page.

Every effort has been made to trace or contact all copyright holders. The publishers will be pleased to make good any omissions or rectify any mistakes brought to their attention at the earliest opportunity.

Map artwork by Jess Macaulay.

10 9 8 7 6 5 4 3 2 1

A CIP catalogue record for this book is available from the British Library.

Hardback ISBN: 978 1 80546 410 5
E-book ISBN: 978 1 80546 411 2

Printed and bound by CPI (UK) Ltd, Croydon CR0 4YY

Atlantic Books
An imprint of Atlantic Books Ltd
Ormond House
26–27 Boswell Street
London
WC1N 3JZ

www.atlantic-books.co.uk

Product safety EU representative: Authorised Rep Compliance Ltd., Ground Floor, 71 Lower Baggot Street, Dublin, D02 P593, Ireland. www.arccompliance.com

This book is dedicated to two transcendent figures of light, Dietrich Bonhoeffer (1906–45) and Etty Hillesum (1914–43), both victims of Nazism.

God is light; in him there is no darkness at all.
1 John 1:5

Contents

	Preface	1
1	Crossing the Rhine	11
2	Black Forest, White Rose	39
3	Swiftly Flows the Danube: Ulm to Donauwörth	73
4	One Way, Four Paths: From Donauwörth to Nuremberg	99
5	The Road to Flossenbürg	129
6	Sudetenland: From Flossenbürg to Prague	175
7	Prague, Lidice, Terezín	209
8	Central and East Bohemia: Prague to Pardubice	241
9	Into Moravia: Pardubice to Ostrava	271
10	Silesia, Poland, Auschwitz	307
	Epilogue	351
	Illustration Credits	365
	Notes	367
	Acknowledgements	385
	Index	387

Preface

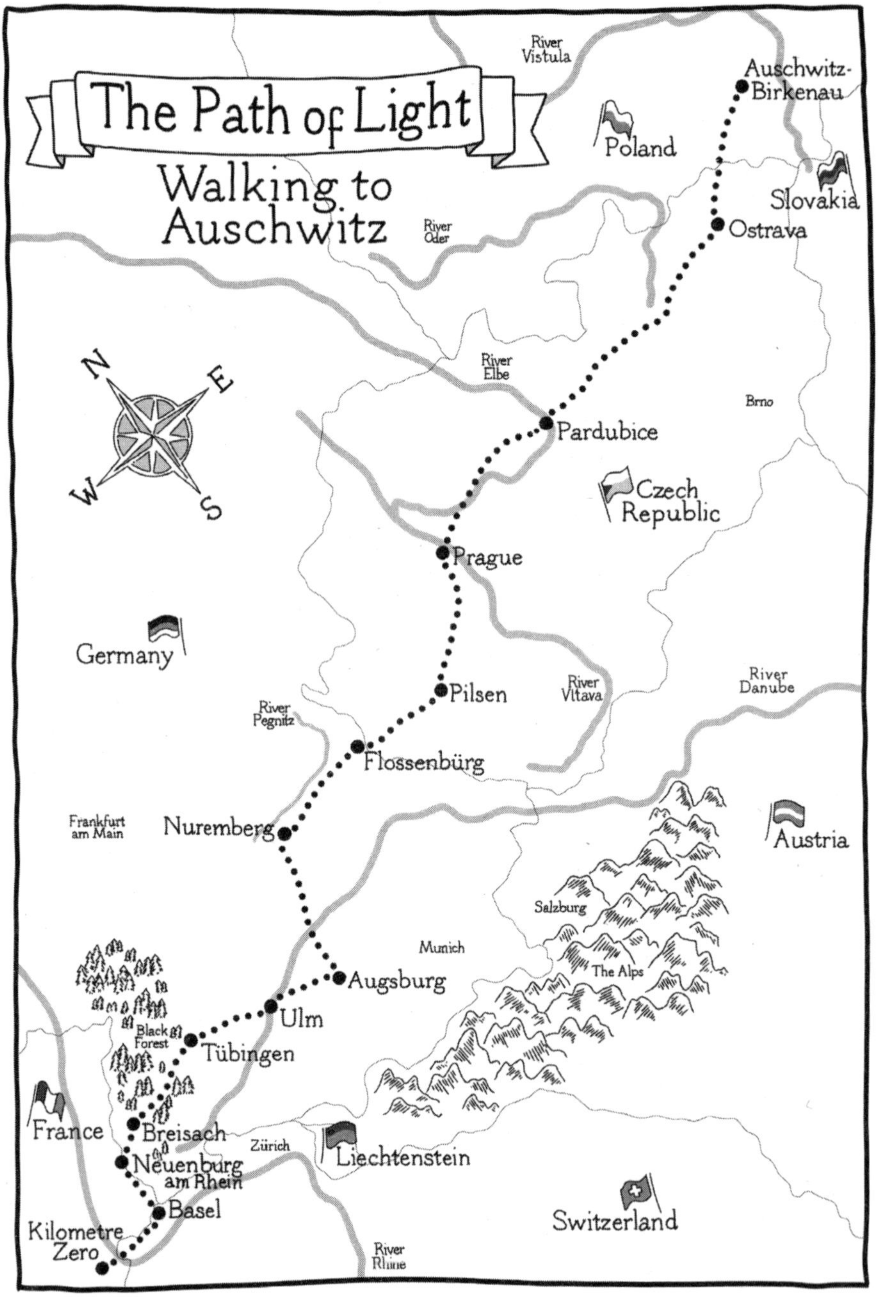
The Path of Light
Walking to Auschwitz
River Vistula
Auschwitz-Birkenau
Poland
Slovakia
River Oder
Ostrava
N
E
W
S
River Elbe
Brno
Pardubice
Czech Republic
Prague
Germany
River Vltava
River Danube
Pilsen
River Pegnitz
Flossenbürg
Frankfurt am Main
Nuremberg
Austria
Salzburg
Munich
The Alps
Augsburg
Ulm
Black Forest
Tübingen
France
Breisach
Zürich
Liechtenstein
Neuenburg am Rhein
Basel
Switzerland
Kilometre Zero
River Rhine

I MUST WALK TO Auschwitz. I will have failed the biggest challenge of my life if I don't. Since my mid-teens, the concentration camp has possessed me. I have never understood why. Visiting it, as I had done on five occasions, hadn't provided answers. Might travelling to it the long way, by foot, confronting my own inner demons as I did so, unlock any light? Step by painful step, I thus decided to walk across Europe till I arrived in south-eastern Poland where Auschwitz and its string of subordinate camps lie just 200 kilometres short of the border with Ukraine.

Auschwitz is the darkest example in history of intentional mass barbarity. The apex of evil and cruelty. Would I be hearing in the villages, towns and cities along my route yet more stories of man's inhumanity during the Nazi era (1933–45)? In the eighty years since the war ended have we heard enough perhaps about human depravity? Is a rebalancing needed? So I decided instead to unearth stories, if I could, of human goodness, compassion and courage along my trail. I wanted to be uplifted on my way by learning about men and women of honour who at great risk protected those deemed by the Nazis to be 'others'. I craved not more tales of human darkness, though inevitably and for contrast my story would contain some, but human light. I am going to walk to Auschwitz in search of light. To create indeed a 'path of light' across the heart of Europe to uplift others, perhaps even to lighten their darkness. To provide a different narrative to the light of despair of the Auschwitz crematoria whose chimneys belched out burning human embers, illuminating even the darkest night skies between 1941 and 1945.

I had already walked half the distance. Task half done! During the second Covid summer, 2021, I travelled by foot from 'Kilometre Zero' where the trenches of the First World War abruptly ended at the Swiss border, to Nieuwpoort on the North Sea where the front line began on the Belgian coast.[1] That 1,000-kilometre walk, which took me 1 million steps through soil where 10 million fell, was designed to encourage a permanent path along No Man's Land that we called the 'Western Front Way', conceived originally in a British officer's letter I had discovered by chance when researching a book on the First World War. The soldier with the rousing vision, one of the most uplifting to emerge from the war, Douglas Gillespie, was killed shortly after writing it down; his letter then lay dormant for a hundred years. I recounted the story of its discovery and the walk in *The Path of Peace*, published in 2022. One of the themes is that we are all affected today by the trauma of what happened in those four shattering years between 1914 and 1918; though distant, the Great War's ghosts still linger. This present volume, focused on the Second World War, is a sequel. I would set out on this walk from the exact point, Kilometre Zero, where the first walk started, and where hostilities ceased when the First World War ended.

My intention was to start out in the spring of 2023 and complete the walk before the weather turned, walking day by day east from Kilometre Zero till I arrived some 1,300 kilometres later at Auschwitz. But unlike that first walk, there was no former front line to follow, no line of *villages détruits (destroyed villages)* nor of vast cemeteries. Instead, I would walk east, on as direct a path as possible. I had a vague idea of my travel: Basel, Freiburg, Ulm, Augsburg, Nuremberg, Flossenbürg, Prague and Kraków, but otherwise I did not know what fate had in store. I wanted to walk along as many rivers as possible, a particular passion, through the four countries: France, Germany, the Czech Republic and Poland. The plan was to finish walking by the end of summer, and have the book written by Christmas 2023.

PREFACE

It was nearly time to depart when on the evening of Sunday 12 February, returning from a walk to prepare for the journey, my phone rang. 'You don't know me, but I'm Dr Alastair Wells, chair of governors at Epsom College.' I'd heard of the tragedy at his school the previous weekend from my children. I had been head of two schools and our three children had been brought up in heads' houses in the midst of the campuses. Emma Pattison, Epsom's radiant and brilliant new headmistress, and her seven-year-old daughter had been murdered in the head's house in the middle of the school, presumably by the husband who then killed himself. I thought I was going to be asked for advice on who might come in to run the school. Instead, he asked me if I could take it on myself. I hadn't expected that. 'When?' I stuttered. 'Immediately.' 'Let me talk to my wife Sarah,' I replied. My first wife Joanna, the mother of our children, had died six years before from cancer, and I had married Sarah less than a year ago. We were still building our lives together. I felt instinctively I had to do it, 'running towards the fire' the image in my head. Sarah is far more practical than I am. She saw quicker that it would turn our lives upside down. But she readily agreed. We both knew in our hearts it was the right thing to do.

I was to be at Epsom for eighteen months until the summer holidays of 2024. Being head of a boarding school is a more than a full-time job. The only way I knew how to do it was to throw myself into the life completely, which meant spending most evenings and weekends at school, doing what I could to bring everyone through the tragedy as positively and cheerfully as possible. Not a day went by when I didn't think about Emma and her family. I wanted to preserve her memory as best I could. I didn't even change her study whose redecoration in lily white with lavender curtains had only been completed the week I arrived. I always felt a deep peace in the room: never fear, but a sense of her benign presence. A room of light indeed.

The unexpected job meant that I would have to rethink my strategy for the walk. Very well, I thought. No longer can I do this in one haul as with the Great War walk. I would have to break it up into bite-size chunks, fitting them in around school holidays, book writing and other commitments, all of which had piled up remorselessly. I would try to make a virtue out of necessity, and walk less punishingly than in 2021.

Finding time to juggle running a school with walking proved to be just one of the challenges I would face. I had not grown younger since the first walk and was now on the cusp of my seventieth birthday. Perhaps three score years and ten is meant to be our natural span. Certainly, after a life with barely a day lost through illness, I was to find myself suddenly assaulted by an unexpected health problem, as readers will hear. I would have to learn to take more care of myself this time. I had made so many naive blunders on that first walk which culminated in four separate outpatient visits to hospital. The day after I returned home in late September 2021, I awoke to find I was unable to move more than a few metres. I had pushed myself to the very limits of my endurance, perhaps beyond, and was in a state of physical and mental exhaustion. My body recovered after a few days, but not my feet. Walking for at least six hours a day for thirty-five days with only one short break for my daughter's wedding had stripped layers of skin off my soles and ankles. I had foolishly assumed that, because I could walk 35 kilometres in one day, I could walk that distance day after day. The stupidity of it. Inflexible boots and rough socks added to my folly, and it meant that towards the end of the walk, every time I put my foot down on the ground, searing pain shot from my soles up both legs. Looking back, I could have done myself serious harm, not least walking with a heavy load by the side of busy roads in the heat of the midday sun or when overtired at the end of the day. I was just a stumble away from potential disaster. This time round, I determined, what my body might lack in youth could be made up for in wisdom. Or so I hoped.

The very distance, 1,300 rather than 1,000 kilometres through four countries with no precise route to follow, posed further challenges. So too would be walking eastwards away from home rather than westwards back towards it, as I consciously did on the first walk. Would having as my destination Auschwitz rather than home prove a psychological block? True, I was looking for light on my way, and choosing to enter the camp on foot rather than being herded there at gunpoint in cattle carriages. I could leave whenever I wanted. But my goal of those infamous gates, with the words 'Arbeit macht frei' ('work sets you free') above them, was still daunting.

The hope of establishing a permanent trail had proved vital in keeping me going in 2021, especially after the walk became hard, lonely and painful. The widely publicized mission to raise awareness of the Western Front Way and thereby boost the number of travellers meant I dare not fail. But would I be as fired up by the mission of this second walk as I had been by the first? I wasn't sure. Would I really find telling examples of human bravery and compassion along my route? Thanks to Steven Spielberg's film *Schindler's List*, everyone knew the story of German factory-owner Oskar Schindler, who rescued hundreds of Jewish workers from the crematoria by putting them to work in his plants. But were there others like him, whose stories were untold? Was he really as good a man as has been made out, and could I be sure other figures of light I might encounter were genuine?

The timing of the new book's publication, in the eightieth anniversary year of the end of the Second World War, would be a spur. I wanted to probe what exactly we would be remembering, now the sacrifice of those who had fought was passing out of living memory. Would the anniversary be anything more than an excuse for celebrating a historic victory and indulging in a pageant of nostalgia and films? It made me all the more eager to find or revive stories that would uplift and inspire the young and old. The sorrow I feared is that the names and deeds of many of the most remarkable heroes will have been erased from human knowledge: the million selfless acts by soldiers caring for others on battlefields, of civilians surviving endless bombing raids or protecting victims, and prisoners sacrificing their food for others in the camps, all lost. But if I could highlight the lives of inspiring heroes might it provide an alternative to the toxic and misogynistic influencers filling the minds of young people? To the nihilism of so much of social media?

The walk was under way at the time of the 7 October 2023 invasion of Israel by Hamas and the brutal war that has followed. Developments in that violent struggle were to form its constant backdrop. The sufferings of the Jews have continued throughout history across Europe. Their victimization down the ages would be a leitmotif of the walk. The Holocaust hastened the establishment of the State of Israel in 1948. I am deeply convinced that Israel has a right to exist behind secure borders. But do the country's leaders of today have a duty to conduct themselves in a more enlightened way (that word 'light' again) than Jews themselves have been treated by others? This would be one of the many difficult moral questions I must confront.

I wanted this book to probe the nature of what we mean by goodness and courage. I studied Philosophy as part of my undergraduate degree. Rather than asking us students to tackle questions of good and evil, right and wrong, justice and injustice, we were fed a diet of dry philosophical texts by Hegel and Nietzsche, with, to me, little real world application. This, I suspected, suited the interest of academic philosophers, but was of less interest to young minds eager to engage with the big questions of life. I wanted my book to explore these questions in the real crucible of war, and ask why so few challenged the brutal regime. Why was the Judaeo-Christian injunction to 'love your neighbour' so little followed, not least by ordained ministers? What character and motivation lay behind those who did stand up? How might we react today if we faced the appalling moral dilemmas that Nazism presented? Would we do the 'right' thing if it placed our families or communities at risk? Were those who stayed quiet afraid of the consequences of acting, and why did so many believe that the genocide of an entire race of people, namely the Jews, together with Slavs, Roma, homosexuals, the mentally and physically ill and political prisoners, was justified to build a 'purer' world?

The walk was going to be a personal pilgrimage too. Might it help me become a kinder person, a better husband and face up to my inner turmoil including the fear of failure and inadequacy that has stalked me all my life? I discuss whether I found any answers to the questions I pose above in the Epilogue.

The book was given added piquancy by the rise of populism and aggressively nationalist leaders. The background noise to this book was, besides the Middle East, the war in Ukraine, the emergence of pro-Russia leaders in Eastern Europe, the election of Donald Trump, the ambitions of President Xi of China, President Putin, and the pivot of the United States away from Europe for the first time so strongly since 1945. Key dates like flagstones paved my way to Auschwitz: 24 February 2022, the Russian invasion of Ukraine; 7 October 2023, Hamas's attack on Israel; 8 December 2024, the fall of the Assad regime in Syria; 20 January 2025, the second inauguration of President Trump; 20 June 2025, the US attack on Iran's nuclear facilities, either reducing or enhancing the risk of a Third World War. Each new flagstone was taking us closer to what? And where was the voice of the overlooked men and women everywhere who just wanted peace and friendship, not to go to war at the behest of their leaders? Not for me, leaders who want to separate and divide. I wanted my walk to encourage people to find what they share in common with others, not what divides them. That quest, in a world in which hate and aggressive nationalism are on the rise, would really spur me on.

Finally a confession. I have skin in the game. My father Arthur Seldon was Jewish, the child of Ukrainian immigrants who had fled the pogroms only to perish in East London in the influenza plague at the end of the First World War. My three children would all have been condemned by the Nazis because they had three grandparents who were Jewish. My mother Marjorie Willett was Christian, so in line with Jewish law, I converted to Judaism to marry my first wife Joanna, who was Jewish. I recall Hugo Gryn, the celebrated rabbi telling us about an episode he experienced in the concentration camps in the final winter of the war, 1944–45. During the Jewish festival of Chanukah, the festival of light, it is customary for Jews to light candles. His father lit a wick in a bowl of margarine, only for it to sputter out, because margarine does not burn. Hugo protested and wept at the apparently futile gesture; they needed the food and could not waste it on a candle. His father replied, 'You and I had to go once for over a week without proper food and another time almost three days without water, but you cannot live for three minutes without hope!'[2]

That hope of candles burning dimly is a powerful example of light. Light indeed at the end of the path of light.

1

Crossing the Rhine

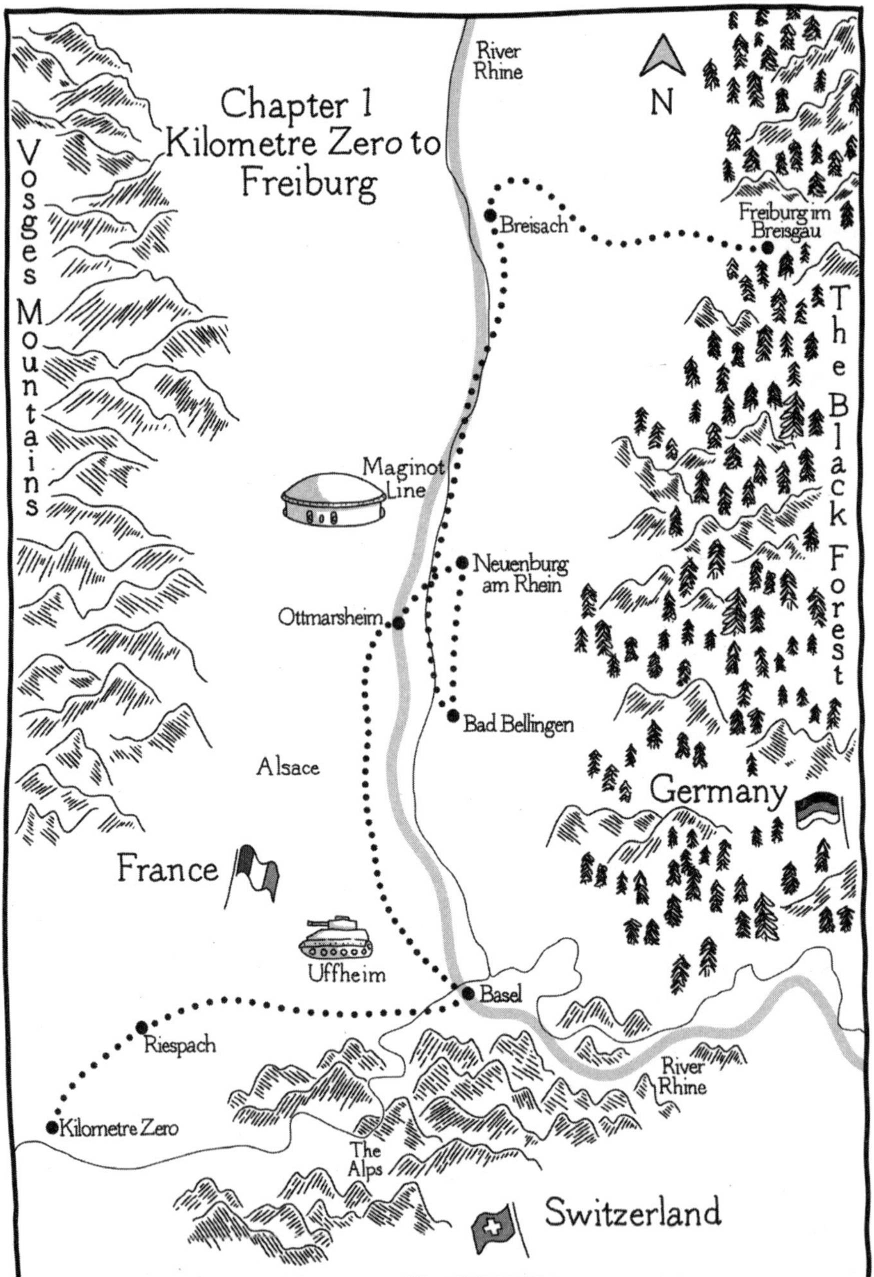

Chapter 1
Kilometre Zero to
Freiburg
River
Rhine
N
Vosges Mountains
Breisach
Freiburg im
Breisgau
The Black Forest
Maginot
Line
Neuenburg
am Rhein
Ottmarsheim
Bad Bellingen
Alsace
Germany
France
Uffheim
Basel
Riespach
River
Rhine
Kilometre Zero
The
Alps
Switzerland

'Do you think you can do it?'

'I've done it before.'

'And look at how difficult you found it! Do you really have to walk all the way?'

'Of course I do,' I shoot back.

'But why? Honestly? It will be so much harder than last time.'

I go quiet. One thousand three hundred kilometres. Route, unknown and perhaps unfindable. Languages I cannot speak. Heroes it may be impossible to find. And time, how will I now find it?

It is the 2023 summer holidays and we are driving across northern France to the Swiss border for the start of the great adventure. Sarah's questions have touched a raw nerve. At heart, I am not confident I can make it work. Is that why, in contrast to the Western Front walk which I told everyone about who would listen, I have kept this walk virtually a secret? Once I started at Epsom College in February, we moved into rented accommodation halfway between it and Sarah's school, complicating her life greatly, and now the summer term is over, whoosh, we are off.

We put on The Rest is History podcast, appropriately about my hoped-for destination, Auschwitz. Journalist Jonathan Freedland is discussing his book *The Escape Artist* about Rudolf Vrba (born Walter Rosenberg) who in April 1944 broke out from the concentration camp and survived, having committed to memory every last detail of the horror that he had witnessed, including the numbers of trains arriving, the origin of the passengers and the fate that befell them, helping himself remember by reciting each morning his accumulating 'mountain of facts'.[1] It gives me an idea.

'Do you think I could count Vrba as the book's first "figure of light"?' I ask Sarah. We talk it over. Technically, my self-imposed 'rule' is that I have to discover a connection with a courageous person along the actual route I am walking, otherwise the book will just become a compendium of heroic people in the Second World War from across Europe. Sarah, as a languages teacher, can be disconcertingly precise. But we decide, yes, he qualifies. I have my first figure of light, and I haven't even started walking yet!

Vrba escaped across southern Poland and into Slovakia, but once in safety found himself caught up in a different battle, to be believed by sceptical authorities who couldn't or wouldn't accept the shocking truth he was telling them. He warned that preparations were being made for the mass murder of Hungary's still untouched Jewish population and that they must be alerted.[2] The Slovakian Jewish Council questioned him for six hours, and he had felt that he had won them round, but was bitterly frustrated when they did not apprise the Jewish Council in occupied Hungary. He and his fellow escaper, Alfred Wetzler, met repeated brick walls even after they subsequently wrote their famous Vrba-Wetzler Report, published in November 1944 by the US government. What clearer example of courage and selflessness could there be to inspire me at the very outset of my path of light?[3]

We break the journey at 8 p.m. at Reims where, for nostalgia, we book into the same hotel, the Campanile on the Aisne-Marne canal, where I'd stayed on the Western Front walk two years before. Enticing champagne bottles are everywhere on offer but we opt for a quiet dinner in the hotel and an early night. The next day, we drive down to Kilometre Zero, the place where the insanity of the Western Front collided with neutral Switzerland's border, covering the sixteen days I spent walking two years before, I noted wryly, in under five hours.

Kilometre Zero, two years on.

By 3 p.m. we are back at the famous if little-visited landmark on the Swiss border, looking remarkably unchanged over the two years. Sarah photographs me with my foot on the same pillbox as in August 2021. This time the sun is shining and we joke together; I note how much more relaxed I am now even if I miss the confident energy of that first trip. Kilometre Zero is as deserted and silent as it would have been on Armistice Day, 11 November 1918. By then, the French and German soldiers here had no appetite left to kill each other. The serious fighting since March 1918 had been going on north-west of the Vosges mountains, starting with the great German Spring Offensive that broke the trench stalemate, followed by an unstoppable Allied counterattack in Champagne, Picardy, Artois and Flanders that ended in Allied victory.

The German army commanders had in fact forgotten Alsace and much of the area had succumbed to anarchy, with a 'Republic of Alsace Lorraine' declared to the raising of red flags in Strasbourg on 8 November. News of the Armistice on 11 November received a mixed response from the German soldiers who were given stern orders to evacuate Alsace altogether within fifteen days.[4] Some were eager to get back to the Fatherland to fight for or against Communist uprisings, most were just happy to have survived, and a few bitterly pined for revenge. Only six days passed before the last of the German soldiers crossed the Rhine, on 17 November. Four days later, the French tricolour was raised in Strasbourg for the first time since the territory was annexed by the Germans in 1871.[5] A rapid policy of 're-Gallicization' took place in this most disputed of European territories: German place names were returned to their original French spellings, and over 111,000 Germans who had settled in Alsace during the previous forty-five years were promptly expelled, foreshadowing the century's later 'ethnic cleansing'.[6]

Twenty-one short years later, following the fall of France in 1940, the Germans were back, and promptly re-Germanized both Alsace and Lorraine, attaching them administratively to Baden-Baden on the opposite bank of the Rhine. French language, press, stamps, currency, street and place names were all re-Germanized. Those people with given names that were French had to have them changed to the German equivalent. Any inhabitants considered undesirable, including Jews, North Africans and Asians, were expelled, some 35,000 in total, the Nazi Party, police and administrators ensuring that the party ruled over all aspects of life.[7]

Alsace was overseen by Gauleiter (Nazi district leader) Robert Wagner, the polar opposite to Auschwitz escapee Rudolf Vrba. Whereas the latter risked his life repeatedly to save as many Jews as possible, the former set great store by killing as many Jews as possible. How did these two men born into similar middle-class homes in Central Europe become such utterly different human beings? Was it their innate characters or life circumstances that made one a fearless hero and the other a vile monster? In the First World War, Wagner had fought in Ypres, the Somme and Verdun and was wounded by gas. A chance meeting with Adolf Hitler in September 1923 captivated him and changed his life. He took part in the Beer Hall Putsch in Munich in November 1923, stood trial with Hitler and was jailed alongside him in Landsberg prison. Soon after Wagner took over as Gauleiter, Hitler told him that he wanted Alsace and Lorraine Germanized. 'Wagner wielded the same powers in respect of Alsace as Hitler did in the rest of the Reich', read the Allied indictment when he was arrested after the war.[8] He responded with relish to the request to rid the territories of all Jews, seven train loads promptly departing for concentration camps in October 1940, with Wagner proud to report to Berlin that his was the first province in greater Germany to be 'cleansed of Jews'. Then in June 1943, he authorized some one hundred Jews to be transferred from Auschwitz back to Natzweiler concentration camp in Alsace where they were gassed, their corpses being sent to a German professor, August Hirt, in Strasbourg for their skulls and skeletons to be studied as evidence for racial theory.[9] As Allied forces advanced after D-Day, Wagner refused to give up the fight until April 1945, when he tried to flee. He was arrested by the Americans in July 1945, handed over to the French, tried, convicted and put before a firing squad at Belfort in August 1946. Unrepentant to the end, 'Long live Adolf Hitler, long live National Socialism' were his final words on earth.[10]

Vrba too stayed true to his beliefs, continuing to state for the rest of his life the uncomfortable, if contested, truth that the authorities were slow to act on their report and alert the world to the fate of the Jews departing in the cattle trucks. With 12,000 leaving Hungary every day to concentration camps after he had warned the Jewish Council in spring 1944, at least some of the 400,000 Hungarians murdered that

*Robert Wagner, left, murderous Nazi ruler of Alsace, and
Rudolf Vrba, right, who tried to save lives.*

summer might have been saved.[11] His unforgiving belligerence, towards both the Allied and Jewish leaders who had not acted on his words, cost him friends and recognition: when he died in 2006, only forty people turned up to a memorial event in his honour in Vancouver.[12]

* * *

So here I am, ready to set off on the second walk. I'm feeling the model of a professional walker, with much suppler boots, super-dry merino socks, ultra-lightweight trousers and top, and an improved direction finder on my phone. What could possibly go wrong? I stride boldly north towards Pfetterhouse. Ten minutes later, Sarah drives past me in the car: 'You know you've set off in totally the wrong direction?' Her calm voice is quite extraordinarily irritating. 'I am not an idiot,' I protest. She shows me her map, I admit I am an idiot, and arrange to meet her at a location due east in four hours. An inauspicious start. I wait for her to drive off so she doesn't see me retrace my footsteps, before walking along winding tracks to the village of Mooslargue, then setting off across fields to Riespach. My confidence takes a second hit as I'm walking on a track past a farm, and I don't hear a small bulldog come up behind me till he has my fist in his mouth. He could have done me some harm but I think he was just seeing if I had any food in my hand: there are no teeth marks. I decide to take a track through some woods, but then totally lose the path, my map is no help, and there's no connection to Google Maps on my phone. I listen for traffic, follow the noise and come out on a busy road, take my bag off to adjust it when an overtaking car on the other side of the road misses me by half a metre. A warning to be more careful. The day finishes along beautiful tracks and lanes into my destination, the Alsatian village of Riespach, after a walk of just over 15 kilometres.

Over a glass of Riesling with Sarah in the square, we take stock. Only now I am back walking has the truth come fully home to me that on this walk, there isn't a No Man's Land, no front lines, nor battles and monuments to guide me. There will be a million ways to walk to Auschwitz, and I'm having to choose one that will maximize historical learning while minimizing distance and difficult terrain. We discuss taking in a few cities, including Ulm, Prague and Nuremberg, while going the most direct way possible. As the crow flies, it is 925 kilometres. I'd be surprised, though, if it takes me less than the expected 1,300 kilometres to get there. A plane would cover the distance in an hour and a half; a car perhaps fifteen hours. But by foot? Anyone's guess. I've got to take this one day at a time. But this evening, it's a half-hour journey with Sarah navigating the car flawlessly to the Rhine village of Bad Bellingen, followed by a warm shower, dinner and bed. Fifteen kilometres might not be very much for Day 1, but I'm on my way. Only 1,285 kilometres to go!

I cannot remember a more blissful day walking along the Western Front than my second day out. I'm heading due east into the rising sun towards the Rhine. If Kent is the 'garden of England', then Alsace is the 'garden of France': I see agapanthus, bougainvillea, hibiscus, dahlias, hydrangeas, marigolds, peonies, roses and zinnias, a blaze of reds, golds, yellows and blues. The half and fully timbered houses with overhanging upper storeys have distinctive steep pitched roofs with *tuiles écailles alsaciennes* (flat clay tiles). All are beautifully maintained, rich in local symbols and decorations, including floral motifs and embedded woodwork in all manner of patterns, including the St Andrew's Cross. Even in the height of summer, the aroma of burning logs lingers. As I walk, I catch glimpses of the Vosges mountains to the west, the Black Forest to the east and, further still to the south, the Alps.

As I approach the village of Uffheim, I chance upon a museum to the Maginot Line. A more futile legacy of the First World War can hardly be imagined than this pre-1939 defensive fortification. When travelling through Verdun two years before, I passed the spot where French soldier André Maginot had been wounded in 1914. While fighting, he had been captivated by the impressively resilient fortresses at Vaux and Douaumont. In the 1920s, Maginot, by now a government minister, campaigned tirelessly for a string of similar fortifications to be built along the eastern border of France. Seventy per cent of French soldiers who fought in the First World War had become casualties, and 1.4 million died, 900 for every day of the war, leaving the nation in widow's weeds.[13] Surely, Maginot asked, there was a better way to defend France, with concrete not flesh?

Fascinated, I enter the museum and find it has much to teach me about his vision. Stretching for 400 kilometres and up to 25 kilometres deep, the Maginot Line was largely completed by the time the Second World War broke out. Its singular aim was to deter a future German invasion, such as France had suffered twice in the preceding seventy years. If there was to be a war, the French soldiers would duly be hidden behind casemate and concrete, saving their precious lives. The massive Maginot defence fortifications included underground electric railways, power stations, 142 major fortresses and 5,000 blockhouses.[14] Additionally, strong mobile forces – drawn from the cream of France's army – were created to protect those parts of northern France that the defensive fortifications did not. The genius of the Maginot Line, it was argued, was that it allowed fewer men to protect more of the country, while the mobile forces could fight the Germans on their own terms.

When the war came, the line did its job superbly well; the Germans never did attack it in strength. It just didn't matter. The Germans instead drove their tanks through the 'impenetrable' Ardennes forest, bypassing the mighty fortifications, before destroying the French army's mobile forces at Sedan between 12 and 17 May 1940. As the German tanks broke through, the British forces escaped to Dunkirk, and the French government began to consider the hitherto unthinkable: capitulation.[15]

Not wanting, after 1945, to waste an asset into which they had pumped so much of their national wealth in the interwar years, the French remanned the Maginot Line after the fighting was over, just in case. But the advent of nuclear weapons, and the abandonment by Germany of any hostile intent to France, meant the line was mostly left to the elements from the 1960s. Now it is a monument to both folly and misjudgement.

The sun is still beating down on Day 3, 10 August. Fortified by a hearty dinner in a rural tavern in the hills above Bad Bellingen where Sarah and I were delighted to find ourselves the only English people, and by a good night's sleep, I set out to reach the Rhine today or tomorrow, before walking into Germany. I only have to work out where to cross the river that forms a 184-kilometre border between both countries from Basel up to Lauterbourg to the north of Strasbourg. As I set off walking this morning I find myself overcome by a wave of emotion to be on the threshold of striding into Germany. True I have only walked 40 kilometres since Kilometre Zero, but putting this and the 2021 walk together, I have now walked across Belgium and France. What will Germany bring, I wonder?

My path takes me to the outskirts of a landmark city where we must linger awhile because it contains several stories that will shed light on my quest. Basel is one of Europe's most beguiling international cities (pronounced 'Basle' in English), and has become the post-1945 Kilometre Zero in the sense that it is the meeting point of the same three countries, France, Germany and Switzerland. The cultural capital of the last and its third largest city (behind Geneva and Zürich), Swiss Basel blends seamlessly into German Basel and a small French town (Bâle), with the houses intertwined over the national borders quite unlike any other city on earth. Why can bricks and mortar achieve what human beings find so difficult? Basel's deep commitment to internationalism and humanism brought a flock of leading thinkers to it throughout the ages, including early-modern Dutch humanist Erasmus, nineteenth-century German philosopher Friedrich Nietzsche and twentieth-century Swiss psychotherapist Carl Jung.

Central to our story, the city is the birthplace of the State of Israel, and paradoxically the location of some of the most virulent antisemitism. Basel was chosen in 1897 as the venue for the world's first Zionist Congress, chaired by prime mover Theodor Herzl, and it became the most popular venue for subsequent Jewish congresses until the objective was achieved, the creation of the State of Israel in 1948.

Herzl had lived in Vienna as a young man, but the rise of antisemitism promoted by demagogue and later Viennese mayor Karl Lueger convinced him that antisemitism could not be erased, that 'assimilation' for Jews alongside gentiles would never work, and that only a discrete Jewish homeland behind its own borders would keep Jews safe.[16] He travelled to London to enlist the support of prominent Jews for his objective, but though cheered at public meetings in the East End (where my Ukrainian grandparents were to settle), his ideas met a mixed reception from the community. Despondent at the response, he decided the best way forward was to organize a World Congress of Zionists to try to win backing from Jews across the great diaspora. Munich was his first choice of venue, given the sympathetic way Jews were then treated in the city; but most Jews in the Bavarian capital were happy with assimilation, and thought that talk of a Jewish homeland was unnecessary and potentially provocative. So Herzl settled on Basel for the Congress, to which came 200 delegates from seventeen countries. After it concluded, he wrote confidently in his diary: 'If I had to sum up the Basel Congress in one word... it would be this: at Basel I founded the Jewish state.' Seven years later, in 1904, he died from a heart condition at age forty-four.[17]

Basel also has a walk-on part in a key piece in the antisemitism jigsaw. At the forefront of Herzl's thinking about antisemitism was the experience of a Jewish Frenchman whose family had moved to Basel, to escape the German annexation of Alsace, and then to Paris, when he was still a child. Alfred Dreyfus went on to have a successful career as an artillery officer until he was arrested in 1894 and accused of selling French military secrets to Germany. Publicly humiliated, he was imprisoned until fresh evidence emerged of his innocence. The army and many at the top of French society nevertheless continued to insist on his guilt. As tensions rose, antisemitic riots broke out across France in 1898 and novelist Émile Zola published *J'accuse* charging the French elite with a mass cover up. Not till 1906 when Dreyfus was granted a full exoneration did the episode that had transfixed France for a decade begin to fade. The political right, though, have refused to let it be forgotten, most recently with Jean-Marie Le Pen, the late founder of France's far-right National Front, spreading suggestions of Dreyfus's guilt alongside outright Holocaust denial. As recently as 2021, ultranationalist politician and presidential candidate (and Jew) Éric Zemmour again questioned Dreyfus's innocence, suggesting that 'we will never know' if he was guilty or not.[18]

Basel was centre stage, alongside the fellow Swiss city of Bern, in another vital part of the antisemitism story, the famous legal challenge to another widely promulgated lie designed to besmirch Jews and spread distrust in the mid-1930s. Two Swiss right-wingers Alfred Zander and Eduard Rüegsegger were brought to court by several local Jewish leaders, accused of insulting Jews by distributing a book called *The Protocols of the Elders of Zion* that had already been proven untrue and defamatory.[19] It was the most influential antisemitic document of the modern era, asserting that Jews were working in secret to take over the world, to dominate world banking, to insinuate their way into every centre of power, and to divide Christendom through war and conflict. The book purported to contain verbatim reports of secret meetings of Jewish leaders planning how to achieve this end.[20] The most likely source of the creation of the *Protocols* is the Russian secret police, the Okhrana, in 1902, in the then Russian capital St Petersburg. Why there? Because Russia at the time had the world's biggest Jewish population, having seized Jewish-populated parts of Poland during the eighteenth century, and antisemitism was rife. Jews could only live in the 'Pale of Settlement', a specified area of western Russia, beyond which they were forbidden to travel. While Tsar Nicholas II, renowned for his antisemitism, was sceptical of the *Protocols*, saying that 'a good cause cannot be defended by dirty means', the text still flourished in Tsarist St Petersburg. When revolution came in 1917, many aristocrats blamed the Jews for causing it, with the result that they suffered further from 'torture, murder and rape' in the ensuing civil war. As one historian writes, 'On seizing a town from the Reds, it was common for the White officers to allow their soldiers two or three days' freedom to rob and murder the Jews at will.'[21]

Following the Bolshevik victory in the civil war, exiled aristocrats took copies of the *Protocols* with them into exile for them to be seized on gleefully by the extreme right across Europe, and in 1920, the first English translation was published in Britain. Hitler wrote in *Mein Kampf* in 1923, 'To what an extent the whole existence of this people is based on a continuous lie is shown incomparably by the *Protocols of the Elders of Zion*.'[22] For a time, the *Protocols* were required reading

Alfred Wiener, who spent his life documenting antisemitism and the crimes of Nazism.

for schoolchildren in Nazi Germany. This was the background to the trial in Basel, which ended in 1936 with an out-of-court settlement. The book's distributor Zander had to pay the court costs, and admit in writing that the *Protocols* had no connection with either the First Zionist Congress or the Basel Jewish leaders.[23]

Enter Alfred Wiener, a key figure in the 1930s who helped prove the *Protocols* were a hoax, and was deeply involved in publicizing the Bern trial.[24] Born in Potsdam in 1885, he had fought proudly in the German army in the First World War. But after the Armistice he became a ferocious and forensic compiler of antisemitic writing and actions that he saw unfolding in post-war Germany and across Europe. In his belief that gathering evidence of hatred and action would alert an ignorant world to the fate of the Jews, he was a mirror image of Rudolf Vrba.

Within weeks of the Nazis coming to power in March 1933, Wiener was summoned to a meeting with the newly appointed chief of the Gestapo, Hermann Göring, who demanded that he destroy his entire archive of 'anti-Nazi' material. Considering it too dangerous to remain in Germany, he moved his family to Amsterdam, long considered a safe haven, where his daughters became school friends of Anne Frank and her sister Margot, and where he continued to inform the world about anti-Jewish activities. However, after Kristallnacht in 1938, when Jewish shops, property and synagogues were smashed across Germany with the authorities' active connivance, the Dutch government began to fear its tolerance of Wiener's activities would be viewed unfavourably by the Germans. In 1939, he therefore moved his information-collecting operation to London. But his family remained in Amsterdam, and despite Wiener securing them visas, were unable to leave in time so they were soon swept up in the horrors that followed. The remarkable story is searingly recounted in the book *Hitler, Stalin, Mum and Dad* written by Wiener's grandson, journalist Daniel Finkelstein.[25]

Before we leave Basel, I have just one final story to recount, about a figure of transcendent moral authority. While Wiener, a German Jew, had been sceptical of Herzl's vision of a Jewish homeland in Palestine, Hermann Maas, a German ordained Christian, had been a sympathizer ever since observing the Zionist Congress in Basel. Influenced by German-Jewish theologian Martin Buber, he became a champion of Christian-Jewish reconciliation. On his return to Heidelberg after a visit to Palestine in 1933, local Nazis demanded that this 'pastor of the Jews' be banished from the Church. Maas became a member of the *Pfarrernotbund*, an association of Protestant pastors and forerunner of the Confessing Church set up by Martin Niemöller, of which more later, in opposition to the pro-Nazi 'German Christians' movement. When the deportations of Jews began in 1940, Maas stood up and protected some of the old and frail. The Nazis' campaign against him intensified and resulted in his forced retirement in 1943 and banishment

Pastor Hermann Maas, little-known hero, who was sent to a labour camp for saving Jews.

to a labour camp aged sixty-seven the following year. He survived to become the first German to be officially invited to visit the State of Israel in 1950, and in July 1964 he was recognized by Yad Vashem, the Holocaust Museum in Jerusalem, as one of the 'Righteous Among the Nations', an honorary title given to some 28,000 people, including 659 Germans.[26][27] For the second time on my walk, I ask myself why Wiener, like Vrba but unlike most Jews, and at great risk to himself and his family, set out to chronicle Nazi evil, and why the equally little-known Maas refused to collaborate as did so many of his fellow clergymen, and stood up boldly against the Nazis for what he knew to be right?

* * *

Leaving Basel behind, I'm back working out where best to cross the Rhine. It is not proving straightforward. There are five bridges across the river in the centre of Basel, but they are going to take me further south than I want to go. So I set my sights on crossing the enticingly named *Passerelle des Trois Pays* (Three Countries Bridge) on the outskirts. Built on the exact spot where a German bridge had been blown up by the French in 1797, and a German pontoon bridge was destroyed by US bombing in October 1944, it has become an emblem of the futility of conflict in this most disputed of territories. For many years after the war a passenger boat plied cars back and forth until the present bridge was completed in 2008. What more fitting passage into Germany for a walk with an international aspiration than a walk across this bridge, especially as it was designed exclusively for pedestrians and cyclists, the two categories of travellers for whom the path of peace is intended. What a celebration of physical engineering too: at 250 metres, it is the world's longest single-span bridge intended solely for those crossing under their own steam.

The previous day, drunk on the freedom of no longer having to follow one set route, I had let my heart dictate my path through Alsatian villages as I wandered casually northwards in the direction of Uffheim. To make it back down to the tri-nation footbridge today, I face one massive obstacle that not even the advancing Allied troops had to reckon with in the autumn of 1944: the impenetrable perimeter fence of the Basel-Mulhouse-Freiburg Airport, a 4-kilometre-long presence that is taking no prisoners. Feeling I need some expert advice, I amble into my first tourist office of the trip. After a good deal of arm waving to indicate mutual fraternal feeling, they suggest I give the iconic walking bridge a miss and cross the Rhine on the next bridge downstream by walking cross-country on the path to Ottmarsheim. Joy of joys, the tourist staff tell me that, once in Germany, I will be able to buy maps showing roads with cycle tracks beside them along which pedestrians can walk with impunity. This very good news lifts my spirits. I am all too aware that, walking togs aside, I had done insufficient research on my route. Almost none, to be precise. Now I know I can walk along cycle tracks, a huge weight is lifted, and despite the sun being very hot and at its peak, the journey feels easy. From Ottmarsheim, the tourist officers suggest I cut due east, and pick up the path on the west bank of the Rhine canal that runs adjacent to the river. Had my French been better, I'm sure the path they recommended would have been easier to follow.

Readers of *The Path of Peace* will know that I am besotted with rivers, and be familiar with the joy I found in the seven rivers accompanying me on that earlier walk west. So I am excited that only three days into this walk, I'm naming the mighty Rhine as path of light river number one! As I write these words, I'm at our first married home into which we moved in the autumn of 2023, looking out over the Thames surging strongly downstream towards London and the sea. From my bank, I observe the river moving; but if I was the swan I see floating regally by, the river would be still and the bank would be moving. Are all moral judgements, I ask myself, relative to the point of observation, or are some moral truths, as I believe, absolute?

I think how different the Rhine and Thames are. It's partly scale: the former at 1,230 kilometres is four times the length of the latter, falls ten times in height, and discharges a hundred times its volume of water at its mouth. The Thames with its system of eighteenth-century locks has no need of an adjacent canal to make it navigable. Navigating the Rhine to Basel with its steep gradient was always difficult and dangerous for boats. The fast-flowing waters downstream of the city were renowned as hazardous making it virtually unnavigable, and in the mid-nineteenth century, attempts were made to deepen the river that backfired by quickening the flow of the water and eroding more of the river's base. So in the years before 1914, the German government, which then controlled both banks, decided to dig a massive canal to the west of the river from Basel to Strasbourg with hydroelectric dams installed at strategic points. The war interrupted the plans, and the Treaty of Versailles made France the exclusive controller of the project and sole beneficiary of the electricity. Known as the Grand Canal of Alsace, construction began again in 1932 and was only completed, at a length of 50 kilometres, in 1959.[28]

A windfall of crossing the river further to the north is that I can walk across the ground that saw the last major fighting on French soil of the Second World War. Hitler invested great importance in keeping this last slither of German-controlled Alsace in his hands, and on New Year's Eve 1944 unleashed a major offensive in what became known as the 'Colmar Pocket', designed to support the larger Ardennes Offensive to the north, which was already stalling. Codenamed Nordwind, it was to be the last German offensive on the Western Front. Defending the bridges at Neuenburg am Rhein, where I am heading, and Breisach downstream, was utterly essential so German forces could keep being supplied.

I marvel at the historical symmetry of this Alsatian countryside where I am walking, which is like a 'then and now' photo negative of the First and Second World Wars. In August 1914, it saw the first skirmishes; in early 1945, it saw the beginning of the end. In 1914, it was high summer; in 1945, a Siberian-like winter. Then the French army was equipped with bright blue nineteenth-century uniforms with Napoleonic breastplates and swords; now drab green utilitarian kit given to them by the Americans. Then the army was horse-powered; now it was supported by tanks, armoured vehicles, trucks and aircraft. Then the French were routed; now the Germans.

The German offensive was petering out by early January 1945, and General Eisenhower, the Supreme Allied Commander, gave instructions for its remaining troops to be captured or destroyed, as he wanted Alsace to be free of all enemy forces before the Allied invasion of Germany proper began. He invited the French forces, fighting together for almost the first time on French soil since the fall of France in 1940, to join battle alongside American forces to complete the task successfully.

The French army was under the command of the flamboyant Jean de Lattre de Tassigny. Wounded five times in the fighting at Verdun in 1916, he became France's youngest general in 1940. He remained loyal to the pro-Nazi French government in Vichy, but in 1942, when the Germans snuffed out its remaining independence, he ordered his troops to fight back, before fleeing to England and then joining de Gaulle's Free French forces fighting in Algeria. He was destined to be the senior French commander at the signing of the German surrender in Berlin in May 1945, and on his death from cancer in January 1952, was given a state funeral in Paris that lasted five days. In him, France found the war hero its national pride so desperately needed after the country's capitulation to the Nazis in 1940 and Vichy's subsequent shame.[29]

I cross the Rhine canal by the village of Chalampé, scene of fierce fighting, crossing canal and river as directed on the Neuenburg Bridge. I stop midway over it and look down at the slow-flowing waters. I've arrived in Germany. I sit down by the banks and reflect again on my mission of finding acts of human goodness, not depravity, during the Second World War, before wandering into the small town of Neuenburg am Rhein, which is set back from the river, my first destination in Germany. One particular resident draws me to it. Born to aristocratic parents, like his older brother who became a fighter pilot, he served throughout the First World War, fighting at Ypres before being wounded in the war's final months. He developed a particular aversion to Hitler, and moved to Vienna then to Prague when war broke out.

Albert Göring hoped his brother Hermann, Luftwaffe supremo and right-hand man to Hitler, would protect him. Famously, after the German annexation of Austria in 1938, the SA (*Sturmabteilung*, storm troopers or 'brown shirts') forced Jews to scrub the streets. On

The two Göring brothers, Albert on the left and Hermann on the right.

one occasion, Albert joined them, getting down on his knees alongside the Jews, the SA knowing that they could not touch him, even after he was later known to have helped some escape to safety. When arrested by the Allies in 1945, he was saved from harm by the testimony of survivors. After the war, when his family name was toxic, he shunned publicity and became an alcoholic before dying in 1966 in Neuenburg an unknown, his anti-Nazi deeds unacknowledged. His last act was one of kindness, to marry his hard-up housekeeper, knowing that his state pension would be transferred to her on his death.[30]

A degree of uncertainty surrounds exactly how far Albert went to save Jewish lives. One biography is named *Thirty-Four*, supposedly the number of lives he saved, leading to a flurry of headlines suggesting 'Göring's brother was another Schindler'.[31] Pressure was placed on Yad Vashem to honour him with the designation 'Righteous Among the Nations', but it declared in 2016 that though there was evidence of him helping some Jews, there was a lack of 'primary documentation' proving he had taken extraordinary risks to do so.[32]

The full truth may never be known. But it is beyond doubt that Albert didn't follow his brother into the Nazi Party, that he defended and protected others who were vulnerable at significant risk to his livelihood if not to his actual life. Hermann said of him: 'He was always the antithesis of myself. He was not politically or militarily interested; I was. He was quiet, reclusive; I like crowds and company.'[33] How can the same parents bring up one monster and another who stands up against evil and protects the vulnerable? Canadian physician Gabor Maté says 'no two children have the same parents.'[34] Both brothers may well have experienced totally different parenting, but both made their choices as adults. An early conclusion emerging is that, whatever the disadvantages people may have endured, we are all responsible for our acts.

My day ends walking for two hours south along the riverside path from Neuenburg am Rhein to Bad Bellingen. I don't pass a single walker, but my eyes keep pinned to the river, a short distance below me, visible periodically through the trees. It is our last night at the Kurhotel Markushof in Bad Bellingen, a welcoming family hotel for the first sojourn on this new trip, many leagues above the places I rested my weary body on the Western Front. In the morning, Sarah drives me back to Neuenburg am Rhein from where I walk by the side of the Rhine to Breisach, a hill city I remember from History A Level. A strategic stronghold commanding the river, it was held by the Habsburg-led Holy Roman Empire till lost in the Thirty Years War and ceded to France at the Peace of Westphalia in 1648. Because I had zipped up the 20-kilometre walk in four hours, we are able to meet for lunch in Breisach's market square, and I am able to fulfil what I had long promised Sarah: walking in the morning and spending the rest of the day together. There is scant evidence today that most of the town was destroyed in the battle in January and February 1945. But it is the earlier history that captures our attention as, even in this land of alternating control, it set new standards. In brief, Breisach was French from 1648, returned to the Habsburgs in 1697, French again in 1703, returned to the Habsburgs in 1714 (which led France to create the Vauban-inspired magical fortress town of Neuf-Breisach on the western side of the river), then retaken by Germany in 1871, and so on, and on...[35]

The one constant? Jews faced persecution, regardless of who controlled the city. In a story repeated endlessly across Europe, the Jewish community was destroyed in 1349 by the Black Death then expelled as it regrouped in 1424. The Jewish population peaked at 564 in 1880, but sank to only 231 by 1933. On Kristallnacht in 1938, the synagogue was burned down, and two years later, the last thirty-four Jews were deported to the Gurs concentration camp in south-western France. Sixty-eight of Breisach's Jews are known to have died in the Holocaust.[36] Of those who had fled before the war, none returned. In the 1960s, the sole Jewish survivor made it her task to tend the two Jewish cemeteries that had not been destroyed.[37] Less than a week into the walk, it is already clear that antisemitism was rife from France to Russia centuries before the Nazis came to power. Why were the Jews so hated throughout history?

It is ironic that in this most contested of cities, a case was heard that was to be an early milestone on the road to establishing the concept of international criminal law and crimes against humanity that found full expression in the Nuremberg Trials of 1945–46. So what happened here? In 1469, a knight called Peter von Hagenbach had been appointed by Charles the Bold, Duke of Burgundy, to oversee the city and surrounding territory. Soldiers under his command soon gained a reputation for rape, violence and murder. Five years later, in 1474, he was put on trial at the mayor's residence in Breisach by the Swiss Confederacy having 'Trampled under foot the laws of God and Man'. 'Everyone,' said a medieval chronicler, 'wished to be present at the death of the tyrant, traitor, sodomite, and ravisher.' Von Hagenbach, in an uncanny precursor of the Nazi defendants at Nuremberg, pleaded innocence arguing he was merely following orders from the Duke of Burgundy. His pleas were rejected and he was duly beheaded in public. Lawyers of course argue about the historical significance of the trial, but most accept that it can be considered the first war crimes trial, and also the first prosecution of a commander for sexual crimes committed by themselves and their troops – an acknowledgement of *command responsibility*.[38]

Day 6 arrives with the news that Sarah's beloved only brother Jeremy has finally lost his battle with cancer. We visited him in Sevenoaks on our way out of England a week ago, talked about Daniel Finkelstein's book which he had been enjoying, and listened together before we departed to a recording of a prayer by Dietrich Bonhoeffer. A truly good and wise man, Jeremy had exceptional courage and resolve during his long illness, ministering to others in need and preaching the gospel to the end. One of his last appearances on a public occasion was leading Sarah down the aisle at our wedding in Bray Church.

Sarah decides not to travel home immediately and we spend the day here very quietly together.

On Monday, refreshed by the day's rest, I walk from Breisach towards Freiburg im Breisgau and the Black Forest, travelling along cycle tracks through vineyards and a succession of sumptuous villages, Ihringen, Wasenweiler, Bötzingen, Gottenheim and Umkirch, then a gentle 5-kilometre walk into Freiburg along the straight Dreisam river (really more of a stream). There is a symmetry between the medieval city of Freiburg with its Catholic cathedral and the city of Canterbury with its Anglican cathedral that has captivated me since I encountered Douglas Gillespie's vision of a 'fine broad road' or Via Sacra, along the No Man's Land of the Western Front, ten years before. Might the Western Front Way be extended at both ends to include a pilgrim path between these two great centres of faith and civilization? One thing I've learned: if something is meant to happen, it will. But human agency helps.

We have booked into the Hotel Hirschen in the western suburbs of Freiburg for what we have decided will be our last night before returning home. Under the trees, we have dinner talking about the 150-kilometre walk so far from Kilometre Zero. What have I learned? The first week has been ridiculously easy compared to two years ago: never longer than 25 kilometres a day, a day's rest (albeit unplanned after the news from home), Sarah ferrying me so I don't have to carry all my possessions day after day, planned hotels to stay in place of constant uncertainty about where to sleep and whether I'd find water and provisions along the way. I know equally that I would be foolish if I were to expect the walk to be this easy again.

I feel I have made only a little progress to date comprehending why some did but so few didn't risk protecting the vulnerable during the Third Reich. So far we have met some remarkable people, from Rudolf Vrba and Alfred Wiener to Albert Göring and Hermann Maas. On the last night of this leg, I want to focus on the story of another such person, Freiburg citizen Gertrud Luckner, born in Liverpool to German parents in September 1900. Early adversity could have stymied her life: an only child, she lost both parents while still young. Ferociously bright at a time when women had few openings in higher education, she studied at Birmingham then at Frankfurt and Freiburg universities, where she obtained her doctorate in Social Welfare Economics. When war broke out, she organized an 'Office for Religious War Relief', which became an operation for smuggling Jews south over the Swiss border, and passing messages from Jews to the outside world until she was arrested by the Gestapo and sent to Ravensbrück concentration camp in November 1943, where she spent nineteen months. She was one of the rare survivors: for the remaining fifty years of her life, spent in Germany, she dedicated herself to good works and building understanding between Christians and Jews.[39]

Why did she do this? Did her early bereavements inure her to fear and enable her to empathize with others' pain? Some who experience

Gertrud Luckner, who protected Jews during the war, and built Christian–Jewish bridges after it.

early loneliness and deprivation become untrusting and self-centred. Why not her? She and the other four are the beacons of light I will need to guide me and help me to understand as I walk on... to Auschwitz.

2

Black Forest, White Rose

Chapter 2
Freiburg to Leipheim

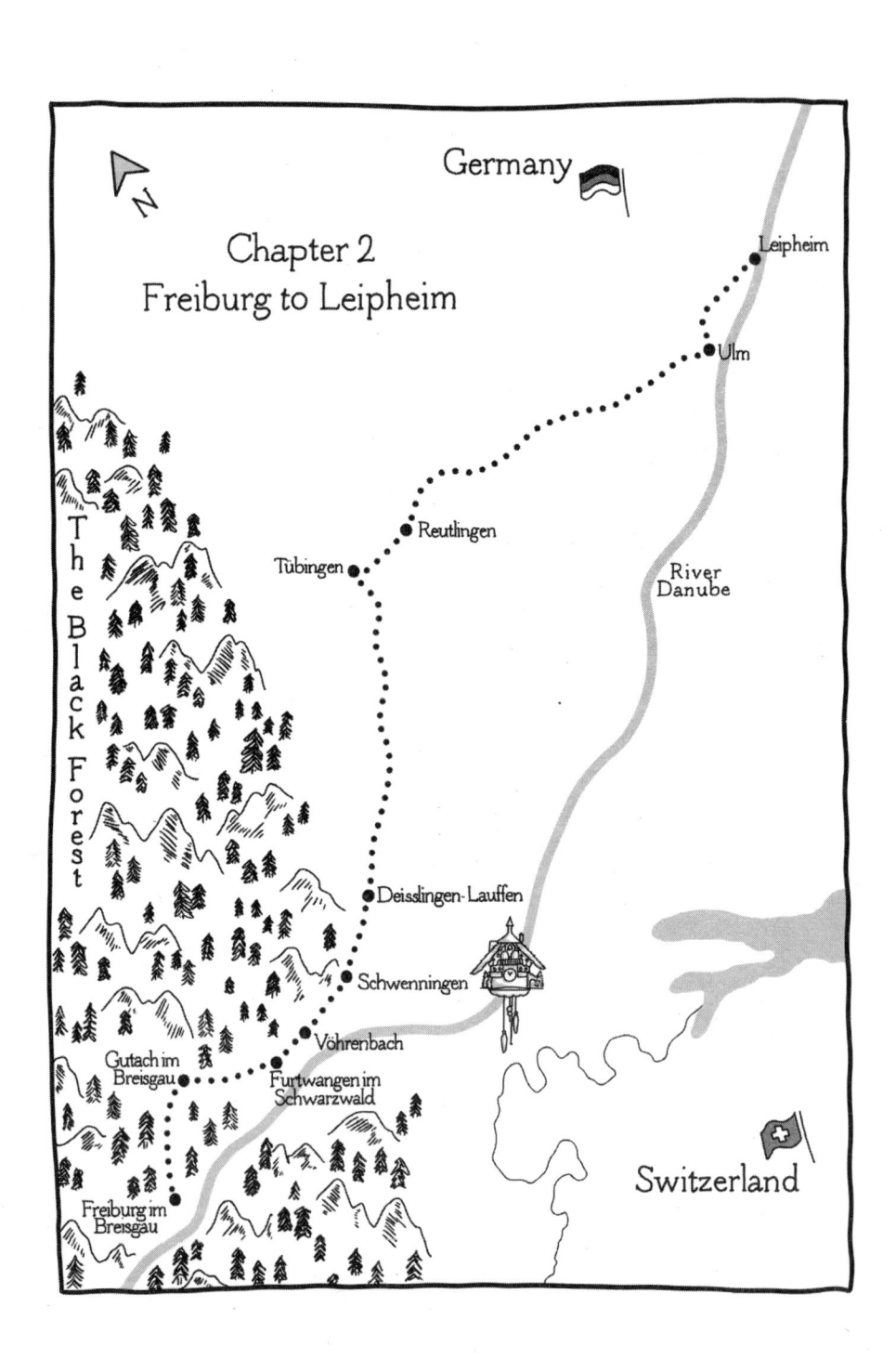

The Black Forest, thick with deciduous trees, firs and spruce, managed what the Maginot strategy never accomplished: it kept out the marauding invader, in this case, the Romans. It put up a pretty good fist of keeping me out as well. Century upon century, the dense wooden wall witnessed French and Germanic warriors slitting each other's throats, the deep undergrowth perpetually stained with blood from some feud or other. The tall trees may have long gone, but the area through which I will be walking retains a sinister air.

The Danube, the longest river in continental Europe outside Russia, has its origins in the Black Forest. The bucolic river has charmed and inspired generations. But our story knows another side. Ulm, the first city on its course, witnessed one of the earliest roundups of political prisoners after the Nazis came to power; on it flows to Regensburg, home to a bestial section of the Flossenbürg concentration camp; on to Linz, Hitler's beloved hometown; then to Vienna from where Adolf Eichmann organized the systematic persecution of Jews and expropriation of their property; on and on it flows into Hungary where on the very edge of its east bank in Budapest is a metal sculpture of pairs of shoes and boots marking the spot where Jews were shot having had their last items of value forcibly removed. Their bodies were carried to the Danube's last big city, Belgrade, which became the first major city in the Nazi Empire to be declared *Judenfrei* in 1942. What darkness this blue river has known as it waltzes its 2,800-kilometre journey from the Black Forest to the Black Sea.

* * *

To my surprise, fully a year has passed before I am again able to resume my search for light in July 2024 as I don my walking kit and pick up the route at Freiburg. Epsom College and Liz Truss were primarily responsible for the long gap in my quest to find remarkable people during the Second World War along my trail. I had planned to do some walking in the school holidays, but Christmas 2023 proved too cold and Easter 2024 too short. My time at Epsom is over; though unexpected, I don't regret the experience one iota. Indeed, of all the institutions I have run, it was comfortably the most enjoyable and fulfilling job. Despite the circumstances that led to my appointment, maybe in part because of it, everyone I encountered, pupils, staff and parents, was generously tolerant of me being placed in their midst. Everything I did was directed towards keeping the school moving, the children and staff busy and happy, and avoiding like the plague anything that might bring fresh trauma, or the public spotlight, into their lives. Never at work have I felt more of a sense of collective purpose and harmony. When my time came to leave after eighteen months at the end of the summer term 2024, I was surprised by the loss I felt at parting with everyone. I was sad, of course, to have left Brighton and Wellington Colleges where I had been the head, and I had nothing but gratitude for my time at both. But leaving Epsom was a bereavement.

Liz Truss was a much more conflicted reason for my inability to get back to Germany to continue the walk. When I arrived at Epsom in February 2023, I was correcting the proofs of my book on Boris Johnson; as I left in July 2024, it was the proofs of *Truss at 10* that I was burning the candle at both ends to complete. I didn't love writing about her; I found no joy talking about a talented, beleaguered woman whose dreams went so badly wrong and inflicted such harm. Her self-implosion after just forty-nine days in Downing Street also meant I had to fast-track a book I hadn't been contracted to write for some while. When I met her at the *Spectator* summer party in July 2023 she pressed her nose towards mine to say, 'I hear you're writing a book about me.' I admired her spirit, energy and self-belief, but not her lack of self-knowledge nor ignorance of how to be prime minister. She had managed to alienate almost all her close team and ministers. This was not, however, unhelpful to my task of research. I spent the next nine months listening to these capable if bruised men and women open up about her days at Number 10 before writing the book about her premiership. Another, much more deserving woman was, of course, Sarah. To her chagrin, she was realizing that circumstances decreed she had married less of a presence than an absence. When I wasn't working flat out at Epsom, I was toiling away every weekend, half term and holiday trying to accommodate this other woman in our marriage, to the detriment of the one I dearly loved.

Sarah. When we set out from home to Freiburg, we had only recently passed the second anniversary of our marriage conducted by two clerics at the church at Bray near our home in Berkshire in April 2022. The Vicar of Bray had been the subject of a famous eighteenth-century satirical song about a cleric forever changing his principles to retain his ecclesiastical position. Was it the groom now changing sides, having converted to Judaism to marry Joanna in a synagogue in 1982, and now reconverting to Christianity and marrying Sarah in a church exactly forty years on? It was a question I asked myself. And yet I felt at peace with the decision. I never rejected Christianity when I embraced Judaism, the religion of my father, my wife Joanna and hence our children, and now, I most definitely was not rejecting Judaism in embracing Christianity, the faith of my mother and Sarah. Indeed, in this story as in my entire life, so too in this book, the two are entwined.

Sarah indeed. Our own lives are entwined forever now too. In marrying her, I had given too little thought in all the busyness about what to expect. I had not absorbed the advice that a second marriage is not remarrying one's first partner in a different guise. Marrying somebody new means seeing them entirely afresh as they uniquely are, and embracing their family, their friends, their work and their interests.

So I am having to rethink who I am and my relationship with my new wife. (Sarah hates it when I introduce her as 'my new wife'. 'I'm not your new wife. I'm your wife,' she regularly tells me. I'm learning.) Joanna had been forgiving and tolerant, supporting me even when she suspected I was wrong. Too forgiving, no doubt, but our marriage was very blessed. We had met while working on plays at university when she was nineteen and I was twenty, and grew up together sharing the same friends and outlooks on life. I encountered Sarah first in my mid-fifties when I was her head and she was one of my colleagues at school, and we became partners when I was in my late sixties. Sarah makes it very clear what is acceptable. And what is not. She doesn't like that I give my everything to work and there's almost nothing left over. She's very different to Joanna but I adore her and I want desperately to make her happy.

Sarah with her beloved border terrier, Tallie.

I'm fairly certain she's not looking forward much to returning to Germany, but she's too kind to tell me outright. It was a hard year for her, juggling her own school teaching with supporting me as a head's wife at a busy day and boarding school. We'd spent very little time together alone for eighteen months. Come the summer holidays starting in early July, she was looking forward to a complete rest, and here I am dragging her off on another long journey. As we travel to the airport and on the plane, I'm still handwriting letters of thanks on my lap to staff at Epsom. We pick up a hire car at Basel Airport, and drive directly to the Hotel Hirschen in Freiburg, from where we left for England eleven months ago. We don't even have time to relax at the hotel before she drops me off at the outskirts of the city, as, anxious to get some kilometres under my belt before dusk, I set off with a new rucksack, shoes and walking poles given to me by my Epsom colleagues as a leaving gift. I strike out along a cycle track, walking north towards the dormitory village of Gundelfingen. Fortified by my splendid new kit I cover the 5 kilometres in just an hour, then wheel north-east through gently rising countryside, passing Alpine-style houses. I'm struck by how much more prosperous the countryside and villages seem than in England, with factories and offices regularly distributed across rural communities. As I approach Gutach im Breisgau, my target for the day at just 20 kilometres, I phone the hotel to book a table for dinner by the pool – OK, but don't be *spät, bitte* ('late, please') – and I begin to realize how colossally anxious I've become about the walk. Crippling self-doubt ranks very high on my inner demon index; masking it as I do with confidence doesn't always work. As if on cue, my habitual fears rise to the surface to attack me: will I lose my way, injure my ankles or knees, be unable to sleep, dodge attacks by dogs and even by humans? On top of this, something else happened last week that has unsettled me. A routine health check picked up clogged arteries, the specialist saying as a result I had 'coronary heart disease'. Bit of a shock: I'd had no pre-warning. I'm slapped on statins and daily aspirin, but will they do the trick? I park it, too much to take on board, and the specialist, I tell myself, did not seem unduly concerned.

I sense a storm approaching, with a harbinger just around the corner. I'd arranged to meet Sarah at St George's Church in Gutach im Breisgau, famous for its monumental eighteenth-century 'Dance of Death' wall painting, depicting dancing skeletons carrying off the great and good.[1] It sounds more like a path to darkness than a path to light. Has it jinxed me? My phone, which has been on the go all day, suddenly dies and I grip it tightly as if to prevent it being carried off by some demon to another world. The minutes pass and there's no sign of Sarah. My mind catastrophizes, imagining something terrible has happened to her driving alone in a strange car. I weave my way through the village to hunt down someone willing to charge an iPhone. But the residents of Gutach seem to have gone away for July. I spy a sign pointing to a restaurant up a country lane towards the forest. More than a little worried, I jog the kilometre to it but find that it is closed. I rush back to the heart of the village, spot a man parking his car, and before he's had time to unlock his front door, I pounce. In schoolboy German and hand signals indicative of an uncharged phone, I indicate my plight. It does the trick, and a few minutes later, I'm on the phone to a very unamused Sarah. I then wait on my saviour's porch for her to drive up and explain to him in eloquent German that she's sorry but she's married an idiot.

Once in the car, the gloves are off. She is completely clear that I gave her a different meeting point. Who'd have known there are two halves of Gutach, each with their own church? Rather than see it through her eyes, I argue with her. I'm totally convinced I told her the church name. But did I dream it? I mean, she might have been right. We bicker all the way back to the hotel, the tensions of the previous days and weeks cascading out into the cabin of the Hertz Kia estate (which, by the way, is far too big for us, and why on earth did I book something so stupid?). Only in the cool of the evening, over a second glass of a particularly elegant Gewurztraminer, do we begin to become friends again.

Too much wine! A restless night. Mind you, nowadays, even three glasses is too much. Unrested, I come downstairs ahead of Sarah to seek strength in *Müsli und frisches Obst* (muesli and fresh fruit). The heat under the trees is already intense. I'm daunted. I have two weeks to walk the 400 kilometres of my chosen southern route to Nuremberg, infamous site of rallies and trials on the far side of the country. That distance should be perfectly manageable if I'm moving normally at 30 kilometres a day. But I fret my energy this year is absent. I pore over maps at the breakfast table, worrying about today's leg to the Black Forest mountain village of Gütenbach, a distance of just 15 kilometres but with a climb of over 600 metres by the side of a busy mountain road with neither pavement nor trail. Sarah, sensing all is not well, sits down beside me and we talk through the options. Start from where I finished last night or skip unhappy Gutach (both of them) and zip by taxi straight up to Gütenbach to start walking from there? I find the idea of missing out chunks very uncomfortable. However jaded I was, I never omitted a section on the 'Path of Peace' walk and I'm worrying about creating a precedent. But it is going to take me four hours to climb up in the heat, and I accept the skip as the only way forward if I'm to keep to my timetable, consoling myself with the thought it is a segment I will walk before the book is published. It will be an exception and, henceforth, I will stick to my rule. After all, even my inspiration, interwar European walker Patrick Leigh Fermor, about whom more later, accepted the odd freebie.

So I hop in a taxi, using the time to catch up on the news. Donald Trump is still dominating the agenda four days after the attempt to assassinate him in Butler, Pennsylvania. Milking the incident, he announces on his social media platform Truth Social (both words misnomers) that 'God alone' prevented his death. Delegates at the Republican National Convention at Milwaukee are wearing bandages over their ear in a show of solidarity with their leader, whose ear was damaged by the bullet. At least I comfort myself that no Trump follower would ever dream of making a Nazi salute in public. The biggest news story in the eleven months between my walks, eclipsing even the US presidential election, has been the horrific 7 October attack on Israel by Hamas, and the Israeli retaliation. It is reported that another fifty people have been killed in Israeli strikes in Lebanon. Where are the voices of peace on both sides, I keep asking? Jews and Muslims alike rank the Psalms among their most holy Scriptures. Very well: Psalm 34 says, 'We should seek peace and pursue it.' Do the fighters and their leaders know the passage, or are they not interested in pursuing it? To the atheist, throughout history war and destruction have been perpetrated in the name of religion, a thoroughly objectionable human creation. That's not how I see it. On this journey, I want to explore whether darkness and evil happen not because of the presence of an all-loving God in the hearts of leaders and religious fighters, but because of the absence.

Weighty thoughts as we come to the end of a long taxi journey wending our way up to Gütenbach. We pull up at the Restaurant Bachhof and I slip out of the taxi €100 lighter into the sweltering heat. I set off in an easterly direction, walking poles by my side, and I find myself in a different world. I have arrived at last in the Black Forest, a much older and hence much lower mountain range than the Alps. The hilltops are generally level and rounded, forming a high plateau renowned for heavy rainfall and melancholy weather. I notice at once that the architecture is very different to the Rhine Valley, with low-hanging roofs protecting the homes from snow, and farmhouses built on sides of hills with the entrances leading directly into large barns so that the dwellers could share the same space as the livestock to take advantage of the animals' warmth in deep winter.

My day starts promisingly with a 3-kilometre walk along cool mountain tracks, but then my track joins a busy road for 3 kilometres into the town of Furtwangen im Schwarzwald, renowned for its clocks.

Of significance though to my mission is a family who found shelter and safety briefly here in the early 1940s. German-born Peter Bielenberg, then studying Law in England, had married British citizen Christabel in 1934 at the German Embassy in London, a ceremony that required her to become a German citizen to marry him. The ambassador was still the old-fashioned career diplomat Leopold von Hoesch (who died in 1936 and whom Hitler replaced with the ultra-loyal Nazi Joachim von Ribbentrop). Firm anti-Nazis, the Bielenbergs settled in Berlin as the Nazi tentacles spread across Germany.

While Peter unobtrusively worked his way up the Nazi bureaucracy as a civil servant, they became drawn into subversive activities. By 1940, now with three children, they started sheltering Jews. When their lives became too precarious, Christabel took the children from the capital, eventually settling in Rohrbach, on the outskirts of Furtwangen. Peter was later suspected of complicity in the plot to assassinate Hitler on 20 July 1944, codenamed Operation Valkyrie, which only narrowly failed because the suitcase containing the bomb was moved at the last moment. No doubt fervent Hitler supporters believed his deliverance too was an act of God, in as far as by then there were any believers left beyond his close circle. In the subsequent roundup, Peter was imprisoned in Ravensbrück concentration camp. At considerable personal risk to herself, Christabel travelled to the camp to persuade the Gestapo that he should be released from what would be almost certain death, managing to get him switched instead to hard labour and then a 'punishment unit' on the Eastern Front from which he managed to escape. Some 5,000 people thought to be involved in the plot were killed on Hitler's orders, but, incredibly, both Bielenbergs survived the war, and, believing all their friends in Germany had been murdered by Hitler, they settled in Ireland where they made a life as farmers.[2]

Christabel's work protecting Jews was featured in the landmark television series *The World at War* (1973–74), and her life was dramatized in TV drama *Christabel* in 1988, where she was portrayed by a young

Resistors Christabel and Peter Bielenberg, rare survivors of the plots against Hitler.

Elizabeth Hurley. *The World at War* made a big impact on me at the time, as it did on the students in my first teaching job in Croydon. I now find myself deeply moved to be standing near the spot where she and her family lived and breathed. In her post-war years, Christabel was to play a prominent role in raising money for the families of those executed in reprisals following the failed assassination, such as that of their close friend Adam von Trott zu Solz. By strange coincidence, the eightieth anniversary of the 20 July plot falls as I am passing through.

Here at least is some light in the darkness, so many brave men joining forces to try to oust Hitler and his murderous regime. But sadly, while Peter Bielenberg himself was evidently a good man, the uplifting story I have clung to all my life of brave democrats trying to bring down a vile dictator is more nuanced. Claus von Stauffenberg, the key conspirator and depositor of the briefcase bomb by Hitler's legs, one of my heroes since my father first told me about the plot, turns out to have been an avowed supporter of Hitler from when he came to power in 1933 till 1943. The motives of the conspirators are difficult to discern, given that the secrecy of their plan meant their reasoning was often unrecorded, and most went to their graves immediately after with their stories untold. But many lead conspirators were complicit in terrible crimes. Henning von Tresckow, the architect of the plot, had served with units that committed atrocities in Poland and Russia.[3] Many of the plotters, desperate to save something of the Fatherland, only turned on Hitler when the tide of war changed. Most were aristocratic, conservative nationalists, not modern democrats or liberals. Author Alfred Werner sees the dying embers of the old Germanic order in their resistance, writing that the bomb plot was 'the last feeble attempt of what was left of Frederick the Great's Prussian army to act as an independent political force'.[4] Courageous yes, but tainted too.

Historians also debate whether Hitler's death would have delivered the benefits the plotters hoped. If he had been killed, and the war had ended at once (a big if), then millions of lives, not least those of the Hungarian Jews and soldiers on both sides of the fighting fronts, might have been spared. But those still loyal to the Nazi regime might have chosen to fight a civil war with the plotters, and they might have won. The Allies had already decided in 1943 on a policy of 'unconditional surrender' towards Germany; they were in no mood to agree an armistice with any plotters. The killing of Hitler in July 1944 might even have led to another 'stab in the back' myth like that after 1918, leading to a continuance of instability. After all, as we have seen in recent years, 'regime change' has seldom gone to plan. Was it therefore necessary for Nazism to be totally and utterly defeated for the world to move on? These are not questions that can be answered definitively, but they run through my mind as I walk on and on.

I hop child-like from sleeper to sleeper along the disused railway track that the Bielenbergs travelled along to and from Berlin, and along which Jews were taken on their final journey to faraway destinations. I am aiming for another small town, Vöhrenbach, spurred on by the prospect of Sarah waiting for me in the square with lunch. I have ensured that my phone battery has not run dry; the wizardry of her tracking my every step too should avoid another debacle. Great joy, she is standing by the car smiling with picnic in hand; better still, she tells me after we have eaten she will join me for the 10-kilometre walk through the forest to Pfaffenweiler where I plan to finish the day. Much of our track takes us through the forest, where, shielded from the heat and firm underfoot, we make swift progress. So happy are we that we fail to notice we have stumbled headlong into mosquito central. Trapped! These little devils are from hardy woodland stock so, standing back to back as in the Battle of Thermopylae, we fire off almost two entire canisters of repellent warding them off. Mission accomplished, we hurry off along the track periodically checking we are not being pursued and descend to the plain where a taxi awaits us. As we drive back for our last night in Freiburg, we listen to The Rest is History podcast (we are hooked on it) about Martin Luther in preparation for arriving in the city of Augsburg in three or four days' time. That night, we have supper on the balcony, no alcohol, and have an early night. Bliss!

The sun is already beating down strongly while we have our final breakfast at the Hotel Hirschen. We're moving on today to the university city of Tübingen. As we lay out my walking kit on the bed, I see that a clip holding the sections on one of my poles, so recently given to me by my colleagues, has dropped off, rendering the device useless. I am irrationally upset. Sarah comes to the rescue and suggests that the omnipotent queen bee of the hotel might be able to fix it. I'm sure she won't, but concurring is my only resort. QB rises to the occasion, summoning one of her technicians who takes the poles, reappearing in ten minutes mended pole in hand and beaming across his face. I take this as a sign that it will be a good day. A miscalculation.

I leave early by taxi, which costs an eyewatering amount to go to another tiny village 60 kilometres up in the Black Forest. I cannot sustain the trip with such bills, but with no convenient trains, and buses taking forever, I am at a loss to know how else I can manage the walk, except moving on night by night, which we decided against. On the journey, I catch up again on the news, full of Gaza (bad) and Ukraine (better), with some rallying by Zelensky's forces. It is very hot. I set off on roads walking due east directly into the sun through more small villages then out into open fields, skirt some woods and decide to take the cycle track, which is flat and regularly signposted. I'm vaguely aware that it's boiling, and that I seem to be doing a lot of walking but not going very far. I'm more concerned by a pain on the back of my ankle. I put my hand down inside my socks and it comes back red. Blast. I can't understand how blood could be present on just my third day walking, and with my new boots. I sit down on some logs and work on my laces, pulling them much tighter. I've only been walking for two hours and I'm feeling lightheaded. I feel instinctively behind me for my water bottles, but all I can find is one and it's half empty. I'd forgotten in the kerfuffle this morning to load up my bottles with fresh water and soluble electrolytes, the perfect answer to dehydration that I started using halfway through the first walk. I am miles from any shop, so there's nothing to do but ration my water, and press on through the hamlets of Rietheim and Marbach till I arrive at the unlovely town of Schwenningen, once the proud cuckoo-clock capital of Germany. To take my mind off my giddiness, I read up a shade manically about how, by the mid-nineteenth century, England was purchasing more of these clocks than any other country. Indeed, 200 Black Forest clockmakers had set up business in London that century alone until demand gradually fell, the victim of changes of taste and cheaper production in East Asia. I recall my father's cuckoo clock, which remained on our sitting room wall long after the cuckoo had omitted its final *cu-coo*, the grey paint on its doors a paler shade with each passing year.

As I trudge on along pavement and track, through village after village, too conscious of the beating sun to absorb anything around me, I'm finding no further evidence of light. In its place, I stumble upon the location of the 'Stalag V-B' prisoner of war (POW) camp. Villingen-Schwenningen was not unusual in housing one, with the 'V-B' camp containing 30,000 inmates at its peak. Some 1,000 POW camps were set up by the Nazis. The news today contains speculation about whether the Israeli captives in Gaza are still alive nine months after 7 October 2023. I wonder how the POWs here kept their spirits going, not knowing if they would ever be released, and with no connection with the outside world year after year. Treatment of Soviet soldiers, who arrived here from late 1941, was notably brutal; whereas some 3.6 per cent of American and British prisoners died in Nazi captivity, the figure was 58 per cent for Soviet soldiers.[5] The Nazis saw their war on the Soviet Union as one of annihilation, in which the Slav population would be destroyed. During their invasion of the Soviet Union, the German army captured 5.7 million Soviet soldiers, of whom over 3.3 million would never return.[6] In late 1941, there were days when more Soviet POWs died in German camps than British and American POWs died in the entire war.[7] Those who were not starved or murdered soon after capture were sent to prison camps like this where Gestapo raids were regular events when Soviet troops and Jews could be selected for removal to concentration camps, beaten up or killed on the spot.[8] I am finding it hard to think such barbarism happened right here. In fact, I am finding it hard to think clearly at all.

My spirits are sinking as I press on along lanes through flat open farmland with trees shimmering in the distance. I continue through Deisslingen till I arrive at my destination at the Krone Hotel, in neighbouring Lauffen, only 25 kilometres for the day but it feels double that. My head is spinning as I sit on the front doorstep waiting for Sarah. I collect my thoughts and gulp down a litre of water. The name Lauffen rings an eerie bell. At school, I studied sixteenth- and seventeenth-century Britain and Europe. The first essay I wrote that won the admiration of teacher Geoffrey Parker was on the Thirty Years War whose devastating mark I had encountered earlier at Breisach on the Rhine. This most extensive, complex and cruel war has captivated me ever since. Ostensibly a religious and political war between Catholics and Protestants, it was fought largely in the patchwork of imperial, ecclesiastical and semi-feudal lands that would much later coalesce to form the nation-state of Germany in 1871. It began, as we shall see, with a defenestration (oh, how my History set loved that word) in Prague, and went on to kill some 15–30 per cent of Germans, with disease and starvation the fate of many.[9] The Swedish army alone destroyed some 1,500 towns and 18,000 villages in German lands.[10] Inhabitants would regularly be massacred, or burned alive in their homes, as in the sack of Magdeburg in 1631. By 1648, vast tracts of German farmland had been abandoned.

The Black Forest bore the brunt of the fighting; some one hundred forts, battlefields and campsites are known to have existed in the region. I realized later, when I had recovered my wits, that this Lauffen was not the strategically significant Lauffen-am-Neckar, 140 kilometres north. But the war still affected this area too. Sixteen thousand French-Weimarian troops camped at Pfaffenweiler, before fighting the Bavarians for Freiburg in August 1644. What followed was among the bloodiest battles of the war, an ugly slugging match that cost the French half their men and the Bavarians a third of their 13,000. In the end, the Bavarians retreated first, but the withered French abandoned their attempt to take the city. Even after the Peace of Westphalia in 1648, with town and fields destroyed, this locale continued to suffer regularly from occupation by unwanted troops. '*Villages détruits*' signs are frequently dotted along the Western Front Way; if the Thirty Years War had bequeathed something similar, I would have passed a myriad along my route.

I'm sure there were countless acts of light, of courageous men and women protecting innocent lives during the Thirty Years War. But the tales left behind are overwhelmingly ones of the absence of mercy. It may have been fundamentally a 'war of religion', but it was not a war of love and nor was it one of neighbourly compassion.

Anxious to escape the heat, and with a piercing headache, I leap into the car when Sarah arrives. I'm gnawing away at myself as she drives the 70 kilometres to our next base camp, the university town of Tübingen. I see the kilometre posts fly past and realize it'll be a long journey back in the morning to pick up my route. I'm already a long way behind where I had hoped to be. We find our boutique Hotel La Casa on the outskirts of the city. To revive my spirits I have a long very hot shower (big mistake) and we saunter in the still evening air into the city by the side of the small Steinlach river, both banks dotted with students lying on the grass sharing food, drink and more. We cross over the larger Neckar and spy an Italian restaurant overlooking the water mid-town. Only once we are sitting on the veranda to eat do I realize I'm giddy and my head is still spinning. We finish up quickly and walk back to the hotel in search of an early night. But I cannot sleep, I'm sweating while also feeling cold. My heart is racing and I start wondering that I might be properly ill. I've never had Covid but have been coughing for the last few days. Perhaps that is the matter? Or sunstroke? Or have I simply worked myself up into becoming exhausted after a year of non-stop toil? Has the emotion of leaving Epsom finally caught up with me? While I was in the school, I was just doing the job, but now it's finished, my mind is turning over what happened that terrible night. Being head had given me an identity and sense of self-worth again; now it is over, the anxious thoughts and fear of failure flood back. It's 3 a.m. and I still haven't slept. I become afraid of going to sleep worrying I might never wake up. Eventually, a mixture of a large glass of white wine and paracetamol, and Sarah's loving presence, do the trick.

Normally optimistic and energetic, I become low and anxious, as I have done periodically all my life, the world is a grey place, all colour drained, a black rainbow indeed. I'm throwing everything at this walk in search of a destination that I might never reach. Morbid thoughts plague my dreams: am I guilty of terrible hubris to think that, at the age of seventy-one, I can do this? What if I fail?

I awake feeling bleak. This trip is not working out at all as planned. We've been out for five days, but I've walked barely 60 kilometres rather than the 150 the timetable requires. I decide with heavy heart that I will do the stretch from Deisslingen-Lauffen to Tübingen at a later date. I'm coughing heavily and in no condition to walk today. So we decide to take it gently, read in the morning in our room, and walk around Tübingen in the afternoon. The decision eases the pressure and gives us time together. The medieval city, nestling between the Neckar and the Ammer, is exquisite, the buildings, streets and squares largely undamaged by developers and bombs (the three Allied air raids inflicted minimal disruption). It feels like a young city, unsurprisingly, as a third of the 90,000 inhabitants are university students, giving it the youngest average age of any city in Germany.

But shining Tübingen is not all it seems: below the surface, it has a sinister history. The city's Jews were expelled by the Duke of Württemberg when he founded the city's prestigious university in 1477, not to be welcomed back till the mid-nineteenth century. After Hitler's rise to power, the university's science and humanities departments enthusiastically contributed to the Nazis' genocidal policies.[11] Of the approximately one hundred Jews in the city in 1933, only two remained in 1945. Lingering antisemitism might explain why it took forty years after the burning down of the city's synagogue on Kristallnacht to see a plaque erected to commemorate it. Indicatively, critics observe, it does not name the perpetrators.

Hatred also motivated one of Tübingen's most infamous residents, Gudrun Ensslin, key founder and guiding spirit of the *Rote Armee Fraktion* (RAF) or Baader-Meinhof Gang. They spread terror between 1970 and 1977, killing twenty-eight people, politicians, businessmen, soldiers and police officers, causing widespread harm and mutilation in a spate of bombings, shootings and bank robberies.[12] A Communist terrorist group, they sought nothing less than the undermining of the West German state and its replacement by a 'red revolution'. Equating post-war West Germany with Nazism, and fired up by Marxist and antisemitic ideology, Ensslin declared in 1967: 'They'll kill us all. You know the pigs we're up against. This is the Auschwitz generation… They have weapons and we have not. We must arm ourselves!'[13] The group caused fear and misery until the leaders including Ensslin took their own lives in 1977. The principal RAF survivor, Horst Mahler, after release from prison, not so surprisingly, started attending neo-Nazi gatherings where he delivered addresses denying the Holocaust and the existence of the gas chambers.[14] He finished his latest prison sentence in 2020.[15] The cause of the RAF (their choice of initials was an intentional reference to Allied bombing) turned out to be total delusion; yet their incoherent ramblings and their nihilistic violence captivated and even inspired millions of mistaken idealists globally.

Gudrun Ensslin, whose Red Army Faction terrorized West Germany, in police custody in October 1972.

What made Ensslin so full of hate? Certainly neither poverty nor a troubled home background can be enlisted as excuses. The fourth of seven children, her father was an evangelical priest. She was diligent and apparently kind as a schoolgirl, winning a scholarship to Tübingen University to read English and German Studies. What drives anyone to embrace an ideology that makes them think that inflicting mass death and acts of terror is the answer? Like all extremists, Ensslin seems to have had a propensity to see herself as a martyr well before she met the people who radicalized her. Most of those who acquiesce in evil, as between 1933 and 1945, are passive and swept along by the current. But to choose deliberately to kill in an open society requires a positive act of will. Understanding that darkness will be the flipside of my quest to discover the genesis of human light.

I am still feeling rough the next day. After much soul-searching with Sarah, I decide to abandon going backwards any distance at all, and we set off walking eastwards in the direction of Ulm. After 5 kilometres we reach the village of Wankheim, pausing only at the site of the synagogue that served the nineteenth-century congregation. Along lanes, fields and through woods we traipse till we reach the industrial city of Reutlingen. We've walked only 15 kilometres but I am exhausted and collapse into a café chair hoping my strength returns. We find ourselves in a long pedestrianized street, Wilhelmstrasse, and the view is uninspiring. Reutlingen had for almost 300 years been a Free Imperial City in the Holy Roman Empire. But a savage fire in the eighteenth century destroyed three-quarters of the old centre, and much of what remained was obliterated by the Allied bombers targeting the factories making the wings for V-1 flying bombs. Little of the medieval splendour of the town remains. I reflect on those British towns and cities whose historic hearts were destroyed in the twentieth century less by fire or enemy ordinance than by avaricious developers and corrupt politicians.

Horror returned to Reutlingen's streets in July 2016 when a Syrian asylum seeker killed his partner with a machete, injuring two others.

Why would someone want to commit murder on these very streets? The attack came days after a gunman killed nine people in Munich, 'inspired', police said, by Anders Breivik, the Norwegian far-right extremist who murdered seventy-seven people in Oslo and Utøya in 2011. The same week as the machete carnage here saw other attacks on German streets perpetrated by individuals with Middle Eastern backgrounds. Together, the violence inflamed a volatile public wary that the horrific terrorist attacks in France, including the Bataclan nightclub massacre in November 2015, might be repeated in Germany too. Populism, on the rise across Europe, feeds off such incidents. No surprise that support for *Alternative für Deutschland* (AfD), the right-wing populist party founded in 2013, received a significant boost from violence as occurred here in Reutlingen. In 2017, the number of seats AfD won in the German federal elections shot up, making it the third largest party in the country. There will be another election in Germany the year after our visit, with the AfD predicted to do even better (as indeed happened).

All I can see around me is dark and listless. I am maybe looking in the wrong places, but ever since I entered the Black Forest, apart from the Bielenbergs, I've been unable to find the uplifting stories I have been seeking. We decide to pack it in for the day, walk to the station in Reutlingen and catch a train back to Tübingen. The next day, a Sunday, I'm still coughing heavily and feeling restless. We go to the Lutheran church in Wankheim where the female pastor delivers a passionate sermon about the exploitation of women. Why, Sarah and I discuss, were almost all the acts of violence in the war, outside of some female guards in concentration camps, carried out by men, while the burden of protecting and sustaining life was carried disproportionately by women?

Monday morning sees another difficult decision. I've lost three days' walking on this trip so far. Reutlingen to Ulm is going to be 70 kilometres, three days' walking, but if I undertake it now, I'll fall even further behind. We decide to pack up early, drive speedily to Ulm, and then I'll get a taxi to take me back 25 kilometres to cover at least some of that ground. We arrive early at Ulm's Maritim Hotel, tall and ugly, where I change into my walking kit and shoot off by taxi back to an upstream point on the Danube. I'm delighted to find the river has a well-marked trail by its side. Before it fully sinks in that I've reached the Danube, river of dreams, a violent thunderstorm breaks out. I shelter under trees, but when the storm finally passes, the mosquitoes come out in force. I have brought no insect repellent with me and have no idea how to stop them biting through my trousers and top. It's a losing battle, and I decide to quit for the day, getting back to town early enough to have dinner with Sarah in the hotel. On offer is an institutional buffet less appetizing than the food the pupils eat at the schools I've run. At €250 for the night, we decide we're being ripped off and will move in the morning.

Up early and beginning perhaps to feel my usual self, I head off while Sarah finds a more congenial hotel and gets to know the city. The one redeeming feature of the Maritim is being able to walk out of the front door straight on to the Danube footpath. After all the angst, it is a joy to walk on a solid path by the riverside, flat, dry and mercifully bend free. I'm sporting my new mosquito-proof shirt – 'it'll be good for eighty washes', said the shopkeeper yesterday. That'll see me out, I reckon. The long-sleeved beige garment with a plethora of buttons leaves only my hands, face and ears in need of anti-insect spray: a big relief. It has been unpleasant and inefficient, covering my upper body in that revolting acidy concoction.

At midday I listen to the news through my headphones: President Biden has announced, far too late, that he is throwing in the towel and endorsing Vice President Kamala Harris as the Democratic Party nominee. I don't think the problem was just his age: Winston Churchill was exactly the same age in his final term as prime minister (1951–55). Yet my first book *Churchill's Indian Summer* tried to argue he still proved a remarkable and far-seeing PM.[16] Churchill too hadn't wanted to disappear into the abyss; but with Biden, it seems to have

The Danube at Ulm, my second river of the walk.

been an arrogance and unwillingness to accept how weak he was. I think history will be harsh on him, and rightly so. The softness of the path underfoot, and the silent urgency of the river on my right, gradually assuage my frustration. Presidents, like PMs, matter. How much worse still might history have turned out, I think, had Biden, born in November 1942, been president during the Second World War, not his Democrat predecessor Franklin Roosevelt, a true leader.

The river is about as wide here, I calculate, as the Thames at Hammersmith, the length of a football pitch, but the water is dark and almost entirely boat free. Another calculation, wildly inaccurate I'm sure, is that the water is moving at 3 kilometres per hour, so will take six weeks to reach the mouth of the river 2,500 kilometres away on the Black Sea, by which time Sarah and I will have long left the country. After five hours and with 25 kilometres covered today, I stop at the small town of Leipheim, which between 1946 and 1950 hosted a displaced persons (DP) camp with over 3,000 Holocaust survivors.[17] I have now crossed into the 'American Zone' of the post-1945 Allied occupation. Whereas the French and British oversaw the areas of West Germany closest to them geographically, the Americans had to satisfy themselves with Bavaria and southern Germany. Together the three Allies found themselves responsible for looking after millions of displaced persons of all European nationalities, including 250,000 Jews who did not believe it was safe to return to their home countries.[18] Many of these survivors were young and angry; they wanted to build new lives, but not here. 'Many Jewish displaced persons... are living under guard behind barbed-wire fences... [W]e appear to be treating the Jews as the Nazis treated them except we do not exterminate them,' was the chilling verdict of the official 1945 US Harrison Report.[19] In response, the United Nations Relief and Rehabilitation Administration introduced housing and food improvements at Leipheim, as elsewhere.

But the torment continued. The Harrison Report had recommended that Jews be allowed to leave for Mandatory Palestine (the region which had been under British control since the First World War). President Truman was sympathetic to the idea, but this created a rift with Prime Minister Clement Attlee, who opposed such an exodus, fearing it would destabilize the region.[20] The fraught diplomacy contributed to misery in the DP camps. In February 1946, the Jews in the Leipheim camp went on hunger strike in protest at mistreatment by GIs whose raids on their accommodation brought back memories of the ghetto and concentration camps: epithets such as 'American SS' and 'American Gestapo' were regularly shouted at the GIs.[21] Across Europe, millions of vulnerable displaced people, damaged physically and mentally, remained unable to resume any kind of recognizably normal life. The idea that their experience was miraculously transformed when the fighting ceased in May 1945 is as fanciful as assuming, after the Armistice in November 1918, that everything was suddenly lovely in the garden for those who had been caught up in the war. Long after the camps were liberated, long indeed after Victory in Europe (VE) Day, the hell for many millions continued unabated. And not just for them, for their children and grandchildren too. Trauma is passed down from generation to generation like unwanted family heirlooms.

With such experience in mind, and wary of being used himself, Ulm-born Albert Einstein declined a personal invitation from his hometown to be granted the right of 'freeman of the city'. This rejection by its most famous son was painful for Ulm. He had said before Hitler's rise to power, 'The city of birth will be as much a unique part of your life as your descent from your mother.' Now he turned his back on it. His relationship with Ulm was in truth always ambivalent. When he was shown a photograph of his old home that had been destroyed by an Allied bomb in December 1944, he wrote: 'Time has affected it even much more than it has affected me.' His thinking was captured in a surreal fountain created in 1984 in which artist Jürgen Goertz features him sticking out his tongue at the town forever.[22]

Einstein sticks his tongue out at Ulm.

I catch the train from Leipheim back to Ulm, marvelling at its punctuality and cleanliness. It is a fraction of the cost of a taxi. Will trains prove my salvation on the walk? I relate my enthusiasm to a middle-aged couple sitting in front of me. They are having none of it. 'Our trains are usually late. This is Germany,' they say, eyes pointing upwards. I debate whether to share stories of British trains but decide against it, and instead murmur something about the beautiful countryside. They are the first people I have heard so brazenly convey their disappointment at today's Germany. As if to prove their point, the train pulls up inexplicably 3 kilometres short of the destination, at Neu Ulm. After fifteen minutes, I've had enough of waiting, get off the train and walk back into the city. Sarah has found a wonderful arty, left-field hotel (Boutique 005) in the middle of the city, which is in the midst of a throbbing beer festival. We have dinner at a table in the street, watching ever drunker partakers sway past us extravagantly late into the night.

Only the next day do I take stock of the extraordinary city in which we have found ourselves. Divided from Neu Ulm on the south bank of the Danube, which is in Bavaria, the medieval city of Ulm on the north side lies in the state of Baden-Württemberg. The city blossomed as the German Samarkand of north–south trading routes from the Netherlands to Italy. Then in the nineteenth century it became Germany's Clapham Junction, an international railway corridor with trains rattling through night and day from Paris to Budapest and from Strasbourg to Vienna, and then on to Lemberg and Odessa, Belgrade and Constantinople. Who would have imagined too that this unassuming city so far from the war's Western and Eastern fronts should have such a deep and complex story to reveal? Ulm blossomed in the fourteenth century, when the massive minster was begun, till the late sixteenth century, after which the city ran out of money. Finance and willpower conjoined to complete the minster spire only 200 years later and in 1890, for four glorious years until overtaken by Philadelphia City Hall, the city rejoiced in having the tallest building in the world (albeit requiring a somewhat flexible definition of the 1889 Eiffel Tower as a 'free-standing structure' rather than a building). Amazingly, the spire remained Europe's tallest building until 1952.

War has been unkind to Ulm. In the fighting following the French Revolution, it was occupied by French and Austrian forces, who wrought much damage, until 1805, when it was the site of Napoleon's masterful victory at the Battle of Ulm. Then during just one night, 17 December 1944, Royal Air Force bombs laid waste to over 80 per cent of the medieval city.[23] The minster itself was later spared when a 500-kilogram bomb in a subsequent raid failed to detonate. My walk does not take me to Dresden and Hamburg, still less to Berlin and Cologne, which all suffered the most from Allied munitions. But it is a reminder, even in this seemingly peaceful corner of southern Germany, of the destructive tentacles of war.

Unlike Reutlingen, Ulm retains its magic, with the medieval winding streets and buildings restored or sympathetically reimagined. Wandering around the lanes, Sarah and I at last find some peace, and my sense of purpose in my walk begins to revive. On this leg so far, apart from the Bielenbergs, I have encountered darkness. But we now find ourselves in Hans und Sophie Scholl Platz, just below the minster square, and this helps restore my zest. The square was named in 2004 in honour of siblings Hans and Sophie Scholl as part of a citywide drive to commemorate them and twenty-six other young people from Ulm who confronted the Nazi regime. The Scholl family moved to Ulm in 1932 with their five children. Nearby lies the home on Münsterplatz where the family lived from 1939 to 1944. Hans was born in 1918 and joined the Hitler Youth early in the Nazi reign. Sophie was born three years later, joining the League of German Girls within the Hitler Youth in 1934. Their experiences disenchanted them with the Nazi regime; after Hans set up an anti-Nazi group in 1936, he came to the attention of the Gestapo, who imprisoned him the following year. In 1939, he left Ulm to study Medicine in Munich, and was joined by

Sophie Scholl, centre, and Hans Scholl, left, with their friend Christoph Probst. All three were part of the White Rose, and all three lost their lives to the Nazis on 22 February 1943.

Sophie three years later, where they both became influenced by the Catholic journalist Carl Muth and university professor Kurt Huber. With fellow students, they started distributing leaflets denouncing Nazi crimes and repression under the moniker 'White Rose' (the origin of the name is obscure even today).

Copies of the five separate leaflets they published were placed strategically around Munich University and beyond. 'With mathematical certainty, Hitler is leading the German nation to disaster. Hitler cannot win the war, he can only prolong it! His guilt and the guilt of his assistants have infinitely exceeded all measure. A just punishment grows ever closer!' read the fifth leaflet.[24] Then on 18 February 1943, Sophie and Hans placed copies of a sixth leaflet in front of the lecture rooms in the university's main building, and then threw the remaining copies down into the atrium. A janitor reported them and they were promptly arrested by the Gestapo. On 22 February, after a 'People's Court' trial in which Sophie repeatedly harangued her accusers, they were executed in Munich-Stadelheim prison by guillotine. In July 1943, copies of the sixth leaflet were dropped by Allied planes over Germany with the heading 'The Manifesto of the Students of Munich'.[25] A rare but uplifting act of cross-national unity during the war.

In Ulm itself, the leaflets were distributed by the Scholls' friends Susanne Hirzel and Franz Müller. When they were tried, the racism of the infamous Nazi 'blood judge' Roland Freisler might even have worked in their favour, because he could not believe that the pretty blonde and blue-eyed Hirzel could possibly have meant ill. He therefore gave them short prison sentences and they survived the war. Müller would have nightmares of being taken to the guillotine for the rest of his life.[26]

Hans, Sophie and their fellow White Rose students were young men and women from unremarkable homes, and I'm again left asking why, if they showed such courage, other students, a group noted for anti-authority thinking and impulsiveness, didn't seek to oppose the regime more widely across Germany. How do you reconcile Sophie Scholl and Gudrun Ensslin, both doing what they thought was the right thing in standing up against an evil fascist state, one seeing the truth clearly, the other, delusionally? One used terror and hatred in pursuit of her objectives, the other words and reason. One bequeathed confusion: the other inspiration.

Sophie and Hans are undoubtedly heroes in my quest, a title that cannot be bestowed upon another celebrated Ulm candidate. On D-Day, 6 June 1944, this figure was celebrating his wife Lucie's fiftieth birthday at a family gathering at home in the village of Herrlingen outside Ulm, having made a stopover in Paris on his way down to purchase fashionable shoes (size 3 and a half) for her from its finest shoe boutique. With her birthday celebrations in full swing, he received the startling news of the Allied landings in Normandy. Erwin Rommel, military commander in North Africa from 1941 to 1943 and now of the defence against an Allied invasion in France, was the man with the best chance of thwarting the landings. On the decisive day, the Allies landed 150,000 men establishing a beachhead. He had travelled to Ulm believing the bad weather in the English Channel would have prevented such an Allied invasion. He was wrong. His Horch 830 staff car drove him at speed along German autobahns and French national roads but it was after midnight when he arrived at his headquarters at La Roche-Guyon, a chateau on the Seine 70 kilometres west of Paris. But eighteen hours had been sacrificed without effective communications. The best German opportunity for repelling the invasion had been lost.

Once he arrived in Normandy, Rommel showed the same talent for inspirational and aggressive leadership that he had previously displayed in the Western Desert and in 1940. But Allied firepower, aircraft and sheer numbers began to turn the tide. The battle to stem the invasion was already lost when, on 17 July, Rommel was wounded in an aerial attack by a patrolling RAF plane. The official story was that he died of complications from the wound, and Hitler ordered he be given a funeral with full military honours in Ulm, where he is buried. The reality is he was suspected of complicity in the 20 July Stauffenberg plot, and was offered the chance to kill himself with a cyanide pill, which he took. For several years after the war, notably in the film *The Desert Fox: The Story of Rommel* starring James Mason, he was portrayed as a 'good' German. The reality is that, though undoubtedly less complicit than most senior Nazis, the film and a host of publications perpetuated a myth. Rommel was aware of the barbarities of Hitler's regime, and turned against him at the end when he realized he was leading Germany to disaster. But in a country and in a world weary of the Second World War, Rommel 'the good German' was for many a convenient model of an apolitical 'heroic' German who had fought cleanly, in contrast to the Nazis.[27]

High on the charge sheet against Rommel was his awareness of the proposed '*Einsatzgruppe Egypt*', charged with murdering the sizeable Jewish population in North Africa and in the British Mandate of Palestine.[28] Walter Rauff, who helped design the gas van to murder Jews at scale, met Rommel's staff and some *Einsatzgruppen* units to discuss how to murder Jews in his territories most effectively. Only British victory at El Alamein and American landings of Operation Torch, both in 1942, which together led to Rommel's total defeat, ensured that the *Einsatzgruppe Egypt* was never deployed.

Einsatzgruppen were special units of the SS. Like all Nazi organizations they had the trappings of a military unit: rank, uniforms, structure, weapons and vehicles. But they did not fight; their purpose was the mass execution of the Jews initially in Soviet territory. They drove from town to town 'liquidating' an entire civilization. Sometimes their victims numbered a few dozen or a few hundred. At Babyn Yar in Kyiv in September 1941 they shot 33,771 Jews in two days, including no doubt some of my family; a few weeks later 14,300 at Simferopol, then two months later at Rumbula 25,000 more, and on and on and on.[29] To the *Einsatzgruppen*, the destruction of a community that had lived in a place for centuries was just a matter of a day or two's work and a little organization. Overall, they murdered 500,000 Jews in Eastern Europe – part of what French priest and writer Patrick Desbois described as 'The Holocaust by Bullets'; namely the murder of 1.5 million Jews, and half a million others, across Eastern Europe in the aftermath of the German invasion of Russia in 1941.[30]

Ulm became the focus of global attention in 1958 over the activities of another *Einsatzgruppe* unit. The Ulm *Einsatzgruppe* trial was the first major Nazi war crime trial to take place under West German law rather than by military or international tribunal as at Nuremberg. Writer Hannah Arendt had written of a visit to Germany in 1950, 'Everywhere one notices that there is no reaction to what has happened.'[31] The country was still numb. 'Denazification' was waning by the mid-1950s, as the Allies wanted to move on and enlist, not further demoralize, the nation as active allies in the Cold War. The 1958 trial changed all that. As historian Tony Judt wrote, the Ulm *Einsatzgruppe* trial began the process of national remembering in Germany. While the world

Two defiant students with a totally different philosophy, impact and legacy. Gudrun Ensslin, left, and Sophie Scholl, right.

watched on, the sixty days of trials proved conclusively that the ten defendants were involved in 5,502 murders, with the guilty sentenced to prison terms of three to fifteen years. The trials marked the first of a series of tribunals carried out by Germans themselves, including the Auschwitz trial in Frankfurt in 1963–65. By the end of the decade, West Germany had announced that schools should teach the history of 1933–45, something that continues to the present day.[32]

Ulm should be seen as a heroic town in my story, one that had known great darkness, but had come to terms with it and moved on. Inge Scholl, Hans and Sophie's sister, founded the Scholl Foundation in 1950 and Franz Müller, the last surviving leader of the student movement, founded the White Rose Foundation in 1987, both of which worked to perpetuate the memory of the Scholls, their group, and the ideals of democracy and courage that they espoused. The city embraces all the best, and worst, of the past with honesty and integrity.

From Black Forest to White Rose. This section of the walk from Freiburg that had begun in darkness closes with optimism, renewed in this city of light.

3

Swiftly Flows the Danube:
Ulm to Donauwörth

Chapter 3
Ulm to Donauwörth

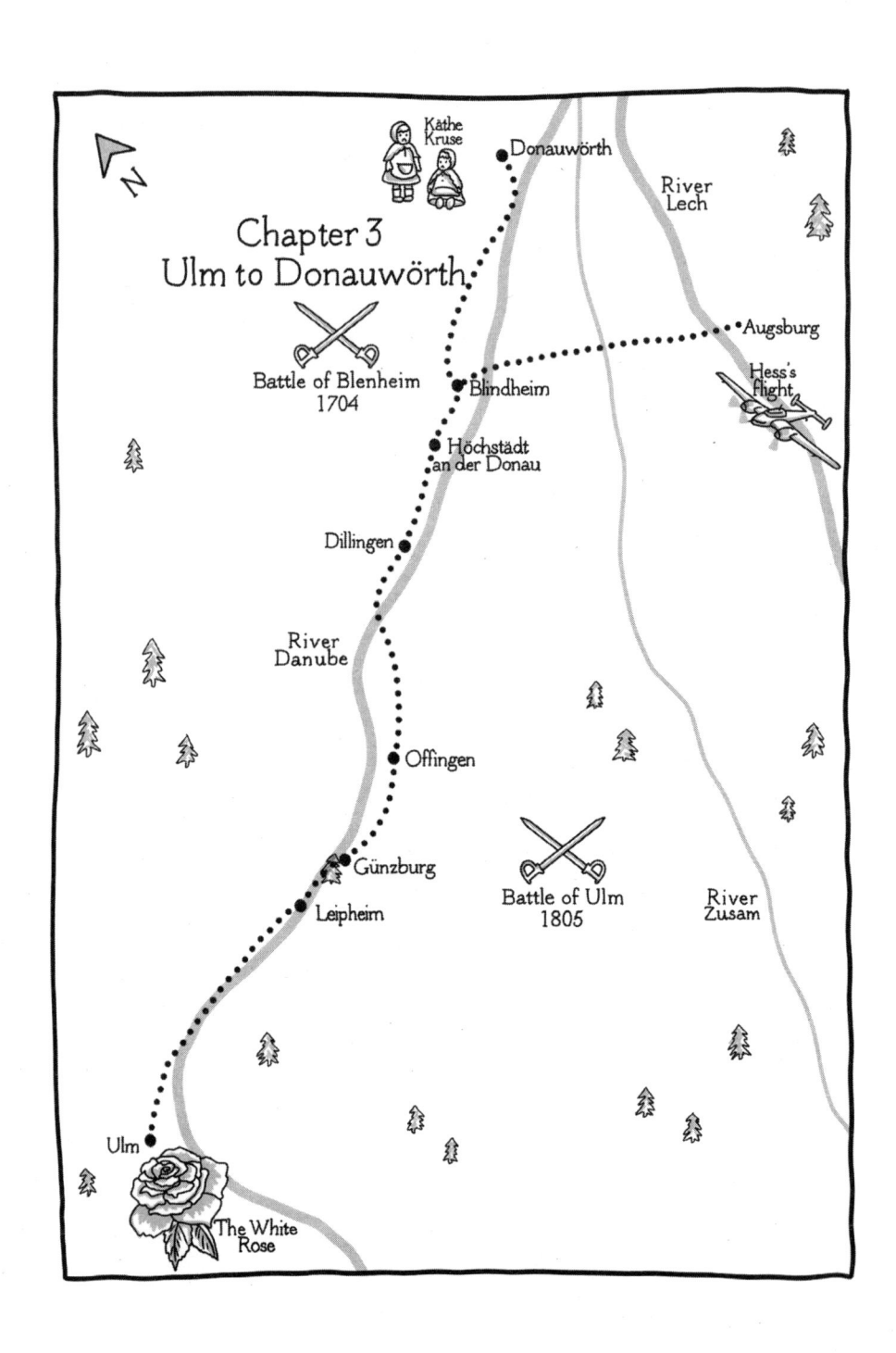

I'm going to have to put everything I have into this walk if I'm going to succeed. Killing the kilometres is the only game in town. Time spent discursively looking at the countryside through which I'm passing will have to take second place. It's the kilometres, stupid.

Walking for the next three chapters will take me through Germany's biggest state, Bavaria, rich in history and cradle of Nazism. So what can be said of my new home for the next 400 kilometres? The same size and of similar shape to the island of Ireland, it borders Austria to the south, Baden-Württemberg to the west, the Czech Republic to the east and the German states of Saxony and Thuringia to the north. An independent duchy from the sixth century, for centuries after it was a staunchly Catholic force within the Holy Roman Empire until its disbanding in 1806 when it became the Kingdom of Bavaria, retaining its title of 'kingdom' and much autonomy even after incorporation into the unified Germany in 1871, finally ending up a full (West) German state after the Second World War. It retains even today a keen sense of its distinctive history and culture, not unlike Scotland within the United Kingdom, including a blue and white flag, though without Scotland's hankering for independence. Yet…

No surprise the Nazi Party was founded in Bavaria's capital Munich in 1920, and that in 1923, Hitler chose Munich as the site for his Beer Hall Putsch, an attempt to emulate Italian leader Mussolini's defining 'March on Rome' of the year before. While Munich earned itself the title *Hauptstadt der Bewegung* ('Capital of the [Nazi] Movement') in 1935 from the Führer himself, Nuremberg, Bavaria's next largest city, was chosen as the site for Hitler's rallies. It was there too that a special meeting of the Reichstag in September 1935 proclaimed the Nazi racial laws: the 'Law for the Protection of German Blood and German Honour'. Hitler built his mountain retreat in Bavaria, at Berchtesgaden, 150 kilometres east of Munich, where he met British Prime Minister Neville Chamberlain in September 1938. As the war came to a close, the Nazis talked of a 'Wagnerian last stand' there in the Bavarian Alps, resulting in two US armies being sent to deal with it. But, when the American 3rd Infantry Division arrived in early May 1945, they found that Allied intelligence had been hoodwinked; there was no *Alpenfestung* (Alpine Redoubt) at Berchtesgaden and, having hardly fired a shot in weeks, euphoric US paratroopers drank champagne in what survived of Hitler's mountain retreat after the RAF had bombed it a few days before. Extensive looting of Hitler's private possessions and paintings took place: today, they are unsavoury collectors' items.

Hitler naturally chose Munich as the location for his plush private nine-room apartment at Prinzregentenplatz 16, in the upmarket Bogenhausen district. When Berlin and Berchtesgaden became Hitler's preferred bases after war broke out, the Munich apartment was regularly used for Nazi guests under special invitation. The iconic photograph of the uninvited American photographer Lee Miller naked in his bath in the flat, with her boots symbolically on his bath mat still muddy from Dachau concentration camp, and a photograph of the Führer propped up by the taps, was shot on 30 April 1945.

Meanwhile, 600 kilometres to the north-east, Hitler shot himself, in the company of another woman, that very same day. The day before, he had dictated his last testament blaming the Jews for the war, and encouraging the Germans to keep up the fight. He put a bullet in his right temple at about 3.30 p.m. with his 7.65mm Walther PPK pistol, deep in his bunker beneath the garden of Berlin's Reich Chancellery. His wife of one day, Eva Braun, selected cyanide as her exit tool of

American photojournalist Lee Miller bathes in Hitler's bathtub, 30 April 1945.

choice. Their bodies were burned by his staff to prevent capture by the advancing Soviet Red Army just streets away in the smouldering city.

Nazism was quite a legacy for Bavaria to live down. But it rapidly dusted itself off, and flourished after 1945, exploiting the independence it was given in the 1948 Constitution as a federal state with a wide measure of autonomy. It helped power Germany's *Wirtschaftswunder* ('economic miracle') spearheaded by a host of Bavarian companies including Siemens, Adidas and Puma becoming household names, and as home to the celebrated *Mittelstand* (small and medium-sized family-owned companies) at the heart of Germany's post-war economic success. But the Bavaria into which I was about to stride was losing its confidence and boundless optimism, no less than the rest of the country.

For as long as I can remember, Germany was a proud exemplar of success in post-war Europe, with a booming economy and stable, sensible political leaders. Whereas Britain's industries continued to decline after the war, Germany's bombed-out industrial sector roared back into life, with more German cars being sold in Britain than British cars. Even the absorption of East Germany's moribund economy from 1989 was barely a speedbump for the Federal Republic. Germany was a beacon to the rest of the world, having recovered from both defeat and division, reconciled itself to its shocking past, and found its place as a peaceful, orderly country, representing the best of modernity, contributing strongly to Brussels, while perched under America's defensive shield.

But Germany, as did Japan, the other major defeated power, had grown complacent. Angela Merkel's sixteen-year chancellorship (2005–21), once seen as the epitome of all that was prudent, had lost its way. Her energy deals with Russia, closing Germany's nuclear power plants and the slashing of the once mighty Cold War army left the country in poor shape for the new age of confrontation. Meanwhile, Germany's industries were rocked by the revelation that the Volkswagen group had been cheating on its emissions tests: so much for German dependability. During the 2020s, German energy costs rose, no longer able to rely on cheap Russian gas, while investment fell, industries shuttered and growth stalled. By 2025, the country was in its second consecutive year of economic contraction and wages in 2024 were 8 per cent lower than they had been in 2019.[1]

All this led to an uncertain political landscape. Chancellor Olaf Scholz's hapless coalition government was in a poor state by 2024, and Germany's future looked more bleak than at any point since the war. Racism too was, as we have seen, on the rise again.

One question I must confront. Did Bavaria hate the Jews more than other German states? Prussia (if not Berlin), Saxony and Thuringia were all early supporters of the Nazis and their antisemitic rhetoric and policies. Bavaria certainly had a long history of victimizing Jews, but not uniquely so. For nearly 900 years leading up to 1933, Jews were subjected to regular expulsions and massacres at the hands of the state or Church, including over 600 killed in Nuremberg in 1298. Some

10,000 Jews are believed to have been murdered in Bavaria when they were blamed for the Black Death during the 1350s. After the Jewish population had been expelled from various cities in the fifteenth century, they settled in small towns and villages developing a patchwork of rural communities exceptional for their cultural significance and economic activity, named the *Landjudentum*.[2] The nineteenth century was a seesaw for German Jews longing for emancipation and full civic recognition under the law, but they had to wait until unification in 1871. Jews who returned to the cities after emancipation drew great strength from the longevity of their communities. For the next sixty years, they were anxious to show that they were good Germans, contributing to civic society as lawyers, entrepreneurs and scholars, dutifully fighting for the Fatherland from 1914.

Jews were much less numerous in Bavaria, though, than in the rest of the country. In the census of June 1933, there were approximately 500,000 Jews in Germany out of a total population of 67 million. But whereas some 160,000 resided in Berlin, 26,000 in Frankfurt and 20,000 in Breslau, only 9,000 were living in Munich.[3] They were all made to suffer terribly in the years that followed. Conclusion? Bavaria was not uniquely antisemitic, though its close identification with the Nazi Party, and its hosting of two particularly virulent concentration camps, Dachau and Flossenbürg, have made it seem so.

Sarah agrees to accompany me on foot for half a day, just 15 kilometres from Leipheim station to Offingen. I'm always happy when she's walking with me. 'I can see why you like walking so much,' she says. 'If only it was always like this,' I reply. We are following rural paths by the side of the river, the temperature warm but not hot. After an hour, we arrive at the village of Günzburg where the small Günz river is swallowed up by the mighty Danube. Since Roman times, it's been a strategic crossing point and the town even today retains a certain air of importance.

How could this small community of little more than 20,000 souls have produced not one but two frightful people? We are shocked at what we learn. Günzburg spawned Franz Schwarz, a civil servant and former soldier who was an early Nazi and took great pride in raising the money for the publication of *Mein Kampf*. Hitler was so impressed he asked him to become national treasurer of the Nazi Party in 1925, a position he held until a week after his beloved Führer's death. Hitler's financier died in an Allied internment camp at Regensburg in December 1947, fully thirty years before a still more sinister child of Günzburg, Josef Mengele, gasped his last breath. The so-called Angel of Death betrayed all the values of his medical profession when, aged just over thirty, he conducted experiments on Auschwitz inmates including rubbing glass shards into their open wounds and personally selecting who should live and who should die. After the war, he was helped to escape to South America where in his final years he was described by his son Rolf as an 'unrepentant' Nazi who claimed he never personally harmed anyone but was just carrying out his duty as an officer.[4] Having been protected by many including the sales director of the family firm in Günzburg, he strung out his years listening to Mozart and watching cowboy films with friends until a stroke did what Allied justice couldn't when swimming off the coast of the state of São Paulo in Brazil in 1979. His final wish was to be buried as a soldier, arms at his side in the coffin as if standing to attention.[5] In 2017, a museum to the Holocaust was opened in São Paulo, as moving an initiative as it is imaginative.

Were those who hid the Angel of Death, securing him another thirty years of life, themselves guardian angels? I think not, though some helpers were no doubt ignorant of the full depth of his depravity. The vast majority, though, knew exactly what they were doing and did so willingly, evil defending evil. I am looking at a photograph of Mengele, boyish, without a hint that he was other than a perfectly normal person, fun to be around even. I think of his young impressionable age, the poison of racial superiority already having seeped into his bloodstream corrupting and hardening his heart.

A smiling, plausible Josef Mengele at Auschwitz in 1944.

We talk about the comparative youth of Hitler's stars. So many had their minds poisoned when they were still young. Mengele was just thirty-two when posted to Auschwitz in 1944; Adolf Eichmann, who ensured the Holocaust's trains reached their destinations even as the Reich collapsed, was thirty-three when war broke out; propagandist Joseph Goebbels was thirty-five when Hitler came to power; Heinrich Himmler, commander of the SS, was thirty-eight when war broke out; his deputy Reinhard Heydrich, architect of the Holocaust and Protector of Bohemia and Moravia, was thirty-eight when assassinated. Their youth is striking. But what of their wives and lovers? Did they not prick their consciences about what they were doing? Does the world have young monsters in the making today, avid for the opportunity to commit similar horrors were it to present itself?

A while later Sarah and I are sitting on a bench where the Danube has widened out into a lake when a German lady comes over to us with her dog and starts chatting. After fifteen minutes, she's told us her whole life story: her failed marriage, two children, how she can't get work as a teacher because she was not born in Germany, nor can she access its social security benefits. 'This country is like the Third Reich but it's now "Heil Amen". The Church runs everything. If you're not male, not Catholic, not local and not young, you are discriminated against.' We are sure Bavaria has its faults, but we're not expecting this total condemnation. She's not picking up our response. On it pours. 'It's the fault of immigrants. They're running crime. We've got the Taliban right here!' Oh, how we wish that she would stop, but there is more anger still, now turning on a target where at least we feel we can empathize. 'The mosquitoes are terrible this year because the Danube flooded. There's an epidemic of ticks. I thought the floods would kill them but they can survive three weeks under the water. My dog is covered with them. Last night I took two out from his neck.' We turn in tandem to look at the unfortunate dog, and edge away down the bench imperceptibly. Suddenly our companion has talked herself out, and the whirlwind of gloom sweeps off in the opposite direction.

Good to her word, as soon as we leave, we are surrounded by swarms of mosquitoes. For the next hour till we arrive at Offingen River Café we battle away, Sarah, sans eighty-wash guaranteed insect-proof shirt, faring less well. When we arrive we spray ourselves liberally from dispensers provided along the counter.

Our taxi takes an age to arrive and when eventually we climb in, we're joined by no fewer than twelve mosquitoes. Dispatching them requires skill and agility in a cramped back seat but when we do, we are verbally assaulted by our voluble driver relishing his captive audience, a German whose parents in Venezuela he regularly visits. 'The country's in a terrible state. Maduro [president since 2013] is the worst criminal of them all.' He sees us looking startled in his rearview mirror. 'Ninety per cent of the world's cocaine comes from Venezuela and 90 per cent goes to the US. I hope Trump wins. He might do something about it.' On and on he talks about the problems over there, balanced only by the even worse problems 'over here'. Crikey. No one we meet, it seems, has a good word to say about Germany today. But worse than Venezuela is quite something. We are not sorry to be dropped off at the station to catch the train back to Ulm, relieved it doesn't break down, isn't full of drugged-up criminals and even pulls into the destination on time.

The next day, I am on my own, taking the train from Ulm Bahnhof back to Offingen. Sarah has fallen in love with Ulm, and wants to spend a day exploring and speaking German while I spend the day stumbling across territory that, in two epoch-making battles, changed world history. The Danube is my obvious route but mosquitoes and ticks still loom too large in my mind so I set off across the fields to Aislingen, a small village where as I arrive, St George's Church strikes nine and a cock crows in unison. A transitory moment of bliss. The lanes I take as I exit have banks populated liberally by cornflowers, knapweed, petunias and peonies. For the first time in a week, I feel a cool breeze blowing on my face, and I feel energized and restored. I branch off across fields through rising farmland with clumps of woods and decide to walk due north along cycle tracks to Dillingen.

This once proud town boasted a university opened in 1549 and was a centre of the Counter-Reformation in Bavaria. But the Elector of Bavaria closed down the seat of learning in 1804 and the town lost its way in history. I walk past the dilapidated barracks, imagining the German soldiers training on the parade grounds before going off to fight in the First World War. Images of the recruits being put through their paces float through my mind in the most faithful 1930 film version of *All Quiet on the Western Front*. I summon all my energy to walk the remaining two hours to Höchstädt an der Donau, leaving little time to envisage not one but the two major European battles fought right here in this most sleepy, woebegone corner of southern

Germany. Forgotten by the world today maybe, but this very same countryside forged modern Europe.

The first, the Battle of Blenheim (1704), saw the Duke of Marlborough being sent by Queen Anne to intercept Louis XIV's French army, which involved a five-week slog with his heavily laden forces on uneven roads from Flanders, where they were stationed, to join forces on the Danube with the Habsburg commander Prince Eugene of Savoy, the military genius who had ended the Ottoman threat to Europe. The two leaders could not have been more different. Marlborough had risen through the army, distinguishing himself by skill and assiduous use of connections, and was keenly protective of his wealth and status. By contrast, Eugene valued wealth little but excess a bit too much. A French prince, he had been expelled from Louis XIV's court due to youthful scandals so resolved to serve the Sun King's enemies. Together, Marlborough and Eugene forged one of the most unlikely but effective military partnerships in European military history.[6]

On 13 August 1704, despite being outnumbered, they engaged the French between Höchstädt an der Donau and the village of Blindheim 4 kilometres to my east, which gave its name to the battle – Blenheim. Over the course of a bloody day, Eugene and Marlborough pressured the French flanks, before delivering a killer blow at the centre in the late afternoon. 'The [French] foot remained in the best order I ever saw, till they were cut to pieces almost in rank and file,' wrote Lord Orkney, who led the final assault.[7] Soon after, the broken French forces surrendered in the burning Blindheim. The battle destroyed the myth of French, and Louis XIV's, invincibility, and paved the way for further allied victories including Ramillies (1706). The humiliation of England's old enemy France was all but complete; the French monarchy in the eighteenth century never recovered its lustre, and in 1792, France became a republic.

Winston Churchill, born in Blenheim Palace, the Crown's extravagant gift to Marlborough, was boundlessly proud of being his descendant. No surprise, then, that he deliberately took time out from being a cabinet minister in H.H. Asquith's Liberal government to visit the battlefield of Blenheim by motor car in 1909. 'In the village of Blenheim, we found an amiable curate and an intelligent postman, both of whom knew about the battle and were able to point out the features of the field,' he wrote excitedly to his wife Clementine.[8] On the same official European tour, he met Kaiser Wilhelm II when observing German army manoeuvres, writing to Clementine that 'these people are so amazingly *routiniere* that anything at least out of the ordinary, anything they have not considered officially and for months, upsets them dreadfully'.[9] Five years later, Churchill was First Lord of the Admiralty and directing the Royal Navy against the Kaiser's battleships in war.

Churchill was back visiting Bavaria in August 1932 while researching his biography of the Duke of Marlborough (published in four volumes between 1933 and 1938), and was disturbed by what he saw the Nazis, still five months from taking power, were doing. While staying at the Grand Hotel Continental in Munich, his son Randolph sought to arrange a meeting with Hitler, who was in Munich, via his foreign press secretary, Ernst Hanfstaengl. The meeting never took place. Hitler, distracted and unshaven in the hotel's lobby, dismissed the idea to his aide: 'What part does Churchill play? He is in opposition and no one pays any attention to him.'[10] History is full of such sliding door moments.

What of the second history-changing event that took place in this sleepy corner of Germany? Churchill dreamed of writing a book about the leader at the heart of this second action, whose bust sat on his desk.[11] In October 1805, Napoleon Bonaparte's army crossed the Danube between Höchstädt and Donauwörth, separating the Austrian army marching from Vienna. Napoleon's plan was to annihilate them before the rapidly approaching Russian forces arrived. Several skirmishes took place in mid-October, forcing the Austrian army to retreat west into Ulm. Napoleon's artillery repeatedly battered the town, leading

Kaiser Wilhelm II and Winston Churchill view army manoeuvres in 1909. Within five years, the Kaiser would lead Germany into war, while First Lord of the Admiralty Churchill directed the Royal Navy against him.

to General Mack's surrender with the Russians still 160 kilometres away. One month later, Napoleon achieved what Louis XIV never did, the occupation of Vienna. With the Battle of Austerlitz following in December 1805, Napoleon's greatest battlefield triumph, the balance in the Napoleonic Wars tipped against France's enemies. 'Roll up the map, it will not be wanted these ten years,' said Prime Minister William Pitt the Younger, when he learned of the defeat, the shock of which helped to kill him a few weeks later. Napoleon's success here on the Danube became a staple of military academies as an example of strategic success with little loss of life. It was a decisive influence too on the formation of the Schlieffen Plan, the blueprint Germany employed for invading France and Belgium at the start of the First World War.[12] History can never be understood in isolation.

History of a starkly more contemporary kind preoccupies me when I arrive back at Boutique 005 in Ulm. I spend two hours sitting up on our bed preparing for an interview on Keir Starmer, discussing his first five weeks for Radio 4's *Westminster Hour*. My theme is how he should be learning more from history, specifically what direction successful prime ministers like Pitt the Younger and Churchill took early on. Starting out with the right message and the right people in place. 'Roll up the map' instead was Starmer's mindset as he became Labour's least-prepared incoming prime minister. How different if he had some of Eugene's or Napoleon's brio, or Marlborough and Wellington's panache.

It's pack-up day, and after a walk around the city that has brought us great joy, we drive to Augsburg; on the way Sarah drops me at Höchstädt, which I now regard with a new respect for its walk-on role in Europe's history. Again I forsake the Danube, less than a kilometre to my right, and walk along cycle tracks the 20 kilometres to Donauwörth, nodding respectfully at Blindheim as I go. I sense a surge of optimism: if I can make it to my destination tonight, I reason, I might make it to Nuremberg, a tantalizing 100 kilometres beyond, in a further four or five days. If I can achieve that target, then maybe, just maybe, I might be able to complete the walk. A gentle sun, only 25°C, propels me on, and in the second half of the walk, I switch to welcoming farm lanes running just to the west of the main road.

After four hours, I arrive at Donauwörth, midway point between Munich and Nuremberg on the confluence of the Danube and Wörnitz rivers. I revel in the ecstasy of two rivers, and the town's medieval buildings. But as I have learned to expect, they belie a bloody history.

Käthe Kruse and a few of her dolls.

In the early 1600s, riots took place when the Counter-Reformation attempted to reconvert the population to Catholicism; at the start of the eighteenth and nineteenth centuries, marauding armies in the Spanish Succession and Napoleonic Wars also skirmished here. Despite heavy bombing in the Second World War, the fourteenth-century town hall, medieval churches, gates and fortifications thankfully survived.

I might be winning the kilometres battle, but I'm really struggling to find evidence of figures of light on this leg. But the city did become the home after 1945 of famous doll-maker Käthe Kruse, whose dolls were renowned for hair that could be combed, their expressive faces, and bodies that are soft and warm. She came to the attention of the Nazis when, having lost two sons in the war by 1944, it was noted that her dolls' facial expressions were growing sad. When she refused to fire her half-Jewish workers or produce politically correct faces, her workshops were closed down. When even a doll can become a 'person of interest', one glimpses how extensive was the demented reach of the Nazi totalitarian state.[13]

I walk to the station to catch a train to Augsburg. But they are not running, an electrical fault we are told. I hop on a replacement bus and hear more complaining about the modern Germany. I want to defend my new home, but think better of it. Instead, I tune in to American tourists chatting excitedly about the presidential election. Today, Biden tells the US it is time to 'pass the torch' to Kamala Harris. Would that it had come sooner, they say. They move on to the pressure that Israel's leader Netanyahu is bringing on Biden to 'close gaps' on policy in Gaza. Even here, I sense global politics' tectonic plates shifting.

A hundred minutes after we set off, we reach the suburbs of Augsburg. Out of the window, I watch helplessly as an out-of-breath middle-aged man chases someone who I imagine is a thief out of a café, his distress palpable. Pockets of deprivation are evident everywhere I look in Bavaria's third largest city, with idle youths hanging around looking for trouble and druggy types looking lost. When I alight at the station, the smell of marijuana pervades the concourse, which has an abundance of tattooed people of all ages amidst the ubiquitous graffiti. Why are the graffiti and drug pushing openly tolerated, I wonder? Both spread if not tackled. It's not that the state is oblivious. 'No marijuana on the platforms', a sign says, a stern warning not to overindulge in the spoils of the hard-won victory of liberty over tyranny.

I'm not sorry that we are staying outside the centre. I take a tram out to our hotel, the Ringhotel Alpenhof, another left-field establishment with rooms in random places, gathered around a swimming pool. While a thunderstorm rages, Sarah and I dine outside under a large umbrella, with Bavarian food, Bavarian wine and Bavarian raindrops splashing liberally on the table.

The following morning in bright sunshine we catch the slick Siemens tram from outside our hotel. We are excited to visit the city, confident that the jaundiced view I had formed last night of the McDonald's,

Starbucks and Subway-littered station concourse (perhaps American occupation never did end?) would be superseded by the majesty of this world-famous city. The day begins well. Augsburg has been proud of its tram network since horse-drawn carriages first brushed the rails in 1881. Our inability to crack the ticket system aside, we marvel at this triumph of civic engineering as we glide silently into the heart of one of Germany's oldest and most influential cities.

The 1555 Peace of Augsburg had always intrigued me. The Reformation had been raging for nearly forty years after friar and reformer Martin Luther had launched his campaign in 1517. The 'Augsburg Settlement', as the peace treaty is also known, seemed to me to be eminently sensible, even in my youth, a nod no less to the 'live and let live' spirit of the 1960s that still had me in its thrall. Good on Holy Roman Emperor Charles V for signing the treaty with the Lutheran princes in the north of Germany (the Schmalkaldic League) thereby ending the Catholic/Lutheran divide and making permanent the legal right within the Empire for rulers to decide whether their states should be Catholic or Lutheran. Very Haight-Ashbury.

Sadly, Augsburg (like San Francisco) presaged neither peace nor settlement. The bloody Counter-Reformation was followed by the Thirty Years War, which, as we have seen, killed and maimed millions. I still struggle to understand the title 'religious war' when the message of Christianity's founder so clearly was to love, not hurt our enemies. Only with the Peace of Westphalia in 1648 did the right of rulers to choose the religion in their lands become permanently re-established.

Had I been pinning too much hope on encountering the pre-1939 image of the 'fascinating city' painted by Patrick Leigh Fermor with 'its abundance of magnificent buildings, the frescoed façade of the Fugger house, the walls canopied with wrought iron'?[14] If so, I had failed to reckon with what happened on 17 April 1942 and 25–26 February 1944. On the first date, the RAF carried out an attack on the MAN company's U-boat engine factory in the city, Germany's largest such plant, to impair the serious harm the submarines were doing to Allied shipping. For the two years of fighting up to that point, night-time, high-level raids by the RAF had resulted in almost no damage to German industrial output. The arrival of the fast, four-engined Avro Lancaster bombers in 1942 made it possible to countenance a more daring strategy. A surprise low-level attack might allow the bombs to be dropped on the factory with pinpoint accuracy, in anticipation of guided missiles. When the plan was put to the test though, only five of the twelve bombers returned to England, and only thirty-six of the eighty-five air crew. The mission was a complete failure. Of the seventeen bombs that hit their target, only twelve detonated, inflicting minimal damage to the equipment and making zero impact on the rate of engine construction.[15]

The 1942 Augsburg raid made a significant impact, though, on RAF strategy, convincing Air Marshal Arthur 'Bomber' Harris that low-level raids in daylight were wasteful and ineffective, and only 'carpet bombing' of German cities should be pursued where crews and planes would be put at less risk, with the targets marked out for the bombers by 'pathfinders' who set fire to the objectives with incendiary bombs. Thus, in February 1944, 594 RAF Lancasters and Halifaxes, and US air force B-17s set off for Augsburg. Three-quarters of the crew were in their late teens or early twenties. Yet their efforts that night achieved what even the Luftwaffe struggled to achieve. German aircraft production was weakened ahead of D-Day: but the centre of the city was completely destroyed.[16] The attack had been unexpected: most of Germany's extensive air defences were on the Rhineland and in northern Germany. Augsburg was considered to be too deep inside Germany to be a significant target. The extreme cold ($-18°C$) meant the water in fire pumps froze, and the significant loss of civilian life led to the Germans labelling the raid 'terror bombing'. Indeed, 'Augsburg might rival Dresden as a tragic victim', wrote historian Robin Neillands in his book *Bomber War*.[17]

Bombed Augsburg in 1944.

The comparison needs tempering, though, with the numbers of dead: 25,000 in Dresden in February 1945, compared to under 1,000 civilians in Augsburg. Dresden, often seen as the most devastating case of civilian and cultural destruction, did not even suffer the worst among German cities which had up to 80 per cent destruction. Indeed, only four German cities with populations over 100,000 escaped significant damage, Heidelberg being perhaps the best known. The impact of carpet bombing seemed apocalyptic to those on the ground. Over 7 million Germans were rendered homeless, and in West Germany, nearly 20 per cent of the housing stock was destroyed, figures that shock even now, as do the 55,000 British Bomber Command crew killed, just under half of the total who flew, the most dangerous raids being the first and last five in the standard run of thirty sorties over enemy lines.[18] For perspective, being a member of a Bomber Command crew was significantly more hazardous than service as a First World War infantry officer.

At the end of the war in May 1945, *Stunde Null* or 'zero hour' ushered in the greatest civilian rebuilding project in history. As after the First World War, cities had the choice of either reconstructing ancient streets and buildings from maps and drawings, funds permitting, or creating modern cities around the needs of the car. In many cases, as here, there was little choice because the destruction of old streets and buildings was so total.

While some of old Augsburg survives, the majority has been rebuilt to fresh designs, the overall impact we find soulless. Parts of the great cathedral remain untouched, including the paintings on the nave pillars and altarpiece by Augsburg's prodigy, Hans Holbein the Elder, father of Henry VIII's portraitist Holbein the Younger, who was also born in the city. We visit the fifteenth-century Fuggerei, the oldest social housing in Europe, and the town hall, both restored after 1945. But we can't find any of Leigh Fermor's mystery and magic. No fascination any more. Now, Augsburg is just a town. And yes, I wince when I think of Britain's undeniable role in its cultural, aesthetic and perhaps even moral decline.

Patrick Leigh Fermor has been haunting me on this journey as he did on the Western Front Way. In December 1933, the eighteen-year-old set off from the Hook of Holland to walk to Constantinople. Three books flowed from his journey, the final volume published posthumously,[19] a reminder to me to get on with it if I am to complete my third walk to the Ukrainian front line. Hitler had only recently come to power as he set out, providing an immediacy to his first volume *A Time of Gifts*, reimagined and published many years after his journey. As he wrote, 'Appalling things had happened since Hitler had come into power ten months earlier; but the range of horror was not yet fully unfolded. In the country the prevailing mood was a bewildered acquiescence. Occasionally it rose to fanaticism.'[20] I envy him many things, particularly his youth and his gift for writing, his address book opening up stays in a range of aristocratic eyries and his freedom from a phone vibrating every few minutes with messages from home. His flights of fancy are captivating, especially when not literally true. As biographer Artemis Cooper says, 'He found the legends surrounding a person or an event every bit as interesting as the truth.'[21] I'm excited to be briefly crossing here in Augsburg and at Donauwörth the 'PLF' line, as I term it, as seen on the map on page 100. He remained throughout an inspiration for this walk, as he has been for countless others.

Leigh Fermor's medieval roofs, cloisters and street corners may have been obliterated forever, but I still search to the city's south for a landing strip that made history, forlornly it turns out. On 10 May 1941, a solitary figure boarded a specially prepared Messerschmitt Bf 110 aircraft on that Augsburg airfield for perhaps the most bizarre journey of the entire war. The pilot, Rudolf Hess, was a slavish adherent to Hitler who dictated *Mein Kampf* to him in Landsberg prison. He was appointed Deputy Führer in April 1933 and was responsible for signing into law much of the Nazis' most venal legislation, including the Nuremberg Laws of 1935. But he was marginalized, and something of an embarrassment, by the time war broke out in 1939, had become mesmerized by the occult, and hatched a crackpot scheme to fly to Scotland to meet the Duke of Hamilton. A deluded belief had grown in his mind that the Duke was politically significant and that he was the best person to whom to convey his 'mission of humanity' to persuade him that Hitler 'wished to stop fighting with England'. Hess took off from the long-disappeared Augsburg-Haunstetten airfield on a foggy night with poor visibility, flew west cross-country and then up the Rhine into the North Sea until he ran out of fuel just 20 kilometres short of Hamilton's country seat, Dungavel House. He was captured by an astonished Home Guard, who could not believe their luck in doing something of which other units could only dream. A bemused Hamilton did agree to meet him, and then discussed it with Churchill, who concluded that Hess was a fantasist. Imprisoned for the rest of the war, he only escaped death at the Nuremberg Trials because of his obvious mental deterioration and his flight taking place before the Holocaust became fully operational. Locked away in Spandau, the former Prussian military prison, he remained incarcerated after the other six Nazi inmates including Hitler's architect Albert Speer had been released by 1966. For the last twenty-one years of his life, until he hung himself aged ninety-three in August 1987, he was Spandau's solitary inmate – defiant and unrepentant to the very last.

I had just written about this creepy man when I had a coffee with a friend, James Cowan, in London's Aldwych. He went very quiet when I told him about it. 'I was a young officer in the last British company in charge of overseeing Hess,' he whispered. The coincidence was riveting. 'Hess had been ill earlier in the year and taken to a military hospital, but recovered sufficiently to come back to Spandau.' The four powers (Britain, France, the US and the Soviet Union) rotated oversight monthly. 'I had recently arrived in Berlin from Sandhurst when a sergeant came to see me. "Prisoner Hess is dead," he told me.' After the medics had completed a postmortem and the body had been taken away, James said his company's immediate task was to implement the contingency plan. The principal fear was of Nazi memorabilia hunters and the risk of Spandau becoming a Nazi shrine. Vast sums were thus spent demolishing the entire prison brick by brick to be crushed, taken to a landfill site and buried forever. The ground was turned into a military café and then a shopping centre – which the British garrison swiftly nicknamed 'Hessco's', after Tesco's.

It suited the Allies greatly to have him dead at last. Family and sympathizers claimed that Hess lacked the strength to hang himself by an extension cable from a window latch. That question may rumble on, as no doubt will the story in circulation for many years that it wasn't Hess in Spandau all those years, although in 2019, a DNA test proved with 99.99 per cent certainty that it was him.[22] To thwart Nazi obsessives, his body had to be disinterred, cremated and the ashes scattered at sea. As I walk away from coffee with James, I contrast the deluded Nazi trophy hunters searching forlornly for their dark bricks with the joyous trophy hunters who, just over two years later, wanted a piece from another structure, the Berlin Wall, as palpable evidence of the victory of true freedom and democracy over tyranny and totalitarianism in November 1989.

James is most definitely a figure of light in my story. A brave soldier, he left the army in 2015 to head up the HALO Trust, the international landmine clearance charity. Landmines are a particularly sinister weapon of war, he tells me, that maim and kill often years after being planted, and which were first developed in modern form in the sixteenth century by military engineer Samuel Zimmermann, in Augsburg no less, another coincidence. He told me that it was only in the Second World War that the mines came fully into their own, with 'hundreds of millions' deployed. The all-conquering Germans had little use for them at first, but as they moved to being on the defensive from 1942, they used them to deadly effect especially after 1944 when they discovered non-metallic mines. The Russians alone laid over 60 million, as they are doing in Ukraine today.

Augsburg produced better souls than mine-father Zimmerman and myth-bewitched Hess. I'm determined to hunt down better people before I leave the city. It is not easy: many of the heroes who hid Jews and political prisoners, or the first responders and medics who fought to save life in the air raids, were killed or are names lost. But we do have a few figures whose names have come down through the years. Walter Groos, an Augsburg resident and builder, was appointed site manager at Oberottmarshausen, a building plant that employed labour from Kaufering, a subcamp of Dachau. The mortality rate among the forced labourers was so high in winter that it won the nickname of 'the cold crematorium'. To shield his workers from the harsh winter and brutalities of their SS overseers, he distributed warm gloves, food and medicine, which he smuggled

Walter Groos, Augsburg factory manager who cared for his prison labourers.

in under the noses of the guards. Had his marriage to a half-Jewish woman opened his heart to their plight?²³

Hans Adlhoch headed the secretariat of the Catholic labour movement in Augsburg after 1918. He fell foul of the Nazis by consistently speaking out against them and was repeatedly imprisoned. He survived Dachau from July 1944 until 1945, only to die on one of the infamous death marches in May.²⁴ Bebo Wager, an Augsburg electrician, fought for better conditions for workers and took over the leadership of the Revolutionary Socialists in 1941. The Gestapo arrested him in 1942, and he was murdered in Munich-Stadelheim in August 1943.²⁵ Finally, Roland von Hösslin, a major in Stauffenberg's old regiment, was told by him about the plot to assassinate Hitler and given instructions to occupy key sites in the event the plan worked. He was arrested in August 1944 and sentenced to death by the People's Court and executed.²⁶ If family helped inspire Groos, was it his Catholic faith that moved Adlhoch, socialist ideology Wager and military honour Hösslin?

I have much more thinking to do. Clearly, many with family ties to Jews, deep Christian faith, passionate ideology and many who were humane German officers did *not* stand up to Nazism. Bavaria so far has yielded some light, but not enough for me to see clearly. I must walk on and probe more deeply if I am to answer the questions that are only growing in my mind, step by step.

4

One Way, Four Paths:
From Donauwörth to Nuremberg

Chapter 4
Donauwörth to Nuremberg

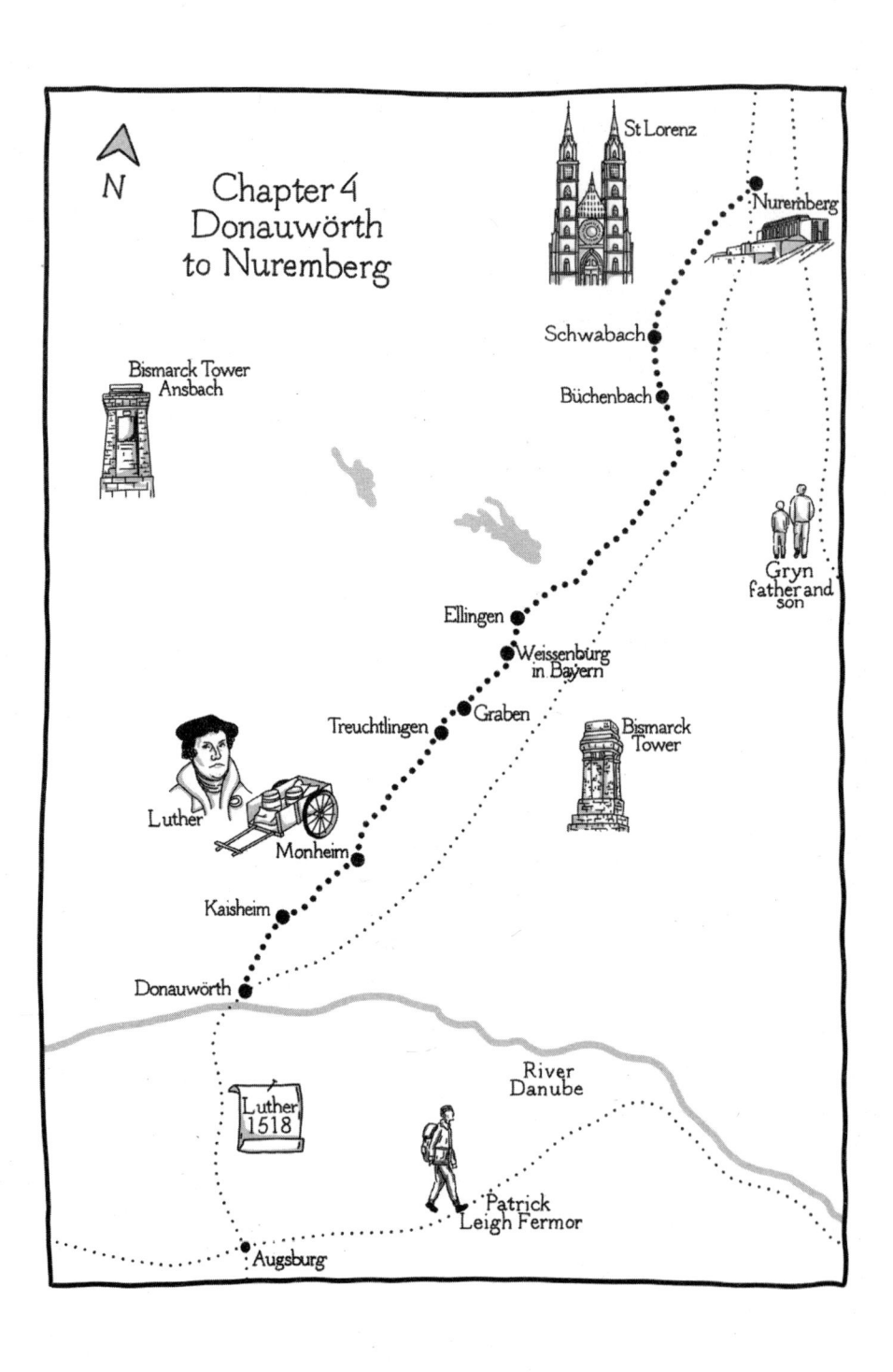

St Lorenz
Nuremberg
Schwabach
Büchenbach
Bismarck Tower Ansbach
Gryn father and son
Ellingen
Weissenburg in Bayern
Treuchtlingen
Graben
Bismarck Tower
Luther
Monheim
Kaisheim
Donauwörth
Luther 1518
River Danube
Patrick Leigh Fermor
Augsburg

I spend the following week battling my way due north through open countryside from Donauwörth to Nuremberg, a distance of just 100 kilometres that in normal conditions would have taken me comfortably under four days. But I make heavy weather of it in July 2024, which shames me when I think that crossing these tracks in earlier centuries, in immeasurably harsher conditions, were a querulous monk, a precocious teenager, and an adolescent boy with a sickly father. I have no excuses!

The first of these three I part company with is the teenager. Patrick Leigh Fermor has been with me on a shared trail since Ulm, but from here he heads off south-east en route to Budapest and Istanbul. From now on his charmed derring-do will taunt me not by his presence but by his absence. I see him disappearing off towards Munich and Austria in his hobnail boots that were to last him the whole journey, his sleeveless leather jacket and riding breeches, his ex-army greatcoat and puttees to keep out the damp. These were all purchased, he tells us, at Millets, the military surplus shop on London's Strand.[1] I imagine him striding to it over Westminster Bridge, gazing down momentarily at the Thames that was shortly to bear him as the solitary passenger on the steamship *Stadthouder Willem* from Irongate Wharf to the Hook of Holland on 9 December 1933 at the start of his big adventure.[2] So fixated am I by his garb that I pore through the internet to discover that there were only three or four branches of Millets by 1933, since the shop first opened in 1893 in Southampton. I search obsessively for photographs of the outlet in the Strand in the early 1930s. There are photos aplenty of nearby Simpson's, purveyor of fine roast dining for one hundred years. But no sighting of Millets. I have to content myself with visualizing him walking in through a uniform-draped portal to emerge translated as a *walker*. Out I see him step into the teeming, fume-filled Strand bustling with red and white London Transport double-decker buses and honking Beardmore taxis spewing their fumes gaily into the air.

It is Sarah's last day. The previous evening, we sat up in bed to watch the rainswept opening ceremony of the 2024 Summer Olympics in Paris, athletes and performers joyously upstaged by the Seine and city. Next morning, we pack up at the Alpenhof and set off for Donauwörth. Before leaving we are fortified by piping hot chocolate in a café where the German waitress with impeccable English tells us that she first learned the language from Harry Potter, starting with the *Philosopher's Stone* at the age of ten even though no one in her family could speak a word of English, working her way religiously through to the final sentence of the *Deathly Hallows*. We wonder whether such an intelligent and engaging person currently visualizes no higher career ambition because of the state of the German economy.

Five kilometres on, we reach Kaisheim whose pride is a giant abbey that dwarfs the small town. Founded in the 1100s and modernized in Baroque style, under the Holy Roman Empire it was one of the dozens of self-ruling imperial abbeys. By the early nineteenth century, its glory days behind it, it became a prison and workhouse for those deemed 'antisocial'. The Nazis used it as a maximum security jail, incarcerating from 1943 several hundred *Nacht und Nebel* ('Night and Fog', or resistance prisoners). Three of the Channel Island 'political prisoners' deported by the Germans were incarcerated here. Altogether, 2,300 were taken from the islands to prison camps in mainland Europe, the only British civilians to be deported from British soil in the war. In April 1945, at the instigation of their guards desperate to flee the advancing Allies, surviving inmates were forced on a death march to

Dachau 100 kilometres to the south-east, a nightmare of endurance that few survived. The elegant white-painted abbey on this bright July morning reveals not a hint of its dark past.[3]

Sarah's imminent departure has unsettled me. We have a final moment: she's unhappy that I've organized an arts festival in August in the small village of Saint-Jean-de-Côle in Périgord Vert where we have a home. 'Why would you want to do that? You've been working non-stop for months. Can't we just have some downtime together without crowds of other people?' They are fair questions and I don't have a good answer. My constant drive to do things doesn't impress her. The last twelve days, which saw my black rainbow emerge then quickly recede, have been the longest we have spent together alone since I started at Epsom eighteen months ago. I have been learning more what a monumental change it is to settle down with another person till death, to take on their life, their hopes and fears, and fit them into a life already well grooved. After all, when I met Joanna, I was only twenty years into my life; now I'm perhaps twenty years from its end. Heck, I was Patrick Leigh Fermor's age. I hardly knew myself and was on the foothills of adult life; now I am trying to ward off a gentle descent. Then I had no real clue what life was or what it would hold; I thought I wanted to be a writer, a farmer, a stage director. I imagined living in an old farmhouse in Devon or Shropshire with a massive inglenook fireplace, surrounded by books, Bernese mountain dogs and bottles of Puligny-Montrachet and Clos Vougeot. So shallow! By the time I reached my present ripe age (did I really think I would make seventy?), I imagined my fears and self-doubt would be behind me. But they're still here, stalking me day after day, which I mask in part with relentless activity. How I wish I understood myself better. This journey, I'm still hoping, will reveal more answers.

It has been wonderful to have Sarah as a companion. We are learning to be with each other, to give space, to sense when to hold back and when to lean in. We're discovering what we bring to the partnership: a heart full of love, practical know-how and emotional intelligence from her. And from me? Well, we're still working that one out.

Walking alone starts out feeling good. The boots are much lighter and tighter fitting than in 2021, the Epsom gifts another boon, and I glide over the terrain. I'm walking mostly along lanes and paths, the air fresh, noiseless bar some distant birdsong and tractors. Given all the miles upon miles I see in all directions of fields and woods in this heartland of Bavaria, I wonder how on earth Hitler could possibly have thought he needed *Lebensraum* ('living space').

The doctrine of *Völkisch* expansion had emerged in the years before the First World War. Plans were drawn up in 1914, when French defeat seemed likely, to seize parts of Luxembourg and northern France permanently and to make Belgium a vassal state.[4] But the real prize was in the east, where the Kaiser's men had crushed the Tsar's. As Russia disintegrated into revolution, here was an empire for the taking. In March 1918, in the Treaty of Brest Litovsk, Germany gorged on Russia's former territory, but it lost every last clod of soil with defeat on the Western Front later that year.

Could the eastern landgrab, which tasted so sweet to the Germanic palate while it lasted, be achieved permanently? The Nazis certainly thought so. They talked of a German destiny in the east, echoing uncomfortably the US conquest of North America during the previous century when lands belonging to indigenous Americans, deemed an inferior people, were seized.[5] In Hitler's ideology, the German peoples were an Aryan master race (*Herrenvolk*) and required *Lebensraum* for survival (survival!). The peoples of these subjugated territories were to be exterminated, sent to work in prison factories or deported to Siberia.[6] The Jews were to be eliminated altogether, along with other 'undesirables'. 'We must be honest, decent, loyal and comradely to members of our own blood and to nobody else. What happens to a Russian, to a Czech, does not interest me in the slightest,' said Reichsführer-SS Heinrich Himmler in October 1943.[7]

'We must be honest, decent, loyal and comradely to members of our own blood and to nobody else. What happens to a Ukrainian or a Latvian does not interest me in the slightest,' Putin might say, as his forces batter Ukraine today. I stop walking, incensed. The deepest instinct I have within me is the polar opposite of that of Himmler and Putin. Caring only for those in your select group and to hell with the rest is a vile philosophy. So, if you are listening, Heinrich and Vladimir, I would say to you, 'It interests me not in the slightest whether I upset you or your cronies in asserting that the very best people in life are the bridge-builders, who reach out beyond tribe to a shared humanity, who make friends across nationality, faith, class, race and gender. You are on the losing side of history.' I'm feeling better now. The thought is clarifying in my mind. Might the men and women of light in this story turn out to have bridge-building in common?

Another thought occurs to me about a controversial bridge-building element in Britain, prompted by the news today about King Charles and Princess Catherine slowly returning to work after their cancer treatments. Monarchy was terminated in China in 1912, in Russia in 1917 and in Germany in 1918. All later saw genocide. Simone Weil, the French philosopher and mystic whose death in England in 1943 aged thirty-four was precipitated by her refusal to eat, in solidarity with the victims of Nazism, argued Britain was exceptional in having a centuries-long tradition of liberty guaranteed by the least powerful part of the Constitution, the monarchy.[8] It's a fair point.

I arrive after two hours at Monheim, a small thoroughfare town of some 5,000, but with a history dating back to the seventh century, another reminder of quite how much history has flowed through the ancient veins and arteries of Germany. This once walled town has much of its medieval beauty still evident, and stood at the cross-section of important trade routes. A plaque records where one traveller in 1518, monk Martin Luther, stayed overnight. He may have been the chief catalyst of the Protestant Reformation that changed world history. But what mainly interests me today is that this man was a serious *walker*.

Between 25 September and 8 October 1518 he strode purposefully from Wittenberg to Augsburg for a hearing with the Pope's representative, Cardinal Cajetan, to defend his Ninety-five Theses that he had posted on Wittenberg's Castle Church the previous year (historians debate the nailing, though not the content).[9] The distance is some 500 kilometres, and covering it in just under thirteen days, he would have had to walk 35–40 kilometres each day. Not for him the easy option of horse and cart: he was going to feel the earth crunch under his feet every step of the way through the cold and rain of a bad autumn, until almost in sight of Augsburg. His biographer says he yielded only when 'Stomach aches had forced him finally to climb on the wagon' that had been carrying his colleague Wenzel Linck on the last leg down from Nuremberg.[10]

Luther was no stranger to long-haul walks: in 1510, he yomped 1,500 kilometres to Rome and back. Walking was in his blood, as if he had something to prove.[11] Earlier in 1518, he had trudged the 500 kilometres from Wittenberg to Heidelberg expecting to be rebuked by the Augustinian Reformed Congregation, but so well did his Ninety-five Theses go down with them that he was offered most monks' holy grail, a lift home. 'I set off on foot,' he announced on his return, 'but I came back *in a wagon.*'[12]

Luther had been expecting until the last moment to face his accusers in Rome itself, so travelling to Augsburg was a breeze in contrast. The interrogation lasted three days and descended into a shouting match, resulting in him being regarded unequivocally as public enemy number one of the Catholic Church and the Pope. Grave offence was caused not least by his vitriolic attack on the abuse of 'indulgences', a pardon that could be purchased to reduce the deceased sinner's time in purgatory, so raising sorely needed revenue for the Church. Zealots wanted him arrested, but in the dead of night, he slipped out of the city. Luther referred to Augsburg as his 'first excommunication', though the deed didn't happen officially until January 1521, when at the Diet of Worms he refused to back down in the face of Emperor Charles V, proclaiming, 'Here I stand. I can do no other.'[13]

My admiration for the yomping monk is tempered by a most unattractive side he developed over time, a violent intolerance of those he disliked, including Catholics ('Romans'), the wrong kind of reformers like Anabaptists, and other races including Turks and Muslims – but none more so than the Jews. Initially a moderate, he wanted Jews to see the light and convert to Christianity to return to their own true faith. But when they refused, anger took over. In his 1543 tract *On the Jews and Their Lies*, he advocated 'that their synagogues be burned down, and all who are able to toss in sulfur and pitch; it would be good if someone could also throw in some hellfire'. His writing contributed significantly to the rise of antisemitism in Germany after unification in 1871: most antisemitic books published during the Third Reich refer to Luther and his writing. Himmler presented a first edition of Luther's *On the Jews* to Julius Streicher, notorious editor of the Nazi newspaper *Der Stürmer*. 'Hitler's fight and Luther's teaching are the best defences for the German people', declared Nazi posters from 1933. German bishop Martin Sasse, acclaimed as one of the foremost Lutheran theologians of his day, is said to have rejoiced in Kristallnacht coinciding with Luther's birthday, 10 November. Sasse edited a pamphlet following it called 'Martin Luther and the Jews: Away with Them!', publicizing his anti-Jewish statements: in it, Sasse praises Luther as the 'greatest antisemite of his time'.[14]

We cannot blame Luther for the way that some people subsequently enlisted him in their cause, though if people of influence espouse hate and violence, others will always latch on to it sooner or later. For sure, Luther was simply provided as an excuse for what the Nazis were intent on doing anyway. Apologists point out that he fulminated widely against all those he disliked, not just the Jews, invective was his style, that much of *On the Jews* was focused on proving Christ's unique divinity and only a small part on attacking Jews, and that his most vitriolic antisemitic writing came only when he was an elderly man and perhaps not thinking clearly. But it still leaves an unpleasant taste in the mouth. I am left with a question I would ask the fervent preacher if he was speeding along by my side today: 'Your core message was that *nothing* should come between a believer and God: so why did so many people who followed you see the world through *your* eyes and thinking?'

'You don't understand,' he replies impatiently. 'The devil, evil are everywhere. We cannot let up for one minute.'

'Why did you change from an advocate of kindness to calling for Jews' homes, synagogues and texts to be burnt and for them to be expelled or serve hard labour?' I see he is framing a reply, but our paths suddenly diverge and I am left not knowing if he regrets the intemperance of his later years which many believe tarnished the reputation of a giant.

Another hour's walking brings me by streams, valleys and hamlets to the peaceful small town of Treuchtlingen, founded in 793 at the time of the first Holy Roman Emperor, Charlemagne. Antisemitic diatribes continue to trouble me as I learn about the community which had 119 Jews in 1933, a presence dating back to the fourteenth century. Violence against them began almost at once Hitler came to power in January 1933, but it tended to be random in the early years. But, in 1937, when Nazi rearmament needed to be funded by expropriation, the rhetoric intensified and Jewish assets were increasingly seized ('Aryanization'). During Kristallnacht in 1938, Jewish leaders and businesses were targeted, and mobs with torches and clubs ran amok smashing windows. Albert Meyer was stabbed and a broken bottle was forced into the mouth of his daughter. After this, those fleeing had to 'run through a cordon formed by the mob'. Under the cover of Kristallnacht, the last six remaining Jewish businesses in the town were seized. In 1946, the largest 'pogrom trial' in the American zone of occupation was convened for crimes committed in Treuchtlingen on Kristallnacht, with thirty-nine found guilty of various acts of violence. Michael Wildt, who wrote a short history of the era of persecution,

An aerial photo of the US bombers hitting the railway line at Treuchtlingen on 23 February 1945.

and whose work informs mine, concluded bleakly, 'there is no Jewish community in Treuchtlingen today'.[15]

Such a gentle town, such horror, and not just at the hands of the Nazis and their sympathizers. At 11 a.m. precisely on 23 February 1945, Allied bombers flew overhead as part of Operation Clarion, involving 900 aircraft attacking transportation centres across Germany. Morning travellers fled the stationary train they were in when they heard the sirens, making for the shelter of the underpass. But it afforded the terrified women and children no safety. Three hundred civilians perished in the subterranean hell and a further 300 in nearby homes and streets.[16]

In other news today, the French rail system is restored after saboteurs' efforts to disrupt the Olympic Games fail, bombs continue to rain down on Gaza, while funerals of Israeli children are being held following Hezbollah's attacks in the Golan Heights. Back home, reports are slowly emerging of a seventeen-year-old male arrested after stabbing children at a Taylor Swift-themed dance class in Southport. It transpires that three young children have been killed and ten injured; the following day, rioters with clubs smash windows, clash with police and attack a mosque. Muslims fear for their lives. Treuchtlingen Kristallnacht reborn? Where is this going?

Such hate, such avid scapegoating, such potency of ideas. I can't let go of those who advanced racial hatred in the name of religion. What was he thinking of? Nazis and racists everywhere are fired up not by the divine, but by anger, resentment and prejudice. I'm trying to find goodness during the war, and here is a massive figure, Luther, who for all his remarkable bravery and brilliant insights, left behind words that were used to justify genocide. The New Testament, though, is crystal clear that we should neither kill nor harm, neither hate nor commit acts of violence. Even those who reject his divinity can see merit in Christ's teaching, the Good Samaritan urging us to care for all, not just those of our tribe, or not throwing stones unless sure of one's own total innocence because we all carry guilt. Then the beatitudes, extolling justice, love, goodness, truth and peace. I suspect it will emerge as I walk on that many of the figures of light in this story will have been inspired by a personal relationship with a God of love.

Nazism divided an already flawed German Church in twain. In a speech in the Reichstag in March 1933, Hitler described Christianity as 'the foundation' of German values.[17] The 'German Christian Movement' was created by the Nazis to unite all Aryan Protestants with National Socialists under one banner. Movement leader Pastor Ludwig Muller helped bring Nazi ideology into line with Christian doctrine, exiling all Church leaders with Jewish heritage, and promising to purge all Jewish influences from churches including removing the 'Jewish' Old Testament. The rallying cry was to be 'One Nation! One God! One Reich! One Church!' Slowly, as we shall see, Hitler's key leaders moved publicly against Christianity; but not yet.

Reaction came in the form of the breakaway Confessing Church under the leadership of Pastor Martin Niemöller, which adopted the Barmen

Pastor Martin Niemöller, an opponent of the Nazi regime and founder of the Confessing Church, but also one who wished he had done more.

Declaration in 1934 rejecting any subordination of Church to state.[18] Roughly a third of the country's 18,000 Protestant pastors supported the Declaration, but it fell far short of a principled resistance movement, seeking rather accommodation for their beliefs and practices within the Third Reich.[19] Niemöller, initially a self-confessed antisemite and a Hitler supporter, became increasingly disillusioned with Nazism, spoke out against it and was imprisoned from 1938 to 1945 at Sachsenhausen as Hitler's 'personal prisoner' and then Dachau.[20] In the camps, he experienced profound remorse for not having done more to help the victims of Nazism and he became a key initiator of the Stuttgart Declaration of October 1945 issued by the Council of the Protestant Church in Germany.

'By us infinite wrong was brought over many peoples and countries… we accuse ourselves for not standing to our beliefs more courageously,' it said. Unlike Christian martyrs Dietrich Bonhoeffer and Maximilian

Kolbe, whom we meet later in the story, Niemöller survived the war, and spent the next forty years touring the world condemning the Nazis and educating the world about persecution and human rights.[21] But he is best known for a poem of little more than seventy words written in 1946, one of the most powerful statements to emerge from the Second World War.

> First they came for the socialists, and I did not speak out –
> Because I was not a socialist.
> Then they came for the trade unionists, and I did not speak out –
> Because I was not a trade unionist.
> Then they came for the Jews, and I did not speak out –
> Because I was not a Jew.
> Then they came for me – and there was no one left to speak for me.

Some of the most profound statements in history are brief: President Lincoln's 1863 Gettysburg address is 272 words. But the truths of its words reverberate down the years. So too do Niemöller's. Every year when I sat with Joanna at the Yom Kippur service, I was minded to read these words as a modern reflection on the ancient words and themes of the Yom Kippur machzor (prayer book).

Catholic complicity in Nazism is equally fraught. In late 1933, the Nazis signed a Concordat with the Vatican that guaranteed the rights of the Catholic Church (one of the only Nazi-era agreements still in force today). A spotlight has been trained on the failure of the Papacy to use the unique moral force of its office to temper the Nazis. Whereas Pius XI released an encyclical *Mit brennender Sorge* ('With Burning Concern') read from all Catholic pulpits attacking the Nazis for 'neopaganism', his successor from March 1939 Pius XII, for all his good work saving Jews discreetly, did not speak out strongly and explicitly against the Nazi genocide whose existence was becoming evident from the early 1940s.[22] Nor did Bishop of Münster Clemens

Bishop Clemens von Galen showed that Church leaders could speak out against aspects of Nazism, and survive.

von Galen who helped draft Pius XI's famous encyclical. In the summer of 1941, von Galen delivered three sermons attacking Nazi terrorist methods, the murder of patients in psychiatric homes and confiscation of Church property. He denounced the maltreatment of Catholics, but regrettably and significantly did not publicly condemn the murder of Jews. The sermons were widely publicized in Germany and abroad; Allied planes scattered leaflets quoting them over Germany, giving heart to many resisting, including the Scholl siblings and the White Rose movement. Yet because of his popularity, the Nazis did not risk arresting him.[23] After the war he was made a cardinal shortly before his death in 1946 and in 2005 he was beatified.

We have already encountered Protestant Pastor Hermann Maas in Basel, and we will hear later about other Christian leaders who risked everything. But it's hard to escape the conclusion that the overall balance sheet of Christian leadership in resisting the Nazis is underwhelming. Historians argue that where there was resistance, it tended to be churches looking after fellow Christians, while those who helped Jews were acting more on their own. The US Holocaust Memorial Museum concludes: 'there was virtually no public opposition to antisemitism… [But there] were individual Catholics and Protestants who spoke out on behalf of Jews, and small groups within both churches that became involved in rescue and resistance activities'.[24]

I catch the train from Treuchtlingen station, site of horror, to Nuremberg, cradle of more horror, the rallies, the Race Laws and the Trials, but now a vital city bursting with life. I'm going to make it my base for the next few days, allowing me time to catch up on my tardy walk diary. I check in at the Novotel Central, everything a corporate hotel should be but which the hotel in Ulm was not. As I settle into my clean and orderly room, I experience a nostalgic twinge for the sheer Gothic weirdness of the Ringhotel Alpenhof in Augsburg with its inexplicable objects round every corner, rocking horses, brass instruments, eerie clocks and stacks of old LPs. My plate glass window looks down on Nuremberg station and railway tracks. I drag my mind away from imagining the trains of prisoners passing through, back to the present. I'm hungry, but am eager to explore. So I set off into the early evening heat and walk to the old city, rejoicing in the dining tables spread across every street in all directions and bountiful street musicians creating a festival atmosphere. I soak it up, feeling intensely alive and emotional, not least walking mid-town along paths beside the Pegnitz river, which I had never seen before. On my way back to the hotel, I stop in front of the church of St Lorenz, whose twin burnt-ochre towers dominate the western facade. Completed in 1477, I wonder whether Luther too gazed up in wonder on his journey south in 1518. What we do know is that the prior of the monastery gave him a new cowl to replace his threadbare head covering, some speculating that this was so he would make a good impression on spectators at his predicted execution in Augsburg.[25]

The Pegnitz flows through the heart of Nuremberg, my photo July 2024.

* * *

I'm into a rhythm. Here's the plan. I catch an early train south on the high-speed Nuremberg to Augsburg line and hey presto, station by station, day by day, I will walk my way back up to Nuremberg. Today is billed as the hottest day in Bavaria all summer, 32°C and more. I am desperate to get ahead of the sun, and every hour counts. So I wake up early, have a quick breakfast and rush to the Bahnhof past the drug fraternity only to see the 7:38, with annoying punctuality, pull out just as I arrive on the platform. I am irrationally upset. I sit down on a wooden bench and immerse myself in writing an article about Keir Starmer's first two months, pouring my frustration into the piece. Diversion therapy for me; less good for the PM. I question his decision to remain at Number 10 and not take a summer holiday, a mistake all premiers tend to make. We are better served by rested not fraught leaders.

The 8:38 pulls in late and deposits me on Treuchtlingen platform at 9:30. I hope it will still be cool, but from the moment the carriage doors open, the heat surges towards me. I scale down my ambition for the day, 25 kilometres, 20, 15: heck, let's just see how far I can go before I evaporate into thin air.

When it's hot like this, what I crave is the kindness of trees. But I can find no shade, my path taking me on a cycle track by the side of the main road (as foretold by the tourist office in Alsace) and then bordering the railway track. I pass through the village of Graben and become ridiculously excited that I have stumbled across the Via Claudia Augusta, the great German road linking Lombardy, via the Alps, to the Danube, marking the northern frontier of the Roman Empire. But… something is wrong here. When I examine it more closely, I see that the Roman road stopped at Donauwörth, which lies to my south. A quick search on Google Maps tells me that there is another Graben lying between it and Augsburg. Wrong Graben. Duh! Kicking myself, I press on deflated along the shimmering, hazy path.

I arrive at Weissenburg in Bayern, a modest-sized town that happens to boast bountiful Roman remains, intact medieval walls, a Gothic town hall in continuous service since 1476, and a 'Bismarck Tower'. These last are structures erected as a tribute to Otto von Bismarck, the Prussian chancellor whose three calculated and successful wars against Denmark, Austria and France had led to the unification of Germany in 1871. Almost 250 such towers were built from 1869, with some 173 still existing today, albeit many in ruins. The idea was that they would be crowned by huge torches at their peak to commemorate the great man, to be lit on select occasions. But there was never a uniform design, and many were constructed as observation towers only, so the dream was never realized. Another incomplete project came 1,000 years earlier at the hands of no less than Emperor Charlemagne. Chroniclers have it that he stayed at an imperial palace in Weissenburg in 793 personally directing his ambition for the *Fosse Carolina*, a canal to connect the

Rhine and the Danube basins. A couple of kilometres of canal were built before the project petered out.[26] It did at least inspire King Ludwig I of Bavaria to build the Ludwig canal connecting both river basins, which opened in 1846, though it was too narrow to be a success.[27]

I stop by a cross in the town. The Nazis encountered resistance here as elsewhere in Bavaria when they began to remove Christian symbols from public spaces, official buildings and schools and to replace them with swastikas, Nazi symbols and portraits of Hitler. By the late 1930s, Nazi revulsion at Christian teaching had grown stronger, and although the party never officially disavowed Christianity, its hostility was increasingly evident. Had Hitler won the war it is likely he would have tried to eliminate Christianity altogether, which he considered weak and decadent, and indeed all other faiths.

Tomorrow is my last day walking. I wend my way along lanes and tracks through the small communities of Büchenbach and Ottersdorf to Schwabach as temperatures climb back to over 30°C. I am troubled by a snail crossing the road, and 50 metres after passing it, I go back to pick it up because I worry it's going to be crushed by the passing cars. But the level of force it takes me to lever it off the road is so great I worry I might hurt it. So we decide to part company, leaving it to its precarious journey while I continue at my own snail's pace.

I listen to the news reports from the Olympics, and updates on the Southport knife attack: the BBC is saying 'people have become simply fascinated by violence'. I don't think that's right: in my experience, most people are revolted not fascinated by violence. I read about fresh stories of children's funerals after the Golan Heights attack and the talk of retaliation. Today is the inquest into the death of Emma Pattison, which precipitated my period at Epsom College. All morning I receive updates on the progress at the court. Then the shattering news comes through with awful symmetry that the chair of governors who asked me to take over, Dr Alastair Wells, died last night. In our short time together, we had formed a deep bond. I am shaken. Chairs can make or break a school or university head. Poor ones, I've had a few. But Alastair was a marvellous and wonderfully kind man, up there with the very best.

Back in the hotel room, I spend four hours in the early evening dealing with the inquest, sending and responding to messages. My core task in the job was protect, protect, protect, above all the pupils, then the staff, the parents. No one needed the school to become associated in the public mind with tragedy. I have come under intense pressure today from media outlets to be interviewed. 'No, look, I'm very sorry, but I really don't want to do that.' 'Head at murder school speaks': good for the media, no doubt, but no good at all for the school and the welfare of those in it. The pupils had had a stellar year in the eighteen months since the tragedy, but the media are never interested in that. They come back at me an hour later: 'We are very keen that you talk to us.' I say a little more emphatically 'no'. I had thought I might be able to answer questions once the job and inquest were over, but now they are, I realize I still can't. I never let what happened unnerve me when doing the job; we all supported each other. But, out here alone, in a strange hotel room, fighting off heat exhaustion, I feel vulnerable. That night, I wake up with an intense headache that won't go away. Waves of panic wash over me. Sleep is hopeless.

The following morning, I catch a train to Schwabach, just 15 kilometres south. It's the hottest day so far, but this time I'm taking no risks, and drop electrolytes liberally into my water which inexplicably I haven't been using this week. Walking by the Donau Main canal is the highlight. A fulfilment of the dreams of Charlemagne and Ludwig I, the canal, completed in 1992, is even more ambitious, and links not just the Rhine to the Danube, but, effectively, the North Sea to the Black Sea. I'm back at the hotel by lunchtime, pack up my motley possessions and catch the train towards Munich Airport.

'Yes, it's often like this,' I am told by two German students, very chatty, with peerless English. I ask them about the late running train and the acute overcrowding.

'This is Germany,' they say.

'But I thought the trains ran on time.'

'That was Mussolini.'

Awkward.

'Is there any air con?' Not my best conversational gambit.

They shrug. It's annoying: I bought a first class ticket as an end of trip treat, but there's no space in first, nor even standing room.

'The economy, it's in trouble,' they say. 'Nothing's working.'

I look sympathetic. The train slows down for their station.

'But it's still a great country,' they call back at me as they disembark.

It is. It really is. Indeed, I have fallen in love with Germany and its people. On this last day I've decided to detour and stop at a city I've been intrigued by ever since I learned about 'The Perpetual Diet of Regensburg', which was, until abolished by Napoleon in 1806, the Reichstag (Parliament) of the Holy Roman Empire. I peer out of the window as the train slows to pull into the station. Regensburg was founded at the confluence of the Regen, the Naab and the Danube rivers to become Bavaria's fourth largest city. One of the oldest in Germany, it survived seventeen sieges throughout history and was never far from strife. A Roman fortress, it had been a bishopric since the eighth century and a stopover point for marauding Crusaders on their way to and from Jerusalem.[28] Hitler himself never warmed to it as he did to Munich. Angry to learn that the mayor joked that Hitler hated the city because the Nazis had not performed well in it in the 1933 elections, he eventually accepted an invitation to speak in the town hall in June 1937. But as he entered the chamber, a heavy chandelier crashed down from the ceiling. Taking it as a bad omen, he promptly turned around, never to return to Regensburg.[29]

One resident stands out for me. Not the famous Oskar Schindler who lived here from 1945 to 1949, of whom more later, but the largely unknown Johann Maier, a Catholic priest at the cathedral. On 22 April 1945, Gauleiter Ludwig Ruckdeschel demanded that all residents defend their city to the very last against the fast-advancing American forces under General George S. Patton. The following day, crowds demonstrated in the town hall square in favour of a peaceful handover. When they began to get angry, because they did not want their city destroyed, Maier called on them to remain calm and spoke of avoiding violence. Promptly seized by the Nazis as a ringleader, he was tried shortly before midnight and sentenced to death. In the early hours of 24 April he was publicly hanged with a sign around his neck bearing the words 'he died a saboteur'. During the night of 26 April, Ruckdeschel and the remaining Nazis slunk away, deciding resistance was futile. The city duly surrendered to the Third US Army on 27 April without a shot fired.[30] The protesters had helped save massive loss of life as well as the historic town centre from destruction. But not before the SS had dynamited parts of the famous twelfth-century *Steinerne Brücke* (Stone Bridge) over the Danube.

When the US forces entered the city, they were surprised to see that most of the historic buildings had survived the intensive air raids

The stunning city of Regensburg in 1930 with the undamaged Stone Bridge behind St Peter's Cathedral.

that had destroyed the railway network, the Messerschmitt factory and freight yards. In the vaults of the city's Reichsbank they found a vast collection of art stolen from across Europe, precious items from murdered Jews and $3 billion worth of Austrian securities.[31]

My trip to the city had been shortened by my train arriving over an hour late. But I still had time to see something of the remaining Roman, Romanesque and Gothic buildings, justifying its status as a UNESCO World Heritage Site. I run down towards the Danube before returning to the station to catch my train to the airport, which, as luck would have it, is also an hour late. And the air conditioning is again broken.

Reading about the death marches in the city brings me back to reality. Surely no more wretched wayfarers could ever have passed through Regensburg than disease-ridden groups of the walking dead in April 1945. They were on one of the infamous death marches as the Nazis emptied out the surviving prisoners from the concentration and extermination camps to flee the approaching Allied armies from east and west. Their aim was to redeploy the still mobile as slave labourers elsewhere, to remove human evidence of maltreatment alongside systematic destruction of the camps, and to hold hostages as potential bargaining counters with the Allies.

Buchenwald, one of the first and largest camps within Germany itself, saw the SS eject some 40,000 inmates, including many Jews, who were made to march south-east to less vulnerable camps, Theresienstadt, Flossenbürg and Dachau (an even earlier camp than Buchenwald). Those who walked close by where I stand in the heart of Regensburg were heading for Dachau, a 400-kilometre walk. They left Buchenwald at the beginning of April, a journey that took them three weeks. How they managed to walk an average of 20 kilometres a day is a mystery. Severely malnourished when they left, the daily ration of a third of a loaf of bread at the start was cut to almost nothing, while water had to be drunk from puddles. The fortunate had wooden clogs that cut their skin, the majority had to walk barefoot. Luther's walk covering much the same ground 400 years before seemed miraculous; but the feat of these remnants of the Shoah (the Hebrew name for the Holocaust) seems superhuman. Any who stumbled and fell and couldn't rise immediately were shot. One recalled an SS officer who would ask prisoners what month they had been born, and if the answer was April, they would be told, 'It is April now and the time for you to die.' They must have passed Regensburg on about the 24th of the month because by the 26th they were in the area of Oberlindhart, 35 kilometres south. Inhabitants of the villages and towns through which they marched watched from pavements and windows in disbelief, shocked and perplexed by the physical and mental condition of the prisoners. Many observers were far too frightened of the heavily armed SS guards to intervene or even to throw crusts of bread if they had any.

But in this forgotten area of the country, three Germans risked their lives to save thirteen Jews. Josef Kimmerling, commander of the nearby Neufahrn police station, had been instructed by SS guards to search out Jews who'd escaped in Oberlindhart, telling him that if he didn't kill them at once, he himself would be executed. Together with Max Maurer, commandant of the Ergoldsbach police station, they managed on 27 April to round up thirteen captives, and together with farmer's wife Anna Gnadl, they decided to help them. Dr Joshua Lustig, one of the survivors, reassured them that they would not try to escape, aware that to do so would put everybody's lives in danger. The three Germans then fed them and let them stay overnight on 28 April in the farm barn rather than shoot them as ordered or turn them over to the SS. Their decision saved their lives because on the morning of Sunday 29 April, the Americans arrived, and the remaining SS guards disappeared.[32]

A cynic might say of these three Germans that they switched sides at just the right moment. No doubt, countless deft switches of allegiance

Josef Kimmerling, left, Max Maurer, centre, and Anna Gnadl, three Germans who saved the lives of thirteen Jews in April 1945.

took place in these final weeks and days right across Germany. But in the case of these three, it seems that their hearts were in the right place. Gnadl came from a family that had a strong aversion to Hitler, which the award of the Nazi 'Mother's Cross' medal, given to mothers bearing six or more children, did nothing to allay. She shrugged off adverse comment from neighbours when she used the traditional Bavarian greeting *Grüß Gott* ('may the Lord greet you') rather than the mandatory salutation *Heil Hitler!* The two local police leaders Kimmerling and Maurer, friends since 1942, had Social Democrat inclinations, were never enthusiasts for Nazism and abhorred violence. None of the three attributed any particular importance to their actions: to them, it seemed to have been an act of natural empathy to which they felt committed because of their Christian faith.[33] Gerhard Strasser, who researched the event, wrote that the motivations of the rescuers 'were based not on politically motivated resistance but on compassion, on altruism, in short on fundamental ethics without any great political claims.'[34]

Maurer was posthumously inducted by Yad Vashem as one of the Righteous Among the Nations.[35] All 659 Germans given this title have had their actions rigorously tested and shown to be worthy of the designation. The figure, of course, vastly underestimates the number of Germans who risked their lives to protect Jews and others who fell foul of the Third Reich. Many of those who performed heroic and selfless acts will never be known to history.

But what of the father and his adolescent son, the third walkers I mentioned at this chapter's start? They left Lieberose concentration camp south of Berlin on a death march on the morning of 2 February 1945. The family had lived in the small city of Berehovo, which had become part of Czechoslovakia in 1919 (and after 1945, Ukraine). The parents, who married in 1929, had two sons. Comfortable rather than well off, the father was a timber merchant, and they played a prominent part in the life of Berehovo, which had 8,000 Jews (only a handful of whom returned after 1945). In 1944, after weeks of warnings and anxiety, the family were deported to Auschwitz, their ten-year-old son Gabi being gassed on arrival. A few days later their surviving son Hugo also entered a gas chamber ante-room:

> I walked in with the other children. We were in a large hall with wooden benches running along the walls. Facing the front door was another double door. A striking feature of the building was the streamlined effect of the contents. I mean, everything looked quite modern, unlike the rest of the camp. Door handles were polished and except for a heap of clothing in one of the corners, the whole look was disturbingly clean... 'Take off your clothing and fold it up neatly. Then line up in front of the door.'

But then, an officer asked him his age, and he lied, saying he was nineteen, rather than thirteen, old enough to be a camp labourer. He was told to get dressed and leave. But before leaving, he watched to see what would happen next. 'The children lined up in twos and the double door was opened. A strong smell came out of the hall beyond. It was a smell I had never experienced before. Sweetish, yet not sweet.'[36]

After several weeks of living in Auchwitz's hell, father and son were then taken by cattle cars to Lieberose, where one memory always stuck in Hugo's head. It is the story I recount at the end of the Preface about the Jewish festival of Chanukah that began that year on 10 December 1944, in which the father spoke about hope when his son berated him for squandering precious margarine on fuel for candles. As they left the Lieberose camp for an eight-day death march to Sachsenhausen, they heard continuous firing and noticed billowing smoke as the guards killed and set on fire everybody not able to move out.[37] Many perished on the 20-kilometre-a-day walk, only to find no respite or protection in their new camp, which revealed evidence of the fast-deteriorating Nazi administration. After Sachsenhausen, they were sent to Mauthausen in Austria by train. Then, shortly after a particularly cold and snowy Passover which ended on 5 April 1945, they were off again. This time, 17,000 prisoners were force-marched to Gunskirchen (a subcamp of Mauthausen). 'This march was even worse than the one to Sachsenhausen because, by this time, practically everyone was sick. There was almost no food at all', Hugo recalled.[38] When they arrived, 'conditions were terrible. What food there was, we were told afterwards on fairly good authority, was being poisoned. There was deep mud, fever and stench and many perished from starvation and the typhoid which by then had infected every one of us.'[39] Thousands of prisoners were compressed into each hut, but there was only one common twenty-hole latrine. The SS had orders to shoot on sight anyone relieving themselves in any place but the latrines, but as so many had diarrhoea, and the lines for the latrines were so long, many could not wait.[40]

On 5 May, 'Around mid-morning we could hear distant gunfire coming closer, the rumbling of tanks. Suddenly our guards… literally the dregs of the SS – dropped their guns, stripped off their death's-head insignia, and started to run. Suddenly there appeared an American tank

Hugo Gryn, along with his mother Bella and father Geza, and his younger brother Gabi murdered in Auschwitz.

and that was, as far as I was concerned, the end of the war,' wrote Hugo. In Auschwitz, his father had told him that they should never let each other out of their sight. The exhortation had seen them both through all the way to the end of the war. A momentous story of father–son love and endurance.

On liberation, the Americans took them to a barracks and put them in clean beds. They had prevailed through months of unimaginable hell to the war's end. 'My father and I shared a bed,' Hugo wrote, '[but] he died in my arms, about three days after we got there. For him, liberation was just a few days too late.'[41]

Hugo, unquestionably a figure of light in the story, came to England in 1946, having been reunited with his mother who had survived the war. He studied Mathematics at Cambridge, became a leading rabbi in London, an influential figure in Christian/Jewish dialogue and a regular contributor on Radio 4's *Moral Maze*. 'Hugo was almost obsessed by reconciliation. He wanted to reach out and touch the humanity in everybody he met,' wrote Michael Buerk, chair of *Moral Maze*, on his death in 1996.[42] A clearer description of human light would be harder to find.

On 11 July 1982, at West London Synagogue, Hugo Gryn married Joanna and me.

5

The Road to Flossenbürg

Chapter 5
Nuremberg to Flossenbürg

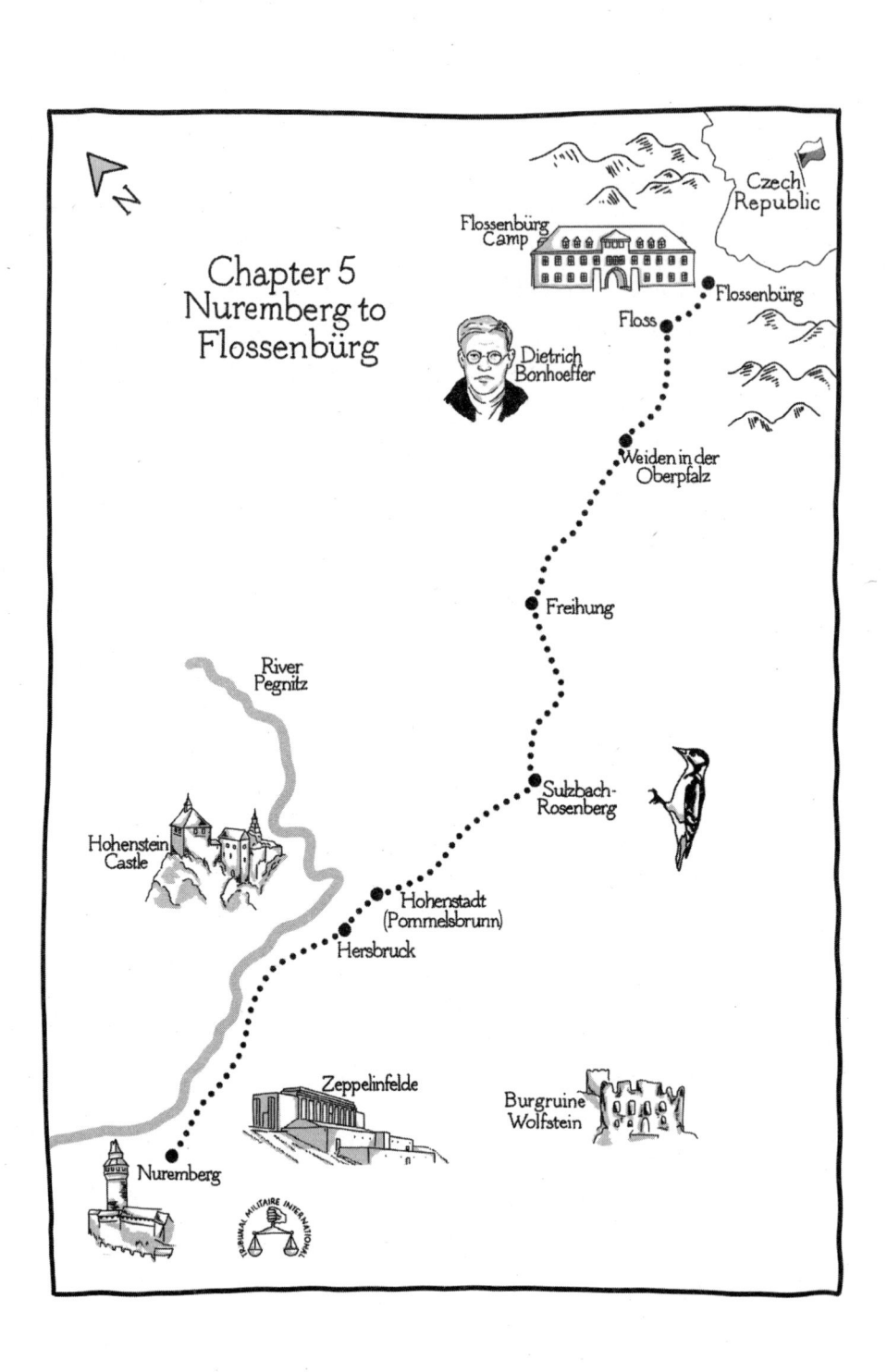

OPERATION BITING, D-DAY: THE *Unheard Tapes, Endgame 1944, The Escape Artist, Cassino '44, Arnhem: Black Tuesday*. I am transfixed by the book titles on display at WH Smith at London's Heathrow Terminal 3 as I loiter in my mosquito-proof battle fatigues waiting to be parachuted back into Germany at the end of August 2024. Almost half the best-seller and recommended book titles on display are histories, guides or novels about the Second World War. Television channels have been thick all summer with documentaries and films about it. Is there anything, I wonder, that holds our fragile country together more than this sense of a shared past when Britain stood defiantly alone, dug deep and emerged five years later on the winning side? The crowning, climactic moment is the black and white shots of King George VI standing with the young Princess Elizabeth side by side with Winston Churchill resplendent on the balcony of Buckingham Palace on VE Day waving to the thronging crowds. Has Britain been prouder or more united since?

How do Germans feel, I wonder, when they enter Britain and the first thing that happens after they pass beyond border control is to come slap bang wallop up against all this? What corresponding event in the 155-year history of their own country can they celebrate with similar pride? Not for them military victories and the vanquishing of enemies, but total and abject defeat and humiliation, not once last century but twice, and having to process personal and family complicity in the most industrially brutal and evil regime in modern history. That's a hard call, and it makes my admiration for the German people all the greater. What they have had to tell themselves is a very different story, one of economic and technological revival, of democratic and cultural regeneration, and exceptional sporting highlights since 1945, a more successful story indeed than post-war Britain, one explanation perhaps for our obsession with the wars. Before and after reunification in 1990, the Germans created a sense too of a shared identity to replace the *Völkisch* ethno-nationalism earlier in the century. That is why it is hard for the Germans that their great post-war economic and political success story seems to be going kaput, as I have been hearing every day. I've experienced nothing on my pilgrimage so far to compare with the convulsions that Leigh Fermor observed as he walked across Germany in late 1933 and 1934; but I've felt tremors, the rise of the radical right *Alternative für Deutschland* (AfD) being one manifestation, the regular cynicism and social exclusion I've witnessed, the other.

My journey this leg is north-eastwards from Nuremberg to the Czech border. I finish at Flossenbürg, such a pretty name, in the remote Fichtel mountains of Bavaria that rise to over 1,000 metres. In May 1938, this innocent town was chosen by the Nazis as a site for a concentration camp, initially to mine granite for grand Nazi architecture, and from 1943, to produce Messerschmitt Bf 109 fighter planes and other armaments for the war effort. By the early 1940s, a series of subcamps, sprawling like the ubiquitous mountain flowers, grew, reaching at their peak to more than one hundred.[1] Some 100,000 prisoners passed through Flossenbürg, and 30,000 died. In late 1941, the SS began experimenting with mass murder at Flossenbürg, when they began killing Soviet POWs. Initially, prisoners were systematically shot, with the SS ordering other prisoners to sing loudly to drown out the noise. But, after angry complaints from local residents about blood and body parts being washed up in the streams, its favoured method of execution was switched to lethal injections.[2]

I will be walking to Flossenbürg following ancient tracks and villages, a distance of 120 kilometres. My path will be winding and indirect. But the road from Nuremberg to Flossenbürg, as to Theresienstadt and Auschwitz beyond, could not have been straighter nor more inexorable.

No German city has been more associated with the Nazi regime than Nuremberg. Why not Berlin, the country's capital since 1871? Hitler never countenanced making Berlin the Nazis' spiritual heart, his relationship with the city being always equivocal, for all his need to have his control centre there. The capital had a much weaker Nazi base than solid Nuremberg, and was polluted by the presence of Communists. In the Nazi mind, it would always be associated too with decadent Weimar artists and interwar sleaze, well captured by Christopher Isherwood in his 1939 novel *Goodbye to Berlin* that inspired the 1966 musical *Cabaret*. Worse still, Berlin was home to a quarter of German Jews. No surprise Hitler had plans to raze the centre of the degenerate city and replace it with a pure Aryan 'Germania', global capital of the thousand-year Reich, with granite from Flossenbürg no less, a project that set his chief architect Albert Speer's heart racing with anticipation.[3]

Why wasn't Munich, cradle of Nazism, selected with preferred status as the shining Nazi city on a hill? In part because Nuremberg's location was more central than Munich, which lay far to the south. The Nuremberg chief of police was also a particularly eager Nazi, Heinrich Gareis, happy to help.[4] Far more important though, Nuremberg had played an evocative and central role in the Holy Roman Empire, the 'First Reich' consolidated by Emperor Otto I in 962, which Nazis revered as a precursor to their own Third Reich from 1933 (the 'Second Reich' had been created with the unification of Germany by Bismarck in 1871). Nuremberg had been designated as a Free Imperial City as early as 1219, giving it significant privileges under successive emperors. The city frequently hosted Imperial Diets and was home to the Imperial Court of Justice. Economically and culturally in the late Middle Ages and Renaissance, it was the imperial nerve centre. Its status as the Empire's symbolic and political centre was confirmed when, from 1424 to 1796, it was the official depository of the Imperial Regalia, including the Holy

Roman Emperor's crown, sceptre and sword. The Nazis adored such symbolism; after the Anschluss (annexation) of Austria of 1938, Hitler ordered the Regalia removed from Vienna and returned to Nuremberg.

By choosing to hold their annual rallies in Nuremberg, the Nazis were deliberately seeking to conjoin their movement to this rich imperial past. The rallies were all about showcasing Nazi ideology, bolstering and inspiring followers, deepening unity, and providing an overwhelming demonstration of the power of the party and above all of its leader, Hitler. The first Nazi rally was a makeshift affair, held in Munich in 1923, the same year as the Beer Hall Putsch. After three years, it was decided to move the rallies first to Weimar and then to Nuremberg. The 1927 rally was the first in the new location to the city's southeast, and the event steadily grew in ambition and fame until it became state-sponsored after the Nazis came to power in 1933.

To help showcase the rallies, Hitler's architect Speer designed the *Zeppelinfeld* in the Nazi Party's 'Rally Grounds'. Greek architecture was a principal influence, specifically the Pergamon Altar built in the second century BC which had been excavated by the Germans in the 1880s in western Turkey, with elements reconstructed in the Berlin Museum. Speer, captivated and inspired by what he saw, designed it with a large swastika atop, finishing it in time for the rally in September 1937. With military demonstrations, light shows and fiery speeches punctuated with regular applause, it was political theatre at its most high octane. Documentary maker Leni Riefenstahl famously turned the 1934 event, known as the 'Rally of Unity and Strength', into one of the most mesmerizing propaganda films ever created, called *Triumph of the Will*. American journalist William L. Shirer caught the scene:

> Two hundred thousand party officials packed in the Zeppelin Wiese with their twenty-one thousand flags unfurled in the searchlights like a forest of weird trees. 'We are strong and will get stronger,' Hitler shouted at them through the microphone, his

words echoing across the hushed field from the loud-speakers. And there, in the flood-lit night, jammed together like sardines, in one mass formation, the little men of Germany who have made Nazism possible... Later they recovered enough – fifteen thousand of them – to stage a torchlight parade through Nuremberg's ancient streets, Hitler taking the salute in front of the station across from our hotel[5]

I am standing in front of Nuremberg station across from our hotel (less posh than the Grand Hotel opposite where Shirer was most likely staying), trying to work out where exactly Hitler stood to take the salutes. The quest is attracting unwanted attention, including arm movements from car drivers that could certainly not be described as salutes. My erudite and delightful friend John James, who's joining me for the walk to Flossenbürg this week, suggests tactfully we are getting nowhere. Sarah is back at home, relaxing after the arts festival

The Nuremberg Rallies showcasing Nazi might and ambitions.

in St Jean de Côle at which she performed non-stop translation, and preparing for her new term. John and I have just arrived in the city and decide to drop our bags back at the Novotel Centre Ville and rush off to the Rally Grounds before dark. We venture inside the *Kongresshalle*. Modelled by architect Ludwig Ruff on the Colosseum in Rome but *obviously* larger, it was intended to seat 50,000 Nazis for congresses, but its upper levels and roof were never completed.[6] We walk around in silence lost in our thoughts. We then walk back to the *Zeppelinfeld*, and are taken aback at the sheer scale. After the landmark event in 1934, four further annual rallies were held here, the last one in 1938 to celebrate Anschluss. The 1939 rally was planned to be the greatest and biggest ever, to be called the *Reichsparteitag des Friedens* ('Rally of Peace') but was cancelled at the last minute because of the outbreak of war on 1 September 1939, when Germany invaded Poland.

It is hard on this darkening evening with the only sound the *caw caw* of carrion crows to imagine Hitler's crowing peroration in 1934 as night fell, the whole area lit by 150 anti-aircraft searchlights pointing vertically into the sky. The beams formed what Speer was to call the world's 'first luminescent architecture' with vast columns supporting a dark blue dome to complete a 'cathedral of light' to a God in whom none believed, the glow seen in Frankfurt 200 kilometres away.[7] Who would have guessed that within just a few years, the burghers of Frankfurt would see the sky lit up again by distant illumination from Nuremberg, as Allied bombers rained down fire on the medieval city night after night.

After the war, the question of what to do with the principal emblems of Nazism was a challenge for the Allies, rarely more so than in Nuremberg. The Americans exploded Speer's giant swastika adorning the stadium (and gave the medieval Imperial Regalia back to Vienna) while the remaining Nazi iconic structures have been left slowly to crumble.

But the evil brewed here in this crucible of Nazism, and on show in these demonic annual displays to promulgate Nazi ideology to the

The US army blew up the swastika above the Zeppelinfeld *on 25 April 1945, having captured Nuremberg five days before.*

masses, lives on in the damaged lives and hopes of millions reaching down even to today. We return by tram to our hotel in silence, aware that what we have seen is almost beyond comprehension.

What we are about to learn, though, hits us even harder. The climax of the rally in Nuremberg in September 1935 left a particularly sinister legacy. The tone had been set by Hitler opening the rally with an attack on 'Judaeo Bolshevism', an antisemitic conspiracy theory that states the 1917 Russian Revolution had been masterminded by world Jewry to destroy Western civilization. Then on 15 September, as the climax of six days of frenetic activity, the 'Nuremberg Race Laws' were theatrically unveiled as Germany's grand national vision for the future.[8] They adjudicated on whether Jews could any longer be full citizens of Germany and thus be entitled to political rights.[9]

This nightmare had long been feared by the Jewish population of Germany. Following emancipation in 1871, Jews felt reasonably confident of their place in German society, not least because so many had integrated deeply into middle-class life, and their total numbers were comparatively small, just over half a million or 0.75 per cent of the population, concentrated, as we have seen, in large cities, especially Frankfurt, Breslau and Hamburg, as well as Berlin. The concentration meant that the vast majority of Germans had never met a Jewish person and had no reason for personal antipathy. By contrast, in Austria, Jews constituted 2.8 per cent of the population in 1933, almost all living in Vienna. In Hungary in the year that Hitler came to power, 5 per cent of the population were Jewish, and in Poland, almost 10 per cent (over 3 million).[10]

An initial panic among Jews when Hitler came to power in January 1933 subsided quite quickly. Even as late as early 1935, the regime's attitude towards Jews was one of 'diffidence', wrote historian David Cesarani, and the community had reasons to think that the Nazis might leave them be. After all, Germany was still powerless militarily, its forces depleted after the First World War and by severe arms limitations imposed by the Treaty of Versailles. This was not the time to risk international opprobrium by overt racism, nor to deprive the country of Jewish talent. Hitler and his generals knew that if the Allies had joined forces to attack in their early years in power, the country would quickly have succumbed. Diplomatic voices in Berlin also cautioned against too obvious antisemitism in the build-up to the Olympic Games in Berlin in August 1936, which Germany had won the right to hold in 1931, before the Nazis came to power.[11]

The turning point came in January 1935 after a referendum in the Saarland, an area rich in coal mines on the Franco-German border. By a majority of over 90 per cent, the territory voted to be returned to Germany. The overwhelming victory emboldened Hitler to reintroduce conscription and pursue industrial mobilization to prepare for war.

By mid-1935, pressure was mounting within the Nazi Party to provide consistency in its policies on race and Jews. Local authorities wanted to know whether the sporadic violence against Jews of the thuggish SA was supposed to be prosecuted or applauded. A *casus belli* was needed to justify and catalyse a new uncompromising line. Hitler thus seized on an event in New York on 26 July 1935, when the German steamship *Bremen* had its Nazi flag torn down by trade union activists, which resulted in a diplomatic incident whipped up by the Nazis against the US. The case was revealing too in how it divided US opinion, with isolationists and Nazi sympathizers lined up against Jews, labour activists and anti-fascists. Hitler promptly blamed the incident, without any evidence, on 'international Jewry'.[12]

Following it, lawyers and officials were instructed to work flat out to produce a set of laws to be announced at the rally just six weeks away, with Minister of the Interior Wilhelm Frick a key orchestrator. The Nuremberg Race Laws that the drafters produced just in time were to assume great significance because they institutionalized racial

SA men implement a boycott against Jewish businesses in April 1933, soon after Hitler became chancellor. The sign says: 'Germans! Defend yourselves! Don't buy from Jews!'

discrimination within German law, above all against the Jews. The drafters had faced a particular challenge in reversing the emancipation whereby Jews had full German citizenship confirmed in 1871. The difficulties stemmed from Jews not always being easy to identify by sight; additionally, many had given up religious practice and were integrated into society, did not live in Jewish areas and celebrated Christian holidays. The drafters thus had to fathom how to separate out citizens who were genuinely of 'German or kindred blood', i.e., Aryan who were entitled to be full citizens, from the Jews who were not.[13]

As confirmed in November 1935, a person was a 'full Jew' if they had three or four Jewish grandparents, even if they had converted to Christianity and had practised the faith for many years. A person with two Jewish grandparents was still termed a Jew if they had married a Jew or belonged to a Jewish community, but were deemed 'of mixed race' if married to an Aryan. Even those with just one Jewish grandparent were deemed to be *mischlinge* or Jews of the second degree. To protect the purity of Aryan blood, all sexual relations between Germans and Jews were forbidden with severe punishment for anyone disobeying.[14]

For the first time in history, Jews were to be persecuted not for what they believed but for who they or their parents were *by birth*. In earlier historic times of Jewish persecution, as in Spain in the late fifteenth century, Jews who converted to Christianity were spared the mass expulsion in 1492. But now Germans who had never practised Judaism, who were respected members of society in senior positions in medicine, business, law and academia, found themselves overnight stripped of citizenship, rights and protections, and in mortal danger.

Back in the hotel, John and I talk about the echoes of these laws in our lives. He and his wife Louise were Joanna's and my closest friends for over twenty-five years, from when we first met at Tonbridge School till her death in December 2016. Our children grew up together and shared countless holidays. One of the reasons Joanna so loved them was she never felt a scintilla of the discomfort that Jews can sense even in a highly assimilated society. They always embraced her Judaism, wanting to celebrate it with her. My generation had it easy. It was more difficult for our parents. Joanna's father, whose biography she wrote in the last year of her life, was told in the 1930s he would never rise up the medical ladder in England 'because you are a Jew'. My own father too chose to conceal his Jewish parentage, conscious no doubt correctly that it would not have helped his career as an economist in post-war London. I know, though, what deep pleasure it gave him when I married Joanna. Antisemitism had barely touched her life or mine. Very occasionally, as when boys at school called me 'hooknose junior' (I never did find out who my senior *doppelgänger* was), did I experience antisemitism firsthand, and then, never seriously. When I first started going out with Joanna, my Catholic landlady in Westminster had staunchly antisemitic views, and we concealed from her the fact that we were getting married. When eventually we told her, she couldn't have been nicer. Perhaps we weren't like the Jews she didn't know but still loathed. I was so happy to be married in a synagogue by Hugo Gryn, and it is a source of pride now that, even though I am a practising Christian and married to Sarah, the Race Laws would still have condemned me.

There is no escaping the unfathomable misery that was unleashed on the world in this city ninety years ago, and how these Laws legitimized ghettoization, deportation and genocide. The Nuremberg Race Laws indeed have now become a case study and warning of state-sanctioned dehumanization and murder. It is getting late. We have talked ourselves out after a long day, and we finish up our last glass of *Weissburgunder*. But before we turn in, we decide we need to walk in the fresh air and put aside for the time being the last of Nuremberg's roles in the Nazis' story, the Trials, which blend unimaginable darkness with heroic human resolve. We are up early the next morning and our path will be clinging tightly to the River Pegnitz to soothe our way out of the cauldron to a restoration of sanity.

The Pegnitz, the third river of the walk, is much more modest than the first two, the Rhine and Danube. It begins its 110-kilometre life in the upper Bavarian town of Pegnitz before wending its way due south to Hersbruck, the destination for today's walk, where it bends sharply west and flows on to Nuremberg where it splits into various arms. I had been enchanted by it on my first evening in the city as I lingered earlier in the summer on the single-arch Fleisch Bridge, built in 1598 and which miraculously survived the bombing. The river branches reunite on the other side of the city, and it continues its flow till it joins the Regnitz shortly after, then into the Main and ultimately the Rhine. For all its modesty, the Pegnitz bursts with character and wildlife. We see coots, ducks, gulls and swans as we walk, and some of the most beguiling urban riverbanks of my entire journey.

Our plan to get out of the city into open country is thwarted by Nuremberg's suburbs extending further than we thought. The tram drops us in a still heavily urbanized area. But we walk briskly, the temperature already 25°C albeit eased by a strong wind, and once out in the countryside and on paths, the route is charming. We travel through woods north of Rückersdorf and break at Lauf an der Pegnitz, eating rolls by the riverbank before pressing on to Hersbruck, covering the 25 kilometres in little over five hours. Red squirrels are a highlight of the last part of our journey. Duly fortified, we catch a train back into the city in good time to go walking in search of 'the reckoning', namely the Trials.

Nuremberg's symbolic importance to Nazism is insufficient of itself to explain its choice as their location. The vast enterprise of the Trials was going to require a big courthouse undamaged by bombing, spacious enough to accommodate the military tribunal and with a large and very secure prison complex on site. Stalin, who had argued strongly that the Trials should take place in Berlin, already securely in Soviet hands, was reluctant to concede. Nuremberg's Palace of Justice, completed as recently as 1916, had its 'Courtroom 600' rapidly extended

The Palace of Justice at Nuremberg in November 1945. Note the court buildings in mid-photograph and the spoke-like prison facilities where the accused were imprisoned, behind.

by knocking down internal walls to accommodate the proceedings unprecedented in the entire history of human law. Completing the space on time was touch and go: the court still smelled of fresh paint as the hearings opened.

Every previous war in history had seen atrocities and acts of barbarism. In 1864, the first Geneva Convention established the rules of war governing the treatment of the wounded and prisoners, and had introduced the Red Cross emblem. Further iterations extended agreement of what was acceptable in armed conflict, including the protection of civilians. To understand more of this fraught topic, I seek counsel from my friend since university Steve Crawshaw, rushing to complete his book *Prosecuting the Powerful*.[15] The First World War, he tells me, had seen some devilish new ways of killing, including poison gas from April 1915, expressly forbidden by the Hague Conventions of 1899 and 1907.[16] The Treaty of Versailles of 1919 required that war crime trials of German soldiers take place. But there was little appetite to deliver on it. Despite the Allies listing over 1,000 alleged offenders they sought to prosecute, when the trials were held in Leipzig, only six of the twelve accused were convicted.

Article 227 of the treaty, however, charged the abdicated Kaiser Wilhelm II with 'a supreme offence against international morality and the sanctity of treaties', and called for him to be brought before a special tribunal overseen by the victorious Allies. British Prime Minister David Lloyd George was willing to do so, as were other Allied leaders. But the Netherlands, which had been neutral, refused to extradite their new resident. George V was shocked at the prospect of his cousin being placed in the dock, especially coming so soon after the murder at Ekaterinburg of another cousin, Nicholas II, the Russian Tsar, together with his family, in July 1918. The King thus asked his Cabinet allies, including the former Viceroy of India Lord Curzon, to intervene on his behalf. Lloyd George turned his attention elsewhere, observing that the Kaiser was in a form of permanent exile anyway in the Netherlands. He never did return to Germany, dying in 1941 untried and unwanted.[17]

The Second World War was altogether different. Even while being fought, it was evident that new depths of depravity had been reached, and the question of trials and justice could not be fudged as after the First World War. The leaders of the main Allied powers, Franklin D. Roosevelt, Winston Churchill and Joseph Stalin, discussed from 1943 what might be done. British Foreign Secretary Anthony Eden cautioned, 'I am convinced that we should avoid commitments "to try the war criminals" and to "hang the Kaiser" [Hitler].' When the 'Big Three' met in Tehran in late 1943, Stalin proposed a toast that 50,000 Germans should be shot. More sober cogitation went into their jointly agreed Moscow Declaration on Human Atrocities, but how exactly to deal with Nazi crimes in the event of an Allied victory was still left up in the air.[18] The Big Three returned to the subject when they met at the Yalta Conference in February 1945. Churchill remained enthusiastic for 'bumping off' the key Nazis. But Roosevelt had moved in favour of war crimes trials and due process, while Stalin insisted he'd been only 'joking' about the 50,000. He had come to see the political advantage to be gained with a well-publicized 'show trial', having orchestrated so many of them in the Soviet Union over the previous twenty years.

The whole subject was only finally resolved at the London conference in late June 1945.[19] Differences, including the Soviets' wish that the accused be treated as guilty from the start, were thrashed out, aided by lunch at the Savoy on the Strand, and a black-tie dinner at Claridge's in Mayfair (at which the Russians protested at the poor quality of the vodka). Awareness of the very different levels of sacrifice in the war by the three big powers was never far below the surface: whereas the total Soviet loss of life is estimated to be between 26 and 27 million, the British suffered 450,000 military and civilian deaths, and under 200,000 US soldiers were killed fighting in Europe. The deliberations were codified in the London Charter of August 1945 that established the International Military Tribunal.[20]

Massive decisions were being taken under great pressure, and the jurisdiction of the investigation was curtailed in some significant ways. Soviet war crimes including mass killings and innumerable rapes by the Red Army were not to be on the agenda. The Soviets' brutality and arbitrary killing rival that of the Nazis, so the exclusion was a very significant curtailment of the integrity and fairness of the entire war crimes tribunal. The extensive Luftwaffe bombing campaign, anticipated for many years before in Downing Street, was not to be included either. The reason was because the Allied Combined Bomber Offensive had hit Germany much harder, killing over 400,000 civilians, compared to the 40,000 that had died in London's Blitz. The inclusion of strategic bombing would also have cast a spotlight on the Allies' bombing of Japan, including the deployment of the atomic bombs at Hiroshima and Nagasaki in August 1945. This omission was later to be termed 'the silence of Nuremberg' by US prosecutor Telford Taylor.[21] The murder of 22,000 Polish prisoners at Katyn in western Russia, though, *was* included in the indictments, incredibly, as the Soviets brazenly tried to pin the blame on the Germans for a crime they themselves had committed.

The great achievement, however, was that the Trials happened at all, given the difference in perspectives of the presiding powers. It was the first time in history that individuals rather than states were to be prosecuted fairly in open court for crimes against humanity, for war crimes and crimes against peace.

To Nuremberg, before the tribunal's opening day on Tuesday 20 November 1945, by plane, car and train, descended a vast gathering of lawyers, administrators, military personnel, journalists, translators and representatives from the four victorious nations, France being the late addition. But the spotlight was shone squarely on just twenty-two people, the Nazi leaders to be tried. The total had been intended to be twenty-four, but two had died by suicide: Hitler's powerful private secretary Martin Bormann whose remains lay undiscovered until 1972, and the Nazis' head of labour organization Robert Ley who hung himself in Nuremberg the month before the Trials opened. Three principal leaders had taken their own lives earlier too: Hitler on 30 April in the Führerbunker, Goebbels on 1 May having succeeded him as chancellor for one day, and Himmler while in British custody at Lüneburg on 23 May.

The twenty-two Third Reich leaders sat sullenly on the first day to listen to US chief prosecutor Robert H. Jackson deliver what has become one of the defining legal addresses of the modern era: 'That four great nations, flushed with victory and stung with injury, stay the hand of vengeance and voluntarily submit their captive enemies to the judgment of the law is one of the most significant tributes Power has ever paid to Reason.'[22] Jackson was spelling out the new era of international justice and law being born. Hitler at the start of the war had goaded on his generals to believe that they would never be held accountable for their actions, not least because of the collapse of the aspiration after 1918. But following the precedent set at Nuremberg, perpetrators of mass crimes thereafter, from the former Yugoslavia to Rwanda, would have justice, if not perfectly, served on them.

The proceedings lasted ten long months. Feelings towards the defendants darkened all the time. Airey Neave, who had escaped from Colditz prisoner of war camp in 1942 and was in Nuremberg as part of the British delegation, recalled, 'Newspaper reports and films of the concentration camps ensured worldwide loathing for the leading Nazis. Even among the easy-going British there was less talk of "old Jerry"... Those ghastly piles of naked moon-white corpses at Belsen and Dachau would not soon be forgotten. At Nuremberg, they were with us always. It was there that we uncovered the truth.'[23]

Neave's task was to serve the indictments on the Germans. Some of the defendants generated more contempt in him than others. Hess, deprived of collar and tie as a suicide precaution but still wearing the Luftwaffe flying boots in which he had flown to Scotland four years earlier, nauseated him. In Hess's final statement, he declared unrepentantly, 'I was permitted to work for many years of my life under the greatest son whom my people has brought forth in its thousand year history... I do not regret anything.'[24] Spreader of antisemitic hatred Julius Streicher was another to arouse Neave's disgust, especially when 'his little eyes caught mine and I realized the heartless savagery of this man. No amount of compassion, no logic, no reason would have swayed him. I again thought of a mediaeval torturer bared to the waist, pitiless and enjoying the smell of burning flesh.' Streicher, when presented with his indictment, told Neave that 'I need a lawyer who is anti-semitic... A Jew could not defend me... I am told the judges are Jews.' Neave's conclusion on him? Streicher was a 'filthy old man.'[25]

The backdrop to the court proceedings was the bombed-out city, which had recently suffered its worst raid of the war on 2 January 1945 when 500 RAF bombers dropped 2,000 tons of incendiaries and high explosives, reducing much of the city to smoking rubble, killing nearly 2,000, with 100,000 losing their homes.[26] The raid inflicted devastating cultural loss too, and one wonders whether the minimal disruption to its industry could justify it, not least in the city where just nine months later such sensitive moral questions were being weighed. Rebecca West, described by *Time* magazine in 1947 as 'the world's number one woman writer', was covering the Trials for the *New Yorker*. She wrote: 'To arrive at Nuremberg was like stepping on to the set of a science fiction film: the extreme of unreality... The name of the town was familiar but nothing else. The picturesqueness which had impressed its image on the minds of the world was now a core of rubble.'[27] The legal proceedings with all the grim detail week upon week, she continued, was leaving those attending it 'permanently depressed... Every one of them longed to go home to his native country... Their eagerness for repatriation was frantic.' She captured the different responses of the four victors in her book *A Train of Powder*. While the Russians kept themselves to themselves, and the French 'rested and read', the British 'reconstituted an Indian hill station' with echoes of Kipling, and the Americans splashed 'huge parties.'[28]

The verdicts were delivered on 30 September and 1 October 1946 after 218 days of deliberation. Twelve defendants were to be sentenced to death, including Governor of Poland Hans Frank, Luftwaffe chief Hermann Göring (who swallowed a cyanide capsule hours before execution), head of the *Einsatzgruppen* and SS leader Ernst Kaltenbrunner, army chief Wilhelm Keitel and Foreign Minister Joachim von Ribbentrop. This last name sent a tremor down some spines in Britain. As German ambassador (1936–38), he had pursued a relentless charm offensive with those upper echelons of society such as Lord Londonderry who were sympathetic to fascism and favouring an accommodation with Germany. He made a beeline to Edward VIII, provoking widespread,

The Nuremberg defendants in November 1945. At the top left Hermann Göring sits with his head on his hand. Next to him is Rudolf Hess. On the back row, third from the right, with a pencil in his hand, is Albert Speer.

if fanciful, gossip about a possible sexual liaison with the King's amour, Wallis Simpson.[29]

Two gallows had been constructed some weeks earlier in the prison gymnasium, the executions taking place in the early hours of 16 October 1946 in the presence of a select group of officers and journalists. The prisoners were led to the gallows one by one and were allowed a short final statement in an atmosphere described as 'sombre and clinical'. By all accounts, the American hangman John C. Woods was incompetent: 'The hangman was an American sergeant who meant no harm but had not fully benefited by the researches of Marwood and Berry [nineteenth-century practitioners who perfected the 'long drop' method]. The ten men slowly choked to death.'[30] Some expressed qualified regret, notably Ribbentrop who said, 'My last wish is that Germany realize its entity and that an understanding be reached between the East and West. I wish peace to the world,' and Keitel who said, 'I call on God Almighty to have mercy on the German people.' Kaltenbrunner denied responsibility: 'I am sorry... that crimes were committed of which I had no knowledge.' While Streicher, true to the end to his 'filthy old man' moniker, shouted out 'Heil Hitler!' to the watching journalists and declared, 'The Bolsheviks will hang you one day!'[31] The dead bodies were taken down and photographed, cremated and the ashes were then scattered in the Isar river so there would be no graves to become a future site of Nazi pilgrimage. Instead, their last mortal remains were carried by the innocent Isar onwards till the waters merged with the Danube to end their journey with natural justice in the Black Sea.[32]

No figure who escaped the hangman has caused more consternation than Albert Speer, who had made a show of contrition and regret during the trial, but denied knowledge of the Holocaust. Airey Neave was perturbed that, while his 'unattractive and plebeian' deputy Fritz Sauckel was sentenced to be hanged, his boss was let off the hook, sentenced to twenty years in Spandau prison.[33] He found Speer untrustworthy, describing him as 'beguiling and dangerous'.[34] On his release, Speer became a regular feature on Second World War documentaries, famously appearing as a respected witness in the television series *The World at War* in 1973. Subsequent evidence, including documentation revealing his involvement with the expansion of Auschwitz, his presence at a meeting in 1943 when Himmler discussed the extermination programme, and his own private confession in a letter to knowing about the death camps (not made public till 2007), suggests he was lucky to escape the gallows.[35] He lived a full life dying in 1981 in London after recording another TV interview. By two years, Speer outlived Neave, who became a close aide to Margaret Thatcher until he was murdered by an offshoot of the IRA in March 1979 just weeks before she became prime minister.

From 1946 to 1949, the International Military Tribunal would conduct twelve subsequent trials, with further investigations and tribunals in individual countries focusing in particular on crimes against their own citizens.[36] Ultimately, some 500 Nazis and military figures were executed by the Allies, and 6,656 sentenced under West German law, with another 10,000 being imprisoned in East Germany. Most of the sentences were comparatively light, with the majority serving less than three years in prison.[37]

The Nuremberg Trials were milestones in their insistence that the principles of justice and due legal process be followed even in war and that justice be provided to those who would never have granted it to those whose lives they controlled. Yes, mistakes were made – arguably they were too limited and the justice was selective – but in any survey of moments of enlightenment in history, the Trials should rank high.

They also threw up many admirable figures from all nationalities. If I had to select just one figure of light among them, it would be the only German to give evidence voluntarily for the prosecution: 'I watched a family of about eight persons… The father was holding the hand of a boy about 10 years old and speaking to him softly; the boy was fighting his tears. The father pointed to the sky, stroked the boy's head and seemed to explain something to him.' These were the reminiscences in Courtroom 600 of Hermann Graebe, a German civilian and a Christian working as an engineer in what is now Ukraine. His evidence continued: 'At that moment the SS man at the pit shouted something to his comrade. The latter counted off about 20 persons and instructed them to go behind the earth mound. The family I've described was among them. I well remember a girl, slim and with black hair, who as she passed close to me, pointed to herself and said, "23 [years old]".'[38]

Graebe's haunting recollection was about the mass murder he had observed of Jewish men, women and children at the Ukrainian town of Dubno. His words were read out by the lead British prosecutor in his epic closing speech when this brilliant advocate was at his most persuasive summarizing the case against the defendants. The lawyer was Hartley Shawcross, Attorney General in Clement Attlee's Labour government

Hermann Graebe, whose haunting recollections were a defining moment of the Trials.

that came to power in July 1945. Shawcross placed the suffering of the Jews at the centre of his argument, describing the Holocaust as 'the most frightful crime the world has ever known'. He continued: 'This Trial must form a milestone in the history of civilization, not only bringing retribution to these guilty men, not only marking that right shall in the end triumph over evil, but also that the ordinary people of the world… [should know that] the state and the law are made for [them]'.[39]

When I returned to the UK, I met up with his son, writer William Shawcross, godson of Attlee's wife Violet. He first encountered the Graebe story when a schoolboy, listening to forgotten 78 RPM shellac records brought back by his father from the Trials. William reminds me how his father wound up his closing address: 'You will remember, when you come to give your decision, the story of Graebe, but not in vengeance – in a determination that these things shall not occur again.' William has been fascinated all his life by Graebe, and plans to write more about him. From late 1941, Graebe was using his protected status as a German civilian to hoodwink the Nazi authorities into giving him more Jews as his workers, often for fictitious plants, where he protected them by giving them non-Jewish identity papers. 'He bears comparison to Oskar Schindler: he risked his own life and saved hundreds of others,' William believes. It begs the question again. If Graebe did it, why didn't others? We've seen that there were many concerned Germans, even just along the route I'm taking. But why were so many passive? Germany under the Third Reich was full of good men and women, religious and not, who were appalled by what the Nazis were doing. Where were they at the moment of greatest need? My quest continues.[40]

In a BBC documentary to mark the seventy-fifth anniversary of the Trials, William spoke to one such person who was revolted by the Nazis. This was Niklas Frank, youngest son of Poland's brutalizer Hans Frank, who told him that he was glad his father was hanged at Nuremberg because it 'saved his life' by preventing his father 'poisoning his brain' as he had done with his elder siblings who came more under their father's thrall. Another who William interviewed was Israeli actress Hadas Kalderon whose grandfather had wanted to deliver in Yiddish his testimony at the Trials about the horrors of the Vilnius ghetto. He wanted to force the Nazi prisoners to listen to the language Jews had spoken in Central and Eastern Europe for generations, and which they had wanted to wipe out. But the court didn't have a Yiddish translator so he had to give his testimony in Russian, which he did standing up for its entirety. Hadas's mother and twelve-year old niece were later to be murdered in the Hamas terrorist attack of 7 October 2023.[41] The horror rolls on.

Today, Courtroom 600 is a museum space, the last trial having taken place there in 2020.[42] It is smaller than I expected, in part because the wall removed to accommodate the press gallery was subsequently put back. The building looks much the same as it did in 1945, albeit cleaned up, but the prison where the Nazi leaders were held out at the back was demolished during the 1980s. A museum display discusses the Trials in sober German fashion. A US army box that was used for transporting the highly secret documents catches the eye, while the bench on which the defendants squirmed and scowled leaves much to the imagination.[43]

* * *

The weather has at last turned and I'm overjoyed. As our train pulls into Hersbruck it is raining. Raining! I stand on the platform and let the cool water run down my face (not my clothes, protected by a waterproof kagoule and leggings from, yes, Millets: following the master). After the harshness of the sun, anything is bliss. John, meanwhile, is busy keeping dry the new paper map he has bought. He is routemaster for the next five days and he's taking his responsibility very seriously.

Before we go anywhere we need to reckon with Hersbruck, which seemed an oasis of tranquillity when we left it yesterday afternoon. But today we learn that it housed one of the archipelago of Flossenbürg subcamps for 10,000 prisoners. A Nazi sign erected in May 1935 stated: 'This lovely city of Hersbruck, this glorious spot on earth, was created only for Germans and not for Jews. Jews are therefore not welcome.'

I shift uneasily in my boots. Jews most certainly were not welcome: 4,000 of the prisoners were murdered or died here. A tasteful exhibition and memorial rose garden have been created by the side of the path. We are struck by a bronze sculpture called *Ohne Namen* ('Without a Name') created in 2007 by Vittore Bocchetta. The inscription tells us that members of the Italian resistance were imprisoned here, with many set to work building a vast underground cave. The Italian artist was himself one of the political deportees who managed to escape in April 1945 during a death march from Hersbruck to Dachau when the camp was evacuated. Four-sided stone pillars have been erected by the side of the path with metal models of cattle carriages atop. Carved on the plinths are the names of those transported out, including 'Richard

A memorial at Hersbruck.

Outside Hersbruck, a sign in May 1935 states: 'City of Hersbruck. This lovely city of Hersbruck, this glorious spot on earth, was created only for Germans and not for Jews. Jews are therefore not welcome.'

Schmitt, * [born] 4.3.40, *ermorted* [murdered] Juli 1944 Auschwitz-Birkenau' and 'Johanna Lehmann Tachter *15.5.40, *ermorted* 17.1.44 Auschwitz-Birkenau'. Whatever may have been true of the town's antisemitism seventy years ago, it's hard not to applaud the respect and honesty that this memorial displays.

The rain is easing as we reach Hohenstadt, where the Pegnitz abandons us in search of better company to the north. To console ourselves, we break for a coffee at a wayside petrol station on the outskirts of the town, marvelling at its cleanliness, the freshness of the food, the welcoming tables and staff. Why, we wonder, is the experience so different to cafés in most British petrol stations?

Fortified, we press on along a cycle track beside the main road, but then peel off at Weigendorf to go up into the hills. Maps in hand, with all the cunning of a contestant embarking on *Race Across the World*, John strides forward. He guides us expertly through the hill villages of Haunritz, Bachetsfeld, past the pilgrim church of Simultankirche St Margareta where for a time Protestant and Catholics worshipped together, and safely down into Sulzbach-Rosenberg, our destination for the day. A connoisseur of nature, John cements his credentials by identifying the birdsong of green and great spotted woodpeckers, a kingfisher, nutcracker and nuthatch, and points out to me a heron, buzzard, blue tits, great tits, a treecreeper and a kite (the last one I knew, having been well schooled by Sarah). We talk about swallows and why they leave the south of England after swifts, and we notice still more red squirrels as well as hares darting here and there, lost in their own worlds, as are we deep in conversation.

We talk about how my father and his Jewish family would never buy German products, a practice shared by many Jews at the time. So Germany had behaved badly, I understood that. But I was puzzled when in the Easter holidays of 1966, we went on a road trip through Holland expressly to visit Bonn and the Rhineland. He was not always consistent, but who is? I remember how moved my father was by seeing Bonn, capital of West Germany, the country he admired above all for its free market policies. I now understood; its adherence to the free market had redeemed it. He loved classical music, and I recall too how much it meant to him to visit Beethoven's home in the centre of Bonn. The arts in general passed Dad by: I never remember him reading a novel or visiting an art gallery, but music he loved, and we left the museum clutching bundles of records of Beethoven's concertos. Dad had a visceral dislike of the Soviet Union. I remember him agonizing for weeks about whether he should go with my mother on an 'Intourist' visit to Moscow; with only days to go, he pulled out. Whether it was because he thought the KGB might imprison him for his pronounced anti-Communist views, or because his Ukrainian parents had abandoned the country, as indeed had the Muscovite stepmother who raised him, I was never certain. He loathed tyranny and Communism.

John and I talk about an extraordinarily powerful evocation of the Holocaust we heard given by actor Dirk Bogarde when I invited him to visit Tonbridge School in 1991. His story of being one of the first to witness the liberation of Bergen-Belsen, delivered in the sixth form lecture slot, was spellbinding. So compelling indeed that I asked my magisterial head Martin Hammond (Boris Johnson's unimpressed housemaster at Eton) whether the whole school might hear him after lunch. When again might they hear first-hand testimony from one of the first people to tell the world about the concentration camps? He readily assented, even though it meant the pupils would have to miss games that afternoon, which shows what a big deal it was for the school. Bogarde declined to join us in the dining hall to eat, preferring a sandwich with his chauffeur in his car. But his return to the stage post-sandwich was every bit as mesmerizing as in the morning. 'I remember the day very well, even after all these years', the great actor declared. 'It was a clear, cold April morning. Someone in the unit to which I was attached as an intelligence officer had said the Germans had abandoned a large concentration camp and we ought to have a look. I didn't know what to expect. I'd known for some time that the camps existed – we saw aerial photographs often enough – but it didn't really occur to me I'd be entering a hell which I would never forget and about which for many years, I would be unable to speak.' His testimony about the camp where Anne Frank and her sister Margot had died weeks and possibly even just days before was delivered to a silent audience listening intently. 'It had been a bit of a battering for the boys who had never even heard of the Holocaust,' Bogarde later recalled of his visit. He was pleased to tell his interlocutor that he had noticed 'blubbing' among the younger boys, adding, 'This is not as unkind as it sounds: it merely proves that somewhere a nerve had been touched.' He intended to make a big impression and, boy, he most certainly had.

I was overjoyed by his visit. Bringing in extraordinary speakers to talk to students has been one of the activities I have loved most about teaching. The Second World War was a particular enthusiasm: Tonbridge boys thus heard from Leonard Cheshire, who witnessed the dropping of the bomb at Nagasaki, Rudolf Peierls who helped build it, and even from Vera Lynn, who *sang* to them. Here they were learning about the Holocaust, an event of inestimable significance, and recounted by one of the most gifted actors of his generation.

The problem, and it is quite a significant one, is that he was making it up. As his biographer John Coldstream told me when researching his book several years later, large parts of Bogarde's recollections to the school were fabricated, or at least very heavily embroidered. At first Coldstream thought Bogarde had never visited Belsen, but subsequently conceded he probably did set foot in it at some point. There was one eyewitness, an Austrian Jew named Andrey Kodin, serving with British intelligence, who recalled seeing Bogarde there.[44] But it seems his storytelling greatly eclipsed the reality of what he witnessed.

While all historical recreations involve an element of artistic licence, it's hard to resist the conclusion that he was milking the tragedy to provoke an emotional impact in his young male audience. A compassionate response is that he was a lonely old man, his acting and writing days mostly behind him, his partner Anthony Forwood recently deceased and he was desperate for human connection, to feel that he could still move an audience. Bogarde had indeed given a magnificent performance as an actor. But this wasn't a show. He had been asked to speak as a witness. Truth matters.

Bogarde's obfuscations contrast starkly with the genuine evidence provided by one of the greatest of British broadcasters: Richard Dimbleby, who entered Belsen on 19 April and delivered an eleven-minute broadcast that was to change forever the perception of people in Britain and across the world about the true nature of the Nazi regime and its use of mass extermination. He spoke of the 'cold fury' of the soldiers who were the first to liberate the camp, and how the camp's 'dying and living dead' made a more powerful impression on him than anything he'd witnessed in the previous five years of war. When BBC managers initially told him that they were not certain they could broadcast it until his extraordinary story had been independently corroborated, he told a fellow BBC journalist that he would never broadcast again if it was not.[45]

One passage was particularly searing: 'One woman distraught to the point of madness flung herself at a British soldier... she begged him to give some milk for the tiny baby in her arms. She put the mite on the ground, threw herself at the soldier's feet and kissed his boots... She put the baby in his arms and ran off saying she would find milk for it because there was no milk in her breast. And when the soldier

Richard Dimbleby, BBC war correspondent, who broadcast the horrors of the liberation of Belsen in April 1945.

opened the bundle of rags to look at the child, he found it had been dead for days.'[46] That pitiful story, and Dimbleby's broadcast, have never left me.

The liberation had some happy endings, though not many. Fourteen-year old Susan Pollack was one of the few. Another unknown British soldier sent into Belsen had noticed her body twitch and extracted her from the mud hole in the ground in which she lay dying, gently placing her in one of the ambulances. Through that brief action, she discovered that, despite all the horrors of her life to date, 'kindness and goodwill had also survived'. She had been the recipient of thousands of acts of cruelty in her first fourteen years. But it was that one act of compassion that counted. For the rest of her life, she has asked herself, 'What part of that goodness with your heart do you take from that soldier?'[47] Lieutenant Colonel Mervyn Gonin, a peacetime GP who led a field ambulance into Belsen, learned too the value of hope when an unrequested supply of lipstick suddenly arrived at the camp. Three-quarters of the survivors were women and Gonin was amazed at how it transformed the starving inmates: 'At last someone had done something to make them individuals again. They were someone, no longer merely the number tattooed on their arm. At last they could take an interest in their appearance. That lipstick started to give them back their humanity.'[48]

* * *

We have walked nearly 30 kilometres and are ready to rest on the train journey from Sulzbach back to Nuremberg. The journey gives us a chance to catch up on news. Israel and Hezbollah are exchanging heavy fire in a major escalation of the war. Police have arrested a twenty-six-year old Syrian national, reportedly inspired by ISIS, who killed three people at a festival in the German city of Solingen. Trump is steadily gaining ground in the polls after the initial Kamala Harris honeymoon.

This is our penultimate night in Nuremberg and we walk through the town to the string of fortifications that constitute the medieval castle, the heart of the Holy Roman Empire, from where we survey the rebuilt city before dinner on the patio of the Goldenes Posthorn restaurant. Eager to celebrate more heroes from the city, we find out about two exceptional Germans who stood up against the Nazis. Hermann Luppe had been an active and respected mayor of the city from 1920. But from 1933, he was engaged in a bitter fight with Julius Streicher, from which only one victor was ever likely. Luppe's attempts to ban Nazi newspaper *Der Stürmer* rebounded against him. Denounced as a 'Jew lover', Luppe was hounded out of office and forced to leave Nuremberg to live in Berlin and Hamburg, his ousting hailed as one of the first Nazi successes in the city. In 1939, he returned to live in Kiel, his birthplace, where he continued to be a person of interest to the Gestapo, was placed under surveillance and frequently interrogated. Irony of ironies, he was killed with his wife in one of the very last

Hermann Luppe, Mayor of Nuremberg, who stood up to Nazi propagandist Julius Streicher, only to die at the very end of the war in an Allied bombing raid.

RAF bombing raids of the war on 3 April, just a month before British troops marched into the city. The aim had been to destroy German warships which intelligence indicated had slipped into the port to outwit a last-ditch naval battle in the Baltic, and to stop key Nazis escaping from Germany's last functioning harbour. Not forgotten by post-war Nuremberg, a street near our hotel was named in honour of brave and principled Hermann Luppe.[49]

Liselotte Flemming, wife of a Wehrmacht major, was caught by the SS sharing her rations with a Jewish woman in Riga who had been born in her hometown Nuremberg. Fortuitously, Liselotte was able to slip away from their clutches because of a message that she must return urgently to Nuremberg where the family house had been hit in a bombing raid. Her husband, who similarly felt compelled to care for the vulnerable, was denounced for giving food to prisoners, and saw no way out but to take his life. Liselotte survived the war, discovered that the Jewish lady she protected had survived the war too and again befriended her. In 1984, Liselotte was recognized by Yad Vashem as Righteous Among the Nations.[50]

These are better notes on which to leave Nuremberg. That question keeps coming back: are human beings essentially good or essentially bad? I still think the former, but I cannot resolve why the Third Reich years didn't throw up more Graebes, Luppes and Flemmings.

Today is to be a day of hard walking, from Sulzbach-Rosenberg north-east to Freihung. John is in charge, and steers us through the 25 kilometres flawlessly. My diary note records merely: 'We press on for five hours without stopping for anything more than pees. It's a focused day, relentlessly driving forward.' The one town we pass through is Hahnbach, but apart from the pretty Church of St James, the main attraction is a 1994 statue of a rider holding his bike aloft, erected in celebration of the ferociously uneven cobbled roads in the town where cyclists often have to dismount. John, a genuine cyclist, finds a fascination in the story that escapes me.

John receiving a gift of home-grown tomatoes.

The next day it's a similar distance from Freihung to Weiden in der Oberpfalz. I remember more of this day, highlights being a stopover at a remote *Gasthof* in a hamlet. The proprietor and his family are having lunch and tell us very nicely they're closed. John speaking his best German asks winsomely if we can sit in the shade to have a fizzy drink. '*Erfreut,*' ('pleased') they respond. After they finish their meal, they want us to talk to them: their daughter tells us about a school visit to London, and John draws them into conversation about all the different German words for 'kind'. They are very taken with him and rightly so. A while later, in another remote village too small to have a name, John calls out '*Grüß Gott*' to a lady tending her market garden. She too is enchanted and insists that we take five of her most succulent and fresh-tasting tomatoes. We are bowled over again by the kindness of strangers.

This is the day when we have our one disagreement. I'd been navigating since leaving Kilometre Zero using Google Maps, which is generally sound, and it is saying a proposed path ahead is a dead end. John is emphatic that his paper map shows that there is a path through woods. Up and down the road we go seeking out where his path through the forest might begin. We spot a family in a cottage dining at a table by the stream in their garden, the scent of woodsmoke in our nostrils, the drumming of a woodpecker in our ears. They take pains to confirm that there is indeed an ancient pathway through the dense trees. Still not entirely convinced, I surrender my will to paper and print, and we discover what looks as if it was once a path through the undergrowth. It is tense for half an hour and more, with the trees threatening to close in on us, and the brambles reaching menacingly across the diminishing path. Slowly, very slowly, it broadens out, but only after we have stumbled or climbed over several tree trunks blocking the way. I repeatedly lose my connection on the phone, but John never loses his connection with his map, and forges ahead. It looks like we will miss the train, and might have to backtrack, assuming we can find the way back. Suddenly, we are in a clearing where several tracks converge into an identifiable farm lane. The last part of the journey through the woods is a delight in contrast. At one point we walk straight through the centre of an ancient barn heavy with hanging bats, but arrive at the station just in time to catch our train.

John's attention is caught by a young family bidding fond farewells to an elegantly dressed older woman with whom they've likely been staying. When we board the carriage, the family come and settle next to us in our empty compartment. They seem as curious about us as we are about them. They explain that they are Berliners taking advantage of a reduced fares offer on the railways designed to encourage families to spend their holidays in their homeland rather than join the surge of cars hurtling down the autobahns to foreign seaside resorts. Their son and daughter, maybe ten and twelve, conspicuously are not buried in their iPhones but seem eager to engage us in a mix of German and English. The parents are liberal Berliners, professionals who had indeed been to stay with the children's grandmother in the south and have relished the opportunity to explore their own land. The conversation moves to Germany's European identity now threatened by the rising insularity and simmering violence associated with the AfD. The journey passes quickly and soon we must go our separate ways, reminded of our common European destiny.

The last day's walking that will take us to Flossenbürg threatens to be overshadowed by noise from London, and I don't want to let that happen. *Truss at 10* has started serialization today in *The Times*, usually a source of celebration for any author after years of work. But my last book to be serialized, on Boris Johnson about whom it was highly critical, unleashed a storm of protest centred around the principal himself, and I've been apprehensive for some days about what this new serialization might bring. Sure enough, regular phone vibrations portending angry messages wake me up early. For all the care I take to check and recheck each paragraph in my books, I know I'm fallible, and mistakes will slip through. The pushback this time comes not from serialization, but from the press who had read the advance copies, and focuses on whether Truss had considered cuts in cancer treatment among the emergency measures to save billions of pounds following her flawed budget. I spend much of the day while we're walking and wanting to savour the experience, sending messages back and forth with my research team, publisher and agent. By mid-afternoon, the storm seems to be quietening, the truth established. But it's been unpleasant and unnerving.

I hate being criticized for not being professional: is it the blood in me that fears I won't be liked? These two books on Johnson and Truss were never going to end well for their subjects because, despite being formidable talents, one was not morally fit and the other not personally suited to be prime minister. The role has two entry-level requirements:

be good at the job, and be a good human being. Neither were willing to learn. Out here, coming to terms with all that happened under the Nazis, I'm more convinced than ever that moral and competent leadership matters at national level, as elsewhere.

I worry I haven't been good company these last few hours for John, but if he has minded, he hasn't shown it. I speak to Sarah, who always calms and reassures me. She has attended the funeral today on my behalf of Epsom chair Alastair Wells and tells me all about it. Sad though the event was, it's almost a relief to immerse myself in a totally different world, if only for a while.

On the train back to Weiden on our last morning, when the conductor asks us to pay, my credit card falls between the seats. I try to extract it, but it looks as if it will be too difficult and I imagine having to cancel the card with all the attendant kerfuffle. But the conductor gets down on her knees and looks under the seat with her torch, as does another passenger who turns out to be an off-duty train driver. Between them, they manage to extricate it from an almost impossible position. John seizes on the opportunity of finding a hundred ways of saying 'kind'. They spring up together, card in hand, smiles across their faces. Would it have happened in Britain? My sense is that this would have been an exception, but here in Germany, it seems the rule that people want to help.

One low spot on our walk is our stopover in the town of Floss: not a hint of George Eliot, flies all over the bakery café tables and suspicious glares from other customers. The German miracle seems to have bypassed this town, even before the current downturn. It cannot have helped that it was only 10 kilometres from a fearsome and treacherous border from 1948 to 1989, the Iron Curtain no less, separating NATO countries from those of the Warsaw Pact, and the road beyond Floss went nowhere except to a former concentration camp and a one-time quarry. The end of the Cold War brought the district fresh difficulties because the military bases dotted all over the area to defend NATO were cut drastically, and economic life receded.

It wasn't always like this. For much of its history Floss had been just south of the 'Golden Road', on which more next chapter, from the castle in Nuremberg to the castle in Prague. It thrived in the seventeenth to nineteenth centuries, with its own Jewish colony numbering some 200. That rich life ended abruptly on Kristallnacht. But not the influence of Floss on the course of Jewish history. Joseph Schwarz, the first person to map Palestine in the mid-nineteenth century, which helped shape hopes for a Jewish homeland, originated from here.[51]

Reinforced by Capri-Sun Orange, we power onwards to stumble exhausted into Flossenbürg camp, which is not a bit as we expected. It is certainly not heaving with visitors like the most lethal camp of them all, Auschwitz. More like Treblinka, in silent forest country north-east of Warsaw, the camp that saw the second highest number murdered (between 700,000 and 900,000). The Saturday afternoon I visited it in the last year of Joanna's life to see where her family were murdered, we were the only visitors. Here in Flossenbürg, John and I seem to be alone too. Nor can we see an open visitors' centre. We are surprised to find instead a new housing estate built on the hill immediately overlooking the bleak parade ground where prisoners stood for roll call every morning and evening. We walk in silence around the main sites, past the laundry, the piled ashes memorial, the church, synagogue and crematorium. We pause at a memorial to Dietrich Bonhoeffer and study a plaque dedicated to him bearing the names of Donald Trump and his then vice president, Mike Pence. We wonder whether the great man knows who Bonhoeffer was or that a plaque to him had been erected in his name. On the other side of the Atlantic today, Trump is lashing out on Truth Social against the 'witch hunt' being prosecuted against him.

Arriving at Flossenbürg reminds me that my journey is half complete. What am I learning? The best were bridge-builders reaching out beyond their own tribe, like Gertrud Luckner, fearless in standing up to power like Mayor Luppe, and passionate about communicating the terrible truth like Hermann Graebe and Richard Dimbleby. Flossenbürg is about to teach me more before I exit Germany. But my quest is far from over.

After the war Flossenbürg never achieved the same reputation for unimaginable suffering as did some other German camps, notably Dachau, Buchenwald and Ravensbrück. So what was special about Flossenbürg that meant it did not become a byword for inhumanity? While never an extermination camp like Auschwitz, it was a particularly brutal 'work camp'. Political prisoners formed the bulk until 1944, after which Soviet prisoners and Jews joined the ranks, swelling numbers to some 50,000, of whom 75 per cent were in the subcamps, and some 25,000 perished altogether, a tenth of whom were Jews. When the US army liberated Flossenbürg main camp, they found only 1,500 prisoners, most of whom died in the following days.[52]

After liberation, Flossenbürg was used as an internment camp for Nazi prisoners, and then taken over by the German military. The decades during the Cold War saw the site, under the shadow of the Iron Curtain, neglected, dismantled and falling into decay. Some landscaping of the grounds took place, and while three of the watchtowers were left standing, the rest were taken down and their stones used in a chapel next to the memorial officially inaugurated in 1947. The commemoration of victims that did occur focused on celebrated figures like Bonhoeffer and on high-profile enemies of the Third Reich like leader of the Abwehr (military intelligence) Admiral Wilhelm Canaris. Jews, Roma and less prominent political prisoners received scarcely a mention.[53]

Underlying post-war tensions were exacerbated by prison guards and administrators continuing to live openly in the vicinity, and by a low level of indictments against high-ranking SS figures who oversaw the main camp and the subcamps. The site was rented out to commercial operations, often on the very land where atrocities had occurred, causing serious offence to survivor groups. Further affront was caused by the adjacent housing estate built in the 1950s and 1960s, justified by the scarcity of available land for homes. The former SS mess was converted into a café and restaurant, and SS villas became private homes. Only a small part of the cell block was spared demolition. To families of the survivors and to Jewish groups, it seemed that Germany's long history of antisemitism and racism had not been killed off after 1945: it had gone underground. Feelings ran strongly on both sides, and for forty years, no resolution seemed in sight.[54]

Reunification in 1990 ushered in a new era of thinking about the country's past. Discord gave way to constructive engagement out of which emerged a dignified memorial and an impressive education centre. The mini-memorials we passed four days ago in Hersbruck were a fruit of the same impulse. Too little and too late for some, but a significant and worthy step nonetheless. In 2007, a greatly refreshed documentation (visitor) centre was opened in the former laundry block devoted to the experience of Jews, political prisoners, forced labourers and other victimized groups. Ukraine's then pro-West president, Viktor Yushchenko, whose father had been a Soviet POW incarcerated for four years (the final months of which were at Flossenbürg), was one of the dignitaries present at the opening ceremony.[55] So the camp got there in the end, even if more needs to be done to attract tourists and extend the visitor centre.

And so we finish this leg of the journey focusing on two very different people, both Germans, one a senior military officer, the other, a pastor. Admiral Wilhelm Canaris is the more problematic because the secrecy of his intelligence work means it's hard to distinguish fact from make-believe. His biographer Richard Bassett describes him as a slippery and enigmatic figure. His highest cause was always Germany: 'I die for my fatherland. I have a clear conscience. I only did my duty to my country when I tried to oppose the criminal folly of Hitler,' he declared at his execution.[56] Equally, he was brave, and where the vast majority of his fellow officers were content to condone the brutality, he was appalled. A turning point was his witnessing at Będzin, near Katowice in Poland, the SS setting fire to a synagogue and burning alive the 200 Jews driven inside.[57] After that, he turned against the Nazis.[58]

To an unknown extent he helped Churchill realize how ill-prepared the Germans were for Operation Sealion, their proposed invasion of Britain in 1940. After the war, a journalist asked Churchill how he had been so well informed about Germany's invasion plans, and he pointed to a biography of Canaris.[59] The German spy chief explored several times whether the Allies would be interested in a compromise peace that would spare Germany from being invaded. He was involved in the 'Smolensk conspiracy', the attempt to assassinate Hitler on 13 March 1943 by placing a bomb in his aircraft when he visited German troops in Russia, which failed because the detonator did not ignite.[60] To maintain his credibility with the ever suspicious SS, he needed to display loyalty, as when he represented the Third Reich at the funeral of Kaiser Wilhelm II in the Netherlands. Fog surrounds his motives too in fooling Moscow into complacency before Operation Barbarossa,

Canaris, far left, at the Kaiser's funeral. in June 1941 in Holland. Hitler had wanted for propaganda reasons to hold the funeral in Berlin. But the Kaiser had stipulated only if the monarchy was restored.

the German invasion of the Soviet Union in 1941. Was he avoiding suspicion, or did his dislike of Soviet Communism eclipse his dislike of Nazism, and he hoped for the operation's success? We can never know.[61]

Events were beginning to catch up on Canaris. The failure of his Abwehr to alert Berlin to a whole series of Allied initiatives, including the invasion of North Africa, began arousing suspicions. Eventually, on Himmler's insistence in February 1944, he was dismissed, and the Abwehr was placed under SS command. Suspicion pointed to his being implicated in the July 1944 plot on Hitler, not least through his relationship with key conspirators. He was arrested, but the investigation proved lengthy and inconclusive until his private diary came to light which implicated him. He was sentenced to death, and was sent naked to the gallows, a butcher's hook, on 9 April at Flossenbürg. At the Nuremberg Trials, a junior officer testified persuasively how Canaris had tried to warn army chief Keitel that the army would be held responsible for the atrocities that had already been committed, and future atrocities that were planned for Poland.[62] So a complicated figure, but a brave and principled one too in a world where he had to constantly deceive to survive. Why were there not many more such figures like him in the military, intelligence and government?

Why too were there not more like Bonhoeffer, the standout Christian of the Nazi era, a figure of astonishing courage, intellect and spiritual depth, to whose memory this book is jointly dedicated?

Born in 1906 as one of eight children, he pursued a career in theology, studying at Tübingen and Berlin. He earned a doctorate in 1927, at just twenty-one. After that he briefly lived in New York, where he became sensitive to social and racial divisions, and more sceptical of his youthful nationalism, especially after reading Erich Remarque's *All Quiet on the Western Front*. He returned to Germany in 1931 to teach at the University of Berlin.

Not for him the equivocations of others who took time to accept the evils of Nazi philosophy. Not for him either the response of so many

Dietrich Bonhoeffer c.1938, a leader of towering moral, intellectual and religious strength, to whom this book is co-dedicated.

fellow church-goers that you care for other Christians alone. From the moment the party came to power in January 1933, he was vocal in his opposition to antisemitism. He spoke out courageously and repeatedly against the accommodation with Nazism chosen by other Church leaders, and tried to persuade his fellow Christians that the Nazi definition in the Race Laws of Jews by blood was wrong, and that Jews who converted to Christianity were entitled to the same rights as all Christians. In 1935, he became a leader of a new seminary of the Confessing Church, which he continued even after it was proscribed in 1937. He considered exile before the war began, but decided that he had a duty to share the hardships that were engulfing Germany. In 1940, he helped Jews escape to neutral Switzerland, declaring the Church 'was silent when [it] should have cried out because the blood of the innocent was crying aloud to heaven'.[63]

In October 1940, he joined the Abwehr under Canaris, and made several trips outside the Reich in 1941 and 1942 informing Christians, including George Bell, Bishop of Chichester, about Nazi crimes and the resistance in Germany. In contrast, though, to Canaris, he argued that it would be necessary for the Allies to totally defeat and occupy Germany for the evil to be extinguished.[64] The net was closing in around him, and in April 1943, sure enough he was arrested by the Gestapo for his involvement in Operation Seven, a plan to get more Jews out of

Germany. He too was charged after the failed 20 July plot, imprisoned initially by the Gestapo in Berlin, then taken to Buchenwald in February 1945, and in early April, to Flossenbürg. He was hanged on 9 April, along with his brother Klaus, executed for resistance activities, as were two of his brothers-in-law.[65] Eyewitness accounts describe him being dignified and calm, his final words, according to the camp doctor: 'This is the end. For me, the beginning of life.'[66]

Two weeks later, on 23 April, American Jeeps drove into the camp.

6

Sudetenland:
From Flossenbürg to Prague

Chapter 6
Flossenbürg to Prague

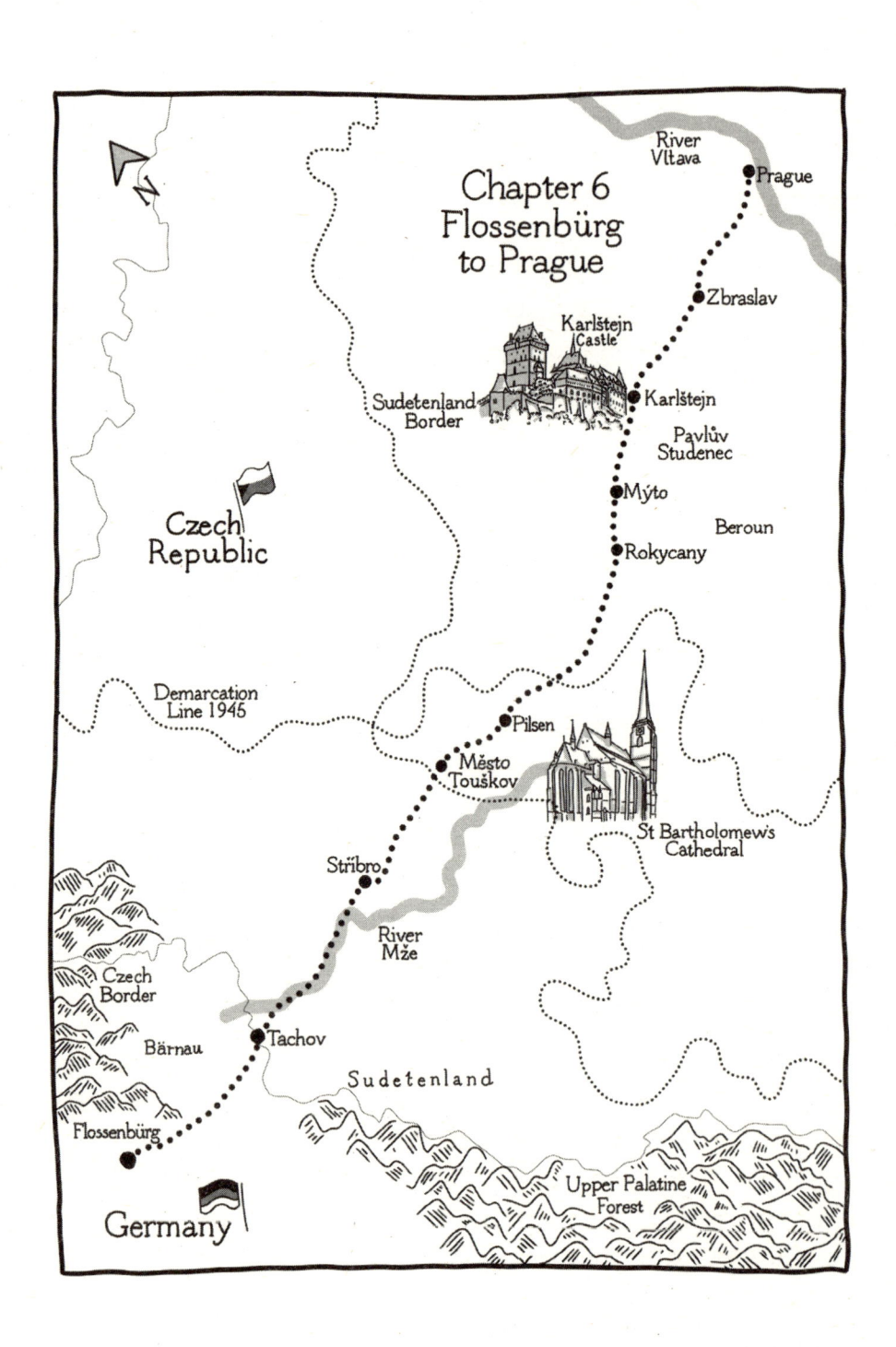

'I'm going to go back out in forty-eight hours whatever you tell me,' I say to the coronary specialist as, glasses perched on forehead, he studies the CT scan of my heart.

He rocks slowly backwards and forwards on his chair.

'I thought you might say that,' he murmurs, eyes glued to his screen.

'Sorry to be predictable,' I reply. 'The tickets are booked, arrangements made.' He doesn't respond.

Six months have passed since I flew home last August having reached Flossenbürg. It is now March 2025, and I'm in a coronary care unit.

His examination over, the specialist turns to look straight into my eyes.

'It's not good news, I'm afraid.' In his lovely reassuring way, he points out to me on his screen the narrowed artery leading to my heart.

'How would you describe it?' I ask.

He chooses his words carefully. 'You have significant heart disease.'

'That doesn't sound good.'

'I'm afraid the position has deteriorated since the scan eighteen months ago.'

'But I've done everything right since then!'

'You have. You're slim, you exercise regularly, you look after yourself, you've got a lot going for you.'

'I've not had more than two days off work in my entire career. I've never been ill...'

He looks to say something, but thinks better of it.

'... My parents lived forever and never had a murmur from their hearts,' I add, willing him to change his verdict.

'That's not how it works, I'm afraid. It's the combination of genes from both parents that make up the mix.'

He tells me I will need a stent to dilate the constricted artery and to have it done quickly.

I go straight for it. 'What's my chance of succumbing when I'm back out in the Czech Republic walking?'

'That's not something we can predict, I'm afraid.'

My mind casts me back to when I was in a French hospital in Lens, desperate to complete the Western Front walk in 2021 and arguing with the doctor who was telling me to stop. Then it was my feet. A bit of a mess, but only feet.

I'm thinking quickly. 'Am I more likely to have an incident out walking than if I stayed at home?'

'That's something I can answer. Walking is good for you. The issue is if you are in a remote place and something happens.'

Something *happens*? I go quiet.

'The Czech Republic has excellent coronary care, as good as here.'

This isn't entirely reassuring.

'Well, I'm off anyway in two days,' I say. 'What can you give me?'

He quadruples my statins, gives me a replacement blood thinner instead of aspirin, and a spray to squirt into my mouth if I feel an attack coming on.

'Anything else?' I'm reeling a bit.

'No, that's all. Try to avoid straining the heart. Take it day by day. Don't overdo it.'

I thank him and make my way back home. The significance has yet to sink in. My walking friends are already *in situ* awaiting my arrival. I'm way behind schedule on the walk and I've barely done a third of the writing. The book is due to be published in nine months. I had negotiated Epsom and writing on Truss. I hadn't banked on anything else coming up. I am only halfway through the walk. I've done the easy part, Alsace and Germany. Now I have to venture into two countries I barely know: the Czech Republic and Poland. The spectre of failure looms large.

I wait till I'm home to tell Sarah the news face to face. No, I don't know how much risk I am under. I try to reassure her, but she is still upset. No, I am not having the procedure done privately even though they would rush it through. I can't afford £15,000–£20,000, period, and my insurance doesn't cover it. I'll have to wait my turn on the NHS. She doesn't want me to go back out, but she knows I won't listen to her. I feel really torn. She's had so much loss in her life and now her mother is desperately ill. We talk it through. We pray together. We have found happiness in the last few years. For the first time since Joanna died, I am looking forwards with real optimism. I desperately want to live longer, to spend more time with her, with my three children, my first grandchild, to realize some new projects I care deeply about. I'm just finding my voice. I find it hard to think that my life is seriously at risk. In fact, it's a totally ridiculous idea.

Forty-eight hours later my defiance has been replaced by anxiety, excited anticipation superseded by gloomy thoughts. I am off today. Sarah has left for school and I feel no pleasure as I go through the now familiar routine of packing my rucksack. My spirits pick up once on the plane when I meet a feisty American-Czech father and daughter in row 17 who remind me why I am doing this. For the next two hours, they give me a double-barrelled tutorial on the feelings I will be encountering as I travel through their country. Betrayal is their constant theme, the British, the Nazis, the Soviet Union and now Trump's America. The man's father had been deported by the Nazis from his hometown of Brno to Buchenwald for eighteen months for 'lack of cooperation' with the regime. When the Soviet-dominated Czech government came to power in February 1948, they withdrew his welfare benefits, as they did to other Czech ex-prisoners who had been in camps liberated by the Western

Allies, not by the Soviets. They talk with pride about the assassination in 1942 in Prague of the country's Nazi supremo Heydrich, but tell me that, had the two perpetrators Jozef Gabčík and Jan Kubiš survived, the Soviets would have locked them up at once. 'Why?' I ask. 'Because they'd been trained by the British. This was the Cold War.' I'm learning quickly. 'The assassination showed Britain that we Czechs were not weak and could achieve heroic acts, even though the retribution against our country was terrible.' They wax lyrical about the contribution of Czech pilots to winning the war, like Josef František, the most successful non-British pilot in the Battle of Britain (and did I know that eighty-seven Czech pilots flew in *four* Czech squadrons in the battle?).[1] Now it's the US's turn under the cosh. They are livid at President Roosevelt's sellout of Czechoslovakia at the Yalta Conference in February 1945: 'The American forces were at the gates of Prague but they were told to hang back and to let the Russians take the city.' Father and daughter save their absolute fury, though, for US Vice President J.D. Vance whose speech in Munich the day before appeared to belittle the seriousness of the current Russian threat. This same raw vulnerability fuels their outrage at British perfidy: as the plane slowly dips towards Prague, the daughter launches into a full scale attack on Chamberlain for selling out her country to Hitler. It's been a heck of an education. History I can see is still very raw for Czechs. In fact, not history at all. Or as American novelist William Faulkner put it, 'The past is never dead. It's not even past.'[2]

The chance conversation makes me realize how different the country I'm going to be walking through will be to Germany and France. I am ashamed about my patchy knowledge, so my long-standing researcher Jonathan Meakin patiently talks me through it, filling in many gaps in its romantic if fraught history. A political construct named 'Czechoslovakia' only from 1918 to 1992, its origins can be traced back to the Duchy of Bohemia, founded during the ninth century, and soon to be recognized as a distinct land within the Holy Roman Empire. The core territory was divided into three regions: Bohemia in the west and centre, Moravia in the east, and Czech Silesia, a narrow slither of Silesia that today is mostly in Poland. Charles IV (1346–78) was Bohemia's most significant monarch: after he became Holy Roman Emperor in 1355, Prague became the capital of the whole Empire.[3] He founded the famous Charles University and built the much-loved Charles Bridge over the Vltava. Silver mining and trade underpinned the economy, and towns with graceful architecture and arcades sprouted across the country. The idyll was stalled in the Hussite Wars (1419–34) between the Catholics and the followers of reformer Jan Hus that turned most of the country against Rome. In 1526, left in debt by the ineffective (albeit wondrously named) Jagiellonian dynasty, and fearful of the looming threat of the Ottoman Turks from the south-east, the Bohemian nobles voted for order, and put a Habsburg from Austria on the throne.[4]

But in 1618, the Protestant Bohemian nobles rebelled against the Habsburgs. Prague has history when it comes to defenestrations, and that May, two Catholic imperial emissaries were ejected by Protestants from a window in Prague Castle, helping spark the Thirty Years War. The Protestants were defeated at the Battle of White Mountain in 1620, the whole country faring badly in the ensuing conflagration, as did Germany. In London, James I (1603–25), whose daughter Elizabeth had married into the Bohemian royal family, agonized for the final five years of his reign whether to become involved; wisely, he sat it out. The Bohemian nobility was crushed, with those not killed fleeing into exile, and for the next three centuries, the country was recatholicized by the Austrian Habsburgs governing from Vienna, and by their local loyalists.[5] The nineteenth century saw rapid industrialization and the powerful rise of a Czech national consciousness, with a desire to revive and create Czech literature, language, music, art and architecture. The region became a tourist destination, with spas like Marienbad and Karlsbad fashionable with wealthy Europeans – Edward VII, whose statue graces the former, for one. Towards the end of the nineteenth century, Alphonse Mucha's Art Nouveau creations enhanced the appearance and artistic style of

Prague (to be dubbed 'Paris of the East') and inspired Czech modernist art (the word 'Bohemian' to denote arty, louche types derives from the French word *bohémien* for Roma gypsies originating from Bohemia, and gifting Puccini the title of his opera, *La bohème*).

In the First World War, Czech soldiers largely fought for the Habsburgs, side by side with their German allies, and 140,000 were killed. But with news of horrifying slaughter at the front, cracks in the Empire began to show, and over 60,000 Czechs and Slovaks switched sides to join a 'Czechoslovak Legion' that fought with the Allies. In October 1918, as the culmination of centuries of struggle to establish a distinct national identity, an independent 'Czechoslovakia' was born when Bohemia, Sub-Carpathian Ruthenia and Czech Silesia joined with Slovakia. The Allies wanted the new country to have defensible mountainous borders and with the Sudetenland, the German majority-inhabited areas bordering Austria, Germany and Poland, controversially

The Nazis drive into the Sudetenland in 1938.

becoming part of the new state. By the 1930s, the unified country had become one of the most highly industrialized regions in the world, one reason Hitler itched to grab it.

The Nazis thus seized the Sudetenland in October 1938 and the rest of Bohemia and Moravia in March 1939. Under the *Generalplan Ost* ('Masterplan for the East'), the Czechs were to be expelled or exploited: as 'Slavs' they had no place in German *Lebensraum*. Hitler initially appointed Konstantin von Neurath as Protector of Bohemia and Moravia (the name 'Czechoslovakia' was expunged, and a Nazi puppet 'Slovak' state created in the east). But von Neurath was not brutal enough, so in September 1941 Hitler and Himmler brought in *Einsatzgruppen* and Holocaust chief instigator Heydrich to boost Czech armaments production vital to the war effort and eliminate any resistance with his manifesto 'we will Germanize the Czech vermin'.[6] Meanwhile, a Czech government-in-exile was established in London under President Edvard Beneš. Immediately after the country had been liberated in 1945, the government returned to Prague to pick up the reins, one of its first actions being the summary and brutal expulsion of all Germans from the Sudetenland and elsewhere (on which more later).

For many European countries, the end of the war ushered in enduring stability. Not so for Czechoslovakia. The national name and borders were reinstated and all initially looked well in Prague. But not in Moscow, which poured money in to support the burgeoning Czech Communist Party, which in February 1948 engineered a coup d'état.[7] Beneš resigned as president and died in September, while his assertive foreign minister Jan Masaryk was found dead in his Ministry's courtyard having fallen from a window; whether suicide or murder has never been conclusively proved.

Twenty years later, Moscow thought the regime too liberal. Hundreds of thousands of Warsaw Pact troops with tanks thus arrived on the streets in August 1968 to snuff out the popular 'Prague Spring'. The brave leader of the time, Alexander Dubček, was sidelined as Moscow

Soviet tanks approach Wenceslas Square. The liberalizing 'Prague Spring' of 1968 ended abruptly, to the sound of Warsaw Pact tanks driving through the streets. The Soviet invasion in 1968 led to widespread fear about what Moscow might do again.

reasserted control. The country's liberation had to wait till the 'Velvet Revolution' at the end of 1989, mass popular demonstrations having made the Communist leadership realize the game was up. Then came the 'Velvet Divorce' on the final day of 1992 that saw the harmonious separation of the Czech Republic (or Czechia) from Slovakia, which became two separate and friendly states, neither large, with populations of 10 and 5 million respectively. When the Russian bear started to reassert itself under Putin after 2000, the Czech Republic managed to remain relatively free from Moscow's attention, in contrast to Ukraine, Moldova, Belarus and the Baltic republics. The Czechs found in writer-leader Václav Havel a new hero, president till 2003 but remaining a huge figure thereafter till chain smoking contributed to his death in 2011. The country joined NATO in 1996, and has prospered after joining the EU in May 2004. But today, despite being a beacon for liberal values and a leading Central European country in standing up to Russia, as I am realizing, chill winds from Moscow are blowing again.

I speed through immigration at Prague's Václav Havel Airport and take a taxi to Pilsen. I'm thrilled my driver is another Czech with fluent English eager to engage, as I am bursting to show off my newly acquired knowledge of his country. I have no opportunity before he pours his heart out about how vulnerable his country has been made to feel, although given its history of repeated betrayals, perhaps I shouldn't be so surprised. 'Appeasement' is back in Prague's air. Chamberlain's dismissive remark about it being 'horrible, fantastic, incredible' that Britain should be girding itself up for war because of 'a quarrel in a faraway country between people of whom we know nothing' could have been uttered yesterday, so great is my driver's indignation at the apparent appeasement of Russia today by the Trump administration.[8] The Czechs are no fools: they know that without US arms and dollars in the future, Central Europe will be far more vulnerable to Putin's ambitions. I commiserate with him about Trump and Vance, whose motives and endgame remain a mystery to me, but I can shed more light I hope on Chamberlain's thinking.

The elderly British PM was aware, I pointed out, that British armed forces were not yet ready to take on Germany, that public opinion favoured peace, and he trusted Hitler's words that his appetite would stop with the Sudetenland, which had a high German population anyway. 'He faced strong Cabinet disagreement at the time, and many Brits today are not proud of his appeasement,' I add.[9] 'Please tell me,' the driver asks, his blood up, 'how can it have been right to abandon an ally to appease an enemy and then impose the solution on us?' I try a different tack. 'With Ukraine today, it is different, there is a unified will from the West and the military might to help it resist Russia, unlike—' 'No longer,' he interjects. 'Well, maybe,' I say. I am in an unfamiliar role trying to explain Chamberlain's thinking, and I am not

Hitler and Chamberlain in Munich, September 1938. The Czechs were totally excluded from the discussions about the future of their country.

convincing. Even if he was buying time in 1938 so Britain could rearm, there was no excuse for his dismissive language about Czechoslovakia. I'm relieved when we arrive in the suburbs of Pilsen, the torture almost over. The driver gives me his card. 'This is my number if you need me on your walk to Prague,' he says. It's clear he's no more convinced by my walking potential than he was by any of my arguments. And off he drives into the night. This really is a country on the edge, where the past is palpably present.

I stride into the jauntily named Hotel Rango to be greeted by two old friends, John Ashton and his wife Maggi Morris, who were with me in the summer of 2016 on our first attempt to navigate the Western Front Way. John, a force of nature, led public health in the northwest of England for many years, while Maggi is a pioneering social scientist. We are joined by another Brit, Paul Antrobus, who came out to Czechoslovakia thirty years ago shortly after the Velvet Revolution to set up a business and never returned. Paul was recommended to me by the British Embassy as someone who knows every track in the country; intrigued by the project, he has offered to act as guide. I have my team: medic, psychologist and pathfinder! We descend into the hotel's sixteenth-century cellar for dinner. Surprise all round when I decline the wine and other stronger stuff. 'You were drinking in *The Path of Peace*,' they protest. I worry I have let down the welcoming party, especially after I break the news about my needing to go gently.

We talk about our host city Pilsen, the Czech Republic's fourth largest, best known today for its Pilsner lager and Skoda factory. Paul says there's a lot more to the city than is at first obvious. After dinner, I survey Pilsen's roofs from my garret bedroom, looking forward to getting to know the city better, thankful I can spot no bell towers to chime all night. I'm the first down to breakfast and am reminded how difficult it is to find a good cup of English breakfast tea this side of the Channel. The staff are eager to get the tea right and are desolated when I reject the hot milk on offer in favour of cold. The real problem is the water isn't hot enough nor the teabags sufficiently fertile. I give up after some watery sips and ask for coffee just as the others clump down the stairs. We plan the day: Paul and I will be the advance group driving back over the German border and we'll meet up together later in the day.

We drive west for an hour till we reach the hills just above Flossenbürg in a car park used by cross-country skiers, for which the region is celebrated. I am thrilled to be setting off again after a break of six months, and I'm just hoping my ticker behaves. Paul is the real thing, complete with lightweight equipment, great boots and a total mastery of terrain. After a while we set off on a long straight track through a forest, which is covered in packed ice. The altitude is only 800 metres but it's noticeably colder than in Pilsen. We persevere for several minutes but it's not easy as the ice is rock hard and very slippery. I sense Paul becoming concerned. 'I can't see this getting any better. It could be like this for the next seven kilometres.' 'Righto, you're the boss.' So we backtrack to the car, and drive to Bärnau, closer to the Czech border. For the first 2 kilometres the path is uphill and, blithely ignoring the medical advice, I forge ahead up a long avenue of lime trees. 'Are you sure the pace isn't too quick?' enquires Paul. For a man who has ascended twenty of the highest peaks in the Alps, he is a model of patience. 'I'm feeling fine,' I say, which I am, but when I reach the Baroque Steinberg church and press on to the summit beyond, which is really no big deal, my heart is racing and I'm not feeling so good. After a rest, we proceed more slowly but I let the experience get to me. I have never been good at identifying a genuine health concern, and I'm no good at it now.

We take stock and press on up the hill to the Czech border a kilometre beyond. The point about the border is that there is no border. Cars swish back and forth regardless. The only indication is a small sign with the words 'Česká Republika' in white lettering circled by twelve golden EU stars against a blue background, the design unchanged since adopted by the Council of Europe in 1955. More intriguing is an old stone marker a short way beyond it with the initials 'B' for Bohemia and, carved above it, 'D' for Deutschland, while on the other side a more recently carved 'S' for Sudetenland.

The big surprise is I can see no evident sign as we cross the frontier of the menacing Iron Curtain, the 7,000-kilometre barrier dividing Communist from non-Communist Europe, with its lethal electric fences, tank traps, minefields and guard towers manned by heavily armed soldiers. It was designed to stop people from the East escaping to the West, and ideas from the West filtering into the Eastern Bloc. Even as a rebellious teenager who planned an anti-Vietnam War demonstration at school, I remember thinking Communism must be a bit rubbish if people were desperate to escape from it and barely no one, bar a few of my grandfather's Marxist friends, wanted to go the other way.

Operation Border Stone run by Czech Communist intelligence from 1948 to 1951 was designed to root out and trap potential defectors before they attempted to cross into Germany. But from 1951 the Czechs, under Soviet influence, changed tack and invested in fences and fortifications to deter the escapers who attempted to swim, dig tunnels and even use hot air balloons to escape. The 800-kilometre Czech border was often manned by teenage national service trainees; if they killed escapees, 'they either got promoted or some kind of non-financial awards, or holiday time', said one historian.[10] An estimated 282 Czechs were killed trying to escape between 1948 and 1989, with 145 shot, 100 electrocuted, and the rest drowned or dying through other misadventures.[11] One young man, František Faktor, was pursued by guards a short distance over the border, on to Austrian territory, where they shot him and left him to die as a warning to others. This happened as late as 1984.[12] But several thousand nevertheless managed to slip out of the country, though few by directly attempting to cross the fortified borders. All physical evidence of the fortifications may have gone today, but a certain menace lingers on. In 2014, scientists found that, twenty-five years after the fencing had come down, red deer continued to avoid the former border areas, with unhappy memories of the electric fences and trigger-happy guards.[13]

Crossing into the Czech Republic should have been a moment of celebration, but I'm temporarily preoccupied with maudlin thoughts: should I have come out yesterday, why is my heart aching, what will I do if I have an attack? I kick them back down and distract myself by peppering Paul with questions about the Sudetenland through which we are now walking.

Germans, he explains, formed nearly a quarter of the 13 million population of the newly formed Czechoslovakia in 1918, concentrated in the Sudetenland, which was about 30 per cent of the total country. The name, deriving from the Sudeten mountains that lie along the northern border of the country, only came into prominence when the German population, angry not to be allowed to join Germany after 1918, began campaigning for separation in the interwar years. It was a ticking time-bomb. Chamberlain saw some merit in Hitler's argument that the Treaty of Versailles had been too harsh on Germany and thus in its claim to the Sudetenland. And so, at Munich, at the end of September 1938, Britain, France and Italy agreed on Germany and thus in its claim to the Sudetenland entirely. Though the French had

The older border stone engraved with a B, S, and D.

An image of how the Iron Curtain looked pre-1990. The border fence was only the final line of a deep system of barriers used to prevent escape.

a military alliance with Czechoslovakia, they, along with the British, who had no such alliance, informed Prague that if they fought back, they would be doing so alone. The Czechoslovak government, Paul explains, had no choice but to capitulate.

Their leaders felt totally abandoned and humiliated by being excluded from the negotiations as if their voice did not matter. Worse was to follow. Ethnic cleansing. News that Czechs were being forcibly ejected from their homes in the Sudetenland after the Munich Agreement though aroused little interest in Britain. Most people had other concerns. 'Me fight for Czechoslovakia? Why should I? I should lose my business to begin with', was the opinion of a shopkeeper recorded at the time.[14] The same thought would be echoed by many Americans today about Ukraine's struggle. As Trump very well knows.

Not all in Britain were indifferent in 1938. Winston Churchill, speaking from the backbenches, said that 'we have sustained a total and unmitigated defeat', and that Czechoslovakia would soon be 'engulfed in the Nazi regime'.[15] His sentiments were echoed by Labour leader Clement Attlee, who spoke of 'a gallant, civilised and democratic people betrayed and handed over to a ruthless despotism'.[16] But they were not in a majority in Parliament, nor did such views resonate with the electorate at large.

As Churchill predicted, the Nazis soon seized the rest of the country. Having lost their formidable fortifications when Germany marched into the Sudetenland six months before, and with no allies, Czechoslovakia had little option when German troops advanced in March 1939. They marched into Prague with barely a shot fired. The Czechs would spend the next six years under a bleak and murderous occupation regime, while the Slovaks in the east would live under a separate collaborator government.

During the war, the British were pressured behind closed doors by Beneš about what to do with the German population in the Sudetenland after the war. He wanted them to be expelled, his argument being that the Germans should be punished and should never again be able to challenge the territorial integrity of his country. He realized that he needed broader Allied support for his plan, and in December 1943 flew to Moscow to get approval. Stalin was up for it; he was planning to shift the Polish border west, which would require similar expulsions of Germans from east of the River Oder.[17] Beneš was thus delighted when the Allies confirmed at Potsdam in July 1945 that all Germans outside its national borders would be repatriated, though the violence and murders that took place had not been sanctioned. An estimated 13 million Germans were uprooted from across the whole of Europe, sometimes from communities centuries old, and sent to Germany, with more than half a million dying in the process, figures that still shock.[18]

In May 1945, Beneš made public that 'we have decided to eliminate the German problem in our republic once and for all', a chilling statement with frightening echoes. The 'Beneš decrees', as they were known, led to the forced expulsion of some 2.5 million Germans from the Sudetenland. Many were murdered: tens of thousands according to the Czechs, hundreds of thousands according to some German sources, including women and children, with Czech paramilitary groups guilty of atrocities, all under the benign indifference of the Czech police. Over 1.3 million of those expelled went to West Germany, principally to Bavaria, Hesse and Baden-Württemberg. The Beneš decrees stripped them of their property and rights, though the government in Bonn offered some compensation for lost property. The remaining 800,000 went to East Germany, principally to Saxony and Thuringia where they fared less well financially.[19] The whole experience provoked strong emotions on both sides. Václav Havel, a figure of light most certainly who stands out as a Czech leader long before he became president in 1989, believed that what happened was deeply wrong. He worked hard on forgiveness and healing with German leaders, which bore fruit in the German-Czech Declaration of Reconciliation in 1997.[20] It remains a live and raw issue to this day.

I am staggered by what happened here in 1945–47. Whole ancient German communities – Königswart, Bärringen and Weipert – wiped from memory.[21] I think of the expulsion of Germans after 1945 I learned about when walking through Alsace. Or Trump's proposal in the news this week for the US to 'take over' Gaza, to carpet it with casino resorts and to resettle its 2.1 million Palestinians elsewhere. The concept of 'ethnic cleansing', which first entered popular consciousness in the 1990s in the Balkans, is deeply abhorrent, any time, any place.

Paul points out a memorial by the side of our road, where the border village of Pavlův Studenec once stood, founded in the early eighteenth century on the Bohemia–Bavaria trade route. The population of nearly 1,500 in the interwar years was German with a sprinkling of Czechs who worked at the local customs office and police station. After 1945 and the summary expulsion of the Germans, it was resettled by Czechs, but after the Communist coup in 1948, it fell into the border zone, and all buildings including the village's satellite settlements were demolished except for those lived in by the border guards. Nothing remained bar the church, customs office and several houses. Then in the 1970s when the border zone was expanded, new barracks were required and all the surviving buildings were demolished; the last to be blown up was the church in 1977. 'The Communists stamped out the Church wherever they could across the country: it still hasn't recovered,' Paul tells me. In its place they substituted the 'Soviet dream'.

We must press on to meet John and Maggi in Tachov, still 10 kilometres away. I ply Paul with questions about the country under Charlemagne, the Holy Roman and the Austro-Hungarian empires. The conversation switches to the 'Golden Road' built by Charles IV to stimulate trade between Prague and his German imperial lands. The route flourished just as the Silk Road (or 'Silk Routes') connecting the eastern and western worlds through Samarkand were beginning to decline in the fifteenth century. Legend has it that Charles IV himself travelled down this road fifty-two times. It was certainly popular,

A small memorial is all that remains of the community of Pavlův Studenec.

allowing traders to travel from Prague to Nuremberg without paying customs duties, protected by a network of fortresses and castles, with special religious sites for pilgrims. Into Bohemia poured spices, wines, fabrics and weapons, while the German lands gained grain, and other foodstuffs including malt, hops and cheeses. But after 1600, rival routes were beginning to open up, and the Golden Road became a smuggling route and footpath between both cities until falling into disuse.[22]

We finish the day in Tachov, the first major town in Bohemia along the golden road. It boasts an imposing thirteenth-century castle and thick stone walls around the town. The glory days, though, are long past. After the expulsion of the Germans in 1945, it was repopulated by Czechs and Slovaks, as well as by incomers from Ukraine and Romania. For long years afterwards, like Flossenbürg, it was forgotten, a town on a route that led nowhere but an impassable border. Prosperity was slow to return after 1989 but can now be seen in the re-cobbling of the main square full of elegant Austro-Hungarian buildings. We meet

John and Maggi in a bar overlooking the River Mže and plan the walk for the next few days. Judging by today, I'm not going to be able to walk uphill nor to cover more than 15 kilometres. They go out of their way to be understanding but for the second time in twenty-four hours I worry I am letting my friends down.

At midnight I awake in my hotel bed back in Pilsen and sit bolt upright. My heart is racing, which is exactly what it doesn't need to be doing, and I don't know how to stop it. I eye the container of glyceryl trinitrate spray I am to use if things get bad – how bad? – and it's not reassuring. I run through all my usual routines, shower, yoga, reading, and I'm still wide awake. So I resort to the nuclear option, a slug of white wine that normally sends me off when my mind won't let me. Not this time, and I'm up early in the morning and walk to Náměstí Republiky, the main square just by the hotel to clear my head. It dates from when Pilsen was founded as a royal town in 1295 by King Wenceslas II (not the tenth-century Bohemian King Wenceslas famous for his kindness to the poor who inspired the nineteenth-century carol). I enter St Bartholomew's Cathedral, which dominates the square; an early service is in progress. I spot nobody younger than fifty, and think again of Paul's observation the day before about the Communist impact on the Church, and wonder what the modern Czech Republic offers in its place: does it help explain why the country ranks at the bottom for religious belief in Europe? The square is made up of Renaissance and Baroque buildings, none more imposing than the sixteenth-century town hall. One building mars the unity, the Hotel Central created in brutalist form by the Communists in 1968. Their crass insensitivity to beauty and style has no clearer landmark.

Breakfast is already in full swing and the dining room smelling of coffee when I come back in. Maggi is talking about her son Dylan, a world-famous sky-diver and BASE jumper who had worked with Tom Cruise on one of the *Mission Impossible* films. A perfectionist on all safety matters, an inexplicable accident caused his death aged thirty-three in the Italian Dolomites three years ago. We talk about loss. 'The grief I feel every day is the inevitable result of the love I feel,' she says. When Dylan's own father died, John stepped in and became a second father. 'I always insisted I had Dylan's exact location tracked on my phone,' she says. 'It was how I knew where he was.' I so admire them both, and I ask them about the work they have done in tragedies as far apart as the Hillsborough Stadium disaster in 1989 and the Grenfell Tower fire in 2017. It's time to set off, Paul driving us back to Tachov.

I'm falling in love with what I'm seeing of the Czech Republic. With one missed chunk, we walk to Stříbro along country lanes and tracks, along avenues of trees, beside streams and rivers. At one point, we walk by a silver lake, covered in ice. John, who is on car duty today, keeps appearing along the route with drinks and sustenance. We barely see anyone else all day, bar one vehicle, a white van driven much too quickly and closely past us, memorable because atypical. I ask Paul about the ubiquitous and beautifully kept paths we have been following. They date back, I learn, to two members of the nineteenth-century Czech National Revival movement, Miroslav Tyrš and Jindřich Fügner, who were intrigued by similar organizations being established in the Austro-Hungarian Empire to promote national cultural identity and physical prowess. So they established an organization called Sokol ('falcon'), which spread throughout the country and was significant in establishing Slav cultural identity and a sense of national Czech solidarity.[23] How unlike the Hitler Youth with its aggressive militarism. Sokol's last pre-war mass display, peaceful in contrast to the rallies, was held in July 1938 and attended by 350,000 members at Prague's Strahov Stadium, still standing today and at the time Europe's largest sporting venue. Marking out hiking trails across the country was one of the Sokol founder's great successes: by 1938, nearly 40,000 kilometres of tracks had been carefully defined across the entire country. Czech émigrés set up similar bodies abroad. The network came to international prominence after 1945, with many other countries seeking to emulate the Czechs in what is considered the gold standard for trails anywhere in the world.[24]

As we approach Stříbro, we notice an increasing number of bunkers and defences, constructed interwar by the government in the event of a German invasion. As most of the defences were in the Sudetenland, they were of no value when the Germans annexed it. The pillboxes and other defences are now painted in a variety of bright colours, yellows, browns and greens. They have found a purpose as colourful memorials to recent history.

Stříbro is the second Golden Road town in Bohemia after Tachov that travellers would have encountered, and it retains a proud presence, with medieval walls and a Renaissance stone-arched bridge spanning the Mže with one of its passage towers still standing. It was completed in the late 1550s just as Elizabeth I (whose distant cousin Elizabeth Stuart, James I's daughter, was later to be Queen of Bohemia) was being crowned Queen of England. The town is built on high ground surrounded by the river, with a large square and well-preserved buildings on all sides, as in Tachov. No eyesore Communist buildings here, but equally no local stories I can find of wartime heroism by Czech partisans. What I do learn, though, is that there were some 150,000 ethnic Germans in the Sudetenland who detested Nazism, mostly Social Democrats and active Christians, who engaged in sabotage, hid Jews and aided refugees. An exhibition called 'Forgotten Heroes' toured the country in 2007 highlighting their actions, such as eleven-year-old Bedřich Dedek and his father who thwarted Nazi attempts to destroy flood defences in 1945. Despite the active resistance of many Germans, and the friendship they showed to native Czechs, all but a handful were forcibly thrown out in the mass expulsions after 1945.[25]

As we walk along the river out of the town the next day, we pass the silver museum with narrow gauge rail tracks and small carts by the side of the river where mining, which started in the twelfth century, continued until late in the last century. Our conversation turns to the

The Renaissance bridge at Stříbro, over the Mže river.

Mže. If there was a Mže supporters' club (there might be), Paul would be its president. The river rises in Bavaria, and is our on/off companion all the way to Pilsen where it is renamed the Berounka, before finally merging with the mighty Vltava in Prague. Today is a Mže off day, for me at least. As it flows downstream, it cuts through hilly country, and my heart is finding the constant rise and dip of the path testing. We decide it would be prudent for John to meet us and drive us on to flatter ground for the walk into Město Touškov.

A community of just over 2,000 inhabitants today, this one small place epitomizes the entire history of this troubled but indomitable country. A flourishing market town in the fourteenth century, it was destroyed in the Hussite Wars the following century, becoming a mere village again. It recovered to become a busy market town again in the 1500s, until savagely destroyed in the Thirty Years War in the early 1600s. German settlers were invited in to build it up again, where they lived alongside the small Jewish community. Five fires ripping through its timber houses, followed by plagues in 1680 and 1713 that killed perhaps a third of the population, were further body blows, but the town bounced back. Then when the Sudetenland was annexed in October 1938, the town's Czechs and Jews fled eastwards, and in 1945 it was the Germans who were expelled. The cowed population then had to endure forty years of unwanted Communist rule.[26] Living all my life in Britain, this level of impermanence is hard to grasp.

Back to Pilsen for our last night, and a final chance to get to grips with this surprising town, European Capital of Culture in 2015 no less. Sitting just outside the Sudetenland, it was the first city seized by Hitler in March 1939, and the first (and last) Czech city taken by the US army in 1945. As a show of the continuing gratitude of the city on the sixtieth anniversary of liberation in 2005, a museum dedicated to the flamboyant US General George S. Patton was opened here.[27] The general, aware of the terrible treatment of civilians by Soviet soldiers, who had gained a reputation for rape and disorder, insisted that his Third Army behave impeccably, which Czechs have never forgotten. Furious at being stopped from taking Prague by Supreme Allied Headquarters in place of the Soviets, Patton said, 'we should have gone on to the [Vltava] river and, if the Russians didn't like it, let them go to hell.'[28] Another general, Heliodor Píka, no less distinguished, was not treated as a hero after the war. A brave soldier, he was chief of the Czechoslovak Military Mission to the Soviet Union on behalf of the Czech government-in-exile in London. That effectively signed his death warrant, and when the Communists took over in 1948, he was promptly arrested, tried for treason and hanged in Pilsen's notorious Bory prison in 1949. His body was never found. He became the first victim of the Communist Party's purges in the country.[29]

John, Maggi and I talk over dinner about the Western Front Way and its progress in the nearly ten years since we first walked it together. The Belgians have been enthusiastic supporters, as they are of all matters to

US soldiers in Pilsen in May 1945.

do with the war and remembrance, and the path is marked out from the North Sea to the Belgian-French border town of Armentières. French engagement with 'La Grande Guerre' is more tenuous. It is taking time, but the pathway is marked with our distinctive four national flowers logo down to Neuve Chapelle (which saw bitter fighting in 1915) and finishes close by the spot where Douglas Gillespie, the inspirer of the walk, fell in the first hours of the Battle of Loos. It might take another ten years or more for the path to be marked all the way down to the Vosges mountains and Kilometre Zero. I'm optimistic. I always am. The initiative's core mission to encourage different nationalities to celebrate what they share in common, though, has not been winning the battle of ideas since we started out, we note wryly. Equally, it makes the walk, and the vision behind it, even more vital. We talk about good and evil people (I have met remarkably few of the latter) and about the difficulties we have encountered speaking truth as we see it in our different professions. None of us is naturally comfortable in closed clubs. 'Have you found any figures of light yet in the Czech Republic?'

John asks as we finish our sticky *trdelník* dessert, a local delicacy. 'Not yet, not yet, but they're out there, I know,' I respond.

The next morning we set out walking from Pilsen to Rokycany. I start each day with such optimism, and today is glorious, warm at last, nature bursting into life: we spot blackthorn, flowering quinces, primroses and celandine. I'm desperate to make the walk a success, but after two or three hours I realize I'm becoming breathless and have an aching chest. I ask Paul if I can take a few minutes to sit down in some woods by the side of our path and put my head between my legs to ward off fainting. After fifteen minutes I realize it's not working: I can't get rid of the nausea. I remember thinking at the time this is the lowest point of the whole walk, and so it was. We meet up with John, talk it through and arrange for me to see a doctor in Prague. I sit in silence as we speed into the capital, worrying whether I'm being melodramatic. Sleep-deprived nights haven't helped me think clearly. The doctor is empathetic, does her tests and gives me a hug: very un-English but probably more help to patients than the rushed patter and the drugs British doctors often prescribe. The verdict? Inconclusive but 'err on the side of caution' is the sense of the meeting. I'm left with a difficult choice. Continue to be a patient and a bother out here with the risk I could push my body too far? A tricky one as I do not know how much risk I am under. Or return home and get back on top of my health? I am beginning to accept I came out too soon after the specialist's consultation and had not given the new drugs time to work or to process the diagnosis. Sarah was right. She usually is.

I can't recall now the exact sequence of what happened next, so I resort to my diary: 'The consultation convinces me I should leave. I break the news to John and Paul who are incredibly generous, and I bid them a sad farewell outside the rather wonderful Pytloun Old Armoury Hotel on the Vltava near the Old Town where we were due to be staying. I feel absolutely wretched because the next four days were full of special places to walk through and people to meet. I don't know where this leaves the walk…' It feels very bleak for a few hours, I

The three of us outside the Armoury Hotel in Prague. Paul Antrobus is on the left, and John Ashton on the right, the day I decide to return early.

have let myself and everyone else down. Is this the end of the project? Absolutely not! That night I am back in the UK, and resolve to grind this through. I will pick up the remaining walk to Prague, which I do a couple of months later. The more this walk has gone on, the more utterly dedicated to it I have become. Even if I have to miss out more sections because of this latest health obstacle, I will walk to Auschwitz, whatever the cost.

The walk goes on. The hunt for answers goes on.

It is when I am back at home that I have my own moment of light. Out walking one day, I am listening to a Tim Keller talk on the famous Corinthians passage about love, read at Sarah's and my wedding, as at so many others'. The truth hits me that I have been looking in completely the wrong place. The answer was under my nose. Literally. My heart is damaged, they say, and if I do have an attack, because of the hardened artery being the principal corridor to my heart, I might not survive. But it's not my physical heart that I should be concerned about but a deeper heart, the human heart. Those in the war whose hearts were open *knew* what to do without thinking. Heart to heart, they loved and cared for others, regardless of any worldly differences that might have separated them. Those with hardened and closed hearts hated, maimed and killed. My path will be to worry less about myself and my physical heart, and to open my human, spiritual heart more with each fresh step in whatever time remains in my own journey from darkness to light.

* * *

I catch up with Rokycany a few weeks later, facilitated by Paul's kindness. This historic city has stunning medieval and Baroque architecture. Rokycany, though, will always be known as the precise location where the US and Soviet forces met on 10 May 1945 (the US army had arrived on 7 May, but had to wait three long days for the Red Army to show up, time they could have used pressing on east). But earlier in the year, Allied high command, eager to avoid clashes with the Soviets, and to ensure that liberation occurred as agreed at Yalta, had decreed that Patton's American forces should stop fighting right here. Troops from both sides duly met each other, exchanged fraternal greetings and shared food and drink. The demarcation line, marked by an inconspicuous low memorial at the side of the road (see photo next page), has none of the lustre of the much celebrated meeting of the two armies at the Elbe, near the town of Torgau in Germany, on 25 April two weeks before. That was the *first* formal link-up of American and Soviet troops as they advanced from the west and the east, celebrated across the world with iconic, and carefully stage-managed, photographs of troops from the two armies greeting each other. But this meeting here in Rokycany, two days after VE Day on 10 May, was the *last* major meeting between both sides, and it is striking not more is made of it. For Czechs, the long agony of the Second World War ended here.

Where the Eastern Front met the Western. The demarcation line memorial outside Rokycany.

The house of Václav Stehlík, the railway worker in Rokycany, where he sheltered Heydrich's two assassins, with a small rectangualr plaque on the wall.

Heydrich's assassins, of whom more later, were sheltered by the family of Václav Stehlík, a retired railway worker, in Rokycany (photo previous page), while the village of Mýto, on the Prague road 11 kilometres outside the town, provides our first figure of light since crossing the border. A memorial to Přemysl Pitter was unveiled in Mýto on the fiftieth anniversary of the end of the war – the time gap is significant. An unusual man, he stood up not only to the Nazis and Communists but also to his fellow Czechs. When fighting as a volunteer in the First World War, he became a pacifist and Christian, founding the Czech branch of the Movement for International Peace after 1918, and starting an orphanage and shelter in Prague for the poorest children, including Jews and Germans. In 1938, he opened a more remote shelter for Jewish children in Mýto, continuing this work until the war ended despite Gestapo harassment, when he set up a series of homes for Jewish children in confiscated chateaux after 1945. But his criticism of the forced expulsion of Germans from the Sudetenland incurred the ire first of the Beneš government, which removed him from membership of its health committee, and then of the Communist government, which interrogated him about his work with pacifist organizations and threatened him with forced labour. He managed to leave the country in 1951 and continued his work from abroad, being a rare recipient of two high honours, from the West German government for 'saving German children' in 1973, and, posthumously, Righteous Among the Nations from Israel. I was hoping to find a figure who spoke out against the Beneš decrees and now I have. Perhaps it needed a person like Pitter, someone who committed themselves to all human life and who refused to divide people by nationality or race, to do so?[30]

Finally some stops that remind us of Bohemia's international importance as I limp into Prague. Beroun, the last major trading town before Prague on the Golden Road, with its medieval walls and two gates, Plzeňská and Pražská (upper and lower gates respectively),

Přemsyl Pitter founded Milíč House during World War II to support Jewish families and after the end of the war organized health and social care for children from the camps.

on either side of the main square is a jewel. On to Karlštejn with its world-famous neo-Gothic castle founded by Charles IV in 1348, at the time Europe's most significant monarch, as the location for the Imperial Regalia. The Hussite Wars put the precious artefacts at risk, hence their removal in 1421, with all the subsequent symbolism for the Nazis, to Nuremberg at the other end of the Golden Road. As I walk towards Prague, a city that achieved fame long before Berlin and even Vienna, I pass the abbey on its outskirts at Zbraslav, built in the thirteenth century by Wenceslas II as the proud burial place for Bohemian kings, who were at the heart of the Holy Roman Empire for so long. On the outskirts of Prague we walk around the site of the Battle of White Mountain of 1620, which turned a regional dispute into the Europe-wide Thirty Years War (one of several defining battles, along with Austerlitz in 1805, fought in Czech lands).

The vanquished Frederick V himself is not buried in the abbey because he was a protestant. But Shakespeare had written *The Tempest* in part to celebrate his betrothal to James I's daughter Elizabeth, and for good measure, he sets *The Winter's Tale* partly in Bohemia (I know he writes about '*the coast* of Bohemia', but who is perfect?). Final reminders, if any are needed, that this faraway country about which the British were told by Chamberlain they knew nothing, was once the beating heart of the known world.

7

Prague, Lidice, Terezín

Chapter 7
Prague, Lidice, Terezín

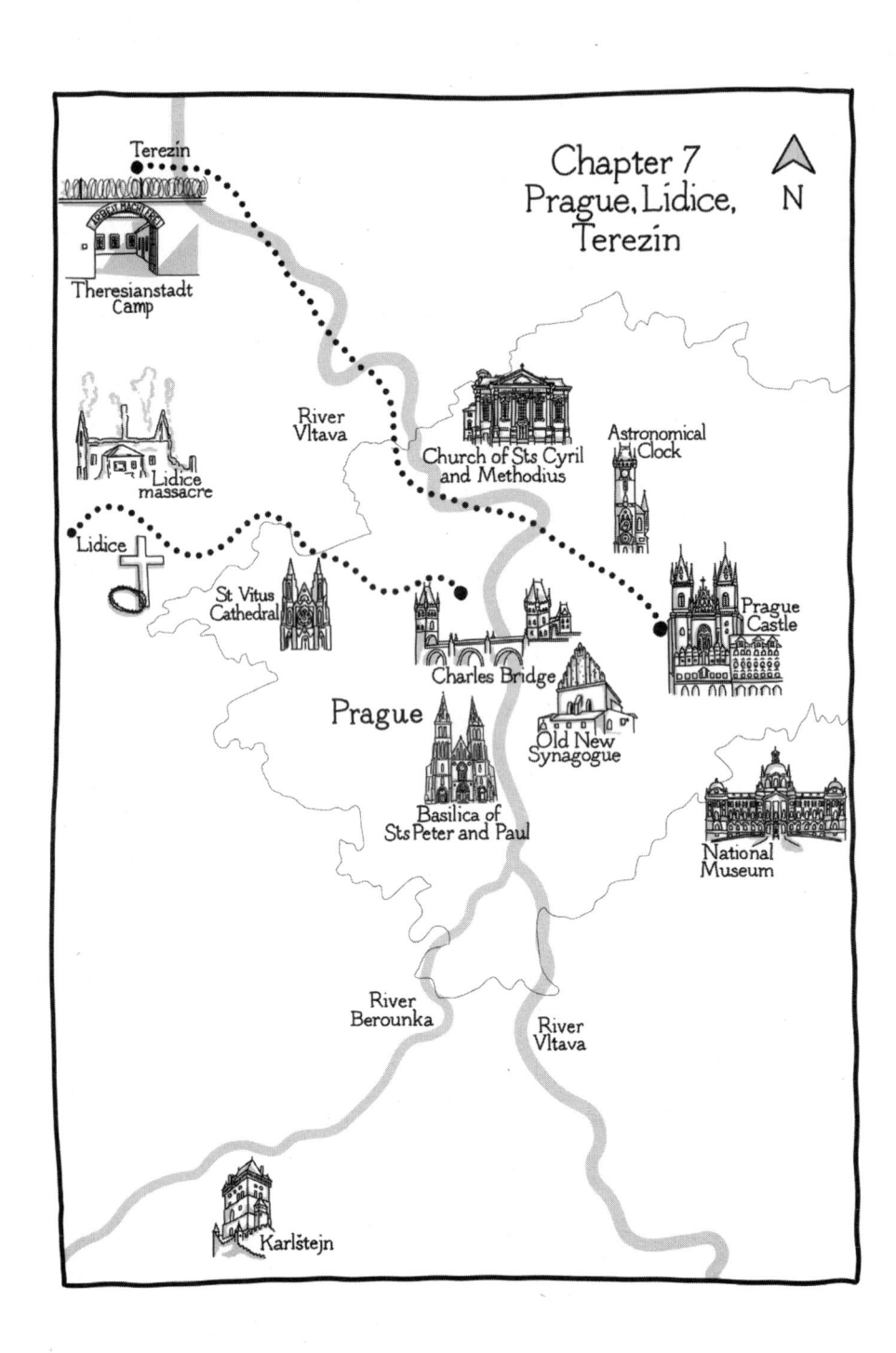

'Fuck off, British, go home.' The message, painted in large letters on a brick wall, certainly got straight to the point. It was April 1991 and I had brought a group of forty schoolboys to Eastern Europe to show them life in the countries behind the newly opened Iron Curtain before they became Westernized. The late 1980s and early 1990s was a glorious time to be a History teacher: in previous years, I had taken groups to Moscow, Leningrad and Berlin. But never to a welcome quite like this. The expletive was daubed on a wall facing the hostel where we would be staying in Prague for the next three days before going on to Budapest. I hoped that the boys wouldn't notice the words. Fat chance. They became a high point of the entire trip.

I never discovered what impulse had inspired the artist. Had forty years of Communist preaching that British capitalists were deplorable engendered resentment against a hostel for Western tourists? Was it a premonition of alcohol-fuelled Brits on stag weekends being sick on street corners? My hunch was an earlier group staying at the hostel had clashed with local youth and this was payback.

Prague in 1991 was stirring but was still overwhelmingly drab and depressed – the only place to get a decent cup of coffee or a drink was in one of the hotels rapidly opening up to foreigners. The city was hauntingly, mesmerizingly soulful nevertheless. For me, it was love at first sight, a love that has grown ever deeper. A teacher colleague on the trip, my mentor Jonathan Smith, author of the novel *Wilfred and Eileen* about my grandparents, had written a landmark Radio 4 play,

The Butcher, The Baker, about the assassination of Reinhard Heydrich.[1] What better way to spend our first morning than to take the pupils to the Church of Saints Cyril and Methodius in the city centre for Jonathan to tell them about Operation Anthropoid, the most successful act of assassination of the entire Second World War, and to hear how Heydrich's killers were tracked down and killed here at this church. For the boys, plucked from the Home Counties overnight and finding themselves in this very different world, it was the perfect introduction to the fraught history of Czechoslovakia.

The plan, Jonathan explained, had been hatched by the Czech government-in-exile in London (the codename 'Anthropoid' was randomly selected). In 1938 and 1939, the Czechs had seen their country invaded by the Germans without their firing a shot or offering any resistance. President Beneš had fled to London and his government-in-exile had taken time to establish credibility: it was only properly recognized by Britain in July 1941 despite the Munich Agreement still being in force. It wanted to hit the Nazis where it hurt most to display to the Allies and to the Czech people its presence and potency, to discredit the Munich Agreement, and to bolster Beneš's own profile for when the war finished. The Czechs in London decided that assassinating Heydrich, acting Protector of Bohemia and Moravia since 1941, was the ideal target, monstrously daring and dangerous though it was. Heydrich was hated and feared for his brutality – his nicknames were the 'butcher' or 'hangman' of Prague – and for his attempts to eliminate Czech culture and morale. The killing of the Nazis' ruthless strongman, whose swelling influence was soon likely to eclipse that of Göring and possibly even Himmler, if successful, would strike at the very heart of the Third Reich. The depth of Heydrich's importance to the Reich is demonstrated by the fact that he convened and chaired the Wannsee Conference in Berlin on 20 January 1942 to ensure efficiency and speed in achieving the 'Final Solution' to the 'Jewish problem' by transporting all Jews to occupied Poland to be promptly and discreetly murdered.[2]

Jonathan is a master storyteller. The boys remained in the coach after it pulled up by the church while he continued to recount with mounting tension the key events. The two men selected for this dangerous mission, he told them, were Jozef Gabčik and Jan Kubiš.

Kubiš was a Czech, born in Moravia in 1913. Gabčík was a Slovak, born in Rajecké Teplice in 1912. Both men had fled what was left of Czechoslovakia after the Munich Agreement. First, they went to Poland, then France and finally Britain, where they joined the Czechoslovak forces in exile. Both were trained as paratroopers at Cholmondeley Castle in Cheshire. During 1941, further training had taken place in and around Arisaig House in west Scotland and in southern England, supervised by the British Special Operations Executive (SOE).

They took off from Tangmere airfield in Sussex on 28 December 1941 in a Handley Page Halifax aircraft. They were briefly tailed by Luftwaffe fighters over Darmstadt in south-western Germany, before parachuting into Bohemia. Heavy snow cover meant they missed the drop zone, disastrously landing instead near Nehvizdy east of Prague, with Gabčík landing so badly he was unable to walk unassisted for some eight weeks.[3] They met up with the Czech resistance who provided shelter and logistics, and guided them to Pilsen, their intended meeting point. Gabčík and Kubiš's arrival was not uniformly popular: some partisans worried whether Heydrich's killing would merit the terrible reprisals that would inevitably follow, which could rip the heart out of the still young Czech resistance movement.[4] The initial plan, to assassinate him on a train, was dismissed as too difficult. Partisans in Prague then spent weeks studying Heydrich's daily movements. A pattern emerged where he travelled from his requisitioned mansion north of the city by open-top Mercedes to his HQ at Prague Castle with only light close protection, so confident was he that he had eliminated all resistance in his first few months. An ambush site was chosen in the Holešovice district at a tram stop near a hospital, where his car had to slow down for a tight bend. The pupils were sitting forward in their seats totally gripped. Days before the attack, Václav Stehlík, the rail worker and his family who had protected the two men in Rokycany, had been seized by the Gestapo after a tipoff, but despite torture, no details of the mission appear to have been extracted.

Wednesday 27 May 1942 was the chosen day. At 10.35 a.m., Gabčík stepped off the pavement as the black Mercedes slowed for the bend and fired his Sten machine gun directly at Heydrich. But the gun, a notoriously unreliable make, jammed. Heydrich stood up to shoot Gabčík, not noticing the approaching Kubiš, who threw under the vehicle an antitank grenade he had concealed in a briefcase. Its immediate detonation was sufficient to wound the German with shards of metal and debris ripping through the car and into his body.[5] Though wounded, he tried to chase them but collapsed. Kubiš and Gabčík escaped thinking their mission had failed, but a week later, despite Heydrich initially rallying at Prague's Bulovka Hospital, he died on 4 June of sepsis from wounds to his spleen.

All hell then let loose. The two assassins took refuge with five other resistance fighters in the church till the storm blew over. The boys

Heydrich's damaged car.

craned forward looking at it out of the coach windows. For some time, the assassins seemed safe. But the fighters were betrayed ('By who, sir?' 'Karel Čurda.' 'Who, sir?' 'A resistance fighter who went rogue and betrayed the parachutists for one million Reichsmarks.' 'No way, sir.' 'Can I get back to the story, please?'). Jonathan resumed, his voice falling to a whisper. 'On 18 June, large numbers of heavily armed Nazi soldiers surrounded the church. A firefight ensued lasting several hours. The parachutists began running out of ammunition, but still the soldiers couldn't get to them. It ended with the SS flooding the underground crypt where the men had taken refuge to force them into the open. All seven died there from enemy fire or suicide by pulling pins on their grenades.' There was a long silence before the boys trooped off the coach. I remember them looking with particular awe at the bullet holes still very evident on the building. The atmosphere remained sombre as the group walked around the church. I thought how admirable the pupils were, as they remained for the rest of the trip.

Thirty-four years later, I am back at the Church of Saints Cyril and Methodius, this time with Sarah. She is joining me for a week's walking east of Prague and we are starting with a day in the city. As we wander around the church I see in her the same sense of trepidation and disbelief that I saw in the boys all those years ago. We are here as a prelude to seeing the impact of the Nazi retribution, which was every bit as pitiless and sadistic as the Czech resistance had feared. Hitler learned of the attack on Heydrich when at the Wolf's Lair, his military HQ in Rastenburg in East Prussia (today, northern Poland). For Hitler and his senior officers, the assassination was threatening and deeply disturbing: nothing like it had ever happened before. No record survives of his precise words, but he was said to be incandescent.[6] He demanded massive reprisals including the execution of 10,000 randomly selected Czechs, the killing of all Czech political prisoners, and mass deportations of the population.[7] Fearing international condemnation, still a concern in his staff's minds, and the effect it might have on war production as the country provided so many of the Nazis' armaments, he was talked out of such indiscriminate measures in favour of more targeted retaliation, hunting down the assassins and their helpers, and the destruction of villages suspected of aiding the operation.

First, though, Hitler wanted to do the proper thing by his fallen lieutenant, a man after his own heart whom some even talked about as his successor.[8] To begin with, a magnificent ceremony at Prague Castle on 7 June with full military honours, SS guards and eulogies. Then the state funeral in Berlin on 9 June at the New Reich Chancellery, when Hitler placed on the coffin the German Order decoration, the Nazis' highest honour. Hitler described Heydrich as 'one of the best National Socialists, one of the staunchest defenders of the concept of the German Reich and one of the greatest opponents of all enemies of this Reich'.[9] I'd always imagined the funeral would have taken place in a church with a grotesque service overseen by a servile cleric. But Christianity by 1942 had ceased to play any part in Nazi thinking. Hitler and Himmler no longer hid their contempt for Christianity, despising its values and Jewish roots, and looked to its wholesale replacement in the future by a Nazi-rich ideology rooted in paganism. Why the need for faith when you have Hitler giving his life and soul to the cause? For many fanatical Nazis, Hitler was the saviour.

The Heydrich ceremonies over, the SS turned its attention to retribution. On the day following the funeral, 10 June, the village of Lidice was razed to the ground on the haziest of evidence that it had assisted the perpetrators.[10] All 173 men over the age of fifteen were lined up to be executed, the women sent to Ravensbrück concentration camp, and all children bar seventeen taken to Chełmno camp in Poland where they were suffocated with fumes from the specially adapted vehicles.[11] On 24 June, six days after the killing of Gabčík and Kubiš, the thirty-three inhabitants of the village of Ležáky east of Prague were murdered. By the end of the month, aided by torture and threats, virtually everybody involved in the operation was dead, along with their families. Some 5,000 were killed in reprisals, including perhaps 1,000 connected with the Czech resistance, which indeed never properly recovered.[12] Heydrich was succeeded by the equally violent Kurt Daluege as *de facto* Protector who oversaw the reprisals with relish. When a heart attack removed him from office, a grateful Führer gave him a property in which to recuperate. In August 1943, he was replaced by Wilhelm Frick, unswerving in his treatment of dissent, who was sentenced to death at Nuremberg. Likewise, Daluege was hanged in Prague in 1946.

Was the operation worth it? Czechs are mostly of one mind. On 5 August, two months after the assassination, Foreign Secretary Anthony Eden formally and publicly repudiated Chamberlain's Munich Agreement, writing to the government-in-exile that, in the eyes of Britain, Germany had 'deliberately destroyed' it.[13] A month later, Free French leader Charles de Gaulle followed suit, declaring Munich 'null and void'.[14] For most Czechs, the assassination was the beginning of the recovery of national pride: like my new father and daughter friends on the plane from London, they have no doubt that the price was indeed worth it.

We had no idea what to expect when we went to Lidice. I imagined it would be like the countless *villages détruits* I saw on the Western Front, with remnants of shrapnel-battered buildings still standing. Or the burnt-out village of Oradour-sur-Glane in central France, torched by the Nazis on 10 June 1944 with 643 murdered by Waffen-SS, another act of mindless Nazi violence in vengeance for French resistance operations aiding the Allied invasion of Normandy, which began four days earlier. But there is nothing of Lidice left above ground. On Hitler's express instructions, the entire village was to be eliminated. Soldiers set the houses on fire then destroyed remaining structures with high explosives. Nothing was sacred, not even the livestock, innocent as their owners, all slain. Not even the cemetery escaped, smashed to pieces together with the church. When the soldiers left, all that remained was a wasteland

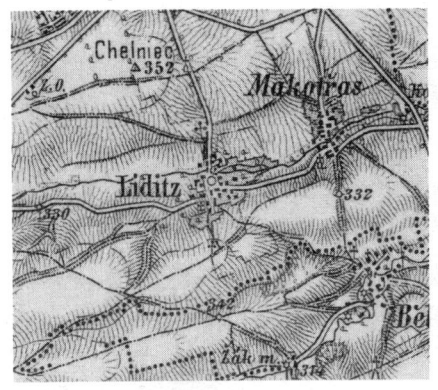

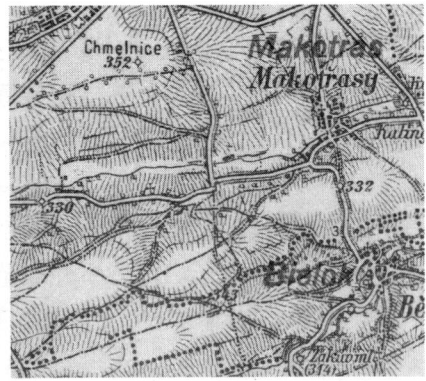

As this comparison shows, Lidice was wiped not just from the earth but also from paper maps by the Nazis. As observed by the cartographer Mike Klein of the US Library of Congress.

hurriedly covered with fresh earth, with prominent signs around the perimeter in German forbidding entry on pain of death. Nazi maps published after 1942 had the town's name obliterated.

A Christian cross with crown and thorns now marks the site of the mass grave of the town's men. A rose peace garden, opened in 1955, contains 25,000 rose bushes gifted from around the world. Particularly affecting is a statue, *Memorial to the Children Victims of the War*, completed in 2000, depicting the forty-two girls and forty boys who were deported. A memorial museum displays artefacts and photos, including a documentary film that the Nazis meticulously recorded during the destruction, perhaps as a gift to Hitler to placate his seething anger. It's no Leni Riefenstahl, but it's certainly graphic. Not for one minute had the Nazis conceived that it would be used as evidence against them. But it was. Document No. 379 at the Nuremberg Trials to be precise. Soundless though the film is, all in Courtroom 600 watched in horror at what they were seeing. There without shame for all to see were monsters at play.[15]

The Nazi high command compounded their misjudgement by then making one of the most spectacular public relations mistakes of

Lidice burns in June 1942.

modern history. In their frenzy to showcase the atrocity as a warning to any would-be resistance across the Nazi Empire, they broadcast the news extensively on radio and in print the following day, with graphic details of the executions and boasts about the town's eradication (in contrast to their normal practice of suppressing evidence of atrocities). It is telling no one in Hitler's inner circle anticipated the abhorrence that the free world would feel. International media picked up on it immediately. Here was undeniable evidence of the demonic brutality of the Nazi regime, not against the Jews – that was already obvious after Kristallnacht – but against unarmed civilians at large. On 11 June, the *New York Times* front page headline blared out: 'Nazis Blot out Czech village. Kill all Men, Disperse Others'.[16]

As the news spread in Britain, miners in Stoke-on-Trent initiated a 'Lidice shall live campaign', pledging to rebuild the village and raising

£32,000 for the purpose.[17] A British rose was named after the town, streets and squares too, as in Goole and Coventry. Churchill condemned the massacre, amplifying its significance. Lidice indeed became a global symbol of Nazi terror and brutality: an inspiration to resistance movements everywhere, and a potent focal point for Allied propaganda. In the US, children, parks and memorials were named 'Lidice'. Cities as far away as Venezuela, Mexico and Brazil renamed public squares after the town. 'Remember Lidice' became an international motto for opponents of fascism and tyranny. It hadn't needed a Picasso, whose famous anti-war painting *Guernica* of the town in northern Spain horrifically bombed by Nazi Germany and Mussolini's Italy in April 1937 brought the crime to the attention of the world. Hitler's vindictiveness had done the job for it.

Lidice tells us much about the Nazi regime and the seeds of its downfall. It shunned all law, moral codes and religion, and replaced them with Nazi ideology, a hollow veil for a state bent upon racial supremacy and a hatred of difference. It believed it was superior to all powers on earth and could act with complete impunity or accountability. The Heydrich assassination had touched a very raw nerve in Hitler and, as thin-skinned tyrants have done throughout history, he overreacted and lashed out, which unleashed forces that proved uncontrollable.

We walk along the linden-lined avenue, which connects the old site to the new Lidice 300 metres away, whose building was announced by the Beneš government at a peace demonstration there on 10 June 1945.[18] We talk about the many acts of remarkable human sacrifice and courage that came out of the tragedy, but I focus here on just one figure, a survivor who came back to live in the newly built town after the war. To understand her story, we need to revisit the seven children not murdered by inhaling carbon monoxide into their young lungs at Chełmno. Marie Doležalová was born in Lidice, and was just ten when the Nazis came. Within hours, her father had been shot. Her brother was subsequently executed. Her mother was taken to Ravensbrück.

Marie was transported with the eighty terrified children to the town of Łódź in Poland. 'We were alone and didn't know what to do,' she later recalled, 'with lice, hungry and longing for home.'[19] The seven children were picked out to live because their 'Aryan' looks suggested potential to be 're-educated' as Germans. For a year they were moved to a school near Posen in eastern Germany (now Poland), until suitable German couples could be found to adopt them. Her step-parents, Alfred and Isla Schiller, gave her a new name, Ingeborg, a box room behind the kitchen to live in, while she was told by her adoptive mother, 'if I ever hear the word "Lidice" in my house, I will beat you half dead'.[20]

In 1946, a Czech children's charity tracked her down and the Schillers were ordered to release her. Back in Prague, she was reunited with her mother: 'We recognised each other instantly, but we couldn't talk to each other because I spoke only German and I had forgotten the Czech language,' she later told the BBC.[21] Her mother, already severely ill with tuberculosis contracted at Ravensbrück, died four months later. The orphaned Marie went to live with an aunt.[22] At the age of fifteen, she testified in October 1947 at a trial in Nuremberg of members of the SS's 'Race and Resettlement Office', one of only three people, another teenager and a middle-aged woman, to give evidence that day about what happened on 10 June 1942. She subsequently graduated from a nursing school in Ostrava, a town through which I will pass.[23]

On her marriage, she became Marie Šupíková. 'When I had my own family, I often thought of that moment when our mother had to let us go, what must have passed through her mind in those few seconds.'[24] She moved back to the rebuilt village where she worked for the Lidice Memorial and subsequently became, for sixteen years, the dedicated secretary of its national committee. Revenge, rage and depression would have been all very natural emotions for her to feel, expected even; but in her quiet, dignified way, she simply got on with her life, determined to be a witness, and to care for others. She lived to see her great-granddaughter born, before dying in 2021, aged eighty-

Marie Doležalová, aged 15, giving evidence at Nuremberg, 1947.

eight, living proof of the comprehensive failure of Hitler's diabolical revenge and of the transformative power of love.[25]

We race back from Lidice in time for me to speak at the British Embassy in Prague, situated in the magisterial Thun Palace in Malá Strana ('lesser town') just below the castle. It is the only moment in my walk when I taste the high life that Leigh Fermor periodically enjoyed, and we revel in every moment of it. Ambassador Matt Field and his wife Martina have asked me to speak on British prime ministers: successes and failures. There is respectful silence from the audience of notables when I run through the latter, until I mention one name, when there is an electric reaction. Most prime ministers, I explain, faced one principal challenge in office; the judgement of history is heavily weighted towards how they responded to it. 'Neville Chamberlain simply couldn't rise to his challenge,' I say. I can't resist a provocation.

'Of course, no Western leaders today could possibly be so gullible in the face of ruthless tyrants.' The murmurs climax at the image I simultaneously project on the screen, US Vice President J.D. Vance, who had recently made famously provocative comments at the Munich Security Conference. At the reception afterwards, the guests tell me about the Czech contribution to the British war effort, like Jiří Kafka, a recent guest at the embassy now aged one hundred who flew for the RAF, and Elsbeth Hamilton, a Czech-born radio operator who worked for the RAF's Women's Auxiliary Air Force, and went to live in Oxfordshire (she died aged 104 in May 2025). But what they really want to talk about is the Trump administration and what it is doing to Europe. Is he planning to abandon us?

I need to explore this matter further and so arrange to have coffee with one of the embassy guests, Michael Žantovský, a leading figure

Ambassador Matt Field, left, former minister Greg Hands, who accompanied us on this part of the walk, right, and author by the Churchill statue close to the British Embassy in Prague.

behind the Velvet Revolution, spokesperson (and biographer) of Václav Havel, and formerly Czech ambassador to the UK, US and Israel. He chooses our venue, Café Slavia on the Vltava's east bank, the celebrated café opposite the National Theatre where Havel would regularly be spotted through thick clouds of cigarette smoke on Saturdays, surrounded by the Czech literary and political elites. 'How seriously worried are Czechs by Trump and Vance?' is my opener. 'There are justified fears and suspicions. These Americans think by parleying with Putin, they bring peace closer – an unbelievable spectacle!' His derision for Trump's special envoy, real estate businessman Steve Witkoff, is unprintable. 'Can Trump's cosying up to Putin in any way be compared to Munich?' I ask. 'Munich is still a wound in the Czech psyche. It is still seen as a betrayal. We are not yet at those levels, but there's genuine apprehension that Trump might make a deal that gives Putin what he wants, i.e., Russia's sphere of influence over Central and Eastern Europe back as it was during the Cold War.' Czech and other European governments, he explains, are locked out of US–Russian discussions. The exclusion explains much of the bitterness over Munich. 'Czechoslovakia was not allowed to play any part in the discussion, even though it was this country that would lose out.' He's dismissive of the hopes some Czechs place in Trump's inner Czechophilia by dint of his three children with Czech-born first wife Ivana: 'I think that's clutching at straws, to be honest.'

Changing subject, I ask him about Havel's significance. 'He was the only one who could have united the country in 1989, with the stature, the intellect and the moral authority from his multiple incarcerations by the Communists as a political prisoner when he could have been released. He alone had the breadth and tolerance to unite the conflicting interests that for years had been suppressed under Communist rule,' he explains. He highlights Havel's seminal 1978 essay *The Power of the Powerless* that prophesied the ultimate fall of the Communist government because of its disregard for truth. By the same logic, Trump's blithe disregard for truth – indeed, his shameless lying – will inevitably spell his own fall, he concludes. It's been a political masterclass from polymath Žantovský, whose own literary output includes translations of Norman Mailer, Toni Morrison and Tom Stoppard. I wonder whether we have anyone in Britain who combines his wide intellectual gifts and record in public office. Iain Macleod for the Conservatives perhaps, who landed on Gold Beach on D-Day, then as Colonial Secretary significantly accelerated the process of British decolonization, went on to edit *The Spectator*, and whose premature death in July 1970 when Chancellor of the Exchequer fatally weakened the government of Edward Heath. Or Labour's Denis Healey, who had an equally brilliant mind, turned down an academic career at Oxford, had a heroic war record as beach master (military landing officer) at Anzio, was a commanding Defence Secretary and Chancellor and then wrote a string of books, including one of the very best political memoirs, *The Time of My Life*. The Liberals' Paddy Ashdown comes close with his exceptional service as High Representative for Bosnia and Herzegovina (2002–06). Britain is very much the poorer for being unable to attract giants like these into politics today.

It is time for Sarah and I to beat the streets of Prague. A striking contrast to the German cities is the absence of war damage; the Gothic, Baroque and Art Nouveau architecture survive intact. The Nazi annexation in 1939 and the Soviet liberation in 1945 saw little fighting, the only aerial bombardment of the war coming in February 1945 when a detachment of the US air force mistook it for Dresden. Given they are 150 kilometres apart, it was some miss. Sarah and I are splashing out and staying in the Paris Hotel, inspired by none other than Alphonse Mucha. Having immersed ourselves in political Prague, we are now in search of exploring why the city has been so prominent in Jewish history. A ten-minute walk through the Old Town takes us to the Jewish quarter, which nestles in the bend of the Vltava as it makes a sharp turn east. Jews are known to have lived here from the tenth century. By the twelfth century it had become a celebrated centre of learning, attracting some of the most significant scholars of the Middle

Ages. The Jewish population swelled further following massacres in Poland during the 1640s and their expulsion from Vienna in 1670. Empress Maria Theresa briefly exiled Jews in 1744, but she rescinded the ban soon after, though not the obligation for Jews to pay a special tax and to display gold stars.[26] Better times were to lie ahead. Her son Joseph II issued an Edict of Tolerance in 1782, which allowed Jews to play a full part in the life of the state: the quarter was renamed 'Josefstadt' after him. The ghetto was abolished in 1848, and legal emancipation followed in 1867, making the Jews equal citizens in all aspects of public life. A golden era had begun, with world-renowned Jews, including Sigmund Freud, Franz Kafka and Gustav Mahler born in the country in the mid- to late nineteenth century. Jewish life was renowned for being more secure and less traumatic in the Czech lands than elsewhere, notably in the Russian Empire.[27]

Antisemitism, though, was never far below the surface, notably among some of the German population in the country, numbering a third. It exploded to the fore in a legal case in 1899 where Leopold Hilsner, a poor Jewish man, was accused of the ritual murder of a young Christian woman, and who was convicted in a sensational antisemitic show trial. Hilsner was publicly defended by philosopher and politician Tomáš Garrigue Masaryk, then a professor at Prague's Charles University in an episode that had much in common with the contemporary Dreyfus affair raging in France. Labelled a 'Jew lover', Masaryk's reputation suffered badly. But he nevertheless went on to become the first president of the new country, Czechoslovakia, from 1918 to 1935, and is one of its most universally revered figures, his insistence on justice and human rights further setting him apart from many of his contemporary leaders in interwar Europe. His son Jan became Foreign Secretary in the exiled government from 1940 to 1948, until his untimely and mysterious death as the Communists took power.

We walk around what remains of the Jewish quarter, home to 18,000 Jews in the nineteenth century, which was mostly demolished from 1893

The Old Jewish Ceremonial Hall in Prague. The Josefov (or Jewish Quarter) of Prague is one of the best-preserved Jewish monuments in Europe.

to 1913 at the height of the frenzy for Prague to model itself on Paris (whose own medieval buildings had been mostly destroyed in the great Haussmann reconstruction). Only six synagogues remained, the most important being the Old New Synagogue dating from the 1200s. The cemetery is the oldest surviving Jewish cemetery in Europe, with up to twelve layers of graves. As Jewish tradition forbids destruction of existing tombs, and with space in the quarter so limited, fresh deposits of soil were regularly heaped on existing graves to allow new ones to be built on top.

Particularly chilling is learning about the potential Nazi plans for the 'Museum of the Extinct Race' to be housed in the ghetto, a scheme on which historians remain divided, with some disputing that any such museum was real.[28] The plan was said to be a permanent museum to document the culture, 'features' and history of the Jewish people when they no longer existed (at least not in continental Europe). It was to be partly a celebration of a job well done by the Nazis, but also a justification for why the Final Solution was necessary. What is known is that for several years, items including holy manuscripts and books, Torah scrolls and ceremonial objects were shipped from all over Europe to Prague, some 140,000 artefacts altogether. One wonders why the Nazis would invest so much effort bringing all these items to Prague, and having them so meticulously catalogued, if there wasn't to be an exhibition.

Jewish curators and scholars were, we do know, forced to work under SS direction at the Jewish Museum, originally founded in 1906, which became the centre for the storage and cataloguing of the items arriving by the week (seven of the eight Jewish curators were later murdered by the SS). Prague was selected as the showcase city because it had one of the oldest, most important and best-known Jewish communities in Europe, it had the existing museum and some of the best-preserved Jewish buildings, and because of its centrality in what would be the new German Empire. The Nazis' museum was never opened, the war ending before the work of the Final Solution was complete. Heydrich's drive at Wannsee for efficient coordination had been insufficient to complete the task. Ironically, many of the objects the Nazis pillaged are now displayed in this museum to living Judaism, while others have been returned to the communities from whom they were taken.

The Holocaust managed to all but destroy Jewish life in the country, one of the most assimilated and integrated Jewish communities in all of Europe. Some 118,000 Jews had lived in Bohemia and Moravia before the war. Before 1941, around 26,000 were able to emigrate. Of the remaining 90,000, best estimates suggest 77,000 perished in the camps. After 1945, most of the 10,000 survivors left for Mandatory Palestine. Today, there are only some 3,500 Jews living in the Czech Republic.[29] We meet a Jewish man from North London who regularly visits Prague, he tells us, out of respect for his relatives, and I ask him about antisemitism in the Czech Republic. 'Even though I wear a yarmulke [a skull cap worn daily by Orthodox Jews], I hardly ever encounter antisemitism in this country. It's completely unlike London, which has become unpleasant,' he says, adding 'though nothing like as bad as France.'

Cheating the SS's mission of total annihilation were 669 children, the majority of whom were Jewish. Key to their survival was a young British stockbroker and socialist, Nicholas Winton, one of the better-known saviours but still a most worthy figure of light. Born of German Jewish parents, he was urged by a friend in December 1938 to cancel a skiing holiday to come to Prague to see for himself the dire conditions of Jewish refugees arriving by the day from the annexed Sudetenland. Winton, aged just nineteen, was perturbed at what he saw, and on his return to London lobbied the British government to allow Czech children to be added to the established *Kindertransport* programme that was bringing a limited number of children from occupied Europe to the UK. It agreed, but only on the condition that each child was matched by a host family to care for the children until they were eighteen, and a guaranteed fee paid by the family. Throughout 1939 until Britain declared war on 3 September, Winton worked tirelessly with volunteers including his mother to find them loving families and to raise funds to cover travel expenses. The last train was due to leave Prague station on 1 September 1939 but was held up because of the deteriorating diplomatic position. It never left, Winton believing that 'none of the children on board was heard of again'. Publicity-shy Winton resumed his normal life after the war, believing that what he did was no 'big deal' and he was merely 'in the right place at the right time.'[30] His modesty does nothing to explain why he acted when so many didn't. Again the question. Why him? Plenty with Jewish backgrounds remained bystanders. What would I have done is a question that comes to me with increasing insistence as I learn about these remarkable people. It wasn't vainglory that drove Winton on, or a desire to impress. Fame and honours nevertheless flowed to him when the BBC television programme *That's Life* reconnected him in 1988 to many of those saved, sitting unbeknownst to him in the seats beside and behind him. His tears moved all who saw the programme because he so obviously was not a self-seeker, and had no wish for his story to be told.

Sarah and I read the simple Winton Children Farewell Memorial plaque on Prague station dedicated to the parents whose children departed from there on trains heading west to safety, not east where, without Winton, they would have gone and almost certainly perished:

> This Farewell Memorial is a symbol of courage and love of parents who in 1938 and 1939 regardless of what their own fate awaited them, boarded their children on trains and with heartache and tears in their eyes waved good bye, sending them away to safety to save their lives. Most parents perished in the Holocaust.

Nicholas Winton with one of the Jewish children he saved.

Swallowed up by the concentration camps alongside those parents were Kafka's three sisters, as well as his lover Milena Jesenská, but not before they saw his posthumous fame as a writer, above all with *The Trial* and *The Metamorphosis*, spread across interwar Europe, to the extreme displeasure of the Nazis. Kafka himself had perished from tuberculosis in 1924 largely unknown, with no inkling that his writing would transform European literature and thinking. So much of the glory of Czech life disappeared forever between 1939 and 1945. Sarah and I are now on a journey to the place through which almost all the country's Jews were funnelled, to learn more about what exactly happened here.

* * *

Theresienstadt (Terezín in Czech) is a name I had first heard in my twenties but hadn't realized till Sarah and I visited it on a bitingly cold spring afternoon that it is two separate camps. Built ironically by prosemitic Austrian Emperor Joseph II as a fortress to honour the name of his mother Empress Maria Theresa, the complex defended the confluence of the Ohře and Elbe rivers from the ever-present Prussian threat. Sixty kilometres north of Prague, nestling under the magisterial Central Bohemian Highlands just 10 kilometres away, it is too far to walk, so we are driving.

We visit the Gestapo prison camp first, originally for political dissidents, Czech resistance and prisoners of war, situated in the Small Fortress east of the Main Fortress that housed the Jewish ghetto. We join a group of some twelve English-speaking visitors shown around the prison by an erudite Czech guide wearing an incongruous black spider top. In the later nineteenth century, when international relations were more peaceful, it began to be used as a jail. The Gestapo seized it in 1940 as a ready-made answer to their need for a secure unit to dump political undesirables. We are shown prison cells, guard blocks, torture rooms, shower and feeding facilities. All relentlessly grim. Our attention is caught by the swimming pool, built near the prison blocks by prisoners under inhumane working conditions to enhance leisure for the Gestapo and their families. More disturbing still is the execution wall. Our guide tells us that, in the final days before the camp was liberated, fifty-two prisoners were shot dead here. 'Why?' we ask. 'Because they could,' was his matter-of-fact reply. 'There was no other reason.'

Emperor Joseph II could never have suspected that his Small Fortress would incarcerate the assassin of his great-great-great-nephew Archduke Franz Ferdinand, whose murder in faraway Sarajevo in June 1914 sparked the First World War. As we gaze at Gavrilo Princip's cell in this bleak desolate place, a chill runs through my body at this unsuspected connection between both world wars. Twenty-five conspirators were tried in Sarajevo in October 1914, all nationalists wanting to liberate Bosnia from Austro-Hungarian rule. At his trial, Princip expressed no regret at killing the Archduke with a bullet in his neck, but was apologetic that he shot his wife Sophie, killed by his bullet to her abdomen.[31]

Three of the accused were sentenced to death, but Princip, twenty-seven days shy of his twentieth birthday, the legal age requirement for the death penalty in the Empire, was sentenced to twenty years in prison. Subjected to solitary confinement, he became dejected and riddled with tuberculosis. By 1916, he was reported to be a 'living corpse', his torso wrapped in bandages covering ulcers.[32] His condition gradually declined, but he remained unrepentant to the end, protesting that the war was not his fault (quite a burden of responsibility to carry), and that 'the Germans would have started it anyway'. He died at 6.30 p.m. on 28 April 1918, at a time when it seemed that Germany might even win. Five Czech soldiers took his body to a nearby cemetery with instructions to inter it in an anonymous grave. The officer in charge made a note of the precise location, and when the war ended in November 1918, he went back to the cemetery and planted a Czech flag above his body. Two years later, it was dug up and reburied in the 'Heroes Chapel' in Sarajevo, the city where his two bullets six years before had changed world history.[33]

We pull our coats tight as we proceed over the River Ohře to the Main Fortress. Seven thousand had lived in the town before the war, but the Nazis expelled the inhabitants and Heydrich had it prepared for use as a ghetto in 1941. By September 1942, 60,000 were imprisoned, with 4,000 dying that month alone.[34] Heydrich had three aims for the ghetto: as a transit camp for Jews awaiting deportation to the east and north; as a deception device, with Jews from Germany, Austria and Czechoslovakia selected on account of their artistic or other distinction to showcase that the treatment of Jews met acceptable international standards; and as a destination for elderly Jews, the camp being described as a 'spa town' where elderly German Jews could 'retire' in safety. As the Nazis wanted to maintain the fiction that Jews were being deported from Germany to be 'resettled in the east' where they would be put to work, and as it was implausible that elderly Jews would be suitable for such work, the ghetto was a convenient dumping ground for them till they fell victim to the terrible conditions. Death was just a matter of time.

On 23 June 1944, two weeks after D-Day, the Nazis succumbed to international pressure to admit the International Red Cross. The SS seized on it as an opportunity to counter growing international concern about its maltreatment of Jews, stalling for several months to allow time for preparation, with the ghetto cleaned, flowers planted and cultural activities arranged. Shops, a bank, a model school and cafés were erected. Under fear of death, prisoners were instructed what to say and what not to say to the visitors. Many thousands of inmates deemed to be problematic, notably the sick and elderly, were hastily dispatched to Auschwitz. Finally the day came. Into Theresienstadt swept Swiss physician Maurice Rossel at the head of his inspection team. They were guided along a preordained route by the hosts who directed them to the prisoners and the activities they should see. The visitors were impressed. When the Red Cross report arrived, it said inmates were well fed, healthy and were looked after culturally and educationally in the largely self-directed camp. There was no probing

The entrance to the Theresienstadt Small Fortress camp.

about deportations or conditions of the prisoners at large. The fact of the Red Cross visit, and Rossel's apparently favourable impressions, was beyond the wildest dreams of the Nazis, who exploited them extensively for propaganda. But for those who were suffering at their hands, it did incalculable damage. It stymied the case that was slowly building against the Nazis for their treatment of Jews. The Red Cross accepted the inspectors' conclusions without great probing, for which it subsequently was heavily criticized, as it was for its refusal to release the report for many years.

The Rossel Report stands out in history as a casebook example of weak and defective investigation by humanitarian bodies charged to search out the truth in lawless regimes. Was Rossel naive, ill-prepared or

A street in the Theresienstadt ghetto.

unsuited to the task? He refused to admit responsibility, maintaining he merely reported what he saw and it wasn't his job to probe further (the defence of the slippery and weak all the way down to the contemporary hospital, social care and Post Office scandals in Britain and beyond).[35]

As the cars carrying the delegation swept away, and the Nazis' celebratory bottles of Schnapps ran dry, the iron glove immediately descended. Fresh deportations to concentration camps promptly resumed, including those who had helped in the grand deception. In total, 140,000 Jews passed through Terezín, nearly 90,000 deported to Majdanek and Treblinka as well as to Auschwitz, the last transport leaving in October 1944. In the ghetto itself, some 33,000 died mostly from disease and starvation.[36] Adolf Eichmann had been intrigued and impressed by the great deception of June 1944, and as late as March 1945 visited it to explore the possibility of it being shown to international commissioners as an example of 'Nazi humanity'. The impulse perversely may even have saved the lives of remaining inmates as conditions improved in anticipation. When the Red Army arrived in May 1945, some 30,000 prisoners were found still alive.[37]

Among the most distinctive and heroic features of Theresienstadt was the cultural life that flourished within it, and the dogged refusal of a collage of artists, musicians, actors, writers and academics to stop singing, dancing, drawing, painting, writing and giving lectures. Almost all of this prodigious body of work is lost forever. Of the fragment that survives, most affecting perhaps are the artworks of the 15,000 children who passed through the ghetto, 90 per cent of whom perished there or in the camps.[38]

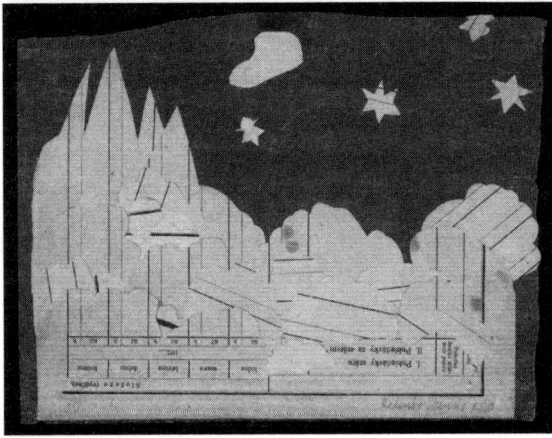

Examples of art created by children in the Theresienstadt ghetto.

Two transcendent figures represent all those who brought light into the desperate darkness of the Terezín ghetto. In the midst of the depravity, they soared above, finding within themselves almost superhuman depths of humanity. Ilse Weber was one of the tens of thousands of selfless people who tried to make these children's lives more bearable. A night nurse in the sick area, her task was made more difficult because the Nazis forbade medicines for Jewish prisoners. A well-known Jewish poet and musician, the medicine she could offer was singing the children songs on her illegal lute and guitar, strumming throughout the dark nights to lighten them with her melodies. Her family had lived in Vítkovice on the Polish border. When annexed by the Nazis, she managed to place one of her sons on the Kindertransport to London, but in February 1942, she, her husband and remaining son Tommy were taken to the ghetto. When in early 1944, the entire children's infirmary was deported to Auschwitz, rather than abandoning the children, she volunteered to go with them to hold their hands, to sing and hug them. She and Tommy were murdered soon after arrival, but her husband survived. Having managed to hide some of her poems and songs in a garden shed, he retrieved them in late 1945. Here is a fragment from 'Musica Prohibita':

> I wander through Theresienstadt,
> A policeman's glance makes my flesh crawl,
> the lute I found is concealed, held tight
> wrapped like an infant in a shawl...
> We must be strong within ourselves,
> lest in despair and dread we drown.
> Must sing until the song dissolves
> these walls, and our joy tears them down.[39]

The same artistic defiance can be seen in Romanian Rafael Schächter, raised in Brno and receiving his musical education at the

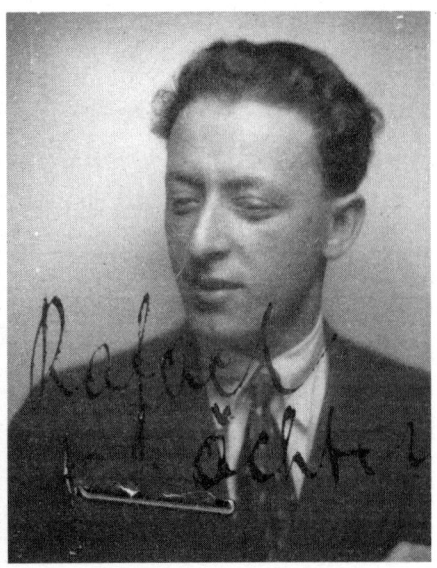

Ilse Weber, left, a musician who dedicated her time to making the lives of children at Theresienstadt more bearable. Rafael Schächter, right, who put together operatic performances at Theresienstadt, even after entire choirs were murdered.

Prague Conservatory. Soon after being sent to Terezín in November 1941, he began to seek out singers and instrumentalists. In no time, he had assembled a choir around a smuggled piano in the men's barracks, transforming their spirits, as it did when he gave the guards the slip and set up an equivalent female choir in the women's barracks.[40] His irrepressible zest became celebrated across the ghetto. In the summer of 1942, he started to rehearse Smetana's *The Bartered Bride*, which premiered in November. Initially staged illicitly, the authorities gave permission for an official premiere three days later, and it was reprised thirty-five times. So struck were the SS by Schächter's virtuosity, they ordered him in September 1943 to conduct Verdi's *Requiem*. With no option but to accept, he told his hastily assembled choir that 'we will sing to the Nazis what we cannot say to them': the performance electrified all who listened to it.[41] Hopes began to grow that the musicians might be spared the gas chambers, but shortly after, his entire choir was deported to Auschwitz. The SS wanted more Verdi, but a second choir was also sent to Auschwitz that December. A third choir lasted long enough to give fifteen performances, including to the Red Cross delegation. Time was running out, though, for Schächter, and in late 1944, he too was deported along with his leading musicians to the east, from where they never returned.[42]

His memory lives on. Celebrated American conductor Murry Sidlin conceived and produced *Defiant Requiem: Verdi at Terezín* about, he said, 'an unsung hero, Rafael Schächter, a passionate conductor, a risk taker and a man motivated by music to serve humanity'.[43] The performance combined Verdi's music with recollections of survivors and extracts from the propaganda film the Nazis shot during the Red Cross visit. It premiered in Portland, Oregon in 2002. Among the performers were three Theresienstadt survivors including one, Eva Rocek, who sang in the chorus.[44]

It makes me think about the healing power of the arts. Did the Nazis who heard Schächter's singers in the ghetto have their hearts melted even if just a little? The Nazis might have rejected religion but they loved classical music (as long as on the Nazi-approved playlist). To Hitler, composers such as Beethoven and Bruckner were very proof of German cultural and racial superiority. Wagner was a personal obsession, and he was thrilled to see *The Ring of the Nibelung* at Bayreuth in the 1930s, which became a spiritual home to the Nazis.[45] Orchestras were approved at concentration camps, famously the Women's Orchestra of Auschwitz that played as the prisoners left and returned from work.[46] Beethoven was found particularly useful in other camps to mask the sounds of executions. No senior Nazi genuinely loved music more than the Governor-General of occupied Poland, Hans Frank, a talented pianist. The debate on whether music was central to the Nazis for ideological and transactional, not humanizing, reasons, and whether Wagner was exalted for his antisemitism, will run on and on. It shouldn't. Music can stir all kinds of emotions, from the most atavistic to the most sublime.

Edward Said, left, and Daniel Barenboim, right, who formed the West–Eastern Divan Orchestra in 1999.

On the day Sarah and I visit Terezín, Trump calls Zelensky 'a dictator', and Israeli Prime Minister Netanyahu praises Trump's 'bold vision' for the future redesignation of Gaza. In search of hope on the future course of Arab-Israeli relations, and in pursuit of a way to conclude this light and dark chapter, I can think of no better resolution than a musical one, and no more fitting an initiative than one that fortuitously has been a highlight of the annual Prague Spring International Music Festival. I am thinking of the West–Eastern Divan Orchestra. The brainchild of Argentinian-Israeli conductor Daniel Barenboim and Palestinian-American academic Edward Said, its whole aim is to nurture empathy and coexistence between Arab and Jew, and to have Israeli and Arab musicians perform side by side in the hope of finding a peaceful resolution to the divisions between them. Even amid the ongoing conflict, the orchestra has continued to play on, gracing the Royal Festival Hall in November 2024.[47] A more optimistic and uplifting initiative that epitomizes the whole spirit of my pilgrimage is hard to imagine. Many of the people and stories I am encountering along my journey move me to tears, but this modern response, from the same school of thinking as Gillespie's 'Via Sacra', is right up there.

8

Central and East Bohemia:
PRAGUE TO PARDUBICE

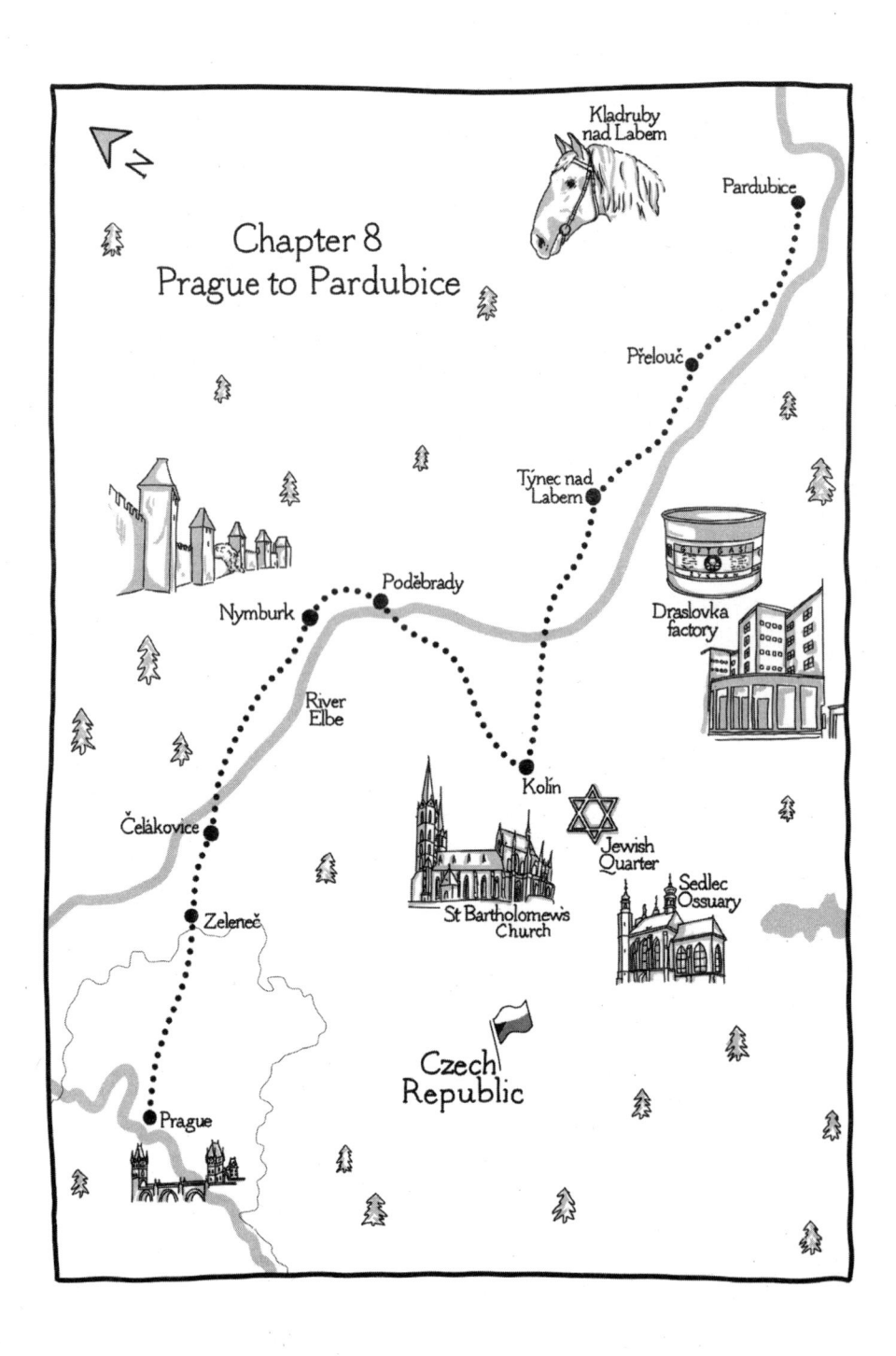

Chapter 8
Prague to Pardubice

'I THOUGHT YOU SAID the weather was going to be spring-like.'[1]

'Did I? I thought I said it would be like it normally is in Prague in February.' I'm on the defensive because I think I've messed this up.

'Well, I'm cold. In fact, I'm absolutely freezing.' We are dashing across the icy tarmac at Václav Havel Airport heading for the terminal.

Sarah's confidence in my meteorological forecasting has still not recovered from our delayed honeymoon to Australia in July 2022. When I first mooted the plan she had asked, 'But won't it be winter in Australia?'

'Yes, but don't worry: it'll be like Greece in January, you'll love it,' I'd replied. I had no real idea what Greece's weather was like in January, but I'd discovered on Google that Athens was a lot closer to the North Pole than Australia was to the South Pole, so it stood to reason it'd be a whole lot milder down under.

We'd arrived in Melbourne in a blizzard, our hotel by the water's edge turned out to be partly boarded up against the elements, and we were the only residents. Throughout our fortnight away, Sarah's bulging suitcase full of summer dresses remained firmly closed.

She has agreed to join me over her spring half term in February 2025 and has been looking forward to relaxing with a bit of walking together and seeing something of the Czech Republic after a flat-out six weeks of school since Christmas. I myself have been asked back by Wellington College to help rethink its wide family of schools. We had arrived yesterday, on Sunday morning, and walked around a freezing

Approaching Čelákovice station: only one of us is wearing a hat.

Prague before the visit to Terezín. Sarah is now contemplating five days of walking eastwards in Alpine temperatures without the skiing. 'Remind me,' she says. I know what is coming. 'Isn't the whole purpose of this walk to find examples of human kindness?' 'It is.' She doesn't need to finish her train of thought.

She has a point. The plan to walk 120 kilometres across Bohemia to its border with Moravia was manageable, but we had picked what turned out to be the coldest February week for several years, dipping below −12°C in Prague on 16 February, which happened to be the day we arrived.

I had chosen to make this leg the first walk of 2025 along what would be a fairly straightforward path by the River Elbe (or 'Labe' as the Czechs call it). My plan was then to pick up the preceding leg from Flossenbürg to Prague, covered in Chapter 6, a few weeks later as the terrain was higher and more testing, the route less obvious and the weather would be warmer. What I hadn't foreseen was the health diagnosis in early March and the severe curtailment of how far I could walk each day. But for this leg across Bohemia, blissfully unaware of the impending health news, I would be romping flat out, max 25 kilometres a day with rucksack braced against the cold, setting off each morning from the Hotel Paris and walking to the mainline station to take me onwards, with Sarah joining when she could.

The first morning we take the Prague metro to Černý Most, the end of the line in the eastern suburbs. As we emerge up the escalator to ground zero, we find ourselves in driving snow. Sarah as always is better prepared; ever the optimist, I have donned an overcoat, and, on her insistence, purchased some woollen gloves, a scarf and a bobble hat in Prague last night. In learning to understand Sarah, I'm having to appreciate that headwear, including bobble hats, looms large in her outlook on life, especially when cold. The ever-resourceful Paul Antrobus has provided us with a planner for each day on the excellent Mapy.cz, otherwise known as Czech Maps. What none of us had anticipated was the difficulty reading a map on a phone in subzero temperatures. Within two minutes, my gadget has frozen over and our fingers are numb with cold. We fall into a shop, thaw out, the map flickers back to life, and we're off on our big adventure! The first hour takes us along pavements in the suburbs through unlovely Horní Počernice and out into open countryside. The temptation to call in for a hot chocolate at a bar with a roaring log fire is too great and in we pile. Loud music is blasting out of the speakers. 'Van Halen,' Sarah says, noticing me trying to guess the band and betting that I will get it wrong. '"Jump",' she adds, with the merest hint of triumph.

Refreshed, we set off, bobble hat still on table, and cut across fields to the village of Zeleneč and pick up the Elbe, whose riverside route is covered in snow. While icy in mid-path, we quickly work out that it's

Our snowy track on the banks of an icy Elbe.

thawing on the grassy edges and quite safe to walk along, if slightly hard work . Rivers in the Czech Republic are regularly dotted with picnic facilities and we settle down on a bench to have lunch, the temperature having risen to just above zero, and enjoy the total silence.

The tension of the last twenty-four hours suddenly dissipates and I feel a surge of joy at reaching the Elbe, river number five on the journey (a reminder for those not keeping the tally: the Rhine, Danube, Pegnitz and Mže/Berounka/Vltava). Our guide in Prague yesterday became quite irrationally emotional when we asked about the Elbe: 'The river should be called the Vltava. It's an insult to the Czech national river. The Vltava is much bigger than the Elbe when they meet 30 kilometres north of Prague.' Sarah and I nodded our heads we hoped empathetically. But a quick check in the guidebook later revealed that, while the Vltava is longer, the Elbe is the larger when they converge; besides, the Germans would never have let their second longest river bear a Czech name. The

Elbe is indifferent to national claims: it rises in the mountains in the Sudetenland, flows due south then makes a dogleg west at Pardubice before absorbing the Vltava, crosses the German border just south of Dresden, then on to Wittenberg, where Luther dipped his toes into its frothing water, on through Magdeburg and Hamburg before surging out into the North Sea at Cuxhaven.

We are struck by the ubiquitous huts (called *chaty*) that run almost continuously along one side of the river. They are almost entirely empty, and only later do we learn that Czech families commonly possess one of these cabins, often without mains electricity or sanitation, and come up to them for the weekend. They are simple in design, often made of wood or local stone, with small gardens leading down to the water's edge. They were beloved rural getaways from the nineteenth century, but they grew in popularity during the Communist era (1948–89) when foreign travel to the sea was difficult, and money was in short supply. Like many such second homes across Europe, they are passed down through families. Russian dachas are similar in that they are rural idylls by rivers, lakes or up in the mountains, and enjoyed a heyday under Communism. The dachas, though, which can be palatial and located near the most expensive cities, exchange hands for serious money, unlike the plentiful, and more modest, Czech *chaty*.

The sun is already sinking low and the temperature dropping back below zero when we approach Čelákovice. We had a difficult moment when Sarah asked why I wasn't wearing my bobble hat and the dreadful story of its loss emerges, but her humour is fully restored by a swish double-decker train that arrives promptly at the station, though not before we'd called into the platform shop that sells piping hot chai lattes. We speed back towards the capital past fields covered with snow lost in deep winter. On the train, Sarah smiles at me. She has enjoyed the walk. Everything will be all right.

That evening we go for dinner in the Old Town Square, ten minutes' walk from the hotel and a critical location in the Prague Uprising of

Resistance fighter Marie Kudeříková, beheaded by the Nazis in 1943 aged 22, inspired many women to support the Prague Uprising.

May 1945. Public gatherings, barricades and skirmishes took place in the square, and after the liberation, it was a focal point for euphoric celebrations.

The Prague Uprising of 1945 is as remarkable as it is unusual. It was the very last European capital to be liberated from Nazi control: Rome had been delivered fully eleven months before on 4 June 1944, Paris on 25 August and Brussels on 3 September 1944, five years to the day after Britain declared war on Germany. By the time of the Prague Uprising, Hitler had already killed himself on 30 April and Berlin had surrendered to the Red Army two days later.

The Prague Uprising was also considerably briefer and less bloody than the battles in the adjacent capitals Budapest and Vienna, both of which saw intense street fighting. In Paris, the French Resistance rose up with singular ferocity to attack the German occupying forces. General Eisenhower, the Supreme Commander of Allied forces, had wanted to bypass the French capital, but when the Uprising began in mid-August, anxious to avoid a bloodbath, he instructed General Leclerc's Free French forces to enter the city and to take the surrender of the remaining Germans on 25 August, a victory that had cost the lives of some 1,500 resistance fighters and civilians.[2]

Massively more costly was the Warsaw Uprising begun by the Polish underground army on 1 August 1944, a bitter fight against the Germans while the Red Army waited on the other side of the Vistula river refusing to help. Stalin wanted post-war Poland to be a client state and to be liberated by Soviet not partisan forces; if the cream of the Polish underground army and intelligentsia was wiped out in this struggle, so much the better. He despised the Poles, and never worried about the loss of anybody's life but his own. His indifference to casualties was one reason why up to three times more Soviet soldiers lost their lives on the Eastern Front than Germans. The Poles eventually surrendered to the Germans in October; half a million civilians were then forcibly expelled and sent to transit camps, and when the Soviet forces entered Warsaw in January 1945, it was a pile of ruins. Some 200,000 fighters and civilians had died in the Uprising.[3] One can well understand Polish bitterness. The ferocious two-week Battle of Berlin, which began in earnest on 16 April 1945, saw 300,000 killed. The Prague Uprising in contrast had lasted just four days and resulted in 3,000 to 4,000 deaths on both sides.[4]

The Czech resistance may not have fully recovered from the Heydrich assassination reprisals, but it was determined to show its potency before the war was officially declared over, which would have left Prague liberated by default if it did not act. By early May, the Soviets were advancing towards the city on three sides, with forces converging from southern Germany, Slovakia and Austria. Now is the time, the resistance told themselves, to make the stand.

The Uprising began on the morning of 5 May. Rumours had been spreading for days, and Prague citizens came out into the streets, defiantly tearing down German flags and signs, and openly flying the Czechoslovak flag across the city for the first time in six years. Things rapidly escalated when German soldiers were assaulted and some killed, and civilians began throwing their long stored-up Molotov cocktails and deploying other carefully hidden weaponry against them. For the resistance fighters, the focal point became the Czech Radio Building, famously broadcasting 'Calling all Czechs, come to our aid' after they took it. The building is venerated today as the originating point of the Uprising. The Germans managed to recapture it, but not before the resistance removed enough equipment to set up other broadcasting operations elsewhere, telling citizens to set up barricades to slow down expected German reinforcements: some 2,000 such defences were erected overnight on 5–6 May. Key strategic targets for the resistance fighters were: the main railway station to stop German reinforcements arriving; the Charles Bridge, to prevent it from being demolished or being used as a conduit for German reinforcements; the Nazi secret police headquarters at Petschek Palace, the regular site of torture which the resistance seized; and Pankrác prison, which was stormed and 3,000 prisoners released, Prague's own Bastille moment.[5]

By 6 May, the resistance had taken back much of the city east of the Vltava. But on 7 May, a Waffen-SS counterattack punched through many of the hastily erected barricades and began to reclaim lost districts. The intervention of the Russian Liberation Army (ROA) at this point proved decisive. These were ex-Soviet soldiers who had agreed to fight in the German army after they had been captured, but who switched to supporting the Uprising. For several key hours that day, they held the SS at bay. The Czech resistance only lost ground when, towards evening, many of the ROA departed west in the forlorn hope of surrendering to the Western allies (when the Americans refused to welcome them,

Citizens' barricades during the Prague Uprising, May 1945.

they were handed over to the Soviets who transported them back to Moscow where they were treated as traitors and many executed).

On the pivotal day, 8 May, the battle in Prague swung both ways: the resistance was weakening, the Americans were not going to be coming and the Red Army was still a day or more away. Defeat was in the air. But the Germans equally were in trouble with further support not transpiring. So a truce, only partly honoured, was hammered out whereby the Germans agreed to lay down their arms and the Czechs promised them safe passage out of the city. The last Germans left Prague in the early hours of 9 May, and almost simultaneously, the first units of the Red Army arrived at dawn. Then at 8 a.m., Soviet tanks rumbled into the city to mass civilian applause. The Soviets lost only ten soldiers in their 'easiest victory' of the war.[6]

Fighting had been intense with atrocities committed on both sides. The Germans used Czech civilians as human shields and indiscriminately murdered others, including fifty resistance fighters at Masaryk train station on 8 May, while the Czech government-in-exile sanctioned brutalities against Germans during and after the siege. Both sides had been frustrated by lack of external support: the remnants of the Luftwaffe were summoned up by German forces on the ground, but their bombing of key strategic points taken by the resistance made little impression.

We need to examine more deeply why the Americans had not come to the rescue when poised nearby. The Czechs had urged Patton, whose Third Army had crossed into Czechoslovakia on 4 May, to rush to their aid. But Churchill was the only one of the Big Three to have argued for the West to take Prague. Stalin maintained it was a job for the Red Army, while President Truman, only three weeks into office following the death of Roosevelt on 12 April, was content to leave the decision to General Eisenhower, to whom Churchill sent his historic and far seeing telegram, stating that the liberation of Prague by US troops 'might make the whole difference to the post-war situation of Czechoslovakia and influence that in nearby countries'.[7] With the Uprising in the balance overnight on 5–6 May, Patton was fuming and pleaded by phone to Eisenhower for permission to relieve the resistance fighters, just a day or two from where American forces were holed up at Pilsen. 'I'll call you tomorrow from Prague,' he daringly told his supreme commander. But Patton could not budge his determination to stick by the demarcation line agreed with the Soviets. General Bradley, one of Eisenhower's senior commanders, read Patton the riot act: 'The halt-line through Pilsen is mandatory for V and XII Corps, George. Moreover, you must not – I repeat not – reconnoiter to a greater depth than eight kilometres northeast of Pilsen. [Eisenhower] does not want any international complications at this late date.'[8] Eisenhower was worried about US soldiers accidentally clashing with the Red Army.[9] The prudent course, which would save American lives and avoid diplomatic embarrassment, was to wait.[10]

The Prague Uprising, for all its limited scale compared to the liberation of other national capitals, had a deep and enduring significance for the country and beyond. The victorious struggle became the proud

Wenceslas Square during the Prague Uprising.

emblem of the new Czechoslovakia post-1945 and is commemorated as the single most significant military action by the Czechs themselves to achieve freedom and independence for their country. In contrast, Eisenhower's blanket refusal to let Patton advance was widely regarded in the country, as we have seen, as yet another betrayal by the West, on top of Munich seven years before. Not overlooked either was that Moscow had refused to accept the Munich Agreement, which made the case easier for Czech Communists in the years immediately following 1945 to argue that the country's natural ally was Moscow, whose forces had liberated their capital, as opposed to the US, which did not.[11] Churchill was not the only figure in Britain to foresee the damage: Foreign Office senior official Orme Sargent said that the West's failure to support the Uprising was the moment that 'Czechoslovakia was now definitely lost to the West'.[12]

Prague's women had suffered particularly under the Nazi occupation. Many were subjected to forced labour in war production factories, sent away to work on the land or enlisted in other ways to the Nazi war machine, always under brutal conditions. They were separated from their husbands, daughters and sons, and placed under constant Gestapo surveillance. Those who managed to send their children abroad on Kindertransport and other schemes suffered from not receiving any information about them, while those with young children were constantly tormented by their diet, safety and health. The women involved as couriers and overseeing safe houses were regularly arrested, tortured and executed. The Nazis very deliberately set out to destroy women's education and cherished rights, Czechs being a people for whom they had no respect. Sexual abuse and violence was common during interrogation, with women forced to work in military brothels in Prague and beyond.

Prague had many heroes during the Uprising. While the lion's share of the fighting was undertaken by men, women built and defended the barricades. But their principal contribution was as medics, couriers, intelligence gatherers and radio operators. Given their importance in those four days, and during the occupation in the years preceding them, the three remarkable figures of light mentioned here are all female.

Marie Kuděriková is Czechoslovakia's best-known female resistance fighter. She was born in Moravia in 1921, and the Nazis invaded Czechoslovakia just a few days before her eighteenth birthday. From an early stage she was involved with the Youth Union, which was connected to the banned Communist Party, and took part in a series of acts from sabotage to distributing anti-Nazi leaflets until seized by the Gestapo in 1941. Despite repeated torture, she never revealed the names of any of her resistance colleagues, but wrote a series of letters from prison that became celebrated, after 1945, as embodiments of the Czech spirit and pure courage. 'Don't cry, I don't cry. Without a lament, without a shudder of fear, without pain,' she wrote in her last letter.[13] Unable to break her will after multiple attempts, the Nazis beheaded her on 26

March 1943. It was just two days after her twenty-second birthday. I pause every time I think about her, wondering how she sustained herself in the years of loneliness, pain and terror at an age when young women should be setting out excitedly on their lives. Marie inspired many women to support the resistance movement and the Prague Uprising.

The second figure, professor of art history and public intellectual Růžena Vacková, did witness the Uprising, if only just. She was born in 1901 near Brno, where she went to school, and moved to Prague in 1920 to study at the Faculty of Arts. She earned a doctorate in 1925 and travelled to Rome to write about the Classics. During the 1930s, she focused her work on Czech art, literature and theatre.[14] When Czech universities were closed by the Nazis, she continued to educate students, clandestinely. Her championing of Czech cultural identity and forthright opposition to Nazi oppression had done much to fortify and embolden others. She was arrested in 1944, and both her brother and brother-in-law were executed, but her death sentence was averted by the Uprising. Her post-1948 refusal to accept Communist restrictions on freedom of speech resulted in her being sentenced in 1952 to twenty-two years in prison.[15] Even inside prison she continued to run classes and to write, including these words: 'Freedom is not something we are given. It is something we must carry within ourselves – even in prison, even in silence,' a way of thinking that chimes closely with that of Holocaust survivor and psychiatrist Viktor Frankl, who wrote *Man's Search for Meaning*, published in 1946, in which he champions caring for others and stoicism in the face of suffering.

The third figure is Milada Horáková, another academic, who, in 1918, had been expelled from school at age seventeen for protesting against the First World War. During the 1930s, she worked as a lecturer and promoted women's rights. When the Nazis annexed the country, she was forced to resign from Prague University. She quickly joined a resistance group, housing those wanted by the Nazis and passing along information. But she was arrested in 1940 and spent five grim years in prison camps, including Theresienstadt. Liberated by the US army in 1945, she returned to a radically different Czechoslovakia. She won a seat in the National Assembly and fought for democracy and women's rights but resigned in protest after the Communist coup in 1948. A year later she was arrested, and tried on wholly fabricated charges of treason. She told the court, 'I take full responsibility for my actions... I stated to the authorities that I stand by my beliefs.' Despite Churchill and Einstein, among others, urging clemency, Horáková was hanged sadistically in Pankrac prison in Prague on 27 June 1950. Her last words were, 'I lost this fight but I'm leaving in an honourable way. I love this country, I love its people; do build prosperity for them. I don't feel any hatred towards you. I wish you, I wish you well...'[16] 75 years on, the dignity of her last words, her life, her death, inspire and contrast with the rabid rants of her prosecutor at the show trial, Dr Josef Urválek.

* * *

It's been a long day and we walk back through the city centre, still vibrant at ten o'clock on a Monday evening. Where there were barricades on the approaches to Old Town Square, the streets are now blocked up by café tables, chairs and heated parasols; where anxious citizens stood tensing themselves to defend their city to their deaths, tourists are now celebrating life.

The next morning, I'm walking alone while Sarah explores the city. I rush to the station, but as I emerge up the escalator on to the platform, I see the 8:46 to Čelákovice pulling out. I saunter back to the main concourse. There's no visible evidence I can see of the fighting that took place here during the Uprising, but a plaque commemorates those who fell during it by the station's enormous Art Nouveau dome. I wander off searching for some coffee; still grappling with the puzzle of which part of which platform trains depart from, I nearly miss the 9:16. But I love the Czech train system, which is more punctual, cleaner and more ubiquitous than what I had experienced in Germany (indeed, it has the densest rail network of any country in Europe). It's still −8°C as I set off from Čelákovice, a town that the Prague tourist office promotes as having 'the largest vampire graveyard in the world'.[17] This claim is based on the discovery in the 1960s of a series of medieval skeletons that had nails and rocks driven through them. The modern explanation is that the dead were either socially excluded, or the victims of a plague, explaining their unconventional burial.[18] No need then for vervain or garlic to ward off vampires still lingering in the vicinity; though, that said, the shop on the station platform that sold us the resplendent chai lattes last night has an entire wall offering customers a wide range of herbs, exotic plants and spices. Just in case.

I set off down Rooseveltová Street, following Paul Antrobus's route, and join the river path, trying to keep up 5.5 kilometres per hour, but finding it hard with the slush underfoot. I am cautious about slipping, reflecting that just one misstep of the 1 million-plus strides on this walk could twist an ankle and destroy my already stressed timetable. But on the positive side, I rejoice that, despite the snow and the cold, it's so much easier walking now than in the draining heat of high summer, thick with mosquitoes and insects. I walk 18 kilometres by the riverside barely passing a soul till I reach Hradištko where Sarah joins me with a very welcome feast for lunch: white *rohlík* bread rolls filled with vegetables and local cheese. We then walk together along the river path to Nymburk as Sarah tells me about her morning wandering through the capital, and negotiating the heaving crowds on the Charles Bridge. We'd been expecting Nymburk to be a showcase medieval town, but are disappointed to find much of it dates back only to the late nineteenth and twentieth centuries, totally missing the city's secret as I discovered the following morning. Back to Prague, we walked to Wenceslas Square, another focal point for the liberation celebrations on 9 May 1945, but also full of darker memories twenty-three years later of the Soviet tanks returning on 21 August 1968 to crush the Prague Spring.

Nymburk's city walls concealing the architectural riot behind them.

I'm back in Nymburk soon after eight the next morning as the town is waking up, the shops clattering open, coffee and tobacco smells oozing from the wealth of cafés on the long walk from station into town. I aim for the thirteenth-century walls begun under the reign of King Ottokar II, destroyed by Saxony's army in the 1630s and rebuilt early in the twentieth century. I enjoy climbing the steps and walking the ramparts, but they're no more impressive than the countless city walls I've already seen across the country. No, the real delight of Nymburk is it being the embodiment of the spirit of Czech nationalism in the late nineteenth and early twentieth centuries. The fifty years from the 1880s to the 1930s are romanticized by Czechs today as their golden era, before the tragedies of the Nazi and Soviet occupations. The town is a riot of eccentric facades and buildings, witness the white Art Nouveau water tower still functioning today, as is the extravagant mock-Gothic hydroelectric dam across the width of the Elbe, the Hotel Ostrov, built in 1922 in Imperial style and set in parkland, and the Hálkovo Town Theatre, with its white cube shapes and large windows. It reminds me of another admirable feature of this country: the palpable affection the Czechs have for live theatre, a passion that makes the emergence and continued veneration of the playwright Havel all the more understandable.[19]

As I make ready to leave this extravagantly bonkers town, I notice the path from walls to river is blocked by engineering work. I see an elderly lady with a dog, and I ask her in perfect English how I can reach the river path, and she responds in perfect Czech how to do so. Neither of us understands a word that we said to each other, but we both understand each other entirely. I turn to thank her and she gives me the most radiant, heartwarming smile. I walk along the north bank of the river, which, receiving more sunlight than the south bank we were on yesterday, is mostly free of snow, making progress today much easier. The strong sunlight dances on the water, which in several places I see is frozen over on both sides, leaving just a narrow channel for the surging water to pass through in the middle. The observation is germinating a thought. I am noticing that something isn't quite right inside: I have had an ache in my chest that I've been ignoring these last few days. It is eighteen months since the heart specialist told me I had a problem with a restricted artery and put me on mild medication and one aspirin a day. But I'd stopped taking the latter a while back, too much faff I stupidly thought, so I phone Sarah and ask if she can pick some up. The aspirin will thin my own surging blood to let it pass more easily through the constricted space.

I decide to stop at Poděbrady, which is appropriate, as it is a national centre of cardiology ('Poděbrady is good for the heart' is the town's motto). Its international renown dates to the establishment of its Cardiological Institute in 1926. The town's coronary specialism originated when it became central Bohemia's main spa resort following mineral water springs being discovered before the First World War. The owner of the imposing castle on the Elbe, Count Hohenlohe, had asked a dowser friend to search for an underground spring as the town had a serious water shortage. The artful dowser obligingly found one in the castle's courtyard, and the canny Count decided to develop a spa resort in the shadow of his castle. Poděbrady boomed after 1918, when the town's opulent spa buildings and colonnades, parks and promenades were constructed, reminiscent of England's spa towns Harrogate, Tunbridge Wells and Cheltenham, but in fact modelled on the country's own famous spas, Mariánské Lázně (Marienbad) and Karlovy Vary (Karlsbad) so beloved by Edward VII. National leaders from Masaryk to Beneš, famous musicians and writers flocked to Poděbrady, where they enjoyed the spa water 'high in iron, carbon and great for the blood flow'; I resist the temptation to join them in a glass. But the town has given me a different medical message, and one I have to take seriously.[20]

'Here are your aspirin,' Sarah says, passing me the packet. The writing is all in Czech, but it's unmistakably the same product. We are back

The Elbe frozen at both banks at Poděbrady, restricting its flow.

in the hotel. 'I don't think you're very good at looking after yourself, are you?' 'I think you may be right.' But a day after taking the pills, I notice the chest ache and heart fluctuations easing. I'm back in action!

Sarah had insisted on some quiet time to rest, so we settle down for a couple of hours into the cosy chairs in our bedroom. While I catch up on my diary, she is deeply immersed in Frank Gardner's thriller *Crisis*, regularly reading out extracts before we dress up against the cold to go out for dinner. My spirits have taken a slight knock from my own more immediate crisis and I'm far more alert to the darker side of Prague. Everywhere I look, I see graffiti, its wretched spray paint eating into historic buildings, bridges and monuments. 'When the Prague city council meets,' I ask her, 'do they ever discuss the graffiti, or have they decided it's a lost battle?' She looks at me patiently, familiar with my restless desire to make things better. 'You're not Prague's headmaster, you know.' Sarah has become adept at gently bringing me down to earth. 'I know, but I can't understand why it's not cleaned off at once, or surfaces treated with anti-graffiti coatings.' We pass four men crouching together in a shop front making demented noises, with a strong smell of cannabis wafting from them. I have seen too much of the damage this Russian roulette 'recreational' drug can do to fragile minds. In Charles Square (Karlovo Náměstí), the largest in medieval Europe, a party of young Brits are swigging spirits gaily in preparation for a stag night on the town. The graffiti, the drugs and excessive drinking are all expressions of personal freedom. Of course, doing things to excess is a rite of passage for young people, I know that. I did it. But a society without a deep sense of responsibility to others will rot from within. Are these actions expressions of the freedom that Růžena Vacková wrote about from her prison cell? Was this the freedom those brave Czechs fighting Nazi and Soviet authoritarianism had in mind? Does Trump, who yesterday dispatched 'real estate mogul' Steve Witkoff to clear the tracks on Ukraine with Putin, understand how fragile liberty and human rights are for those who live in Central Europe?

In the morning, I decide to miss out a particularly beautiful chunk of river walking from Poděbrady due south to Kolín which I had planned for yesterday afternoon. I had set out from home at the weekend determined not to miss any sections of the walk, so the 15-kilometre missing gap along the Elbe hurts. There's no time to get upset. Sarah is right about taking care. I still have a good walk ahead today to Přelouč. First, though, I have to see stunning Kolín, founded in the thirteenth century on the principal trade route from Prague to Pardubice and onwards into Moravia. Kolín's main square, full of Renaissance and Gothic buildings, and colourful merchant houses dating from the sixteenth to the eighteenth centuries, catches my eye, as does the imposing Gothic St Bartholomew's Church, redesigned by celebrated architect Peter Parler who had worked on Prague's St Vitus Cathedral. Gothic too is the nearby ossuary with piles of skulls and bones dating from the 1700s and the excavation of a 'cancelled' medieval graveyard.[21]

As a centre of Jewish life, Kolín was second only to Prague, with Jews approaching 20 per cent of the town's population by the mid-nineteenth century. I wander around the Jewish quarter lost in thought, looking at the synagogue, the cemetery and houses in the narrow ghetto streets. Jews suffered over the centuries in Kolín as elsewhere from the usual round of expulsions, racial attacks and false accusations, as when a young Catholic priest in 1913 implicated a Jew in a blood libel charge after a young girl killed herself, before it emerged that *he* had made her pregnant. But it is the resilience of Jewish life here that uplifts the spirit, the constant determination to bounce back, to give to the community, to study and create. After Jews fled the Sudetenland in October 1938, it was in Kolín that many sought refuge in vain. A plan was hatched for 600 to settle in the French colony of New Caledonia in the Pacific, a scheme thwarted by the outbreak of war. On 13 June 1942, seven centuries of Jewish life abruptly ended in Kolín, because on that day most of the remaining Jews were sent to Terezín, before being transported to Poland. By

Kolín's Jewish quarter, once teeming with life. No Jewish community now inhabits the city.

diabolical irony, the Zyklon B hydrogen cyanide gas that killed them was partly manufactured at Kolín's Draslovka chemical factory.[22]

Hitler had no knowledge of Kolín, but he idolized one man who very much did. This was Frederick II, King of Prussia, who fought and lost the Battle of Kolín in 1757 at the start of the Seven Years War. What captivated the Führer was that twice during that war, in 1759 and again in 1762, Frederick's fortunes had changed very quickly for the better. The first, when the Russians failed to follow up a crushing victory at Kunersdorf, and the second when the death of Empress Elizabeth of Russia elevated her nephew Peter, a huge admirer of Frederick, to the throne. In his office in the bunker in Berlin, Hitler had a portrait of Frederick on the wall. Likely he glanced at it with increasing desperation, hoping a similar miracle would spare him the inevitable in his own (nearly) seven years war. When Roosevelt died, Goebbels had tried to cheer Hitler up by reminding him of Frederick's turning disaster into triumph. With less than three weeks to live himself, Hitler's mind was becoming increasingly delusional, trapped in the bunker; witness his belief that the West might join forces with Nazi Germany against Stalin, which Laurence Rees describes as 'perhaps the most significant example in twentieth-century history of cognitive dissonance'.[23]

I walk out of Kolín along the north bank of the Elbe, coming off after 8 kilometres because my pace is too slow with the slush underfoot. Sarah phones: 'How are your boots today?' I look down at my feet. 'They seem fine. Why are you asking?' 'Because you've taken mine.' 'Really? I'm so sorry, I didn't want to turn on the lights as you were asleep. I couldn't see.' I feel frustrated with myself and notice for the first time the boots starting to be uncomfortable. I press on, negotiating my way through a quarry, the tracks deeply rutted with ice shards, then along farm tracks to the hamlet of Veletov. The map suggests the busy road might have a cycle track beside it, but annoyingly it doesn't, so I have a 5-kilometre walk to the hill town of Týnec nad Labem along the gutter of a busy main thoroughfare. Taking this risk had been common on the Western Front walk, but I had hoped to avoid it this time, as heavy lorries swish past with their fumes and spray. It's over quickly enough and I pick up the Elbe again at Tynéc, seeing otters, geese and ducks. I cut across fields to the village of Selmice and then I'm on a dead straight lane to Kladruby nad Labem, known to horse lovers across the world as one of its oldest stud farms and home to the celebrated Czech indigenous breed of horse, the Kladruber. Emperors throughout the centuries relied on horses from Kladruby for state occasions. When the Nazis invaded in March 1939, they expressed keen interest in breeding a Nazi-branded 'Aryan' horse, with Kladruby's stallions deemed particularly promising. What?! I understand about selective animal breeding, but had never realized that the Nazis applied their psychopathic theories of racial purity to *animals*. But Himmler's crazed interest in eugenics extended beyond humans. The Nazis promptly commandeered the Kladruby stud farm, transporting some of its finest horses to SS stud farms in Germany. Just outside Prague at Hostouň, 5 kilometres south of Lidice, they also established their equine breeding, training and logistics base. Out of the craziness came something elevating, Operation Cowboy, almost unique as an instance in the war of the combatants cooperating in a worthy cause. Wehrmacht officers, who wanted to surrender to the West, contacted US officers to say they were fearful that the animals might be slaughtered by retreating German or by advancing Soviet units. Given that Hostouň was due to be conquered by the Soviets, Patton's permission was sought and given for this mercy mission to cross the lines. Thus, 1,200 rare horses were spirited away by the Americans to safety, thereby preserving bloodlines that might otherwise have been lost forever.[24]

I wander around Kladruby's elegant buildings, to where some of the horses were later returned, and decide I've probably had enough for the day, still 7 kilometres short of Prělouč. But I've walked for over five hours, my nose is streaming and the chest ache is back. I'd made a note of a taxi driver's number that morning at Kolín, so I phone him and ask him to drive me back to the station. I'm always surprised by how long a car journey lasts back to base after a day's walk. It gives me time to talk to my driver Daniel, whose English is strong (it's his third language after German). He loves his country and tells me about his anxiety about America's intentions. I ask him what he likes to do when he's not driving and he tells me he loves to paint. So I ask him what he most enjoys painting, and he says 'walls'. His other job is as a decorator.

The next day, our last, sees another dash in −10°C to Prague station. We board our train to Prělouč only to learn from fellow passengers it may not be running. A Czech conductor comes up to us to explain and walks with us to another platform to see us on to a fast train. Yet again, we're impressed and grateful. We have a coffee when we arrive at Přelouč, a suggestion that always goes down well, and off we set for our destination, Pardubice, along the Elbe's north bank. A mistake. The going is heavy underfoot in the snow, and it's not clear that the track won't disappear. So we walk back to Přelouč and take country lanes to the village of Valy. Then over slushy fields to the village of Srnojedy where we pick up the Elbe for a final and glorious walk into Pardubice, delighted to find the station is on the right side of town. The train arrives almost as soon as we step on the platform, and we sit in a discrete compartment on our own with a sliding door on to the corridor which we close, a layout that sadly disappeared from British carriages at the beginning of this century. My head is spinning, my nose is still running, but I'm wearing the right boots. Sarah is looking very content, the walking mission for the week completed. It's been a good time for us together too. We are learning to share more of the things that really concern us. Sarah's even forgiven me for the bobble hat.

I'll engage more with fascinating Pardubice when I return in April. But I can't leave it now without mentioning the work of one of its residents, photographer Štěpán Bartoš. He became interested in what happened to the 400 synagogues that once stood in today's Czech Republic, many destroyed in the lead up to and during the Second World War, and in the Communist era that followed. His project, 'Invisible Synagogues', documents all the blank spaces left where they once stood. Initially when he set out in 2021, he took photographs of the blank spaces, letting the emptiness speak for itself. Now, he engraves on to the photographic prints the outlines of the former synagogues, reminding people of the truth of what once stood there, often for centuries, and of the stories behind them now lost to human memory.[25]

His work recovering the truth of what has been destroyed won't leave me, and it makes me reflect on today's unparalleled assault on truth. The powerful have always sought to control it, but social media and the abuse of it by some contemporary leaders has brought it to a

Photographer Štěpán Bartoš's stencil drawing of the synagogue that once stood in Pardubice.

point of crisis. In this book, I'm walking from one truth, Kilometre Zero, where the First World War fighting finished, to another, Auschwitz, the biggest factory of murder in history.

Even during the time taken to write this book, assertions that the numbers killed at Auschwitz (some 1.2 million people, 80–90 per cent of them Jews) and indeed whether the Holocaust itself is a fabrication have continued unabated.[26] Aside from conspiracy theorists whose grasp of the truth is never secure, two main groups have perpetrated Holocaust denial. The far right, who want to rehabilitate the Nazi legacy, and antisemites who, as throughout history, abominate Jews and want to diminish them. To the latter can be added those who want to destroy the State of Israel, whose establishment in 1948 was underpinned by international revulsion at the treatment of the Jews at the hands of the Nazis.

Even while the war was still being fought, aware that light was beginning to be shone on their atrocities, the Nazis took pains to destroy evidence of the Final Solution. The top-secret *Sonderaktion 1005* ('Special Action 1005') was set up in mid-1942 by the SS to expunge all physical evidence of mass murder, including exhuming bodies from mass graves as at Babyn Yar in Kyiv, burning them and grinding the remains into powder, before disposing of the slave labourers forced into executing the task.[27] As the tide of the war on the Eastern Front turned at Stalingrad, the Nazis became concerned about the Soviets discovering their extermination camps. First to be sanitized was Treblinka in the far east of Poland, and most at risk of discovery. The killing was stopped, the buildings torn down, the ground ploughed over and replanted. Today, there is surprisingly little to see where up to 900,000 people were murdered. Sobibor and Belzec camps were next to be flattened.[28] At Auschwitz-Birkenau, the crematoria and gas chambers were partly blown up. Documents everywhere were systematically if not thoroughly destroyed: no single piece of paper thus survives of Hitler ordering the extermination of the Jews.[29] The death marches, as we have seen, were designed in part to kill remaining witnesses through exhaustion and starvation.

It's easy to underestimate the shock that the West felt on hearing about the Holocaust and its sheer scale in mid-1945. We have seen that in the sceptical responses that greeted the evidence gathered by Alfred Weiner, or to the Vrba-Wetzler Report, and the incredulous reaction to the Richard Dimbleby broadcast from Belsen. Lies about the camps began circulating as early as the second half of the 1940s. Prime among the non-Nazi promulgators was Frenchman Paul Rassinier whose writing had a credibility because he had been interned as a political prisoner in Buchenwald.[30] To those not wanting to believe the scale of the Holocaust, or who dismissed it as yet more Jewish whining, such reports were lapped up. Other deniers followed in Rassinier's footsteps, such as fellow Frenchman Robert Faurisson, American Professor Arthur

Butz who published *The Hoax of the Twentieth Century* in 1976, and the British historian David Irving.[31] I spotted Irving on a train up from Sussex when I was a doctoral student in the late 1970s. His sympathetic best-seller *Hitler's War* had been published in 1977 by my own publisher, Hodder & Stoughton. I sat down opposite him, genuinely wanting to understand his mind: was he deluded, mad or bad? I remember little of what he said beyond his repeating that Hitler never gave the orders; what remains with me, though, was his deep suspicion of me, and the thin film of sweat stretching over his mouth and pronounced chin.

Pushback against the deniers had been encouraged by many countries, including Germany, Austria and France which introduced laws criminalizing Holocaust denial. The landmark libel trial was in 2000 where Irving was shown to have falsified history, in a case he brought against American historian Deborah Lipstadt and Penguin Books. Irving's manipulation of the historical record showed beyond doubt that he was indeed a Holocaust denier, the judge concluding that he was also a racist and an antisemite.[32] The case and the appeal in 2001 further discredited those academics who had sought through spurious scholarship to undermine trust in the evidence.[33] One might think that objective truth would be on a surer footing in the new millennium. But no. The attack on libraries, librarians and archives, in short on truth, carried out by Hitler and Stalin described in these pages has continued apace, in no decade more than in the 2020s. 'Titles banned, data deleted, the nation's librarians sacked without explanation.' The words of a lefty crackpot? Written about Russia? Well no, on both counts. They are written by the distinguished head of Oxford University's libraries Richard Ovenden, who continued: 'Donald Trump's war on books is a threat to democracy across the world.'[34] The invasion of Israel by Hamas on 7 October 2023, the ensuing war and the uncompromising response by the Israeli government, which has been the backdrop of my entire walk, have greatly fuelled activity, much of it on the internet, that seeks to deny or minimalize the Holocaust.

The brutal hanging of Milada Horáková by the Communist regime in Prague in 1950 deprived the post-war world of a leader of extraordinary courage, dignity and humanity.

The leaders of light who have peopled this story so far are all dead. There are no Churchills today, no Havels; no Marie Kuděřiková nor Milada Horáková who we met in this chapter. I crave figures of light and justice today, national and international leaders, public intellectuals, influential figures of compassion who know violence and hate will only beget more violence and hate. Where are the big-hearted national leaders? Where are the religious leaders to rival Pope Francis? Where is the UN? In their place we have shrill leaders, polarized debate and an absence of reason and compassion. In the remaining chapters I must probe further what the Second World War might still teach us as we grope our way to a brighter future.

9

Into Moravia:
Pardubice to Ostrava

Chapter 9
Pardubice to Ostrava

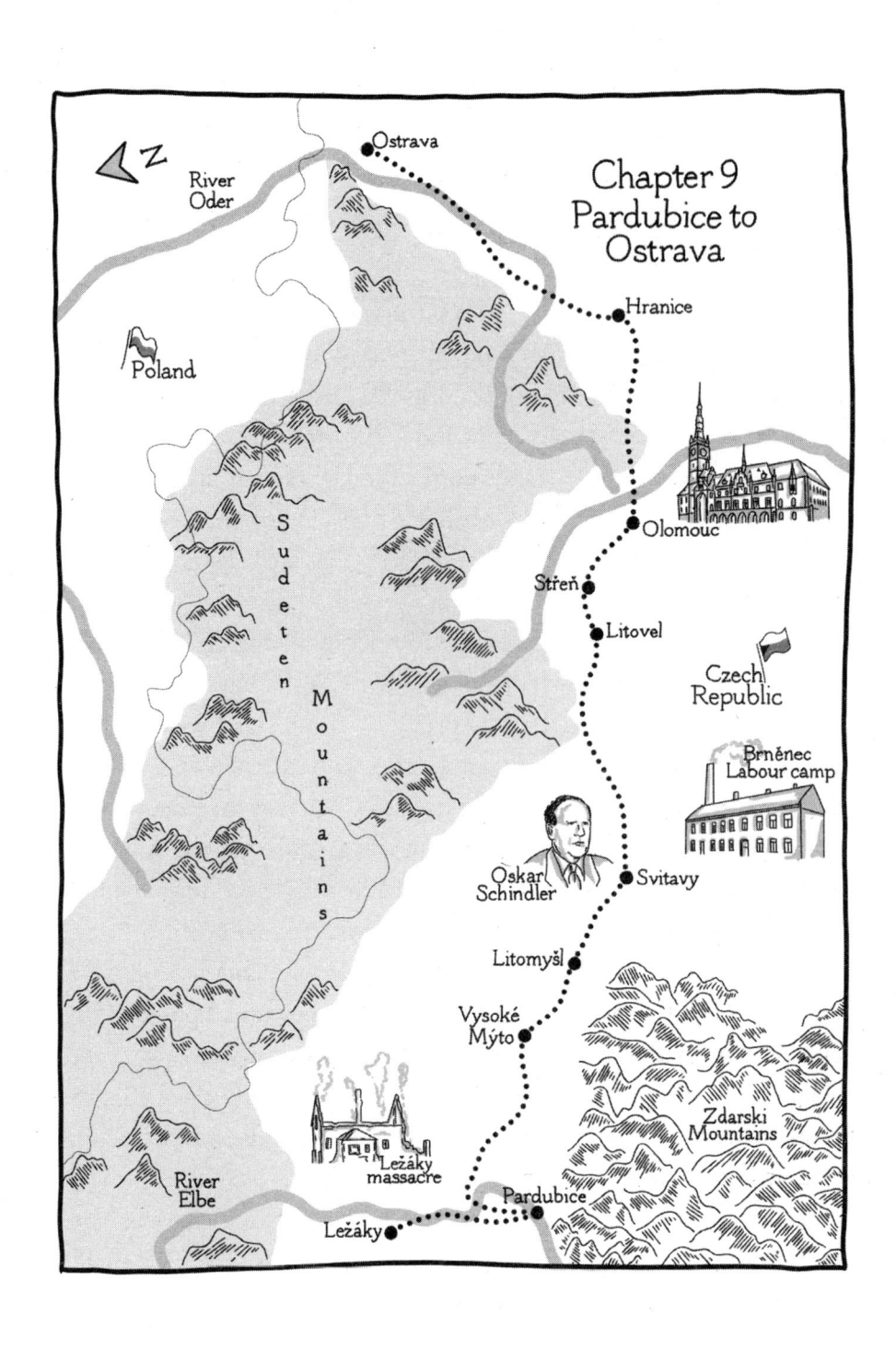

I CAN SENSE WAR edging closer. When I complete this next leg at the Moravian town of Ostrava, I will be less than 400 kilometres from the Ukrainian town of Lviv, and just 1,000 kilometres from the Russian border at Popivka, to the north of the Ukrainian city of Kharkiv. Reaching this far east has been much trickier than I had imagined when I set out. Slowly, slowly, as the world moves closer to all-out war, I am edging closer to *the bear*.

Who would have predicted just a decade ago that in 2025 the world would be hovering on the edge of a Third World War? Increasingly it seems it has already started by proxy. With talk, as I write this, of Putin considering using tactical nuclear weapons at NATO's eastern flank, and President Xi planning how to take Taiwan, I ask myself, yet again, what have we learned from the Second World War, and what are we celebrating on this 80th anniversary beyond individual heroism and victory? Along my journey from Kilometre Zero, I have encountered over forty stories of remarkable men and women from that war. I'm moving closer to answering the questions I posed at the outset: who are the overlooked heroes of the Second World War and what can we learn from them? One lesson is already crystallizing: people at large were passive and failed to speak out against the crushing of democracy and the rule of law during 1939–45. The quest is urgent. Democracy is under threat, as the widely acclaimed book *How Democracies Die* analysed.[1] Much has deteriorated internationally since its publication in 2018 and since I started this walk two years ago. Wisdom, goodness and justice are themes that are emerging strongly from our figures of light. They have much to teach us to help us avert another catastrophe.

I'm thinking, as our train pulls into Pardubice station on the morning of Easter Monday, about my remaining hunt for heroes to shed light on my unresolved questions. My phone starts vibrating. It is Sky News. The Pope has died, can I do a live interview in ten minutes? I pause before declining. The bulletin needs someone much better versed in papal history to comment. But it gives me the chance to reflect on leadership. Francis, Pope since 2013, was a truly good man, his humility, compassion and lifelong example the polar opposite of today's secular leaders. He oversaw the lives of some 1.3 billion Catholics, a similar number to Xi's flock in China and Modi's in India. 'How many divisions does the Pope have?' Stalin allegedly sneered during the Tehran Conference in 1943. But the office has huge influence over Catholics and beyond (would that it had been put to better use in the Second World War), encouraging service, charity and compassion. Might an answer to my quest be that, whereas Putin and other dictators have massive coercive power over the behaviour of their populations, they can never change the hearts of their followers as Pope Francis and other leaders moved by the spirit can.

John James, who has come back to the Czech Republic to walk with me, meets up with maestro route-planner Paul Antrobus in the station forecourt. We hurriedly chuck our bags into his car boot. What a difference two months can make! The mid-Czech Republic town of Pardubice is gleaming in midday sunlight, unrecognizable from the ice-dripped town into which a frozen Sarah and I had stumbled in late February. We make for the main square, drop our bags in the nearby Hotel Atrium and make for the Elbe to get in some walking before dusk. 'How's it going?' they ask. I take it to mean they're asking about the book. 'Good, lots of extraordinary people I've been finding. I just need to make some kind of sense of it all.'

Tree blossom along the river and across central Bohemia, white cherry, pink cherry, pear and apple, will be the defining visual memory of this spring leg of the walk. We walk past lime, oak, sycamore, beech and hazel trees along the banks, we hear a cuckoo, a nightingale (it's a myth they are not daytime singers, especially in spring, John says), a great tit, a great spotted woodpecker and yellow hammer, and we watch a heron slowly descend, a tern gracefully hover, a pheasant run before taking flight, and a young beaver swim innocently out of a stream into the mighty Elbe. When after 7 kilometres the river doglegs north, we carry on walking east till caution tells me that's enough for the first day. Paul had backtracked earlier and collects us in the car to take us back to the city.

Pardubice's fame has always rested upon transport. A principal stopover and market town on the trade route between Prague and Moravia's medieval capital Olomouc, it received another powerful fillip when, in 1845, the railway was opened to great fanfare from Prague to the east. Its transport fame increased further when Pardubice-born Jan Kašpar, inspired by Louis Bleriot's 1909 pioneering flight from Calais to Dover, became the first Czech successfully to fly a plane for a full 2 kilometres at the dizzy height of 25 metres, on 16 April 1910. Then on 13 May 1911, Kašpar flew the 121 kilometres from Pardubice to Prague in ninety-two minutes, the longest powered flight at the time anywhere in the Austro-Hungarian Empire. Tragedy was to follow. Engulfed after the war by financial woes, he took his life in Pardubice in 1927.

Aircraft technology subsequently improved so rapidly that by 1944, heavily loaded Allied bombers were able to fly the 1,300 kilometres from British airfields to bomb the city's oil refinery. An RAF raid on 22 July 1944 missed damaging it, but two subsequent US sorties destroyed the refinery completely, together with the railway junction and the Luftwaffe airport, though at the cost of over 200 civilian lives.[2] The town became a regional hub for both Gestapo and SS operations, known, even against the standards of the time, for its brutal interrogations and executions, masterminded by the infamous Gerhard Clages, who came into his own tracking down the resistance centred in and around Pardubice.

Heydrich's assassins Gabčík and Kubiš were not the only parachutists on the solitary plane that night in late December 1941. Three other Czechs were on board, dispatched by the government-in-exile as part of Operation Silver A, whose mission was to establish a reliable communications network between the country and the Beneš government in London. By mid-January 1942, they believed they had achieved it, having embedded secure radio contacts, and were then starting to coordinate the partisans' disparate resistance efforts. But Heydrich's assassination turned up the heat on the resistance to unbearable levels and in June, the Gestapo discovered their safe house in Pardubice, resulting in one of the three parachutists, Silver A leader Alfréd Bartoš, taking his own life to evade torture and inevitable execution. Gestapo activity in the area intensified further when one of the bodies found in the Prague crypt along with Gabčík and Kubiš belonged to Pardubice local Josef Valčík. Those known to him were rounded up and taken to Larisch Villa, which had been requisitioned by the Gestapo and was known locally as Zámeček. The garden was converted into an execution ground in readiness. Over the next six weeks, 194 members of the resistance were systematically murdered here, their names commemorated today on the Zámeček Memorial.[3]

Josef Bartoň, another leader of Operation Silver A, is one of those named on the memorial. He had graduated from Charles University in Prague as a doctor in 1925, becoming a paediatrician and public health campaigner, setting up the Masaryk League Against Tuberculosis, a deadly killer in interwar Czechoslovakia. Deeply disturbed by the Nazi occupation, he established contact with Silver A in January 1942, providing medical care to the team including Bartoš when they fell ill, and supplying them with a back-up radio transmitter after their original device, codenamed Libuše, malfunctioned. After Heydrich's assassination, the Gestapo found documents in a safe house implicating him, and he and his wife Emilie Welzová, a celebrated singer and actress, were promptly arrested. After his execution on 20 June, Josef Bartoň's body was burned and his ashes thrown in the Elbe while Emilie was transported to Auschwitz where she was gassed on 23 December 1942. Two exceptionally brave, talented and sensitive people who had so much to give the post-war world were thus murdered in the name of evil. They left behind two orphans. Both survived the occupation, Ivan to become a physician, like his father, and Eliška, a teacher.

The Gestapo extracted information from others they tortured, who told them that a radio transmitter used by Silver A was hidden near a village called Ležáky, to the south of Pardubice.[4] Like Lidice, it's been preserved for posterity, the lesser known of the two Czech communities razed to the ground. There's still time for us to head off to see it, where we learn how German soldiers arrived in the village on

Josef Bartoň and Emilie Welzová, both murdered in 1942.

24 June 1942, promptly arresting all residents. In an orgy of violence the troops then looted and burned every dwelling to the ground, before erasing all references to the village on signposts and maps to deny it ever existed. Its men and women were herded into vehicles and taken to Zámeček where they were interrogated, tortured and many executed. Thirteen children were separated from their families, two of whom were selected as fit for Germanization, the remainder sent to Poland where they were murdered at Chełmno in gas vans. We walk around the Ležáky site, which has symbolic foundations marking out where the villagers' homes once stood. The museum is shortly to close for the day and we are the only visitors. What comes across most powerfully from the displays is the quiet dignity of those who once inhabited the community. To name just one, Růžena Šťulíková, who lived with her six children in the mill run by her brother. She and her husband had been arrested on 22 June because parachutist Jiří Potůněk had briefly spent time seeking refuge in the mill. Růžena was transported to Zámeček, then to Theresienstadt from where, on 11 November, she was moved to Auschwitz. Here she is, one of the last batch of incoming prisoners to be photographed before tattooing simplified the laborious procedure; she was allocated the number 24239 and murdered on 21 December 1942. She stands in this book as an emblem of all those millions of inconspicuous women and men going quietly about their lives until so cruelly and capriciously murdered.

We leave Ležáky to its silence, as deeply affected as at Lidice by the senseless violence. Back in the hotel our mood lifts over a Pilsner Urquell before we head out to dinner at the Nejen Dvorek restaurant with smart modern European food, which we consume outside in an imposing garden area. Sarah calls: her ninety-year-old mother, Susan Marshall, has just died after a long illness in Preston, surrounded by her three surviving children. She was a genuinely amazing woman who gave her whole life to serving others. She had met her husband John Marshall at Oxford in the 1950s, both eminently capable of the

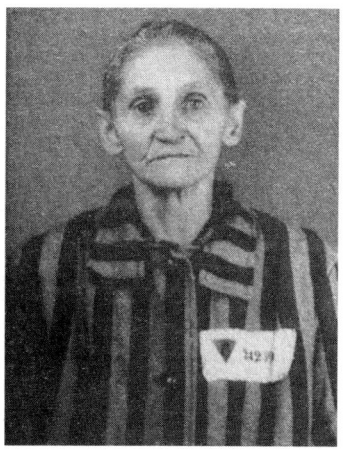

Růžena Šťulíková shortly before the war, left, and her photograph on arrival at Auschwitz, right.

high-powered jobs pursued by their fellow students. But they chose to dedicate themselves to the Christian faith in a Nonconformist church in Hemel Hempstead, where he served as minister for forty-six years. Sarah and I talk again later that evening: she is very strong, but the news, while expected, is a colossal blow for her, coming so soon after the loss of her brother. Only with hindsight did I realize that I should have flown back to be with her. She needed me there not least when she came back down south to our empty home, but she didn't want to ask and, fixated on my project, I was too preoccupied to pick up the signals.

We are up early in the morning, and decide to set off today from Vysoké Mýto, the first significant medieval trading town after Pardubice on the 'Trstěnice Route' connecting Bohemia to Moravia. We enter the main square, one of the largest in the Czech Republic, through the Prague Gate on the town's west side, and select one of the inviting café bars to settle down for coffees and local pastries. Amidst this tranquil urban beauty we talk about the news today from Gaza of further loss of civilian life: the right continue to defend to the hilt every act by Netanyahu as necessary if maybe regrettable, the left to condemn every Israeli action and its legitimacy for existing. Voices of sanity like UN

Secretary-General António Guterres calling for safety for humanitarian workers and for medicine and aid to pass unhindered are not heard as the UN has so little clout.

Louise, John's wife, later phones distraught at the latest Netanyahu-sanctioned attack on Gaza, resulting in widespread loss of civilian life. 'Tell me,' she says, 'what can possibly justify the deaths of children and women?' Unable to make sense of the continuing tragedy ourselves, we leave Vysoké Mýto through the Litomyšl Gate on the eastern side of the town. Old buildings were as vulnerable to fires in this country as in Britain. The gate suffered from several in the early nineteenth century. But unlike in Britain, historic buildings here were regularly restored to the same design, not pulled down and replaced by something often crass. I'm being challenged by my walking companions for being backward-looking. 'Modern buildings can often be more attractive and more practical than those they replaced,' they point out. 'Fair enough,' I respond. 'Here's a challenge. Can you think of any building in London or in another bombed British city erected after 1945 that was aesthetically more pleasing or fitted in better with its environment than the original?' The debate continues as we saunter off along the Loučná river till the conversation switches back to nature, inspired by seeing nuthatches, serin, and a heron rising from the water.

As we approach Litomyšl, birthplace of composer Bedřich Smetana, the conversation turns again, this time to the country's importance to nineteenth-century music internationally, a fruit of the Czech nationalist movement. Smetana wrote eight complete operas, most famously *The Bartered Bride* as well as the renowned symphonic poem *Vltava* (*Die Moldau* in German).[5] While rambling along the banks of the Loučná, a tributary of the Elbe, showered periodically by blossom blown from the trees, John tells us about this most loved composition. *Vltava* imagines in music the course of the river from the twin springs at source on its long journey down to Prague till it is absorbed in the Elbe. Many more I suspect, like me, might recognize its stirring tune than can name it, or its composer. Smetana may be celebrated in this country as 'the father of Czech music', but internationally, co-patriot Antonín Dvořák is the better known, who drew heavily on Czech folk tunes, not least in the *New World Symphony* and *Slavonic Dances*. Leoš Janáček, composer of *The Cunning Little Vixen*, was another distinguished composer born in the country, and much associated with its nationalist romanticism.

John is animated as he enthuses about these Czech musicians. Even Gustav Mahler, the only Jew of the four, was born in the country, though he is known as an Austrian composer having spent so much of his time in Vienna. Significantly, Mahler, born in a German-speaking part of the country, never fully acknowledged his Czech roots, John tells us, and he saw himself following in the tradition of German composers Beethoven, Bruckner and Schubert, even though Czech folk tunes appear in his music, too. Music and Czech identity continue to dominate our conversation over lunch in Litomyšl's Dvorek café on the main square. We're still talking about it as we explore the chateau-style castle, a UNESCO World Heritage Site, built in the 1570s, one of the largest and most treasured Renaissance castles in the country.

We are anxious to make it to Svitavy today, some 18 kilometres south-east, which involves us passing from Bohemia into Moravia. I've never been into this part of the country, and my two companions agree to pose by the border sign in celebration.

Moravia, named after the Morava river that flows through it, is recognizably different to Bohemia – think Wales compared to England (while Slovakia, now a separate country to its east, might be compared to the more detached Scotland). More Catholic than Bohemia with its Hussite and secular traditions, Moravia is proud of its own dialect, folk traditions and festivals. While Bohemia is known for its beer, Moravia is grape country, its vineyards to the south producing much of the country's wine, notably Riesling and Grüner Veltliner. Moravia too is smaller, home to some 3 million compared to Bohemia's 7 million

John James and Paul Antrobus at the Moravia border.

people, and very significantly, it had a prominent German minority population, to whom the town of Svitavy was known as Zwittau, until their expulsion after 1945. During the war, it housed multiple forced labour and prisoner camps, as well as a subcamp of Auschwitz, now coming disconcertingly close on the walk.[6]

Like Vysoké Mýto, Svitavy has one of the largest squares in the country, Náměsti Miru (Peace Square), stretching nearly half a kilometre, and the country's second longest arcade running beneath its Renaissance and Baroque buildings. Until 1945, the town had the biggest German-speaking population in Czechoslovakia outside Bohemia. The Schindlers were one of these families, the Catholic parents giving birth to a boy, Oskar, in April 1908. We begin our quest to understand the town's most celebrated son at a memorial unveiled to him in 1994 to coincide with a special screening in the town of Steven Spielberg's *Schindler's List*.[7] Through a six-pointed Star of David in the heart of the memorial, visitors can see the modest Schindler home on the other side of Poličská Street where Oskar was born. The 1990s owners wanted to avoid any more public attention than the glimpse, suggestive of an ambivalence Czechs feel towards him.[8] We walk back through the town to visit the Schindler Museum: the guide on the front desk is delighted to see us, explaining that while Poles and Germans are frequent visitors, she sees very few British. The museum, a little underwhelming, gives a measured picture of perhaps the most paradoxical figure of light in the entire book.

Nothing in Oskar Schindler's youth and early adult years suggested he was anything other than a self-centred citizen with typical antisemitic views. He attended the local German grammar school, where some of his fellow students were Jewish, as were several of his near neighbours, but he didn't develop a close friendship with any. In 1928, the year after his marriage to Emilie, he became a sales rep, gaining a reputation for being a ruthless salesman and a gambler. He joined the virulently pro-Nazi Sudeten German Party in 1935, and began supplying information to German military intelligence, the Abwehr.[9] Accused of espionage, the Czechs sentenced him to death for spying, but before his execution could take place, he was released from prison when the Sudetenland was annexed in October 1938. He promptly resumed spying on Polish troop movements on the border and may well have aided preparation of the infamous 'Gleiwitz incident', one of the false-flag incidents on the night of 31 August 1939 used by Hitler spuriously to justify the invasion of Poland.[10]

Schindler moved to Kraków in September, using his business activity as a cover for his continued espionage tasks. In November 1939, he took over the administration of a bankrupt enamelware factory commonly referred to as Emalia. Milking his contacts in the Nazi hierarchy to secure favourable business deals, he lived the high life, was notorious

The Schindler memorial unveiled in 1994 in Svitavy's Jana Palacha Park.

Schindler, second from left, at one of his Kraków parties for prominent Germans in 1943.

for his womanizing and unfaithfulness to Emilie, and unscrupulous in every way, showering top brass with generous gifts paid for by his shady deals.

The factory flourished producing kitchenware and ammunition for the German army, and, assisted by shrewd Polish-Jewish accountant Abraham Bankier,[11] was by the end of 1942 employing 800 workers. Some 370 of them were Jews from the Kraków ghetto, which had been set up in March 1941.[12]

Up to this date there was scant evidence, bar his predisposition to treat Jewish workers better than fellow factory owners, that Schindler was anything other than a ruthless hedonist, revelling in the company of high-ranking SS contacts. Inside his soul, though, a transformation was slowly taking place, the genuineness of which his detractors, including many Czechs to this day, like the father and daughter I met on the plane in Chapter 6, deny.

Czech political analyst Jana Kernerova thus argues: 'I see him not as a hero but rather as a practical or even opportunistic man,' and she is critical of *Schindler's List* for offering a simplified and romanticized view.[13] To many Czechs, he was a traitor who abetted the destruction of their country in 1938–39, and who never expressed remorse or apologized for it. I am shocked nevertheless to learn that within days of the memorial's unveiling in Svitavy in 1994, it was daubed with a swastika. This is the Czech Republic: feelings, I keep being reminded, run deep and long. For all this understandable animosity to him, and the truth that he ruthlessly aided the Nazi cause and exploited his contacts for his personal gain, it is equally true that from 1941, he began to use those contacts to bring Jewish workers into his factory, falsifying documents to do so, for humane, not purely economic, reasons. These irregularities brought him to the attention of the Gestapo, who arrested him several times to investigate his actions.[14]

The noose was tightening around Kraków's remaining Jews. Only a fraction of the 68,000 living in the city in 1939 were still alive when, in March 1943, orders were given for the ghetto to be finally emptied. Two thousand women, children and the infirm were gunned down in cold blood, others were sent to the extermination camps, while those deemed able to work were moved to the brutal forced labour camp of Płaszów outside the city. Schindler persuaded the SS commander of the camp, Amon Göth, to let him move his own Jewish workers to a special subcamp at Zabłocie near his factory, freer of SS harassment so he could look after them better.[15] There can be no doubt by now, Schindler was exploiting his cunning and guile to save lives. Then in November 1943, at the invitation of an American welfare committee, he travelled to Budapest to meet representatives of Hungarian Jewry, informing them about the extermination of Jews in Poland and exploring what might be done. This was a perilous and brave enough act. But more remarkable still, in late 1944, as the advance of the Red Army towards Kraków created panic in the Nazi high command, and Płaszów's 20,000 Jews were to be sent off for immediate extermination, he secured agreement for 'his' Jews to be moved back here to his native Moravia.[16] His bargaining counter was that they could continue their essential work for the war machine in a factory he had requisitioned just south of Svitavy at Brněnec. When the 800 men were sent instead to Gross-Rosen concentration camp and the 300 women to Auschwitz, he pulled every remaining string to have them released, including paying for the women's safe passage, the only recorded case in the war of such a large group leaving Auschwitz while the gas chambers were still operating.[17]

One episode not covered in Spielberg's film concerned the fate of 120 Jewish men put on a train to Brněnec in January 1945 as the Soviets approached and who endured a seven-day journey in sealed cattle wagons. Schindler was away from Brněnec procuring food when the train arrived, so initially his wife Emilie, then he himself on his return, had a desperate battle to convince a sceptical SS not to send the train with its human cargo back to the camps. When the frozen doors were prised open, they saw 107 emaciated and barely alive frost-bitten bodies, who they gradually coaxed back to health. A row ensued when the SS wanted to cremate the corpses of those who hadn't survived the journey, but the Schindlers insisted they be buried with full Jewish religious rites in a plot he had bought specially for the purpose.[18] Some weeks later, the Red Army marched into Brněnec; Schindler had left some days before, wisely recognizing, like so many, that he stood a better chance if he gave himself up to the West.

His story was subsequently lost for some years, but in 1961, he was encouraged by Holocaust survivors to visit Israel, the first of seventeen visits to the country, and the following year, a tree was planted in his name in the 'Avenue of the Righteous' at Yad Vashem. On his death in West Germany in October 1974, survivors from his factory arranged for his remains to be brought to Israel to be laid to rest in Jerusalem, the inscription on his grave reading, in Hebrew and German: 'The unforgettable rescuer of 1200 persecuted Jews'. As he, a Catholic, had insisted that the Jewish corpses at Brněnec be buried in a Jewish cemetery, so too did the Israeli government insist that he be interred in a Catholic cemetery, an impressive and moving act. I am left in no doubt at all about the sincerity of his conversion to humanity; I wonder equally if lingering anti-German feeling is responsible in part for the continuing antipathy to him of some Czechs. The key question his life poses, though, is if he, as a fully paid-up and believing Nazi, had his mind changed by personal contact with Jews, realizing that they were not vermin but human beings like himself, why did not more who encountered Jews and other victims of Nazi terror close up undergo a similar transformation?

Publication in 1982 of Australian author Thomas Keneally's novel *Schindler's Ark* helped make Schindler a figure of global renown. For me, a difficult memory: I loved the book and gave my first ever school assembly about it; standing on the school stage in Croydon, a voice in my head said 'You'll muck this up' and my knees started shaking violently. Self-attack is my inner demon. On the eightieth anniversary of VE Day, part of the dilapidated Brněnec factory will be opened as a 'Museum of Survivors'. Keneally's daughter Margaret will read out his message to the world today: 'We need to keep telling the stories.'[19]

Indeed, we do. Another such story of light comes from Louise Freundová, the Jewish sister of Schindler's contemporary at school, Arnošt Freund, who herself knew Schindler. She was deported to Theresienstadt in February 1942, to which her father and brother had already been sent. She only escaped transportation to Auschwitz after them because, devastated by their departure, she had been crying under a coat. When she pulled the coat off, 'My whole transport [had] … simply gone. I learned that only after the war – this entire transport went to Auschwitz and to gas chambers. They probably thought I was dead, they were calling my name and they only saw a bundle covered with a coat.'[20]

Later, though, she was sent to Auschwitz as a forced labourer in December 1943 where she looked after children separated from

The Schindler factory in Brněnec, near Svitavy.

*Louise Hermanová (née Freundová) in 2009,
four years before her death.*

their families till transported again to Christianstadt concentration camp (another, like Lieberose, with a wildly misleading name). When the camp was evacuated in early 1945, she walked 800 kilometres west on a death march, arriving at Belsen dangerously ill. After the liberation of the camp on 15 April, she was marked with a black cross indicating 'no chance of survival'. It took her three months to recover till she was released in July, and travelled to Prague still wearing her prison clothes to learn that her remaining family, including her father, brother, sister-in-law and nephew, had all been murdered. Here was another woman who refused to be beaten or bitter: she married Alexander Hermann, also an Auschwitz survivor, supported him in his work as a Czech doctor, became a mother, and worked fervently as a volunteer supporting Holocaust survivors and countless memorial activities.[21] As Thomas Keneally reminds us, 'we need to keep telling the stories.'

* * *

Up early on Wednesday morning and we collect Greg Hands (former Conservative Party chair under Rishi Sunak), at the station and drive into Moravia for a two-hour walk through a conifer forest, its floor covered by wild garlic and assorted white flowers. John James is leaving us tomorrow, and I sense the conversation will pivot away from music and nature towards politics. But while he's with us John is losing no opportunity, tutoring our ears to a green woodpecker, a greater spotted woodpecker and blackcaps. Trying hard as I do to identify the different birds, I fall short. Today's walk is perfection, a soft carpeted path to walk on, a gentle downhill descent, the air full of the scent of pine and wildflowers, and not a car to be heard. I'm trying not to think about my heart and how it has affected me. The procedure to insert a stent into the narrowed artery near my heart has been fixed for ten days after my return. Till then, 'be sensible' is the advice I've been given, which I am translating as 15 kilometres plus a day, and not racing on as I am wont to do. The good news is that, after the op, I'll be back to full strength, able to positively zip along the final stretch into Poland and on to Auschwitz, covering 30 kilometres a day and more, as I did in 2021. It'll be a relief to be back to normal, not having to ingest so many pills each day nor to carry the dreaded GTN spray in my pocket, 'in case'. As I meticulously lay out my colourful pills each morning before breakfast, I think of Joanna, who was so stoical and uncomplaining as she did the same, despite her own journey having only one destination. Thinking of the letters she left behind for us, I wrote to Sarah and placed it in my bedside drawer before leaving home three days ago. Overdramatic? Perhaps. But I cannot forget the specialist saying that if I do have a heart attack, I might not recover because of where the blockage is.

Being sensible then, with measured pace, I walk down with John and Greg into yet another stunning town, Moravská Třebová, with its perfect market square again delightfully free of Costa, Domino's and Starbucks. Mid square stands a distinctive memorial to the great plague of 1713–15. Those who succumbed to the bubonic plague suffered terribly – what am I complaining about? The region's last major epidemic of the Black Death (a disease that had only recently acquired that moniker) had arrived in the town along the trade routes from the east, transmitted by rats' fleas and caught by a third or more of the population here. As with the Great Fire of London following the Great Plague, a short while after the Black Death finally left the town, a fire ravaged parts of it. I think of the suffering endured by those in the towns through which I have walked, plague, fire, war and famine, and I wonder how much I really understand about the lives of the people who lived in the succession of now gentrified squares and communities through which we are passing.

We sit down in a bakery, spotlessly clean, friendly staff, freshly cooked food. We discuss ethnic diversity: I've only seen white faces since I left Prague. Paul talks about the Roma whose population, some 2 per cent of the country's total but with higher concentrations in Moravia, have never enjoyed a high status in the country. Now that barely any Jews live in the country, have the Roma become the new Jews, we wonder? Nationalism is certainly on the rise. Some nine parties are contesting the general election in early October, Greg says, covering all shades of the political spectrum. The centre parties are being challenged by the right, notably the Slovak-born Andrej Babiš's ANO party and Japanese-born Tomio Okamura's Freedom and Direct Democracy party. As one seasoned Czech watcher to whom I spoke sardonically commented, 'We import everything in Czechia, even our racists.'

Paul drops us at the Morava river, which flows due south from its source in the mountainous border with Poland. The river is narrow on this stretch, but on its 350-kilometre journey it goes on to form the Czech-Slovak and, later, the Austrian-Slovak borders (hence forming part of the Iron Curtain during the Cold War) before joining the Danube near Bratislava. We arrive in Olomouc on foot to rain and make straight for the Hotel Arigone, one of the plushest of the walk: there's a film festival in town so we've had to trade up to find beds. The city might have lost its place to Brno as Moravia's capital after being sacked in the Thirty Years War, but as is already obvious from walking around the streets, this is a place very conscious of its importance in history. Famously, it was here in 1848 that the enfeebled Emperor Ferdinand I abdicated in favour of eighteen-year-old Franz Joseph I, the figure who held the reins of Central Europe in the mid- and late nineteenth century, whose heir's assassination in Sarajevo sparked the First World War. Franz Joseph's sixty-eight-year reign spluttered on till his death at Vienna's Schönbrunn Palace in November 1916. Less than two years later, the 600-year-old Habsburg Empire ceased to exist.

I thought I'd left behind me all figures connected with another assassination, Heydrich's. But I hadn't reckoned with one of that story's greatest heroes; Olomouc's own Vladimír Petřek. Born in the city in 1908, he developed a strongly pacifist stance in response to the rise of fascism. After he became ordained as an Orthodox priest, he was attached to Saints Cyril and Methodius in Prague, helping Jews and others by creating false baptism certificates to evade Nazi Race Laws, and giving succour to the resistance movement.[22] He was one of those responsible for Gabčík and Kubiš hiding in the church crypt. After their deaths he was arrested and repeatedly tortured. Throughout the ordeal he clung to his faith and belief in non-violence, despite the most savage imaginable physical and mental torment, till the Gestapo despaired of him telling them anything of value and executed him on 5 September 1942.[23] What did Petřek and other figures of light like him know that the multitude who claimed they were 'acting on instructions' did not? They knew this: that there is a higher authority and force than a government of the day which holds power illegitimately and uses violence as an everyday tool. I cling to this thought. More prosaically, it showed the Gestapo that no matter how intense the torture, it could not be depended upon to result in reliable truth, its value lying as much in the fear it engendered.

Greg and I bid farewell in the morning to John and drive to Střeň to start the walk. Conversation in the car is about how rapidly, after nearly six years of fighting, the end came. German and Italian fascist forces in Italy surrendered to the Allies on 29 April 1945 at Caserta. Five days later, German forces in the Netherlands, in north-west Germany and in Denmark surrendered at Lüneburg Heath south of Hamburg to Field Marshal Montgomery. Why then, we ask, does the memorial to the Soviet liberation we see at Střeň have the date '9 May 1945', one day exactly after VE Day on 8 May? The monument

Vladimír Petřek knew what his torturers and executioners did not: there is higher authority and truth than the Nazi philosophy.

itself, one of many sprinkled liberally across the country, consists of a grey marbled plinth with a vertical white block above it of some 3 metres boasting a five-pointed Soviet gold star near the top. Different time zones I discover were the diplomatic explanation given for the two different victory days. General Alfred Jodl had signed the Act of Military Surrender on behalf of Germany in the early hours of 7 May at Supreme Headquarters Allied Expeditionary Force in Reims. That document stated that the war would officially end at 23:01 the following evening, 8 May. That was the equivalent of 01:01 on 9 May, Moscow time.

But the real answer is that the Soviets were resentful and suspicious of the treaty being signed at Reims. Why, Stalin asked, was the surrender being signed in the West's zone in France, given the disproportionately large Soviet contribution to the victory? Thus, he demanded a second surrender treaty be signed, but this time in the Eastern zone in Berlin, with Marshal Georgy Zhukov, hero of Leningrad, Stalingrad and Kursk, signing for the Soviet Union and Field Marshal Wilhelm Keitel for Germany. This subsequent signing thus placed the spotlight firmly and squarely on the Soviet Union, 'Victory Day' from that point on being celebrated on 9 May, even if the cessation of hostilities had happened twenty-four hours before as agreed at Reims. Proof if any were needed that long before the Cold War officially began, the seeds were sprouting even as the ink was drying on the documents of surrender.

We start walking due south and in no time are at the tiny village of Lhota Nad Moravou, birthplace of student hero Jan Opletal. Born on New Year's Day 1915 to a family with seven older sisters, he studied Medicine at Charles University from 1936. Indignant at the annexation of the Sudetenland, he was one of 100,000 who protested against it in Prague on the twenty-first anniversary of the foundation of their country on 28 October 1939. Student blood was up and they were ready to challenge the Nazi regime head on. Protesters covered memorials

Jan Opletal was mown down by German bullets on 11 November 1939.

in Wenceslas and Old Town squares in symbolic red, white and blue flowers, the colours of the Czech flag. As darkness fell, they lit candles and chanted for the Germans to leave. The German police ran out of patience and started shooting indiscriminately, one bullet hitting Opletal in his chest in Žitná Street.[24]

He died in hospital on 11 November, the twenty-first anniversary of Armistice Day ending the First World War. Arrangements were made for his coffin to be sent back to Moravia, but, before it left, a funeral was to be held in Prague, with black flags flying from the windows of university dormitories. Large crowds who turned up to see the coffin transported to the station burst into the Czech national anthem, and protesters shouted out again for Hitler and the Germans to leave their country. News travelled fast, and anti-Nazi demonstrations sprung up in other large Czech towns, including Ostrava and Pilsen. Hitler, never able to tolerate dissent, felt threatened by the students and was apoplectic. He demanded an uncompromising and brutal response. Two days later, German soldiers stormed all university dormitories in Prague and across the country, beating up and arresting thousands of students, with many sent to prison. Nine student leaders were executed on 17 November, the first deaths without trial of the occupation, and over 1,000 were sent to Sachsenhausen. Czech universities were shut, and to rub in the humiliation, the Prague Faculty of Law building was repurposed as an SS barracks. On 2 December, the Secretary of State for Bohemia Karl Frank told the Czechs, 'Whoever is not with us is against us, and whoever is against us will be ground to pieces.'[25] It was on the 50th anniversary of Jan Opletal's death that students protested in November 1989 in Prague, to precipitate the Velvet Revolution.

The week before leaving London, I was on the BBC's *Newsnight* to discuss Trump's attacks on universities, specifically his threat to stop Harvard University enrolling overseas students unless it handed over details about them.[26] To even the most sober of academics, it is no longer absurd to highlight some parallels between Hitler and Trump: in April 2025, distinguished Third Reich scholar Richard J. Evans thus added to the apprehensions about the above threats to democracy by drawing attention to both men's systematic dismemberment of democracy and its institutions in their countries.[27] Both leaders are distrustful of objective truth, diversity and challenge in any form, he writes. Parallels can be drawn too between Hitler's chief propagandist Goebbels and Trump's one-time chief adviser Elon Musk, who retweeted a claim that 'Stalin, Mao and Hitler didn't murder millions of people. Their public sector workers did', before deleting it.[28] But whereas Goebbels 'seems to have known that he was lying… Trump doesn't appear to understand the difference between truth and fiction.'[29] Both men cosied up to the leader of the Soviet Union/Russia. But while Hitler always despised and played Stalin, as Putin does Trump, the US president for long has seemed mesmerized by him, susceptible to his charm and flattery as when the Russian leader gave Trump a painting of him punching the air after the failed assassination attempt.

Fiona Hill, who served on the National Security Council in Trump's first administration, has written that Trump is 'terrified' of Putin and the threat of him unleashing nuclear war, and underestimates the much more insidious game Putin is playing of destabilization and corrosion.[30] Vast differences remain, of course, between the two leaders, not least in psychology and style: Hitler was a psychopath and intentional murderer, which Trump is not; Hitler wanted a vast state, Trump a minimalist one. Hitler wanted war: Trump arguably peace. Neither though would have governed if a majority of people in Germany and America, for reasons of admiration, personal gain or fear, hadn't subordinated their qualms and stayed silent.

All night, an intense thunderstorm lit up the windows. In the morning, I go out on the balcony and inhale the newly minted air. My attention is drawn to a garment hanging over the balcony rails. My eighty-wash insect-proof shirt, which I had forgotten to bring in last night, is dripping wet. Ten minutes of energetic use of the hair drier (Sarah would have been proud) does the job nicely, and I'm only a little late for breakfast, albeit I am discreetly informed later, smelling odd. This morning we walk along the River Bečva, a tributary of the Morava, into Přerov, revelling in the blossom and tulips along its banks. The subject of my next prime minister book is Rishi Sunak, who Greg knows well. After writing about his two predecessors, Johnson and Truss, I'm relieved to be writing about a highly intelligent PM serious about the job and who at least tried to do the right thing. We discuss whether Sunak achieved as much as he might have done given the weakness of his 'tail-end' position after 12 years of Tory (mis)rule – jury out; whether he mishandled the timing of the early general election – Greg thinks he did; and whether Starmer's manifest problems since taking office in July 2024 with a fresh mandate reflect favourably on Sunak's efforts – we think they do.

As we sit down for lunch in Přerov's Horní Náměstí (Upper Square) with its typical Renaissance and Baroque buildings, Greg is on a mission. Postcards. He emerges from a shop in a state of some excitement with several in hand, plus stamps. It is the first postcard I've written this century, and I have forgotten exactly how to set out the address and text. Sarah is as surprised the following week to see the postcard on our doormat, the first she has received this century too. Přerov's proudest son Jan Comenius would have approved of Greg's campaign. The seventeenth-century thinker, though largely unknown today (outside of the Czech Republic), is considered the father of modern universal education, at least until in the late twentieth century when exams became the overarching objective of all schools. Comenius pioneered education for all the young regardless of means, lifelong learning rather than memory and recall, and education of the heart and the hand as well as just the head. Well, as AI at rattling speed infiltrates every aspect of education, Comenius, we need you to remind us that human, not machine, intelligence, and human empathy and agency must be at the heart of every good school and university. He travelled widely in Central and Northern Europe, and during the 1640s supposedly turned down the presidency of the newly founded Harvard University, not because of any disapproval by Trump's New World predecessors of foreign intellectuals with radical ideas coming to the country, but to continue his work in the Old.[31]

Přerov made world news briefly on 1 May 1945. With the victorious Red Army approaching from the east it became the first Czech city to rise up against the Germans. Quickly and brutally suppressed by the Nazis on the day, the uprising sparked a series of others across the country, culminating in the Prague Uprising four days later.[32] A darker story about Přerov must be told as well. Known as the Švédské Šance massacre of 18–19 June 1945, 265 Carpathian Germans, including 74 children, were bundled off their train, marched up to the hills, forced to hand over their valuables and undress and were then executed by

Czech partisans.[33] Did none of them wonder in their frenzy whether these terrified civilians deserved this fate, and whether the cycle of violence needed to be perpetuated now that the war was over? The story was suppressed until after the fall of Communism in 1989 that ushered in, under Havel, a new spirit of openness and reconciliation. It is in its way as shocking as Lidice and Ležáky.

We finish the day with an 8-kilometre walk. Paul may have read Chemistry at university but he's really fired up by history: even his dissertation on medieval chemistry was historical, poring over musty volumes in the Bodleian Library in Oxford. The Romans are his first love: as we walk beside the Oder, he expands on how the lands to the south of us saw constant fighting in the second century AD between the Romans and Germanic tribes striving to protect their homelands, in the so-called Marcomannic Wars. The opening scenes of the film *Gladiator* (2000) he tells us, based on the final campaigns of Emperor Marcus Aurelius, took place there, though the film was shot in woods near Farnham, Surrey. We finish the day in Nový Jičín, voted as having the country's best town square in 2015, providing a stunning memory of what will be the last square in an extraordinary sequence that makes me wonder why so few British tourists come. If they did, they would discover the secret of establishing good and attractive communal spaces.

We set off from here on Saturday 27 April, the final day of the walk, much of it along the Oder. All is quiet and peaceful on its banks, but not in the world again at large. Pakistan and India are teetering on the brink of war after a deadly terrorist attack in Kashmir; and Russia claims it has regained full control of the Kursk area from Ukraine. It sparks conversation about the large number of Ukrainians who have left their country since war broke out in 2022, forming now the largest national minority in the Czech Republic, roughly four out of five are refugees, the remainder long-term residents and workers. But they are not integrating well, which could create problems in the long term, for all their being more accepted than the Roma.

We finish the day at the First Czech Tank Brigade monument, commemorating their achievement as the first to cross the River Ostravice into the German stronghold of Ostrava, on 30 April 1945, the day Hitler died. An understated stone monument with gold lettering, it was put up on the sixtieth anniversary in 2005. This leg is thus concluding with a bang, with the largest and bloodiest battle ever to have taken place on Czech soil, the Battles of Opava and Ostrava from 10 March to 5 May. Virtually unknown in Britain, these battles saw nearly half a million combatants, with very high casualties.

Ostrava had been an insignificant Moravian border town, a poor cousin of Olomouc, till the early nineteenth century when the discovery of extensive coalfields right underneath it led to it becoming a bonanza town bursting with coal production, pig iron and steel factories, prompting rapid urban expansion.[34] Together with the adjacent railway junction town of Bohumín, it became of huge strategic interest to the Czechs, the Poles and, from the late 1930s, the Germans. Hence, in the face of the advancing Red Army in early 1945, the German high command decided they had to hold Ostrava, vital they believed to their war production, whatever the cost. If Ostrava fell, not wholly unlike Ypres in the First World War, some asserted it would lead to strategic disaster: in this case, the road to Prague would be opened up.

But by the time the Red Army began to penetrate Ostrava however, the Reich was already being torn apart. Nothing the industrial works produced reached Germany any more due to the shattered railways. Few commanders around Hitler worried any more about Bohemia and Moravia when Russian soldiers could see Berlin's Reichstag in their gunsights. By then, Ostrava was something of a sideshow. But the Germans fought bitterly for the city nonetheless.[35]

But for one group of men, stepping on Moravia's soil for the first time in over five years, it was very far from a sideshow. Vital to the Soviet forces were the little-known 1st Czechoslovak Army Corps, made up of volunteers who for reasons of ideology, patriotism or vengeance against the German occupation chose to fight with the Red Army. They had proved themselves in some of the hardest battles, including in Kharkiv and the liberation of Kyiv in 1943. Then from early March 1945, in conjunction with the Soviets' advance on Berlin, they closed in on Ostrava from the north. Progress initially was slow, the Red Army bogged down in the mud against strongly fortified German defences. But by late April, they advanced into the city, followed by intense street-to-street fighting, until the city's fall on 30 April. The entire offensive, despite its lateness in the war and strategic irrelevance, cost each side horrifically over 100,000 casualties, and left the region devastated.

We enter the town and seek out monuments erected by the Soviets during the Cold War, and see the graphic Red Army Statue, bearing the words in both Russian and Czech:

ETERNAL GLORY TO THE
HEROES WHO FELL IN THE
FIGHT FOR FREEDOM AND INDEPENDENCE
OF THE SOVIET UNION.
GLORY TO THE
RED ARMY, THE LIBERATOR OF CZECHOSLOVAKIA
FROM THE YOKE OF THE GERMAN-FASCIST
OCCUPIERS.

The message that the Soviets, not the West, were the liberators of Czechoslovakia was to ring down the decades. It was those Czechs who fought for the Red Army who would flourish in the post-1948 order, not the men who fought in British uniforms.

We walk along the Ostravice which joins the Oder in the city's north-eastern suburbs to the Memorial of the 1st Czech Independent Tank Brigade on the far bank. This tells a very different history, of Czech heroism in the liberation of their own country. The T-34 tank

People in Ostrava greet the tanks of the Red Army in May 1945.

bestriding the monument in front of a bridge into the town played a key part in the battle. So the story goes, the 1st Tank Brigade was supplied with sixty-five new tanks when it began the offensive. By the end of the Battle of Ostrava, only seven or eight remained in action (out of which only three advanced into Prague on its liberation).[36]

The chapter closes with two figures of light, a seasoned warrior whose life exemplifies the Czech spirit at its best, and a teenager caught up in the fighting. Both lives highlight the evils of the bear with which the chapter opened. Josef Buršík was one of the senior commanders of the Czechoslovaks fighting in Ostrava. His own tank had been awarded the moniker 'Žižka' in 1943, named after the legendary Hussite general 'never defeated by anyone.'[37] Born in Bohemia in 1911, Buršík fled, like so many defiant Czechs, to Poland, where he fought the Germans in 1939, and was then captured by Soviet forces and interned. But, when the Germans invaded the Soviet Union, he got another chance. He promptly joined the 1st Czech Independent Brigade of the Red Army, rising through the ranks to command its second battalion. He distinguished himself with such conspicuous bravery that he was awarded

Josef Buršík in 1944, wearing his Hero of the Soviet Union medal on the right.

the title 'Hero of the Soviet Union', one of the first non-Soviet citizens to receive this highest of military honours in the country.[38]

Post-war, Buršík, never a Communist like so many who fled east, fell out of favour with the new pro-Soviet regime in Prague after 1948. He was arrested in the Stalinist purges of 1949, and imprisoned for ten years after a show trial. Aided by sympathizers, he escaped the following year on a motorbike while under guard in a hospital in Olomouc, and then stole across the border into West Germany, and on to Britain, where in 1963 his daughters joined him.[39] He moved to Northampton, where he lived quietly supporting Czech and Slovak causes, advocating for democracy and exposing Communist crimes. Back in Czechoslovakia, his name was erased and not included in the official history of the war.[40] In 1965 came his proudest moment when he was invited to walk, bedecked in medals, in Winston Churchill's funeral procession.[41]

He had high hopes of the Prague Spring in 1968, and Czechoslovakia's moderate new President Ludvík Svoboda, Buršík's former wartime commander and comrade.[42] But following the Soviet tanks rolling into Prague, he returned his war medals to the Soviets in protest.[43] After the fall of Communism, he was rehabilitated, showered with honours, and is today regarded as one of the greatest military heroes in Czech history. When he died in Northampton in June 2002, he was buried with full military honours, and streets and schools have been named after him in the Czech Republic.

His grandson, also called Josef Bursik, is a professional footballer and played several times in goal for England Under-21s, his performance

Photograph of teenage Štěrbová, emblematic of the millions of children and adolescents traumatised by the war.

never more impressive than in a famous victory in June 2022 over his grandfather's beloved country.[44]

A less happy story is that of Jarmila Štěrbová, whose experience of the battle at a young age of 15 scarred her for life. 'Suddenly at night the shooting started and lasted till morning... I saw dead soldiers lying next to each other in the garden... women... their corpses, piled high on the flatbed trucks.' As the fighting intensified, the family had to hide as their home was seized and burned. 'My mother feared the Germans would shoot us. The experience, night after night, so affected [me] that I don't think I'll be able to recover my nerves till the day I die.'[45]

After 1948, she struggled to attend university because of her religious faith and political affiliations. She later worked as an engineer and as a veterinary researcher. But because neither she nor her husband joined the Communist Party, their son experienced difficulties making progress in his education and career, as had they.

The apprehensions in the Czech Republic, as across Eastern Europe, about the bear's intentions under Putin have become, as I prepare to exit the country, frighteningly and vividly clear. Far clearer indeed than when I entered it talking to the father and daughter in row 17 just a few weeks ago.

10

Silesia, Poland, Auschwitz

Chapter 10
Silesia, Poland, Auschwitz

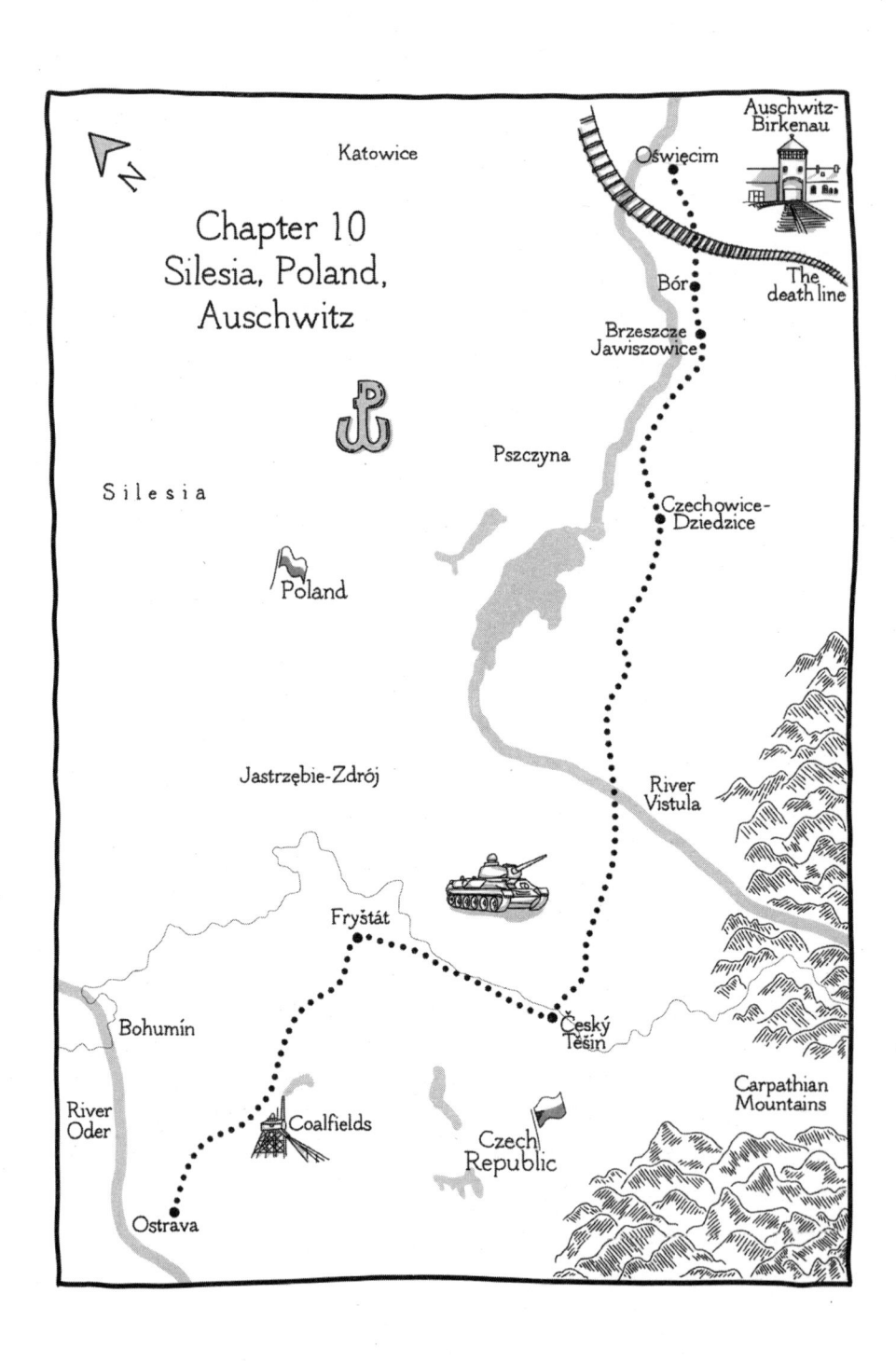

'We're waiting for the Russians to attack us.' The man next to me smelling strongly of tobacco on the late evening London to Kraków flight is emphatic. I peer anxiously out of the window into the dark but see nothing troubling. 'Really, how, when?' I ask, trying not to sound alarmed. Sitting on my other side is a coughing Sarah. She is deep into Percival Everett's *James*, set in America's Antebellum South, but she looks up over her glasses to listen to his thoughts on the Antebellum North. 'They'll attack us from Belarus,' he says, 'and soon, any day, I don't know.' 'With tanks?' 'They've *already* begun to attack,' he replies, 'cyber, misinformation, drones, missiles, balloons… It's happening now.' He pauses to study my reaction. 'We closed down their consulate in Kraków two weeks ago now we have proof they torched our shopping mall in Warsaw.' Intelligence sources refer to these as 'grey attacks', he says, a pattern of Russia probing and undermining Eastern European countries that falls short of triggering NATO's threshold for counterattacks.

My companion is a middle-aged professional returning to his native Kraków with his wife and children after a weekend in London to hear Eric Clapton at the Royal Albert Hall. Planes like trains have become an unexpected research adjunct for this book. He tells me how his country's 400-kilometre border with Belarus has been drastically strengthened: 'Five years ago, there was just a rusting fence to stop the Russian forces marching straight in.' Poles detest the Russians, and can't forgive the West for abandoning them to forty-five years of Soviet occupation after 1945, he declares. Betrayal is very strongly felt among Poles, I am learning, as it was for Czechs: for them, it was Munich; for Poles, it is the Yalta Conference, the finger of blame pointing squarely at Roosevelt for selling them out to the Soviets rather than at the British. But we are still at fault, he says with anger in his voice. 'Why did Britain declare war on Germany in 1939 to protect us, only to abandon us in 1945 to the Soviets?' Sensing raw emotion rising as we descend to land, I change the subject back to Clapton. Did he play 'Let It Grow'? 'For sure: it was his best number,' he retorts. Harmony is restored. The song was the soundtrack to my final year at university. The plane has now docked at the terminal. As we stand up, we sing the lyrics together: 'Standing at the crossroads, trying to read the signs…' We laugh at our rendition. 'We won't see his like again,' he calls back at me, as he disappears down the aisle, followed by his embarrassed children.

* * *

Sarah and I are on half term and we are returning for the final leg, the journey from Ostrava and the north-eastern tip of the Czech Republic to Auschwitz in south-eastern Poland. I'd been eagerly anticipating walking every single step of the 100 kilometres, with the heart problem that had dogged the last half of my pilgrimage since Flossenbürg at last sorted. But the hospital procedure two weeks before hadn't gone to plan. 'I'm very sorry. A stent isn't going to work for you,' the cardiologist announced to his drowsy patient having completed a lot of prodding around in my arteries. I hope he'll say I don't need to have one at all. But he swiftly dismisses the idea. 'I'm afraid it looks like it'll need a rethink.' My head reels and it takes several moments to sink in. Denial is my immediate reaction before I launch into telling him about the comparison of my arteries to the frozen River Elbe: 'I just need the ice on either side to melt and the flow will be back to normal…' He listens sympathetically to the jabber but is thinking it's the drugs talking. When he comes to see me later, I ask him what I can do. Very gently he explains the procedure hasn't worked, it doesn't always, and I'll have to make the most of life while awaiting a more serious heart bypass operation. I refuse to get down about it, and I know many have it far worse; but I can't pretend it's not disappointing. Sarah masks her concern, and is encouraging as ever as we talk through how to manage things. I am not giving up on the walk, not now, not after all the setbacks, even though it will mean remaining on half-power, walking 20 kilometres maximum a day.

One last time we are to be met at Ostrava station by Paul Antrobus, who I have alerted to the heart news and who's amended our itinerary accordingly. As our train speeds south through the Polish countryside, I take stock.

I have known all along that this final leg will be the most significant of the ten, my final opportunity to encounter remarkable people and my last chance to make sense of the enterprise that I never anticipated lasting two years. How will it feel when, or if, I make it all the way to the gates of Auschwitz? I am determined that nothing will stop me reaching it, however I might feel physically, and nothing will impede me drawing lessons from the figures of light. With these thoughts uppermost in my mind, our merry band of three sets off.

We marvel at how Ostrava has been regenerated: the once magisterial iron and steel factory has morphed into the spanking new Industrial Museum, one of the most popular visitor attractions in the country outside of Prague, a triumph of imagination and will. Our route traces the Oder one last time before it curls up north to its source in the mountainous area near the Polish border. Here is another river of great beauty that saw much ugliness in the war. Further downstream, the retreating German army set up defences along its banks in April 1945 in one final attempt to stop the Red Army reaching Berlin. Mass civilian death, rape and looting were committed by Soviet forces, while in the months that followed, German civilians in the areas east of the river were brutally abused and expelled. We then walk along the placid Olše, an Oder tributary, until we arrive at Fryštát, a town whose residents have been very far from free through history in these most liminal lands of Central Europe. We are still in Czech Silesia, where people speak Czech, or Lach, a dialect of Czech with altered vowels and similarities to Polish. Part of Poland until the fourteenth century, it then passed gradually to Bohemia. Subsequently, it became a ping-pong state, with Prussia one of several claimants until, in 1918, it bonded with Bohemia, Moravia, Slovakia and Carpathian Ruthenia to form the proud new Czechoslovakia. We have coffee in the main square brought to us by a chatty Ukrainian, newly arrived in the country, pleased to be here and in work. Paul suggests Ukrainians may be more welcome in this cosmopolitan, liberal part of the country than elsewhere.

On we press to the border town of Český Těšín. Known under the Austro-Hungarian Empire till 1918 by the Germanized name Teschen, it was renowned for its cultural diversity, with thriving German, Polish, Jewish, Hungarian and Czech populations. The abrupt end of the Empire saw local Czech and Polish administrations laying furious claim to the town and the wider region. A division on ethnic grounds was proposed but broke down when the vital railway hub fatally fell into the designated Polish zone, which provoked the outbreak of fighting in January 1919 in the so-called Polish-Czech War. The Czechs made significant inroads into Poland, benefitting from the latter being distracted by a conflict further east with the short-lived West Ukrainian People's Republic. But the victorious powers in the First World War, the US, Britain and France, demanded the fighting cease, and at the Spa Conference of July 1920, they divided the Czech town of Český Těšín off from the Polish town of Cieszyn on the east bank of the Olše. Polish resentment was simmering and, after the annexation of the Sudetenland in 1938, its soldiers promptly seized the areas back, only to lose them to Germany in September 1939. We walk from the Czech to the Polish town over the Friendship Bridge, so named when both countries joined the European

The demarcation line on the Friendship Bridge across the Olše, with Poland to the left and the Czech Republic to the right.

Union in 2004; but the structures at either end still bear the hallmarks of this being an unfriendly and disputed frontier.

I am fascinated by frontiers and learned much from the brilliant book *Borderlines* by Lewis Baston.[1] As a boy I marvelled at how one could catch a direct train from Amsterdam to Poland, a land that seemed impossibly exotic and far away, and here I am having arrived on foot in the final country of the four on the walk. It is the one I know the least about, and I am charmed and intrigued as my journey through it proceeds. Like England, it emerged as a unified country in the tenth century and, like England again, it built a castle on a hill for the King to live in during the eleventh century, respectively at Windsor and at Wawel in Kraków (the capital till 1596, when Warsaw took the mantle). Poland's short-lived 'golden age' from the fifteenth century saw its language, identity and culture flourish. In the Battle of Grunwald in 1410, one of the biggest clashes in medieval Europe, the German Teutonic Order was defeated, the victory becoming a massive symbol of Polish pride and of triumph over foreign invaders. But the glory proved short-lived: the country subsequently lost its way and greedy neighbours pounced, with Prussia and Austria acquiring the parts of Poland nearest to them, while the lion's share went to the Russians. Even today, the once Tsarist domain is less industrialized and more rural than areas ruled by the Prussians and Austrians. The country became a battlefield again during the First World War, with all three of the old imperial powers that had so rudely carved it up – Russia, Austria and Germany – receiving their comeuppance in defeat and revolution. In 1918, after a vigorous lobbying campaign by Polish nationalists, the victorious Allies agreed to reconstitute the country.[2]

Polish celebrations were joyous and prolonged, but as in Czechoslovakia created at the same time, a country whose story so mirrors its own, its independence was to be short-lived. In March 1939, to deter further aggression by Hitler, Chamberlain pledged to support Poland were Hitler to invade. The Führer now faced the nightmare prospect of war on two fronts. So on 24 August, to shore up his eastern flank he engineered an agreement with Stalin, the so-called Molotov-Ribbentrop 'non-aggression' pact. Eight days later, after a series of alleged aggressions by Poles used to justify their invasion, German tanks rolled over the Polish border. On 3 September, Britain and France duly declared war on Germany. The first proper fighting of the Second World War in Europe thus took place in Poland, which saw spirited, but ultimately doomed, Polish defence. On 17 September, the Soviet Union invaded eastern Poland in line with a secret protocol of the Molotov-Ribbentrop pact, precipitating the total collapse of Polish forces.

Poles are ferociously and rightly proud of their bravery in the war. Virtually none of its units saw their colours fall into German hands, and over 100,000 of its soldiers fled via Hungary and Romania, or across the Baltic Sea, to serve with the Western Allies, with tens of thousands escaping eastwards to serve with the Red Army. Poles were to be conspicuous in all three British armed services, serving with the RAF in the Battle of Britain and the army at Monte Cassino in Italy, while at sea, the Polish destroyer *Piorun* took part in May 1941 in sinking the *Bismarck*, the pride of the German fleet, allegedly taunting the stricken battleship with the message, 'I am a Pole'.[3] All this belligerence was combined with a vigorous resistance movement that not only repeatedly hampered the Germans, but also passed on valuable intelligence to the Allies: one British estimate stated that 48 per cent of the 45,000 intelligence reports from occupied Europe during the war came from the Polish resistance.[4]

The Poles suffered proportionately more than any other country during the war. Some 6 million were killed, equivalent to 17 per cent of the country's pre-war population: in contrast, Britain lost just 1 per cent, France 1.5 per cent, Germany 8 per cent and even the USSR 'only' 13.7 per cent. Many of its principal cities including Warsaw were destroyed along with its national treasures. It was invaded by not one but two barbaric regimes under Hitler and Stalin, and it witnessed many of its brightest and best cynically slaughtered, as in the Katyn Massacre and the Warsaw Uprising. And then at the end of the war, after all this suffering, more bitterness. No liberation for the Poles as for France, which had promised with Britain to defend the country's freedom. But forty-four years as a Soviet puppet state.

The Polish government, only twenty-one years old, had been determined to survive. It never surrendered to the Germans in 1939, but slipped quietly out of the country to establish itself initially in Paris and then in Angers in Western France, before escaping a second time after the country fell in May 1940 to set up in London, one of no less than eight European governments-in-exile to operate from the British capital during the war. It fell out with Moscow over Katyn, refusing to accept its lie that the Nazis had been responsible for the murder of 22,000 Polish officers and intellectuals near Smolensk. Then after the war it declined to accept the legitimacy of the Soviet-controlled government in Warsaw. Not till the final end of Communist control did the government-in-exile return to Poland where it officially recognized the legitimacy of Lech Wałęsa, Poland's first post-Communist president, at a moving ceremony in Warsaw in December 1990. Anna Clunes, Britain's outgoing ambassador to Poland, tells me that the bodies of three post-war presidents of the government-in-exile who died in the UK were exhumed and returned to Poland during her time in November 2022, an illustration she says of the enduringly close relationship between the two countries.[5]

Carrying messages back and forth during the war from the government-in-exile in London to Poland was a member of the *Cichociemni* ('Silent Unseen'), Elżbieta Zawacka, known by her codename Zo, whose flawless German and blonde hair provided the perfect cover. On one trip in 1943, she travelled from Warsaw to London via Berlin, Spain and Gibraltar, with smuggled microfilms detailing German military secrets hidden in toothpaste, cigarette lighters and food. She was subsequently involved in the Warsaw Uprising, and in 1945 briefly joined the anti-Communist resistance. Remaining in the country after the war, she was arrested in 1951 by the Communist security service, tortured and sentenced to ten years in prison for treason and espionage. On her release, she remained in the country she had served all her life, devoted herself to scholarship and became a distinguished professor of adult education. She rejoiced in the end of the Soviet regime, and three years before her death in 2009 was promoted to the rank of brigadier general, only the second Polish woman to hold such a high rank.[6]

If Zawacka is one figure of light, Maria Krystyna Skarbek, also known as Christine Granville, is another, also a Polish agent trained by the British SOE. Characterized as 'Churchill's favourite spy' by his daughter Sarah and the 'bravest of the brave' by writer Alistair Horne, SOE colleague Vera Atkins described her as 'very brave, very attractive, but a loner and law unto herself'.[7] The first female agent to

Elżbieta Zawacka, left, and Maria Krystyna Skarbek, right.

be trained by the British to serve in the field, she became the longest-serving of all Britain's female wartime agents.[8] Indeed, her success encouraged the SOE to recruit more women to serve in Nazi-occupied Europe. Skarbek's most daring and celebrated exploit was securing the release of two SOE agents imprisoned in France on the verge of being executed. Using bribes, threats and her famous charm, she bamboozled the collaborator commander into letting them go.[9] Unlike Zawacka, however, she was unable to find her way after the war. Her Jewish identity and the hostile Soviet regime disinclined her to return to Poland. So she moved to London but found it hard to settle, and worked as a waitress, a telephone operator and a ship steward. She was beginning to sink long before her luck and guile, which had served her so well in the war, deserted her. This woman of unimaginable bravery who had come through repeated danger met her end when stabbed to death in a shady Earl's Court hotel by a spurned lover who was subsequently found guilty and hanged. When the hotel was purchased by new owners in 1971, her perfectly preserved luggage was found hidden away in a storeroom. When prised open, it revealed her most precious possessions: her wartime medals and SOE dagger.[10]

Zawacka's mother was Jewish, and she was born into a country that has not always been at ease with its Jewish population. Many Poles of course are not antisemitic: the government-in-exile from 1942, for example, was conspicuous in highlighting the emerging evidence about the death camps, and it supported the clandestine Żegota movement to protect Jews in the country. Ninety per cent of the county's 3 million Jews were murdered by the Nazis in the Holocaust. Helping Jews was punishable by execution, not just of the individual helper but their entire family. Yet Poland nevertheless has the highest number of 'Righteous Among the Nations' designations for saving Jewish lives. But for others, antisemitism was never far below the surface. Many Poles were complicit in betraying and even murdering Jews themselves.

International attention on the post-war plight of Poland's Jews was alerted by the Kielce pogrom in July 1946, in which forty-two Jews were murdered in a refugee centre in the city, the savagery intended to send a clear message to other Jews thinking of returning to the country and reclaiming their property; the Communist government then blamed the murders on agents of the government-in-exile.[11] By 1947, only 100,000 Jews remained in the country, and most of them left subsequently to escape the anti-Jewish Communist regime, largely to Israel. The issue is very much alive today. As I walk through Poland, the lanes and roads are covered with posters for the presidential elections. One of the candidates, Grzegorz Braun of the ultranationalist KKP party, disrupted a Holocaust lecture in 2023, shouting abuse and smashing up equipment before leaving. The following year, in a conspicuously dark act, he used a fire extinguisher to put out menorah candles at a Chanukah ceremony.[12] A fringe candidate? Sadly not. Braun came fourth in the first round of the presidential election in

May 2025, expressing views shared by some other candidates, and millions of Poles.

To understand more about the contradictions in contemporary Poland I turn to my friend the author Edward Lucas. 'The Poles have an ingrained sense of betrayal, chiefly that Western allies betrayed them to the Soviets at Yalta in 1945,' he confirms, 'but – despite all the resulting repression and privation – the country did develop under Communist rule, which forcibly urbanized and industrialized the economy and also educated the population. This enabled Poland to exploit the opportunities of post-1989 opening up and of EU membership from 2004. It's the only European country that has had no recession since 1992.' Putin, he says, is deeply troubled by Poland's success, as well as its role as the hub for aid and supplies for Kyiv. 'That's why the proxy war is under way, with sabotage and cyber attacks.' The victory in the presidential election of right-winger Karol Nawrocki in June 2025, he says, continues the country's crippling political polarization, which enables Russian manipulation and divide-and-rule tactics.

Ben Helfgott, aged fifteen, and his twelve-year-old cousin Gienek Klein only wanted, like other Jewish children after the war, to return home, which, in their case, was near the Polish town of Piotrków. His grandfather, who had been murdered in 1942, appeared to him in a dream urging him to go back home; was he intimating to him, Ben wondered, that he might be reunited there with his family? Ben had been liberated from Terezín in May 1945; most of his family, apart from his sister Mala, had been murdered, in Treblinka. He and Gienek set off back to Poland full of hope. Their route took them across Czechoslovakia where sympathy, food and encouragement helped restore their spirits and health. Elated, they crossed the border by train on the mainline near where Sarah and I walked over the Freedom Bridge at Český Těšín, before they changed trains at the Polish junction town of Częstochowa. Two Polish police officers approached them: 'What are you doing here?' 'We are survivors from the concentration camps and we are returning to our hometown,' they responded. The men beckoned them to follow. After a while, Ben became suspicious, asking, 'Where are you taking us?' 'Shut your f....ing mouth, you f....ing Jew!' came the reply. It dawned on him that they were being taken away to be shot. Their fears were realized when the police took their pistols out, and ordered them to walk to the nearest wall. Ben pleaded with them: 'Haven't we suffered enough? Our common enemy is destroyed and the future is ours. Don't we speak the same language as you?' Eventually one said, 'Let's leave them. They are, after all, still young boys.' 'You can consider yourselves very lucky,' barked the other. 'We have killed many of your kind. You are the first ones we have left alive.' They then disappeared into the night. Ben, who had been close to death many times in the previous six years, had no inkling that danger would come from fellow Poles. 'I was stunned, hardly believing what I had just heard,' he later said of this incident. 'The Nazi cancer was removed but its tentacles were widespread and deeply rooted… I had experienced and witnessed so much cruelty and bestiality yet I refused to accept that man can be wicked.'[13]

They were among the tens of thousands of orphaned children whose return home was cruelly rebuffed: many being killed on their return by Poles. Ben was fortunate: he became one of the first of 300 children to be rehabilitated in Windermere in the Lake District, courtesy of the World Jewish Relief. As a young man, he threw his energy into work in the clothes business and into his chosen sport of weightlifting, representing Great Britain at the 1956 and 1960 Olympics. He lived a long and productive life, dedicating much of his time to community relations, Holocaust remembrance and to working for peace. I met him first when as a student, Rabbi Hugo Gryn asked me to interview survivors, and I was struck by his absence of bitterness and hatred, an absence that amply qualifies him for being a figure of light. Thus began a lifelong bond. I marvelled then, as I do now, how, as a mere child of nine when the Nazis marched into his hometown, and despite witnessing six years of unspeakable terror, violence and death in and out of camps, he was able to face life with such equanimity and affirmation. He rapidly became my go-to person to give talks about the Holocaust, which he did with so much compassion and humanity that even the most detached teenagers were won over. I loved his gentle spirit. We last saw him in his twilight years over Sunday lunch at home in Buckingham with his devoted wife Arza; shortly after, my own wife Joanna, to whom I was married by the Auschwitz survivor who had introduced us all, herself died. We talked at lunch about our visit to Treblinka in her final months when researching her last book. Joanna's family were Polish, another bond between her and Ben. His son Michael encapsulates his zest for life: 'Dad never held his experience at the end of the war against the Poles and always sought their friendship wherever possible. He recognized the importance of the centuries of flourishing Jewish life in Poland, and was very aware that so much abundance was brought to an end by the Nazis.'[14]

Ben aged 15 reclining front right at Windermere

We have reached the Vistula (Wisła in Polish)! It is the seventh and final river of this walk: more than half my journey has been spent on or near one of these magical rivers. The Vistula is a mere stream where Sarah and I are walking along its stripling banks, not wider than 30 metres and completely unnavigable by boat. But it continues to become the longest river in Poland and one of the mightiest in Europe. Yet it is entirely contained within Poland's national frontiers, from its source in the eastern Carpathian mountains to its mouth in Gdańsk Bay on the Baltic Sea. It flows through its three most important cities, Kraków, Warsaw and Gdańsk, tracing Polish history in a similar way that the Danube does Central European history. The river is central to Polish art, literature, music, folklore and trade.[15] At its commercial height in 1618, the year the fearful Thirty Years War broke out, over 300,000 tons of grain were being carried annually by ships along it and out into the Baltic; castles, towns, factories and palaces sprung up along its length.[16] As with the other six rivers, it has a dark history too, never blacker than during the Second World War. Auschwitz is situated at the confluence of the Vistula and the Soła, which flows straight past the camp; the ashes from cremated bodies at both Auschwitz I and Birkenau were dumped in them. It was on the east bank of the Vistula during the Warsaw Uprising that the Red Army cynically waited until the German forces had destroyed the Polish resistance before intervening. Finally, after the sadistic commander of Płaszów Camp, Amon Göth, was tried and hanged without displaying any remorse on 13 September 1946, his ashes were flung in the Vistula, his last miserable remains separated from the ashes of the innocent multitudes murdered under his command not just by time but in spirit and human worth by the width of the entire universe.

* * *

The day's walking over, we bid a fond farewell to Paul, without whose wisdom, generosity and practical help I would never have been able to negotiate my way across his adopted country of the Czech Republic. 'Why is it you always seem to come across people to help you?' Sarah asks rhetorically as we board the train at the Polish town of Czechowice-Dziedzice. Thirty kilometres beyond the Czech border and still just within Polish Silesia, it suffered terribly in the war. The Nazis set out systematically, as in other Polish towns, to extinguish social and cultural life, and to milk its inhabitants and resources of all their value to the Reich. The local population was deported to forced labour camps and subjected to appropriations, roundups and public executions. In 1942, the Germans established two forced labour camps; any Poles who accepted food through the barbed wire fences were shot. On 21 January 1945, surviving prisoners were massacred by the SS.[17] It is surprising then for Sarah and I to see two youths board our train wearing black t-shirts with loud fascist slogans – 'Action' – an ominous echo of the Nazis' 'Aktions'. On the journey to Kraków, where we will be staying, we pass by closed factories and industrial plants daubed with graffiti, a stark contrast to the flourishing overall economy, trumpeted this very week on the front cover of the *Economist*.

Kraków is Poland's, and one of Europe's, jewels. When Poland was reconstituted as a country in 1918, it was Kraków that best embodied the national spirit. It flourished in the interwar years, much like Berlin, Prague and Budapest, its panache and elegance celebrated across Europe. Its renown caught the attention of the Nazi hierarchy who marked it down as their future capital in the east. In the process, its Polish and Jewish history were to be erased, and all Poles and Jews were to be expelled. Its streets and place names were to be Germanized, and a new history written of Kraków as a *German* town. Entrusted with this heavy responsibility was to be Hitler's lawyer, Hans Frank, offered the job of Governor-General of the central chunk of what was once Poland, while the Third Reich directly ruled territory to the west, and the Soviet Union to the east. The brief given him by Hitler in Berlin on 12 October 1939 was to make this portion of Poland 'a colony of exploitation', without legal constraint or mercy.[18] From his base in the Royal Wawel Castle, Frank began his task, the joyful fulfilment of his career's ambition, without a blink.

In October 1940 at the end of his first year, he travelled back to Berlin to dine with Hitler in his private apartment. According to the record made by Martin Bormann, the Führer's private secretary, Frank told him, 'The Jews in Warsaw and other cities were now locked up in the ghettos and Kraków would very shortly be cleared of them.'[19] Hitler was cheered by the progress. The Governor-General returned to Wawel from Berlin with an extra spring in his step. 'The winter here will be a hard winter,' he declared in a motivational speech to his troops at the end of the year. 'If there is no bread for the Poles, there should be no complaints… make short work of the Jews. What a pleasure, finally, for once to be able to tackle the Jewish race physically. The more that die the better.'[20] Not that Hans Frank lacked compassion: in his Christmas message to his troops in December 1941, he implored them to be mindful

Newly arrived Hans Frank in Krakow

about their worried families back at home who will be thinking, 'my God, there he sits in Poland where there are so many lice and Jews, perhaps he is hungry and cold, perhaps he's afraid to write.' But you can reassure them, he told them, that he had the problem under control: 'Of course, I could not eliminate all lice and Jews in only one year's time. But in the course of time, and above all, if you help me, this end will be attained.'[21] Sarah and I read these chilling words in the haunting Schindler museum, opened in his original factory building in 2010. Still reeling, we catch a taxi back to our hotel, the driver pointing out as we do so the perimeter of the ghetto in Kraków's southern suburb of Podgórze, chosen as a location by the Nazis because it was secluded on the far side of the Vistula, and they didn't want to squander the Jewish quarter of Kazimierz by erecting it there, which was on valuable land close to the city centre. The ghetto walls were built with arches at the top, in conscious mockery of Jewish gravestones, giving the message to those inside that they were already dead.[22] Our driver shows us the spot where the women and children were gunned down on 13–14 March 1943 when the ghetto was liquidated, the soldiers' spirits fired up by their historic mission and duty.[23]

The Jewish resistance was determined not to go down without a fight and showed exceptional bravery despite minimal resources. On 22 December 1942, sensing their end was near, they put up anti-Nazi posters and Polish flags, partly to deflect blame towards the Polish resistance rather than the Jews. Then, at 7 p.m. they attacked three cafés frequented by German soldiers with explosives, finishing by lobbing a hand grenade into the busy Cyganeria café where high-ranking German officers could regularly be found. Some ten Germans were killed in the operation, with many more wounded.[24] These acts showed that some kind of armed resistance was possible, and improvised ghetto uprisings later followed in Warsaw in April and Białystok in August 1943.

So many remarkable people perished in the Kraków ghetto, mothers, rabbis, teachers, fighters, doctors, their goodness, bravery and humanity lost forever. The curse of the historian down the ages is that we can only write from what is left behind, which is why archives and records matter so much. Tadeusz Pankiewicz is a rare Kraków ghetto figure whose story *was* recorded. A Polish Catholic pharmacist, he refused to relocate his shop from the middle of the ghetto after it was erected in March 1941. The only pharmacy allowed by the Germans to continue its operation inside, he was also the only non-Jewish male permitted to live and work within its tombstone walls. The Nazis thought he would be harmless. They could not have been more wrong: this wily apothecary dispensed not just drugs, bandages and medication, but food, tools and correspondence, helping to improve the quality of life in the ghetto, even if only marginally.[25] His shop, Apteka pod Orłem ('The Eagle Pharmacy'), became a vital intelligence centre and a precious link to the outside world, in which he was helped by many including courier Irena Droździkowska.[26] He is also known to have saved at least five Jews, four of whom survived the war, from roundups and deportations by hiding them in the pharmacy.[27]

When after two years of unimaginable horror the ghetto finally fell silent after the prisoners, soldiers and dogs departed late on 14 March 1943, Pankiewicz was the witness to all that had taken place. He published his memoirs in 1947 alerting the world to what had happened. Ten years before his death in 1993, he was recognized by Yad Vashem as a Righteous Among the Nations. Inside his still-standing pharmacy a small exhibition on the ghetto was opened, which was greatly expanded in 2003, helped by a donation from controversial filmmaker and survivor of the ghetto Roman Polanski. Like so many figures of light, Pankiewicz underplayed his role, saying of it in his memoirs: 'They [the Jews in the ghetto] had a lot of trust in me and I in them; I shared their happy and tragic hours as if I were a Jew too. I only did what one human should do for other humans who were in a tragic situation.'[28] I am transfixed by his words. Of course it is true that Pankiewicz only did what every human being should have done. But why didn't more act when fellow human beings were screaming out for help? The answer, it is becoming clear to me, is precisely because, unlike him, they didn't put themselves in the shoes of their fellow men. Like the Nazis, they 'other-ed' those they saw as different to themselves.

The following morning I am up early to catch the train back to Czechowice-Dziedzice. Sarah cannot throw off her hacking cough, so she will rest while I walk alone. The good weather of the last few days has disappeared, and as I step out of the hotel, driving rain hits my face. Back I go to reception and manage to procure the last hotel umbrella. Kraków's pavements are heaving with commuters with chins buried deep into their overcoats. I grab some water and chocolate for the walk only when I get off the train at Czechowice-Dziedzice. Google Maps says that I have just a ten-minute margin for error over the 17-kilometre trail, and if I dawdle and miss the train back to Kraków, there's a two-hour wait. The first half of the journey is along roads, with the houses and street corners festooned with more posters of presidential candidates. Much is at stake in today's walk. I'm hoping the rain doesn't stop me reading the map, that I will have phone coverage, and that four hours of non-stop brisk walking doesn't prove too much for my ticker. Cars swish past, each time requiring

Tadeusz Pankiewicz was a Polish pharmacist in the Kraków ghetto. He worked to alleviate the horrors of the ghetto and acted as a conduit for information.

me to step on the verge to avoid being sprayed or, worse in the poor visibility, hit. I keep asking myself as I travel whether any of the lanes were walked along by the 'death marchers' out of Auschwitz in January 1945, or whether the railway tracks I pass were used to convey the cattle trucks with their human cargo into its camps. But I am walking northwards, whereas the death marches and railway lines mostly went east–west. I pass through nowhere of historical interest until I find myself on a long lane called Maksymiliana Kolbe Street, which leads me not just towards my destination for the day, the station at Brzeszcze Jawiszowice, but also further towards answering the questions that the pharmacist Pankiewicz in his memoirs, and this whole book, pose.

Maximilian Kolbe, in whose honour the delightful lane in this quiet corner of eastern Poland was named, had arrived in Auschwitz in May 1941. A Franciscan friar with a German father and Polish mother, his faith gave him a deep understanding of the sacredness of all human life, with no exception, and a belief in the boundless power of love. From the German invasion in 1939, he began to shelter Jews and publish anti-Nazi tracts, resulting in his arrest. Once inside Auschwitz, he continued acting as a priest and inspiration to all inmates, provoking fury and violence from guards. Two months after his arrival, a prisoner escaped, resulting in the authorities selecting ten men randomly from a roll call to be starved to death in an underground bunker as a message to deter any further attempts by prisoners. When one of those selected, Franciszek Gajowniczek, cried out in terror, 'My wife! My children!', Kolbe calmly stepped forward and offered to take his place. The guards, astonished at Kolbe's stupidity, agreed to the switch. Shoved together into a dark and cramped cell, he ministered to his fellow captives' needs and led the singing of hymns and prayers. After two weeks without food and water, only he and three other prisoners were still alive. The guards needed the cell for new inmates, so they injected the prisoners with carbolic acid, which causes extreme pain before death. Kolbe, like Bonhoeffer, was said to have died with calm dignity. He raised his left arm to facilitate the task for the guard with the syringe.[29] The injunction from Jesus, 'Greater love have no man, than that he lay down his life for his friend', though perfectly consummated.

What of the friend for whom Kolbe laid down his life, Polish soldier Gajowniczek? He survived three further years in Auschwitz, a rare achievement, before being transferred in August 1944 to Sachsenhausen camp still not knowing if the wife and sons for whom he pleaded were still alive. After liberation, he was reunited with his wife Helena; his sons had survived almost to the end of the war, but were tragically killed in early 1945 in Soviet bombing. After the war Gajowniczek became a lay missionary dedicating his life to letting the world know about Kolbe. When in 1972, a ceremony in front of 150,000 was held at Auschwitz

Franciscan friar Maximilian Kolbe volunteered to die in place of Franciszek Gajowniczek at Auschwitz in 1941.

in honour of Kolbe's beatification by the Pope, Gajowniczek was one of the first to be invited up to speak. Standing close to where Kolbe had sacrificed his life to spare his own, and overcoming survivor guilt, he told the crowd in words so simple, 'I want to express my thanks for the gift of life.'[30]

The rain has subsided. I arrive at Brzeszcze Jawiszowice station with just under ten minutes to spare, thrilled to have walked so far. A moment of triumph. Then the practical questions begin. Why is there absolutely no one on the platform, and no notification anywhere that my train is coming? A locomotive appears out of the blue and pulls up 100 metres beyond my platform. Out the driver steps onto the ground. As I am about to bellow out to him if he knows if the Kraków train is running, he pulls down his trousers and pees. Satisfied, back he clambers into his cabin and off he calmly drives. Eventually my train appears, very late, to whisk me back. As I pass Oświęcim (Auschwitz) station on the way to Kraków, I catch up on today's headlines: order has broken down in Gaza as starving people search for food, and Netanyahu announces there will be a major expansion of settlements in the occupied West Bank.

Sarah is feeling better. After a short while back in the room, she says I'm to stop writing an article for the *Sunday Times* and take her out for dinner. It's the first evening she's felt fully herself for two weeks, a recovery not helped by losing her dearly loved fifteen-year-old border terrier Tallie, her constant companion. We find an old French restaurant where we eat Middle Eastern food and drink Polish wine. We discuss how the Holocaust could have happened. 'Where was God in Auschwitz?' Jonathan Sacks was asked the question by a student when he was Chief Rabbi twenty years ago. He went quiet for a very long time. 'Where were the human beings in Auschwitz?' was his response. Indeed, where were the Kolbes, and why were there not more figures of light like the ones we will shortly meet? The next morning, we catch a train together to Oświęcim, our attention taken by the number of cadets standing in the carriage aisles, suggestive of a country taking its military strengthening seriously. The local trains are so sparse, we catch a taxi back to Brzeszcze Jawiszowice station to start our walk. Sarah talks to our driver in German: she tells us that her grandparents were farmers nearby and sold their produce to Auschwitz camp. 'There was no choice in these matters.'

* * *

I am so happy to have Sarah with me for the last day of the walk: it is twenty-one months since she saw me off at Kilometre Zero, and drew up beside me in her car a while later to say I was going in totally the wrong direction. Her stride is quicker than mine and I have to ask her to ease back. The rain is just keeping off and she's enjoying the journey: as we pass a lake, she points out entranced as one heron after another glides gracefully past, the geese scattering when they come close. Sarah delights in birds; as does my best friend, John James, and so too did my war-wounded grandfather, who wrote books about birdwatching. Since Alsace, birds have brightened my journey at every turn.

Günther Niethammer walked this very path by this lake when researching his bird survey, 'Observations on the Birdlife of Auschwitz'. It recorded 124 breeding and wintering birds in the Auschwitz 'zone of interest'. A family man, he found it took his mind off the stresses of his day job, working in the camps where he had volunteered as a guard in 1940. On 25 June 1941, he noted the nest of a breeding black redstart constructed from human hair. Two months later, he recorded eight curlews flying over a lake on the day the first prisoners were poisoned with Zyklon B. Auschwitz commandant's son Klaus Höss was one of the companions he took with him birdwatching, Höss senior being pleased that Niethammer's publications served as a distraction from what was really happening. He mourned the camps destroying an internationally renowned wetland for birds, and the untreated sewage killing off biological life for miles downstream on the Vistula and Sola. Tried and imprisoned for his work with the SS after the war, Niethammer later resumed his ornithological research, never fully explaining how his exquisite sensitivity to birdlife squared with his blithe indifference to human life.[31]

We can now sense Auschwitz as one does approaching the sea. We pass at Bór a memorial to the liberation of 1945, which evokes the legendary Battle of Grunwald in 1410, a historical comparison with which the Soviets were comfortable, fought successfully between 'Slav' against 'Teuton'. Indicative of the pride the battle evokes, combatants who fought with the Polish armed forces in the Second World War were awarded in 1945 the Grunwald Commemoration Badge. We stop at a village general store with tables outside to eat our sandwiches, which taste delectable in the fresh air, before I accidentally knock the glass ashtray to the ground where it smashes. The shop owner could not have been kinder and we quickly sweep up the shards together. I look across at Sarah and smile: this walk, and Epsom, and the books have taken a lot away. She smiles back at me. At heart, she doesn't really care about the writing, the jobs, the faff of my life; she just wants to spend more time with me. 'How many books did you say you're writing?' 'Six,' I say guiltily. 'You're mad,' she replies. I think she's right.

After lunch, we pass our first physical evidence of Auschwitz, just 5 kilometres to our east: a 'female penal colony', as a display board outside the closed camp informs visitors. The women, it says, were 'not only forced to work for many hours beyond their physical abilities, frequently in the cold water of the ponds they had to clear, but they were also beaten by the SS'. In October 1942, they murdered ninety women, mainly French Jews. We wonder if Irène Némirovsky, author of the novel *Suite Française*, not published till 2004, was among them. But she seems to have died a few weeks earlier of typhus in one of the main Auschwitz camps.

On we press until we find, just 3 kilometres short of our final destination, that our route is blocked by new highway-building work.

We scramble over mud and ruts to get back on our path, but then come up against a far more serious obstacle, a permanently closed rail crossing. This was the most heavily used line for mass Holocaust transportations, from Upper Silesia and Katowice to Oświęcim station, under the command of the German Reichsbahn, which shared arranging the complex transport operation with the SS. We look at each other despondently as an express train flashes past; we're tired and the nearest bridge over the tracks is a long way round. While debating what to do, an elderly lady on a battered bicycle swerves past us, dismounts at the barrier, ducks under it and pushes her bike forthrightly over the rails. Then, while on the last track, she turns left and pushes it over the sleepers, bang bang bang for 100 metres. She disappears through a gap in the undergrowth and she's back on the saddle and off she cycles. 'Come on,' says Sarah, rushing forward, and before I can stop her, she's striding over the rails looking purposefully left and right. I imagine what I'll tell her sisters if an express train suddenly appears. There's nothing else I can do but follow her, and then we too jump from sleeper to sleeper together emulating our intrepid cyclist. When we're safely on the other side, I ask her what she'd have done if a train came. 'Jump,' she replies. She doesn't explain where.

Sarah's stride is now more determined than ever. In no time we're on a long stretch of road running alongside the River Sola, then looking straight into the private house and garden of camp commandant Rudolf Höss, not unlike the head's house in a boarding school back home. Here lived the longest-serving SS commandant in Auschwitz together with his wife Hedwig, bird-watching son Klaus and his four siblings. On the other side of its high garden wall lay the insanity of the camp. The story has been told and retold often, but nothing has prepared us for the sheer banality of the reality, so close to us we could touch it.

Sarah has never been to Auschwitz. 'With so many concentration camps, why does it loom so large over the others?' she asks. Why indeed, and why has Auschwitz been the destination of this book? Some 44,000 camps and subcamps were established across Nazi-occupied Europe, but there were only twenty-five major *concentration* camps (forced labour units for political prisoners as well as persecuted races) and six main *extermination* camps (principally for Jews and Roma).[32] Bergen-Belsen, Terezín and Flossenbürg were examples of concentration camps.

Auschwitz was both a concentration camp and an extermination camp, and it saw the greatest number of Jews killed (1.1 million) in any camp anywhere. The other Nazi camps in occupied Poland in descending order of deaths were Treblinka, Belzec, Chełmno, Sobibor and Majdanek.[33] The camps were concentrated in Poland because it had significantly the highest number of Jews in 1939 with its 3 million (except for the Soviet Union, no other European country had over a million). But it did not see the greatest proportion of its Jewish population killed: that was Lithuania, which had up to 95 per cent murdered (the precise numbers are disputed), often actively abetted by the local population, compared to Poland's 90 per cent. Czechoslovakia, the Netherlands and Greece all lost 75 per cent of their Jews, which shows the reach of the Nazi killing machine, but also of willing antisemite collaborators the length and width of Europe.[34] Non-Jewish Poles saw the second highest number of deaths at Auschwitz, 74,000, and Roma third with 21,000 murdered.[35] The other four non-Polish camps infamous for murder all had fewer than 100,000 deaths each, Mauthausen in Austria, and the final three in Germany, Sachsenhausen, Dachau and Buchenwald.

In the first phase of the war, 1939 to 1941, bullets in the back of the head (overseen by the *Einsatzgruppen*) were the death mechanism of choice, followed for a while by vans pumping out carbon monoxide gas into their sealed backs, which did for the children from Lidice and Ležáky. Neither was quick enough for the mighty task of cleansing Europe of its 9 million Jews (out of a total of 17 million globally). The Wannsee Conference was thus convened in January 1942, at an idyllic lakeside villa in Berlin, and tasked by chair Reinhard Heydrich with coming up with 'a comprehensive solution of the Jewish question'. Europe would be 'combed through', and the decentralized and chaotic killing to date would be replaced by a proper strategic and bureaucratic industrial process.[36]

Auschwitz had not initially been intended as this place of death. It only came to the attention of the SS in late 1939 when it was reported that a vacant Polish army barracks just outside Oświęcim close to the main Katowice–Kraków railway line would be the ideal location to lock up Polish political prisoners. It was to be another two years before large numbers of Jews arrived.[37] The first camp, where Höss lived with his family, was opened in 1940, and became referred to as 'Auschwitz I'. In August 1941, the SS conducted its first test here of Zyklon B as a potential mass murder agent, using Soviet POWs and Polish prisoners as guinea pigs, as the curlews flew innocently over the water.

Höss agreed that a permanent gas chamber and crematorium were sensible, the first Jewish men, women and children being murdered here in January, February and March 1942. But Auschwitz was still relatively small and cramped, and by 1941, it was accepted that more space was required, so the Germans began construction that October on Auschwitz-Birkenau 3 kilometres away, which was divided into ten sections separated by electrified barbed wire fences. The SS decided in early 1942 to move the principal gassing operation to it, with two gas chambers in operation by the summer. The capacity was still too small, though, so from March to June 1943, four large facilities were built, each with a disrobing area, a gas chamber and its own ovens.[38] To cope with the 440,000 Hungarians Jews who arrived in 145 trains from April 1944, the railway tracks were extended into the heart of Auschwitz-Birkenau, and it was on the shallow platforms that the selections were made for new arrivals, whether sent right for immediate death, or left, to work.[39] The last gassings took place in November 1944, after which the Birkenau gas chambers were blown up, if not totally, to destroy evidence, while the gas chambers and crematorium at Auschwitz I survived intact. Finally, there is Auschwitz III or Monowitz, 6 kilometres away, established by the SS in October 1942 to provide labour for IG Farben's giant Buna industrial complex.[40]

'I could see my mother, my sisters, move to the right... I kept walking, my father holding my hand,' writes Elie Wiesel.[41] Children went right, their death receiving a very high priority from the Nazis, because killing them off ensured no Jewish future. 'This is the reason why three-year-old Emilia [Levi] died: the historical necessity of killing the children of Jews was self-demonstrative to the Germans... Thus, in an instant, our women, our parents, our children disappeared. We saw them for a short while as an obscure mass at the other end of the platform; then we saw nothing more,' wrote Primo Levi, who ranks alongside Wiesel as a writer on the Holocaust.[42] In the Introduction to an edition of Rudolf Höss's biography, he commented, 'It's filled with evil... and reading it is agony.'[43] Two years later, after the illness of his mother brought back desperate faces from Auschwitz, he fell to his death; whether accidental

Primo Levi was an Italian Jew imprisoned in Auschwitz from 1944 to 1945. He wrote about the experience in his book If This Is a Man *(1947). Like many survivors, he was unable to escape the shadow of the Holocaust and his death in 1987 may have been suicide.*

or not has never been proven. 'Primo Levi died at Auschwitz forty years later', was the verdict of Wiesel.[44]

How to pick out individual heroes in such a vast empire of tragedy? Almost all the 1.1 million killed here displayed courage or dignity or selflessness in their own ways, actions and lives that we will only ever know little or nothing about. I think again of those who gave their food to children and the infirm in the ghettos, those who moved aside to let others inhale fresh air from vents in the cattle trucks so their lives could last just a little longer, those who held the hands of the terrified when the doors of the gas chambers clanged shut and the hiss of the descending gas began to be heard…

We have already encountered Ben Helfgott and Maximilian Kolbe. The five whose stories are told below are equally illustrative of the humanity of those in Auschwitz and across the killing fields and camps, and of the millions slaughtered across Europe: slaughtered in the name of what?

Marian Turski became the most enduringly influential prophet among the survivors. Four years older than Ben Helfgott, he was entombed along with Ben's family in the Łódź ghetto in 1940. Marian was in one of the last transports to leave the ghetto in 1944. His father and brother were gassed on arrival at Auschwitz. His mother was sent to Belsen and survived the war. In January 1945, he took part in the death march to Buchenwald and Terezín; when he was liberated, he was on the brink of death with typhus. His body slowly recovered, but it took twenty years for his memory, save one that never went away, to return: 'I could never forget that I was in Auschwitz because I have a number tattooed on my arm and I see it every day.' He remained in Poland, studied History at university, and became an influential journalist and historian. On the seventy-fifth anniversary of Auschwitz's liberation in January 2020, he framed words that went far beyond the sentiments normally voiced at such occasions. 'Auschwitz did not fall from the sky,' he said, repeating a metaphor often used by survivors to illustrate that the camps were not a one-off but the logical conclusion of multiple acts of persecution and dehumanization over many years. The Holocaust, he thus said, had stolen up on the world 'with small steps until what happened here, happened'. An Eleventh Commandment needed to be added to the Bible: 'Thou shall not be indifferent... Because if you are indifferent, before you know it, another Auschwitz will come out of the blue for you or your descendants.' In an open letter, he urged Facebook founder Mark Zuckerberg to remove all Holocaust denial groups, pages and posts from his social media platforms.[45]

Turski was back aged ninety-eight as one of a handful of survivors for the eightieth anniversary in January 2025, very likely the last major occasion when survivors would still be alive. To the world leaders gathered by the gates of the camp, he spoke of a significant rise in antisemitism around the world, the need for compassion and to reject the belief that it was not possible to resolve problems between nations. Chancellor

Marian Turski at Auschwitz in 2020. A Jewish Communist, Turski was imprisoned in Auschwitz, but survived the war. He became disillusioned with Communism during the 1960s and dedicated the rest of his life to commemorating the Holocaust, speaking at memorial events at Auschwitz in 2020 and 2025.

Scholz of Germany, President Macron of France, the presidents of Poland and Ukraine, and the monarchs of the UK, Spain, the Netherlands and Belgium all were present to hear him. But these were not the leaders who most needed to hear Turski, who had consistently campaigned for human rights. Putin was not there to hear him, nor Trump, nor Vance nor indeed Netanyahu, wary of being arrested under an International Criminal Court warrant for war crimes.[46] The following month, Turski died in Warsaw.

Ella Lingens and her husband Kurt were training to be doctors in Vienna. After the Nazi seizure of Austria in 1938, they hid Jews. Arrested in October 1942, Ella was deported to Auschwitz in February 1943. Put to work in the women's camp in Birkenau, she witnessed SS doctors including Mengele carrying out horrific experiments. The SS were incapable of understanding why she, as an 'Aryan German', could possibly have wanted to help Jews in Vienna. As a German woman, and a medic in the women's infirmary[47] in the labour camp, she was able to leverage her position to help other women, including hiding them from SS 'selections' (for the gas chambers). She also altered identities and diagnoses to remove women to safety. In December 1944, she was sent to Dachau, ministering to the prisoners as she went. Her life was still in danger and she was sentenced to death for inciting a strike among the women labourers. She and Kurt survived the war and returned to Vienna where they divorced in 1947.[48]

The following year she published a memoir, *Prisoners of Fear*, which described the horrors. It was not universally well received. Her argument that not all the SS were evil and heartless and that not all the prisoners were saints was not what the world wanted to hear in 1948. Nor did the Austrians want readers to be told that they were complicit and enthusiastic supporters of the Nazis, which clashed with the official narrative that they were Hitler's 'first victim', with the Anschluss in March 1938 known as Hitler's first great land-grab. When after the war she was not devoting herself to healthcare, she kept banging the

Ella Lingens was an Austrian physician imprisoned by the Nazis in Auschwitz and Dachau for hiding Jews. In the infirmary, she worked to save prisoners' lives and alleviate their suffering. After the war, she became the head of an organization for Auschwitz survivors.

unpopular drum about the evils of National Socialism and the horror of the death camps. At the Frankfurt Auschwitz trial in March 1964, she again courted unpopularity by squashing the all-prevailing excuse that those who did terrible things were only acting 'under orders'. Could people *decide* whether to be good or evil in the camps?[49] Yes, they could, she said. As the figures of light have shown again and again.

Lingens was given a voice to pronounce on the most searching of all moral questions: 'If I were to fail, to turn away and thus permit the death of this person who I could perhaps save, only because I was in danger myself, I would be committing the same error as the entire German people.'[50] For the rest of her life, she kept in touch with camp inmates and became the long-serving president of the organization of former Auschwitz survivors. When she died in December 2002, she was buried in an honorary grave in Vienna Central Cemetery, her grave bearing the words: 'She risked her life for the life of others'. Her son Peter later wrote of her inability even to the end to purge herself of the memories: 'A few days before she died, my mother got out of bed again. She leaned on the walls of the room… obviously a bit confused. When each conversation fell silent, she repeated a single sentence, her eyes wide in fear: "You won't burn me? You won't burn me, will you?"'[51]

Witold Pilecki was another Auschwitz survivor whose message was uncongenial to his government after the war. His heroism reminds us, as the numbers of murdered show, it was not only Jews caught up in the miasma of Auschwitz. A small landowner in eastern Poland (now Belarus) and a reserve officer, Pilecki was called up to defend Poland against the Nazis in August 1939. Following its defeat, he managed to reach Warsaw to join the resistance, quarrelling with some units over their scorn for Jews. Soon after, messages started arriving about the treatment of political prisoners in Auschwitz I that troubled the leadership. Pilecki volunteered to investigate personally at enormous personal risk: he is believed to be the only person to have engineered their imprisonment in Auschwitz of their own accord. His mission once inside was to raise morale among the large number of political prisoners and to pass on to the resistance in Warsaw and the government-in-exile in London what was happening, who then transmitted it to the British government. His reports gave conclusive evidence of breaches of all human rights conventions including the early experiments with poison gas on Soviet POWs and sterilization of Roma prisoners.[52] His hope was that, once they knew the shocking truth, the Allies would drop arms on the camps, or that the resistance would storm them from the outside.[53] He endured typhus and pneumonia but it was starvation that he described as 'the hardest battle of his life'.[54] Having helped convene resistance groups inside, and even constructed, despite grave danger, a radio transmitter, he successfully escaped in April 1943. This itself was a rare accomplishment, and he later fought in the Warsaw Uprising. Captured by the Germans, he was imprisoned again and, upon his release, wrote what has become known as the Witold Report on Auschwitz. But rather than the national liberation for Poland he had fought for, he was deeply disturbed by the establishment of the Communist government in Warsaw, and he dedicated himself to the restoration of the pre-war democracy. Captured in May 1947, he was forced under torture to confess to crimes of spying, was found guilty of treason in a show trial and was executed in May 1948 by a bullet in the back of his head. For the next forty-two years he was a non-person in Poland, his achievements blanked out. But after 1990, he was exonerated fully by the Polish government, feted by historians internationally, and praised by Poland's Chief Rabbi in 2012 as the kind of peerless human being God had in mind in creation.[55]

Zalman Gradowski was another seized by a mission to let the world know what had happened and risked his life daily so future generations

Witold Pilecki was a Polish officer who allowed himself to be captured and imprisoned in Auschwitz in 1940, before escaping in 1943 to document what he had witnessed. He was later imprisoned and executed by the Polish Communist regime.

would hear the truth. A Polish Jew deported to Auschwitz, he arrived in Birkenau on 8 December 1942. His family was immediately sent to the gas chambers while he was selected to be part of a Sonderkommando slave labour unit. Made up mostly of Jewish inmates, they were forced, on threat of death, to dispose of bodies from the gas chambers (the SS alone had the task of supervising the killing) until they became too infirm, when they themselves were added to the queue. The knowledge they acquired was dangerous for the SS, as they gained an intimate window on how the extermination system operated. A terrible thought persecuted the Sonderkommando: what would happen if the very last one of them was killed, and no one would ever know what happened here? Thus did Gradowski set about writing his secret diary in Yiddish describing in detail what he saw, burying his wrapped pages in the ground near Crematorium III in a metal canister. As he put it: 'I'm writing these lines in the night. My hand is trembling, my heart is bleeding.' He knew his own chance of survival was minimal, and the likelihood was that his diary would either be discovered by the Germans or never found. But, against the odds, the canister was unearthed during a postwar search of the entire area. Thus was his ardent hope realized, as he expresses in the introduction, that his parents, his wife, siblings and wider family would not be forgotten. 'I pass on to you only a small part of what took place in the hell of Birkenau-Auschwitz… I live in an inferno of death'.[56]

Gradowski had survived nearly two years before participating in the Sonderkommando rebellion whose aim was to end the murder machine by blowing up all the crematoria with charges stolen by women prisoners working in the nearby Krupp munitions factory. The unexpected extermination of 300 Sonderkommandos, with further deaths likely imminent, led to the revolt being brought forward to evening roll call on 7 October 1944. But the plan went awry when German soldiers started to round up prisoners earlier on that day, and the revolt went ahead in an uncoordinated manner. Only one crematorium was blown up,

452 of the Sonderkommandos were killed, including Gradowski, and three Germans.[57] Some eighty escaped through the wire, only a small proportion of whom are thought to have made it to safety. Tragically, the women helpers who provided the explosives, including Shoshana Robota, who lost her entire family in the Holocaust, were discovered. Tortured for many days in the infamous Block II, they refused to reveal names, and were hanged, two at morning roll call and two in the evening in front of their fellow prisoners to taunt them. The date was 6 January 1945, three weeks to the day before the camp was liberated.[58]

The book's final figure of light, Etty Hillesum, came from the city known throughout the centuries as a beacon of sanctuary for its policy of *gedogen* ('toleration by ignoring'). Before the religiously oppressed sought haven in New England, Amsterdam provided a refuge for those persecuted and rejected elsewhere in Europe including Anabaptists, French Huguenots and Sephardic Jews. It was in Amsterdam in the first chapter that we met Alfred Wiener: how natural for him to move his archive cataloguing the rise of antisemitism here from Germany

Zalman Gradowski and his wife Sonia on their wedding day before the war. Gradowski's Yiddish secret diary documented the horrors of Auschwitz. Both Sonia and Zalman were murdered in the camp, but Zalman's hidden diary was discovered after the war.

in 1933 where he assumed his work and family would be safe. It was here that we met Margot and Anne Frank, whose father Otto found it difficult to imagine that the city would ever become unsafe for Jews. They formed 10 per cent of the population of the city, sometimes known as 'the Jerusalem of the West', and many had strong, loving relationships with their neighbours. After the Nazis arrived on 15 May 1940, though, most of their fellow city dwellers became bystanders, a few became collaborators but even fewer became protectors. Conspicuous among them was the ten Boom family in nearby Haarlem, who protected Jews in a secret room in their home, saving the lives of an estimated 800. In February 1944, the Gestapo raided them. The father Casper died ten days later in prison, while the two daughters were taken to Ravensbrück where they rallied spirits with constant prayer meetings. Betsie died there of starvation, while her younger sister Corrie survived to write her memoir, *The Hiding Place*, and to spend the rest of her life preaching her Christian faith, reconciliation and forgiveness, including in Germany in the late 1940s when she famously forgave a former camp guard.[59]

The ten Boom family never, I believe, met Etty Hillesum, separated by a religion but joined by a faith in God and a belief that revenge and retribution are wrong. Like Anne Frank, Hillesum was a committed diary writer, starting hers in March 1941 aged twenty-seven, recording her increasing concern at the closing Nazi net around her fellow Jews, as well as her deepening faith in God. Love, compassion and celebration of life even in intense darkness were the only ways to live, she came to believe. She worked as a volunteer in Amsterdam to help Jews in difficulty, and in June 1943, refusing to go into hiding, to the consternation of her non-Jewish friends, went voluntarily to the Westerbork transit camp where many of Amsterdam's Jews were sent awaiting transport east (Anne Frank's family arrived there a year later after their hiding place had been betrayed).

Westerbork, while palatial compared to the concentration and death camps, and overseen by the Nazi-controlled Dutch government (assisted by Jewish supervisors) not the SS, was a place of torment.[60] Every week, selections were announced for the train leaving on Tuesdays for Auschwitz or Treblinka: 97,000 departed thus; barely a handful returned. Inmates had no choice but to wait passively for their name to be chosen: 'I walk past scenes that loom up before my eyes in crystal-clear detail, and at the same time seem like blurred age-old visions... a dying old man being carried away... a father, ready to depart, blessing his wife and child... [a] few young women are already sitting in a goods wagon... babies on their laps, their legs dangling outside,' she wrote.[61] But she refused to be downcast, writing, 'The sky is full of birds, the purple lupins stand up so regally and peacefully, two little old women have sat down for a chat, the sun is shining on my face – and right before our eyes, mass murder.'[62] At all times, she was imbued by love, for her fellow prisoners and for the guards who she refused to hate. 'I see no alternative,' she wrote in her diary in July, 'each of us must turn inward and destroy in himself all that he thinks he ought to destroy in others.'[63]

Hillesum was in Westerbork less than three months, but as she wrote, 'Despite everything, life is still full of beauty and meaning.'[64] She continued to refuse offers to escape, believing it was her duty to support her fellow inmates, with whom she regularly prayed. In September, she and her family were selected to be deported to Auschwitz, her parents dying three days later. Her diary and letters stopped abruptly the moment she left Westerbork and next to nothing is known about her time following it, but the Red Cross reported her death aged twenty-nine on 30 November 1943, likely to have been in the gas chambers.

The last words she is known to have written were on a card thrown out of her cattle truck travelling east in the vain hope someone would find and keep it. A passer-by did, by the side of the track near Zwolle, en route to the German border. 'Opening the bible at random,' Hillesum wrote, 'I find this. "The Lord is my high tower." I am sitting on my rucksack in the middle of a full freight car. Father, Mother, and Mischa

Etty Hillesum was a Dutch Jewish author who wrote diaries chronicling her experiences in occupied Amsterdam and at Westerbork camp. She was murdered in Auschwitz in 1943.

[sister] are a few cars away. In the end, the departure came without warning... We left the camp singing.'[65]

The seven representative figures of light in Auschwitz each have their own signature: Kolbe's sacrificial love, Helfgott's indomitable will to live, Turski's mission to teach lessons to the world, Lingens's refusal to accept stereotypes, Pilecki's intent to stop the killing, Gradowski's wish to preserve evidence, and Hillesum's limitless love and reconciliation. What do they share with each other, and with those remarkable figures highlighted in the earlier nine chapters? A pattern has become clear as their stories have accumulated throughout the book. A refusal to dehumanize, to belittle or 'other' any person, whether of another faith, nationality or type; a commitment to *act* and to do so with compassion; a blanket refusal to succumb to the forces of hate and negativity; a commitment to all humans, with care and love; and a passionate desire even unto death to discover, to record and tell the truth. They all had a sense that, as human beings, they belonged to something bigger than the confines that time and space, race and group had placed them in, and they had a duty as humans to use their lives to love more than just themselves.

How well do the leaders whose actions have been interwoven like an agitated tapestry throughout these pages, Putin, Trump, Vance and Netanyahu prime among them, compare against these qualities? They have formed the backdrop these last two years of my walk, much as Hitler, Himmler and Goebbels did for Leigh Fermor walking in the 1930s. Should we not expect our leaders to embody some of the qualities of the figures of light? That is a question for the epilogue.

Seven rivers have flowed through this book, from the slow-moving Rhine along whose tranquil banks I walked in Alsace, to the all-Polish surging Vistula. In the two years in between came the sweltering, mosquito-heavy Danube, Nuremberg's autumnal Pegnitz, the Czech's national treasure the Vltava, the iced-over Elbe and the blossom-banked Oder. We have seen too how all seven were rivers of dark secrets in the Second World War, carrying away into distant seas the detritus of Nazism. None of the women and men of light who peopled these pages may still be alive, but the seven rivers most definitely still are, flowing on and on, reminding us that life continues, that we are part of something bigger than ourselves, and that our actions live on after us.

Over the two years I walked the path of light, I was ever mindful of edging closer to Auschwitz's crematoria whose flames once lit up the night sky. There may have been some dark moments on the way. But I was constantly uplifted by the stories of the remarkable people I encountered along the route, none more uplifting than the seven men and women we have met in this chapter. They all put the lie to the 'only following orders' and 'too fearful to act' excuses given by so many during 1939–45. Their lives and actions show that we have agency, and ultimately we *have* the freedom to decide whether it will be darkness or light that will prevail in our lives. Indeed, only now, at the end of these long two years, do I understand that we *all* have our own paths of light to walk in our lives. We may not be living through the unimaginable horrors of the figures in these pages. But we all face our own challenges and difficult decisions, and whether we choose darkness or light will be the most important choice we will ever make. It will indeed define who we are.

* * *

Sarah and I have arrived at the end of the journey at the gates of Auschwitz. The prosaic initially predominates, the tourists leaving at the end of their visits, making their way back to the coach park and the railway station. Then comes a numbness and disbelief that this pilgrimage has reached its physical conclusion. Only subsequently do deeper thoughts flood in. I cannot empty my mind of that last word that Etty Hillesum is known to have uttered: 'singing'. As she and her fellow Jews boarded the cattle trucks at Westerbork to be sent east to almost certain death, she led her fellow passengers in *singing*. I imagine her later on holding the hands of those closest to her as they shuffled in terror into the gas chambers, raising their spirits by encouraging everyone to *sing* prayers, songs and psalms. Here was the love, the light, that no evil could ever extinguish. It is that same spirit that Sarah and I have learned on our way was displayed by Christians Dietrich Bonhoeffer and Maximilian Kolbe as they too were waiting to be murdered, a defiance and faith that love will always prevail, vanquishing indeed the greatest evil the world has ever seen.

Epilogue

It is Saturday morning in Kraków. Sarah is still sound asleep. I've slipped out early from the hotel to walk around the park created in the 1820s to encircle the Old Town to replace its crumbling medieval walls. It's not long after dawn and last night's revellers are still draped around Planty Park, slowly being replaced by well-dressed city dwellers walking their dogs.

We leave the city today at the end of our journey, and I wanted to walk though Kraków one last time and reflect on what the last two years have meant, and whether I have come any closer to answering the questions in my mind as I set out. My head is spinning as I reflect on the remarkable people we have met in these pages. How to make sense of them and of all those I have met on my journey, and of all the international upheavals of the last two years? On the eightieth anniversary of the Second World War's end, what if anything has the world learned from the inferno about facing up to dictators with aggressive ambitions abroad, and about how to treat others, especially the vulnerable? What might the figures of light I encountered on my light and dark journey have to teach us? What can we learn from this greatest cauldron of evil in history about the nature of good and bad and how to nurture democracies and communities amidst today's challenges? And on a personal note, did this pilgrimage, for that is what it has been, help me on my own journey?

'Juden verboten' signs were displayed prominently in the gardens under the Nazi occupation, changing them from a place of harmony to a place of hate. As I approach Podzamcze, I come face to face once again with Royal Wawel Castle and see, through the morning mist rising off the Vistula, Hans Frank coming down its long ramp towards me. After Heydrich's assassination in June 1942, the man Goebbels described as the 'King of Poland' was fearful the Polish resistance would try to kill him too (it nearly succeeded in January 1944 with a bomb under his train). He is heavily protected so I walk towards this epitome of Nazi evil with caution, my head full of questions to ask about his conscience and whether his dreams at night are soaked in blood. But as I approach him, the mist suddenly clears, and he is gone. I'm finished with him anyway. He, along with Heydrich, have shown the extent of the merciless horror that the depraved can unleash if given total power. They prove how bad life can be, not in a far-flung country, but in the heart of Europe.

I take one last look at the Vistula glinting yellow and pink in the morning light before continuing my circle around the city back through Planty Park. As I do so, I think back to how this walk, which I came close on several occasions to never completing, originated. The first walk from Kilometre Zero to the North Sea in the late summer of 2021 had been hard, not the least physically. But as readers of *The Path of Peace* have pointed out, they are not convinced that I found my own inner peace. So I had to set off again on another long journey. I knew I had far to go before I could find meaningful answers. But where exactly should I go, and what would be the mission?

The Path of Peace had been a book amidst and about the First World War, and this is a volume amidst and about the Second World War. It proved to be a much tougher walk and a much harder book to write. But it was a project I knew I had to complete, whatever the cost. It was always more than a physical challenge. I was walking in search of answers.

A core question on the 80th Anniversary is what have we really learned from the Second World War? Like many, I was very moved by the events and the coverage on the anniversary, which produced some fascinating and uplifting television, absorbing writing and excellent new commemorative sites. But I missed serious reflection about what the war taught. Yes, it's appropriate of course to honour those who fought and those who fell: but to honour them fully means that we have to delve deeper, to build that better world that was talked about during and just after the fighting, the world for which they gave their all but which was then lost.

So what do I think the war could teach us today? Above all, the need to stand up to regimes with aggressive ambitions abroad early on to keep them in their box, as the West did successfully with the Soviet Union during the Cold War. Failure to keep Britain on a war footing after 1918 and rearm properly left Neville Chamberlain with little option when squaring up to Hitler after 1937. Similarly today, 25 years have been squandered while Putin's aggressive ambitions have been abundantly clear. Europe failed to rearm sufficiently when the sun shone, relied too heavily on America, and is on the back foot today as a result. It has been a fiasco that could yet be a massive tragedy that was completely avoidable.

Next, even fighting a just war, which the Second World War most definitely was, does not justify unjust actions. The British and Americans overwhelmingly fought within the boundaries of morality that had been delineated by international conventions. As a result, they had clear moral authority in the bank when the reckoning came at Nuremberg and beyond. Not all their actions were just: there will always be questions about the extent of loss of German civilian life in air raids which, as the book shows, massively exceeded the numbers of British civilians lost to German bombs. But this has to be set against the disregard for human life displayed by the Soviets, from mass rape and indiscriminate brutality by its troops on the ground to the sanctioning of repeated mass murder from the Kremlin.

The Second World War teaches us that once the rule of law and civilized codes of conduct are abandoned, as seen equally in the behaviour of Japanese forces in the Far East, then all hell is let loose. As Marian

Turski warned on the 75th anniversary of the liberation: 'Auschwitz did not fall from the sky'. Murderous antisemitism, as seen repeatedly on these pages, has been in existence for 1,000 years and more. State-sponsored antisemitism and anti-Slavism for 12 years after 1933 led to the heartless murder of millions. Human nature has changed not one jot in the last 80 years. Civilization is frail, which is why we need good government, including serious-minded and competent prime ministers in Britain, as well as their equivalents abroad, to ensure reason prevails and the voice of the masses is acted upon before distrust, then alienation, then abandonment of democracy occurs.

What else? That overreaction and the vindictive treatment of others will always fail. The Treaty of Versailles didn't make the Second World War inevitable, but it made it more likely. The German nation was not humiliated after the Second World War, an architecture was put in place within the country, and internationally not least with the United Nations, to help ensure the nurturing of democracy and common prosperity. Has that lesson been learnt? Did the United States overreact, less in Afghanistan but in Iraq, to 9/11? Did the Israeli government overreact after 7 October 2022? As the book shows, the allies were right to totally crush Nazism into the ground but not to crush the German people. In trying totally to crush Hamas, is Prime Minister Netanyahu totally crushing the Palestinian people? Those who have been humiliated will always seek revenge; evil will always beget evil, as the Book of Proverbs tells us.

I reflect back to the world of ninety years ago when Patrick Leigh Fermor was walking across Germany, Austria and Hungary. He wrote about about how Habsburg Europe was being replaced by nationalism, ideology and militarism. Precious few stood up to stop that destruction of decency and democracy, not religious leaders, not writers, officials nor politicians. Almost all acquiesced, while national leaders, notably Chamberlain before the war and Roosevelt during it, gave ground to the dictators Hitler and Stalin.

EPILOGUE

I reflect on the world today, and the wars in Ukraine and in Israel/Gaza, the constant backdrops to the walk. Melinda Simmons, British Ambassador to Ukraine, was under no illusions about Stalin's successor, Putin. In early 2020, she tells me over coffee, she started reporting about signal jamming, and an increase in the numbers of deaths from sniper fire from Russian-backed terrorists and from landmines. Because the numbers were still low, London and other European capitals took time to realize the gravity. So she travelled to the Russian borders with Crimea and elsewhere to see for herself, to keep up the warnings. Slowly the West woke up to Putin's aggressive intent, spurred on by his infamous essay in July 2021 in which he argued that Russians, Ukrainians and Belarusians are historically one people. The chaotic scuttle out of Kabul the following month too jerked the West out of its complacency, and accelerated its plans for evacuation in the face of an increasingly likely Russian invasion. Simmons had been quietly shifting out staff from Kyiv but was insistent she herself remain to show solidarity with Ukraine. But then on 19 February 2022, she received the call from the Foreign Office she dreaded, telling her to evacuate immediately. Initially, she set up her ambassador's base in a hotel on a ring-road on the Polish side of Lviv, making it easier to evacuate further west if needed, given that Lviv's centre was clogged with refugees and supplies. Three weeks later, she pulled back even further and set up camp in the British Embassy in Warsaw.

The Russian invasion of Ukraine on 24 February initially made rapid advances to the north and west of Kyiv, with the city expected to fall imminently. But over the next month, a mixture of poor Russian tactics and logistics, and stronger Ukrainian military resistance than anticipated, turned the tide, and on 29 March, the Russians began to withdraw. Simmons received authority to return to Kyiv in April, driving back under heavy military escort past scenes of terrible military carnage she would never erase from her mind.

'The Ukrainians have no choice, there is no middle ground. They believe they must either fight or they will die,' she says. Already tens of thousands of their children have disappeared into Russia. The Baltic nations of Latvia, Lithuania and Estonia are all under threat, while Eastern Europe teeters on the verge of looking east again rather than west. As I write, there is a serious chance of Putin retaining parts of Ukraine, while the prospect of him facing war crimes charges or accounting for the disappearance of the Ukrainian children is negligible. Who would have predicted this scenario thirty-five years ago when the Iron Curtain came down and, we were told, history was 'ending'?[1]

The war in Israel/Gaza was the other international crisis that never went away. Since the 7 October 2023 Hamas attacks, Benjamin Netanyahu has been responsible for military acts that, justified or not, have lost Israel enormous sympathy and goodwill right across the world. Former Supreme Court justice Jonathan Sumption, no hot-head, argued in July 2025 that the activities by Netanyahu's government are 'revenge, visited not just on Hamas but on an entire population. It is, in short, a war crime.'[2] The UN estimates that 61,400 have been killed in Gaza, compared to under 5,000 Israeli soldiers and civilians killed on and since 7 October. Antisemitism and Holocaust denial have soared and support for Israel fallen very significantly, with Israel's actions affecting Palestinian women and children and hampering humanitarian relief efforts high on the list of reasons given. International sympathy and respect for the Jewish race, and support for the creation of the State of Israel that followed the Holocaust, may take decades to recover.

The news as we leave Poland today is of the 'Proud Boys' who stormed the US Congress on 6 January 2021, in support of Trump's assertion that his victory in the November 2020 presidential election had been 'stolen', and who are now suing the US government for $100 million. When Trump pardoned the Congress rioters, he said, 'What they've done to these people is outrageous. There's rarely been anything like it in the history of our country.' They were, he said, 'patriots'.

Putin is at least behaving as Russian leaders have throughout the centuries. We should not be surprised. But should we be by a US president who openly challenges the legitimacy of the American democratic process, as Trump has done? What happened to the vision for America, as a 'shining city upon a hill', popularized by US presidents including Ronald Reagan in the 1980s to emphasize the nation's role as a beacon and defender of democracy and freedom in a dangerous world? When the president no longer upholds democracy and freedom either in the world or even within the US, and bullies and lies brazenly to camera, can the fragile post-1945 world order still hold together? And what of an Israeli prime minister who has no time for the primary tenets of the Jewish faith, which are to act with justice, charity and love, above all towards the sick, women and children? Another red line? How has Netanyahu been allowed to erect for so long and with such bellicosity his castle on a hill in Jerusalem, sacred city to the three Abrahamic religions? Yet the power and reach of Trump and Netanyahu strengthened while writing this book.

In the 1920s and 1930s, the new technology of radio and film was ruthlessly exploited by the Nazis to gain ground. They knew control of the media was essential to power. In the 2020s, the threats come from artificial intelligence, social media and the systematic discrediting of objective media outlets including the BBC and RFE (Radio Free Europe) as we have seen. In the 1930s, economic instability and uncertainty helped leaders who had no time for the rule of law and democracy to gain power over impressionable minds desperate for strong leaders with compelling stories that allowed them to feel good about themselves. So too in the 2020s. Democracy is far more fragile than we imagine, as historian Laurence Rees reminds us with 'warnings from history', thinking specifically of the Nazi era.[3]

International stability and the ability to stand up against dictators was not helped in the 1930s by the effective collapse of the institution set up in 1919 to maintain peace in the world, the League of Nations, and by the United States levying tariffs and committed to isolationism. International stability and the ability to stand up against dictators is not being helped in the 2020s by the effective collapse of the institution set up in 1945 to maintain peace in the world, the United Nations, and by the United States levying tariffs and threatening a return to isolationism under a president of uncertain moral compass.

Europe, weak militarily and economically, sleep-walked into tragedy in the 1930s; 50 million died before the evil could be exorcised in Europe (if not from the Soviet Union). Europe, weak militarily and economically ninety years on, is sleep-walking towards disaster in the 2020s. Time and again on the trail, I heard about Germany's and Europe's economic and political torpor. Europe must wake up and remind itself what it shares in common (the mission of the Western Front Way) and start acting in concert to protect its common values. This is where the figures of light come in. Ignore their lessons today and tomorrow's light could come from the equivalents of the Nuremberg rally's 'cathedral of light' and Auschwitz's belching crematoria.

I set out worrying whether I could hunt down stories of courageous men and women along my trail and if so, could I be sure their deeds were genuine? I take leave of the book with a profound sense of loss. I will no longer be able to spend time among and be uplifted by them. Looking at their faces, from Rudolf Vrba and Gertrud Luckner's in the first chapter, to Ella Lingens, who remained taunted all her life by the fear that she would be dispatched to the ovens, to Zalman Gradowski, who was, but whose story survived: they all are so vivid and alive to me. What they have to teach us is remarkably uniform. Do not be a bystander to evil. Many of them might have been unremarkable people without the war, but they all responded to the need of the hour. We never know when we will be called upon to step up. They cared for, loved indeed, their neighbours: they were 'obsessed by reconciliation' as Michael Buerk said of Hugo Gryn. They did not just love their own family and tribe: they acted out the Quaker proverb: 'My enemy is someone whose story I do not yet know'. They opened themselves to those stories: they were open, not closed hearted. They felt the pain of others as if it was their own. They were courageous, concerned even unto death to do what they knew was right, just and good. They had a reverence for the truth, even if discovering and relaying it cost them their lives. Unlike their oppressors, they were modest people, failing to see that they had done anything remarkable.

The walk, the last two years, has been a chastening experience. The figures of light have shown me how out of tune my life has been with my deepest values. From my first school assembly 40 years ago, I have always exhorted bridge-building: exhorted it, but done it far too little. The dreams I had to set up a school in Belfast for Protestant and Catholic children to learn and grow up side by side, or in Jerusalem for Arab, Jewish and Christian children, wilted. My aspiration, always, was of helping people understand what we share in common is far greater than what divides us.

I hoped my walk to Auschwitz would at last give me answers to my inner demons, the voice in my head that keeps attacking me. It hasn't. But I'm learning through my illness that having an open heart and caring for others matters infinitely more. Self-interest and self-obsession are paths that lead to misery. I may never understand myself: but in worrying less about it, I can live better.

I will never be a hero now. But I can live better. I will try to follow in the footsteps of the figures in this book, none more so than Dietrich Bonhoeffer and Etty Hillesum.

I conclude with someone who is a figure of light, a surgeon who has saved countless lives, and taught innumerable medics on the front lines in war zones and around the world, including the two, Ukraine and Gaza, that are the backdrops to this book. As I write, David Nott, aged sixty-nine, has just returned from Kharkiv, where he was operating on critically wounded victims of Russian drone strikes. Nott, who says it is his faith in God that sustains him, first came to public attention in 2013 when he testified to the brutality of Bashar al-Assad's siege of Aleppo, and when shortly after he went to Gaza. He was about to operate on a seven-year old girl when he was told the hospital in Gaza City was to be shelled in five minutes. He and the anaesthetist refused point blank to leave: they stayed and they saved the girl's life.[4]

As the Jewish Talmudic saying puts it, 'Whoever saves one life saves the whole world entire.'

'Let there be light'
Genesis 1:3

*The light shines in the darkness and
the darkness has not overcome it.*
John 1:5

Illustration Credits

p. 18 (1) Wikimedia Commons / Public Domain
p. 18 (2) Alamy / Smith Archive (WHACT0)
p. 25 © The Wiener Holocaust Library collections
p. 27 Yad Vashem, Photograph of the rescuer(s), Righteous Among the Nations Collection.
p. 32 (1) Elizabeth Goering via William Hastings Burke
p. 32 (2) Wikimedia Commons / Public Domain
p. 37 Archiv des Deutschen Caritasverbandes
p. 50 Bielenberg Family, Munny House
p. 58 Alamy / dpa picture alliance (D3B6YC)
p. 64 Wikimedia Commons / Nono vlf / CC BY-SA 3.0
p. 67 Alamy / Alpha Historica (2X9HM19)
p. 71 (1) © Ali Limonadi / CC BY-SA 3.0
p. 71 (2) © George (Jürgen) Wittenstein / akg-images (KG894366)
p. 77 © Lee Miller Archives, England 2025. All rights reserved. www.leemiller.co.uk
p. 81 Wikimedia Commons / Public Domain
p. 86 Wikimedia Commons / Public Domain
p. 88 © Käthe Kruse Manufaktur
p. 92 Alamy / Sueddeutsche Zeitung Photo (C460JR)
p. 97 Yad Vashem Righteous Among the Nations Collection, 14471788
p. 109 Alamy / piemags (2K197Y7)
p. 111 United States Holocaust Memorial Museum, courtesy of Sibylle Niemoeller
p. 113 Bildersammlung des Bistumsarchivs Münster / CC BY-SA 2.5
p. 120 Alamy / INTERFOTO (T0MBXR)
p. 123 (1–3) Gerhard F. Strasser, 'The Heroic Rescue of Thirteen Prisoners from a Death March near Regensburg', Wiener Holocaust Library. Guest article. Accessed 18 June 2025.
p. 126 Courtesy of Naomi Gryn
p. 135 Alamy / Sueddeutsche Zeitung Photo (CPM16X)
p. 137 Still from *Here is Germany* (film) / United States Holocaust Memorial Museum / Public Domain
p. 139 National Archives and Records Administration, College Park, MD via United States Holocaust Memorial Museum
p. 143 Wikimedia Commons / Public Domain
p. 149 U.S. Army Signal Corps, Harry S. Truman Library & Museum (Public Domain)
p. 152 Graebe in Zdolbunov, 1941, Yad Vashem Photo Archive
p. 155 (2) United States Holocaust Memorial Museum
p. 159 Photo by Leonard McCombe / Picture Post / Hulton Archive / Getty Images
p. 161 https://kesten.de/station/nurnberg/stadtpolitik/
p. 170 Bundesarchiv, Bild 183-L19106 / Fritz / CC BY-SA 3.0
p. 172 Alamy / World History Archive (2YRYKPH)
p. 182 Bundesarchiv, Bild 146-1970-005-28 / CC BY-SA 3.0 via Alamy / CBW (2R007GT)
p. 184 © Vladimir Lammer / Estate of Vladimir Lammer
p. 186 Bundesarchiv, Bild 183-H12751 / CC BY-SA 3.0

ILLUSTRATION CREDITS

p. 190 Alamy / ČTK (BX47T9)
p. 194 Wikimedia Commons / © Mosbatho / CC BY 4.0
p. 200 *US-Army v ČSR 1945* (film) © Czech Television
p. 206 https://www.kampocesku.cz/article/25527/premysl-pitter (Accessed 7 August 2025)
p. 214 Bundesarchiv, Bild 146-1972-039-44 / CC BY-SA 3.0 via Alamy / CBW (2GFFKRC)
p. 218 3952 (1913 ed.) G6480 s75. A8; 3952 (1942/43 ed.) G6480 s75. A8 / Library of Congress, Geography and Map Division (https://blogs.loc.gov/maps/2021/08/now-you-see-it-now-you-dont/)
p. 219 World War II Today (https://www.ww2today.com/p/massacre-at-lidice)
p. 222 © United States Holocaust Memorial Museum, 1994.A.117
p. 227 © Michal Kmínek / Wikimedia Commons / CC BY-SA 3.0
p. 230 Wikimedia Commons / Public Domain
p. 235 Yad Vashem Photo Archive, 4613/518
p. 236 (1–2) Children's Drawings from the Terezín Ghetto, 1942-1944 / © Židovské muzeum v Praze (Jewish Museum in Prague)
p. 238 (1) https://donne-uk.org/ilse-weber/ (Accessed 15 July 2025)
p. 238 (2) https://x.com/holocaust_music/status/1795131460623421573/photo/1 (Accessed 15 July 2025)
p. 240 Courtesy of Daniel Barenboim Stiftung
p. 248 Základní školy Marie Kudeříkové Strážnice
p. 251 Courtesy of Central Military Archives in Prague (Vojenský ústřední archiv v Praze)
p. 253 Alamy / ČTK (BX59KG)
p. 258 TOBIAS SCHWARZ/AFP via Getty Images
p. 267 © Štěpán Bartoš, Invisible Synagogues (https://unsichtbaresynagogen.eu/)
p. 270 ZŠ M. Kudeříkové Strážnice / Public Domain
p. 277 (1) Wikimedia Commons / Public Domain
p. 277 (2) Wikimedia Commons / Public Domain
p. 279 (1–2) Photographs taken at Památník Ležáky
p. 284 (2) © United States Holocaust Memorial Museum
p. 288 ČTK / Vostárek Josef (0997509794)
p. 289 Memory of Nations
p. 293 Wikimedia Commons / Public Domain
p. 295 Wikimedia Commons / Public Domain
p. 302 Max Alpert / Wikimedia Commons / Public Domain
p. 303 Wikimedia Commons / Public Domain
p. 304 Memory of Nations, Witness's archive
p. 317 (1) © Fundacja Generał Elżbiety Zawackiej
p. 317 (2) Photo by Apic / Getty Images
p. 321 https://x.com/HolocaustMuseum/status/1669754735358881795 (Accessed 11 July 2025)
p. 324 Bundesarchiv, Bild 121-0270 / CC-BY-SA 3.0
p. 327 Wikimedia Commons / Public Domain
p. 329 Wikimedia Commons / Public Domain
p. 336 Wikimedia Commons / Public Domain
p. 338 Alamy / Grzegorz Kozakiewicz (2H20TMX)
p. 340 Yad Vashem Righteous Among the Nations Collection, 14481079
p. 342 Wikimedia Commons / Public Domain
p. 344 Wikimedia Commons / Public Domain
p. 347 Wikimedia Commons / Public Domain

All other images taken and supplied by Anthony Seldon, John Ashton and Greg Hands.

Notes

Preface

1 As detailed in Anthony Seldon, *The Path of Peace: Walking the Western Front Way* (London: Atlantic, 2022).

2 Hugo Gryn with Naomi Gryn, *Chasing Shadows* (London: Penguin, 2000), p. 237.

1. Crossing the Rhine

1 Jonathan Freedland, *The Escape Artist: The Man Who Broke Out of Auschwitz to Warn the World* (London: John Murray, 2022).

2 https://hmd.org.uk/resource/rudolf-vrba/

3 https://collections.ushmm.org/oh_findingaids/RG-50.148.0013_sup_en.pdf

4 https://history.state.gov/historicaldocuments/frus1919Parisv02/

5 https://web.archive.org/web/20170825010138/http://www.twofistedhistory.com/blog/post/the-short-lived-soviet-republic-of-alsace-lorraine

6 https://encyclopedia.1914-1918-online.net/article/alsace-lorraine/ . https://museeprotestant.org/en/notice/the-reintegration-of-alsace-lorraine-after-1918/

7 https://www.memorial-alsace-moselle.com/en/le-memorial/un-peu-d-histoire/1940-germanization-and-nazification-of-alsace-moselle

8 https://www.worldcourts.com/imt/eng/decisions/1946.05.03_France_v_Wagner.pdf

9 https://destinees-juives.expositionsvirtuelles.fr/en/sections/strasbourg/#chapter-4. https://www.holocausthistoricalsociety.org.uk/contents/concentrationcamps/natzweiler.html

10 Robert Wistrich, *Who's Who in Nazi Germany* (Weidenfeld & Nicolson, 1982), pp. 269–70. https://www.leo-bw.de/web/guest/detail/-/Detail/details/PERSON/kgl_biographien/117103896/biografie. https://stadtlexikon.karlsruhe.de/index.php/De:Lexikon:bio-0064

11 David Cesarani, *Final Solution: The Fate of the Jews 1933–49* (London: Macmillan, 2016), p. 710.

12 https://rudolfvrba.com/burial/

13 https://encyclopedia.1914-1918-online.net/article/war-losses-france/

14 https://militaryhistorynow.com/2017/05/07/the-great-wall-of-france-11-remarkable-facts-about-the-maginot-line/

15 For a perspective on the fall of France, see Julian Jackson, *The Fall of France: The Nazi Invasion of 1940* (Oxford: Oxford University Press, 2003), pp. 9–60.
16 https://www.gutenberg.org/files/25282/25282-h/25282-h.htm
17 https://www.britannica.com/biography/Theodor-Herzl. https://www.jewishvirtuallibrary.org/first-zionist-congress-and-basel-program-1897?utm_content=cmp-true
18 https://guides.loc.gov/chronicling-america-dreyfus-affair. https://www.britannica.com/event/Dreyfus-affair. https://www.theguardian.com/global/2021/oct/30/rise-of-far-right-puts-dreyfus-affair-into-spotlight-in-french-election-race
19 https://www.juedisches-museum.ch/en/the-basel-trial-of-the-protocols-of-the-elders-of-zion/
20 https://encyclopedia.ushmm.org/content/en/article/protocols-of-the-elders-of-zion
21 Orlando Figes, *A People's Tragedy: A History of the Russian Revolution, 1891–1924* (London: Pimlico, 1996), p. 242. https://www.state.gov/wp-content/uploads/2024/01/GEC-Special-Report-More-than-a-Century-of-Antisemitism.pdf
22 Quoted in Randall L. Bytwerk, 'Believing in "Inner Truth": The Protocols of the Elders of Zion in Nazi Propaganda, 1933–1945', *Holocaust and Genocide Studies*, vol. 29, issue 2, Fall 2015, pp. 212–29.
23 https://www.juedisches-museum.ch/en/the-basel-trial-of-the-protocols-of-the-elders-of-zion/
24 Daniel Finkelstein, *Hitler, Stalin, Mum and Dad: A Family Memoir of Meticulous Survival* (London: William Collins, 2023), p. 105. https://wienerholocaustlibrary.org/object/3000-7-5/
25 Finkelstein, *Hitler, Stalin, Mum and Dad*.
26 https://www.yadvashem.org/righteous/stories/maas.html
27 https://www.yadvashem.org/righteous/statistics.html
28 https://www.harvardmagazine.com/2006/07/taming-the-rhine-html. https://www.britannica.com/topic/Grand-Canal-dAlsace
29 Christopher Miskimon, 'Destruction of the Colmar Pocket', WarHistory Network, Winter 2023, https://warfarehistorynetwork.com/article/destruction-of-the-colmar-pocket/
30 https://www.whastingsburke.com/albert-goering/ . ttps://www.jewishvirtualmuseum.com/artist/albert-gunther-goring/
31 William Hastings Burke, *Thirty-Four: The Key to Göring's Last Secret* (Sydney: Wolfgeist, 2009). https://www.independent.co.uk/news/world/europe/goring-s-brother-was-another-schindler-7687516.html
32 https://www.timesofisrael.com/top-israeli-honor-eludes-goerings-brother-who-heroically-saved-jews/
33 https://www.theguardian.com/lifeandstyle/2010/feb/20/albert-goering-hermann-goering-brothers
34 https://www.tiktok.com/@dahliakurtz/video/7154725420879875334?is_copy_url=1&is_from_webapp=v1
35 https://blog.nationalmuseum.ch/en/2024/11/breisach-a-hotspot-of-european-history/
36 http://germansynagogues.com/index.php/synagogues-and-communities?pid=69&sid=290:breisach

37 https://www.jewishvirtuallibrary.org/breisachhttps://www.jewishvirtuallibrary.org/breisach
38 Gregory S. Gordon, 'The Trial of Peter von Hagenbach: Reconciling History, Historiography, and International Criminal Law', https://www.legal-tools.org/doc/5cd077/pdf
39 https://www.gdw-berlin.de/en/recess/biographies/index_of_persons/biographie/view-bio/gertrud-luckner/. https://www.yadvashem.org/righteous/stories/luckner.html

2. Black Forest, White Rose

1 http://www.dodedans.com/Ebleibach.htm
2 Christabel Bielenberg, *The Past is Myself* (London: Chatto & Windus, 1968).
3 https://journals.gold.ac.uk/index.php/bjmh/article/view/1605/1719
4 https://www.commentary.org/articles/alfred-werner/the-junker-plot-to-kill-hitlerthe-dying-gesture-of-a-class/
5 https://www.tandfonline.com/doi/full/10.1080/13518046.2024.2340839#d1e869
6 Ibid. https://encyclopedia.ushmm.org/content/en/article/nazi-persecution-of-soviet-prisoners-of-war
7 Timothy Snyder, *Bloodlands: Europe between Hitler and Stalin* (New York: Basic, 2010), pp. 181–2.
8 Geoffrey P. Megargee, Rüdiger Overmans and Wolfgang Vogt (eds), *USHMM Encyclopedia of Camps and Ghettos, 1933–1945, Volume IV: Camps and Other Detention Facilities under the German Armed Forces* (Bloomington: Indiana University Press, 2022), pp. 423–5.
9 Thomas Pert, *The Palatinate Family and the Thirty Years War* (Oxford: Oxford University Press, 2023), p. 230.
10 Michael Clodfelter, *Warfare and Armed Conflict: A Statistical Encyclopaedia of Casualty and Other Figures, 1492–2015* (Jefferson: McFarland, 2017), p. 40.
11 https://muse.jhu.edu/pub/3/edited_volume/chapter/3467257
12 Tony Judt, *Postwar: A History of Europe Since 1945* (London: Pimlico, 2007), p. 470.
13 Quoted in Garth Davies and Vanja Zdjelar, 'The Evolution of Left-Wing Extremism in the West', pp. 23–54, in José Pedro Zúquete (ed), *The Palgrave Handbook of Left-Wing Extremism* (Cham: Palgrave Macmillan, 2023), p. 29.
14 https://www.nytimes.com/2017/05/15/world/europe/horst-mahler-germany-hungary.html. https://www.dw.com/en/german-neo-nazi-horst-mahler-released-from-prison/a-55412553
15 https://www.sueddeutsche.de/politik/mahler-neonazismus-haftstrafe-1.5095092
16 Anthony Seldon, *Churchill's Indian Summer: The Conservative Government, 1951–55* (London: Hodder & Stoughton, 1984).
17 https://encyclopedia.ushmm.org/content/en/article/leipheim-displaced-persons-camp

18 https://encyclopedia.ushmm.org/content/en/article/displaced-persons-administration
19 https://www.eisenhowerlibrary.gov/sites/default/files/research/online-documents/holocaust/report-harrison.pdf
20 https://encyclopedia.ushmm.org/content/en/timeline-event/holocaust/1942-1945/page-from-earl-g-harrisons-notebook
https://www.trumanlibrary.gov/library/public-papers/187/statement-president-problem-jewish-refugees-europe
21 Stephen Fritz, *Endkampf: Soldiers, Civilians, and the Death of the Third Reich* (Kentucky: University Press of Kentucky, 2004), pp. 235–43.
22 https://einstein-website.de/en/ulm/
23 https://www.northlincsweb.net/103Sqn/html/ulm_17-18_december_1944.html
24 https://www.white-rose-studies.org/pages/leaflet-5
25 https://collections.ushmm.org/search/catalog/irn559075
26 https://www.abendzeitung-muenchen.de/muenchen/franz-j-mueller-das-gedaechtnis-der-weissen-rose-art-368327
27 https://encyclopedia.ushmm.org/content/en/article/erwin-rommel
28 Ibid.
29 Anna Reid, *Borderland: A Journey Through the History of Ukraine* (London: Weidenfeld & Nicolson, 2015), p. 155. https://mjhnyc.org/events/rumbula-remembered-80-years-since-the-mass-executions/
30 https://encyclopedia.ushmm.org/content/en/article/einsatzgruppen. Patrick Desbois, *The Holocaust by Bullets* (New York: Palgrave Macmillan, 2008).
31 Judt, *Postwar*, p. 810.
32 Ibid., p. 811.

3. Swiftly Flows the Danube: Ulm to Donauwörth

1 https://www.atlanticcouncil.org/blogs/new-atlanticist/germanys-economy-has-gone-from-engine-to-anchor/
https://www.foreignaffairs.com/europe/what-germanys-economy-really-needs
2 https://www.bavarikon.de/object/bav:BSB-CMS-0000000000010135?p=6&lang=en
3 https://encyclopedia.ushmm.org/content/en/article/germany-jewish-population-in-1933
4 https://www.latimes.com/archives/la-xpm-1985-06-19-mn-9209-story.html
5 https://www.nytimes.com/1985/06/08/world/mengele-s-son-linked-to-man-buried-in-brazil.html
6 https://www.military-history.org/cover-feature/marlborough-and-eugene.htm
7 James Falkner, *The War of the Spanish Succession 1701–1714* (Barnsley: Pen & Sword, 2015), p. 72.
8 Randolph S. Churchill (ed.), *Winston S. Churchill: Volume II Companion, Part 2 1907–1911* (London: Heinemann, 1969), p. 912.
9 Ibid., pp. 910–11.
10 Katherine Carter, *Churchill's Citadel: Chartwell and the Gatherings before the Storm* (New Haven: Yale University Press, 2024), pp. 7–10. Martin Gilbert, *Churchill: A Life* (London: Pimlico, 1992), p. 508.

11 https://winstonchurchill.org/publications/finest-hour/finest-hour-157/france-and-the-french-a-tale-of-two-statesmen-churchill-and-napoleon/
12 Richard Brooks and Ian Drury (eds), *Atlas of World Military History: The Art of War from Ancient Times to the Present Day* (4th ed.) (New York: Barnes & Noble, 2000), p. 156.
13 https://www.dw.com/en/doll-making-pioneer-k%C3%A4the-kruse-celebrated-50-years-after-her-death/a-44744732
14 Patrick Leigh Fermor, *A Time of Gifts* (London: Folio, 1986), p. 86.
15 Robin Neillands, *The Bomber War: Arthur Harris and the Allied Bomber Offensive* (London: Hodder, 2001), pp. 290–91.
16 https://www.northlincsweb.net/103Sqn/html/augsburg_25-26_february_1944.html
17 Neillands, *Bomber War*, pp. 112–14.
18 https://www.iwm.org.uk/history/life-and-death-in-bomber-command
19 Patrick Leigh Fermor, *A Time of Gifts*, 1977; *Between the Woods and the Water*, 1986; *The Broken Road*, 2013.
20 Leigh Fermor, *A Time of Gifts*, p. 120.
21 Artemis Cooper, 'Patrick Leigh Fermor: Mythmaker', *History Today*, vol. 62, issue 12, 2012.
22 https://www.bbc.co.uk/news/world-europe-46964928
23 https://collections.yadvashem.org/en/righteous/4015126
24 https://www.gdw-berlin.de/en/recess/biographies/index_of_persons/biographie/view-bio/hans-adlhoch/?no_cache=1
25 https://www.gdw-berlin.de/en/recess/biographies/index_of_persons/biographie/view-bio/bebo-wager/?no_cache=1
26 https://www.gdw-berlin.de/en/recess/biographies/index_of_persons/biographie/view-bio/roland-heinrich-von-hoesslin/?no_cache=1

4. One Way, Four Paths: From Donauwörth to Nuremberg

1 Leigh Fermor, *A Time of Gifts*, p. 14. Artemis Cooper, *Patrick Leigh Fermor: An Adventure* (London: John Murray, 2012), p. 37.
2 Leigh Fermor, *A Time of Gifts*, pp. 18–19.
3 https://www.frankfallaarchive.org/prisons/kaisheim-prison/
4 https://encyclopedia.1914-1918-online.net/article/war-aims-and-war-aims-discussions-germany/
5 https://encyclopedia.ushmm.org/content/en/article/lebensraum
6 Ibid.
7 https://ghdi.ghi-dc.org/sub_document.cfm?document_id=1513
8 William Shawcross, 'We need the monarchy more than ever', *The Spectator*, 24.08.19.
9 Scott Hendrix, *Martin Luther: Visionary Reformer* (New Haven: Yale University Press, 2016), p. 73.
10 Ibid.
11 Eric Metaxas, *Martin Luther: The Man who Rediscovered God and Changed the World* (New York: Viking Press, 2017), p. 56.
12 https://gcdiscipleship.com/article-feed/martin-luther-theologian-of-the-cross
13 Metaxas, *Martin Luther*, pp. 144–52. https://www.1517.org/articles/luther-at-augsburg

14 https://www.ajc.org/news/on-luther-and-his-lies. Susannah Heschel, 'Kristallnacht and Its Aftermath', *Jewish Quarterly*, May 2013.

15 Michael Wildt, 'Violence Against the Jews in Germany 1933–1939', in David Bankier (ed.), *Probing the Depths of German Antisemitism: German Society and the Persecution of the Jews, 1933–1941* (Jerusalem: Yad Vashem, 2000), pp. 181–209.

16 https://100thbg.com/mission/?mission_id=305. http://www.br-101.de/start.php?n=2&s=foto_gal&thema=mtlmdt

17 https://encyclopedia.ushmm.org/content/en/article/the-german-churches-and-the-nazi-state

18 https://cathedralofhope.org/wp-content/uploads/2019/03/The-Theological-Declaration-of-Barmen.pdf. https://encyclopedia.ushmm.org/content/en/article/the-german-churches-and-the-nazi-state

19 https://encyclopedia.ushmm.org/content/en/article/martin-niemoeller-biography

20 Ibid.

21 https://marcuse.faculty.history.ucsb.edu/projects/niem/StuttgartDeclaration.htm

22 https://www.vatican.va/content/pius-xi/en/encyclicals/documents/hf_p-xi_enc_14031937_mit-brennender-sorge.html

23 https://www.gdw-berlin.de/en/recess/biographies/index_of_persons/biographie/view-bio/clemens-august-graf-von-galen/?no_cache=1

24 https://encyclopedia.ushmm.org/content/en/article/the-german-churches-and-the-nazi-state

25 Charles L. Mee, *White Robe, Black Robe* (New York: Putnam, 1972), p. 217.

26 https://www.spp-haefen.de/en/projects/fossa-carolina/

27 https://www.hmdb.org/m.asp?m=142632

28 David Stafford, *Endgame 1945: The Missing Final Chapter of World War II* (New York: Hachette, 2007), p. 144.

29 https://www.tracesofevil.com/1995/07/remaining-nazi-sites-in-upper-palatinate.html

30 https://www.gdw-berlin.de/en/recess/biographies/index_of_persons/biographie/view-bio/johann-maier/?no_cache=1

31 Stafford, *Endgame 1945*, p. 144.

32 Gerhard F. Strasser, 'The Heroic Rescue of Thirteen Prisoners from a Death March near Regensburg', Wiener Holocaust Library, 2021, https://wienerholocaustlibrary.org/2021/06/14/the-heroic-rescue-of-thirteen-prisoners-from-a-death-march-near-regensburg/

33 Ibid.

34 Ibid.

35 https://www.gedenkstaette-stille-helden.de/en/silent-heroes/biographies/biographie/detail-145

36 Gryn, *Chasing Shadows*, pp. 190–91. Hugo's daughter Naomi has questioned his account of entering the ante-chamber of the gas chambers, believing that this, and some other incidents, might have been partly fictionalized or exaggerated. 'He writes in the voice of a thirteen-year-old trying to make sense of the drama unfolding around him, as the fragile mask of civilization begins to crumble.' See the note in Gryn, *Chasing Shadows*, p. 173.

37 Ibid., p. 237.

38 Ibid., p. 239.

39 Ibid.

40 Ibid.

41 Ibid., p. 241. Naomi Gryn writes that Ge´za almost certainly died twelve days after liberation, on 16 May 1945, which was the date that Hugo gave to interrogators in July 1945. That he later condensed this to three days was probably an issue of memory. However, as this text quotes Gryn's book, I have left it as he remembered it.

42 Michael Buerk, Foreword, in Naomi Gryn (ed.), *Three Minutes of Hope: Hugo Gryn on the God Slot* (London: Continuum, 2010), p. xvii.

5. The Road to Flossenbürg

1 https://encyclopedia.ushmm.org/content/en/article/flossenbuerg
2 Ibid. Nikolaus Wachsmann, *KL: A History of the Nazi Concentration Camps* (London: Little, Brown, 2015), Kindle location 5939–5972.
3 https://www.washingtontimes.com/news/2012/dec/10/book-review-hitlers-berlin/
4 Stephen Brockmann, *Nuremberg: The Imaginary Capital* (New York: Camden House, 2006), p. 136.
5 William L. Shirer, *Berlin Diary: The Journal of a Foreign Correspondent, 1934–1941* (New York: Alfred A. Knopf, 1941), p. 21.
6 https://museums.nuernberg.de/documentation-center/the-site/the-nazi-party-rally-grounds/information-system-rally-grounds/point-02
7 Albert Speer, *Inside the Third Reich: Memoirs* (New York: Macmillan, 1970), p. 59.
8 Cesarani, *Final Solution*, pp. 103–06. https://encyclopedia.ushmm.org/content/en/article/the-nuremberg-race-laws.
9 https://encyclopedia.ushmm.org/content/en/article/the-nuremberg-race-laws
10 https://encyclopedia.ushmm.org/content/en/article/germany-jewish-population-in-1933. https://encyclopedia.ushmm.org/content/en/article/jewish-population-of-europe-in-1933-population-data-by-country
11 Cesarani, *Final Solution*, p. 94.
12 Ibid., p. 104.
13 Ibid., pp. 103–6.
14 Ibid., p. 106.
15 Steve Crawshaw, *Prosecuting the Powerful: War Crimes and the Battle for Justice* (London: Bridge Street Press, 2025).
16 https://www.opcw.org/about-us/history
17 For the full story see William Schabas, *The Trial of the Kaiser* (Oxford: Oxford University Press, 2018). Heather Jones, *For King and Country: The British Monarchy and the First World War* (Cambridge: Cambridge University Press, 2021), pp. 307–8.
18 https://www.cvce.eu/en/obj/moscow_declaration_on_atrocities_1_november_1943-en-699fc03f-19a1-47f0-aec0-73220489efcd.html
19 https://avalon.law.yale.edu/imt/jack_preface.asp
20 https://www.un.org/en/genocideprevention/documents/atrocity-crimes/Doc.2_Charter%20of%20IMT%201945.pdf
21 Telford Taylor, *Nuremberg and Vietnam: An American Tragedy* (New York: Bantam Books, 1971), p. 142.
22 https://www.robertjackson.org/speech-and-writing/opening-statement-before-the-international-military-tribunal/

23 Airey Neave, *On Trial at Nuremberg* (Toronto: Little, Brown & Company, 1978), p. 63.
24 Ibid., p. 79. https://www.roberthjackson.org/nuremberg-event/hess-final-statement/
25 Neave, *On Trial at Nuremberg*, pp. 93–6.
26 https://www.roberthjackson.org/artifact/cathedral-in-ruins/
27 https://thebookerprizes.com/the-booker-library/judges/rebecca-west Foreword to Neave, *On Trial at Nuremberg*, p. 7.
28 Rebecca West, *A Train of Powder* (New York: Viking Press, 1955), pp. 9–13.
29 https://www.theguardian.com/uk/2002/jun/29/research.monarchy
30 West, *A Train of Powder*, p. 72. https://www.kansas.com/news/local/article193628024.html#storylink=cpy
31 http://law2.umkc.edu/faculty/projects/ftrials/nuremberg/NurembergNews10_16_46.html#:~:text=His%2
32 https://encyclopedia.ushmm.org/content/en/timeline-event/holocaust/after-1945/verdicts-international-military-tribunal
33 Neave, *On Trial at Nuremberg*, p. 313.
34 Ibid., p. 138.
35 https://www.theguardian.com/world/2007/mar/13/secondworldwar.kateconnolly https://www.spiegel.de/international/spiegel-s-daily-take-speer-s-hidden-hand-at-auschwitz-a-355376.html
36 https://www.trumanlibrary.gov/education/presidential-inquiries/justice-nuremberg
37 https://www.timesofisrael.com/historian-examines-germanys-minute-number-of-convictions-for-nazi-war-crimes/
38 https://avalon.law.yale.edu/imt/07-27-46.asp
39 Ibid.
40 https://www.yadvashem.org/righteous/stories/graebe.html
41 https://www.bbc.co.uk/programmes/m00100rd. https://www.bbc.co.uk/news/videos/c625nlxjpz7o. https://www.bbc.co.uk/news/world-middle-east-67339008
42 https://www.dw.com/en/nuremberg-trials-courtroom-witnesses-last-ever-judgement/g-52445080
43 https://museums.nuernberg.de/fileadmin/mdsn/pdf/Memorium/Infobroschueren/exhibit-brochure.pdf
44 https://dirkbogarde.co.uk/dirk-bogarde-and-belsen/. https://www.iwm.org.uk/collections/item/object/80030022
45 https://www.bbc.co.uk/news/av/stories-63317358
46 https://www.bbc.co.uk/videos/c87z7p0j3g5o
47 https://hmd.org.uk/resource/susan-pollack/. https://www.theguardian.com/books/2025/mar/22/what-is-the-meaning-of-life-15-possible-answers-from-a-palliative-care-doctor-a-holocaust-survivor-a-jail-inmate-and-more
48 Phil Craig, *1945: The Reckoning* (London: Hodder & Stoughton, 2025), p. 284.
49 https://www.gdw-berlin.de/en/recess/biographies/index_of_persons/biographie/view-bio/hermann-luppe/?no_cache=1
50 https://collections.yadvashem.org/en/righteous/4014845
51 https://www.jewishvirtuallibrary.org/floss

52 Geoffrey P. Megargee (ed.), *USHMM Encyclopedia of Camps and Ghettos, 1933–1945, Volume I, Part A* (Bloomington: Indiana University Press, 2009), pp. 561–3.
53 https://www.dark-tourism.com/index.php/218-flossenbuerg-concentration-camp
54 Ibid.
55 https://www.gedenkstaette-flossenbuerg.de/en/history/prisoners/andrij-andrijowytsch-juschtschenko
56 https://www.jewishvirtuallibrary.org/wilhelm-canaris
57 Ibid.
58 Richard Bassett, *Hitler's Spy Chief: The Wilhelm Canaris Mystery* (London: Weidenfeld & Nicolson, 2006), pp. 178–80.
59 Ibid., pp. 194–5.
60 Michael Thomsett, *The German Opposition to Hitler: The Resistance, the Underground, and Assassination Plots, 1938–1945* (London: Crux Publishing, 2016), Kindle location 2763–2825.
61 Bassett, *Hitler's Spy Chief*, p. 221.
62 Ibid., p. 178. https://www.jewishvirtuallibrary.org/wilhelm-canaris#google_vignette
63 https://www.britannica.com/biography/Dietrich-Bonhoeffer
64 Thomsett, *The German Opposition*, Kindle location 2685.
65 https://encyclopedia.ushmm.org/content/en/article/dietrich-bonhoeffer
66 Eric Metaxas, *Bonhoeffer: Pastor, Martyr, Prophet, Spy* (Nashville: Nelson Books, 2010), p. 528.

6. Sudetenland: From Flossenbürg to Prague

1 https://www.rafmuseum.org.uk/blog/poles-and-czechoslovaks-in-the-battle-of-britain/
2 William Faulkner, *Requiem for a Nun* (New York: Random House, 1951).
3 https://www.britannica.com/biography/Charles-IV-Holy-Roman-emperor
4 Martyn Rady, *The Habsburgs: The Rise and Fall of a World Power* (London: Allen Lane, 2020), pp. 75–8.
5 Rady, *The Habsburgs*, p. 134.
6 https://www.britannica.com/biography/Konstantin-Freiherr-von-Neurath. https://encyclopedia.ushmm.org/content/en/article/reinhard-heydrich-in-depth. Ian Baxter, *Heydrich: The Butcher of Prague* (Barnsley: Pen & Sword, 2022), p. 37.
7 https://www.historytoday.com/miscellanies/who-lost-czechoslovakia-communism
8 https://www.oxfordreference.com/display/10.1093/acref/9780191826719.001.0001/q-oro-ed4-00002794
9 Tim Bouverie, *Appeasing Hitler: Churchill, Chamberlain and the Road to War* (London: Penguin, 2019), pp. 271–4.
10 https://english.radio.cz/killings-czechoslovak-border-during-communist-era-examined-new-report-8093711
11 Ibid.
12 https://magazin.pametnaroda.cz/pribehy/umiral-v-lese-nekolik-dni-jedna-z-poslednich-obeti-strelby-na-hranicich. https://www.dw.com/en/former-minister-on-trial-for-border-deaths-in-communist-era/a-65697901. https://www.jsns.cz/projekty/pribehy-bezpravi/den-pb-2024

13 https://www.bbc.co.uk/news/world-europe-27129727
14 John Charmley, *Chamberlain and the Lost Peace* (London: Macmillan, 1989), pp. 133–5.
15 https://api.parliament.uk/historic-hansard/commons/1938/oct/05/policy-of-his-majestys-government#S5CV0339P0_19381005_HOC_216
16 https://www.findmypast.co.uk/blog/history/clement-attlee-labour-party
17 Alfred J. Rieber, *Stalin and the Struggle for Supremacy in Eurasia* (Cambridge: Cambridge University Press, 2015), pp. 327–8.
18 https://www.dhm.de/lemo/kapitel/der-zweite-weltkrieg/kriegsverlauf/flucht-der-deutschen-194445
19 https://english.radio.cz/memories-world-war-ii-czech-lands-expulsion-sudeten-germans-8097851
20 https://mzv.gov.cz/file/198499/CzechGermanDeclaration.pdf
21 Judt, *Postwar*, pp. 22–7.
22 https://www.gabreta.info/gabreta/fr.asp. https://www.academia.edu/4401298/Die_Goldene_Stra%C3%9Fe_Zlat%C3%A1_cestaLauf_HersbruckHersbruck_HirschauHirschauHirschau_Sulzbach_Sulzbach_Sulzbach_RosenbergRosenbergFuhrwerke_zur_damaligen_Zeit_Fl%C3%A4mische_Miniatur_von_Jehan_de_Grise. https://ec.europa.eu/regional_policy/en/projects/europe/golden-road-history-park-to-boost-tourism-and-culture-on-the-czech-german-border
23 https://sokolmuseum.org/history-of-sokol/
24 https://www.czech-stuff.com/czech-hiking-signs/
25 https://english.radio.cz/forgotten-heroes-maps-stories-sudeten-anti-fascists-8601369
26 https://www.touskov.cz/mesto/o-meste-touskove/historie-mesta/
27 https://www.tracesofwar.com/sights/11772/Patton-Memorial-Museum-Pilsen.htm
28 Don Fox, *Final Battles of Patton's Vanguard: The United States Fourth Armored Division, 1945–46* (Jefferson: McFarland & Co, 2020), p. 273.
29 https://english.radio.cz/june-21-1949-general-heliodor-pika-executed-after-a-show-trial-8820535. https://english.radio.cz/heliodor-pika-general-who-became-communist-regimes-first-judicial-murder-victim-8127867
30 https://www.holocaust.cz/en/history/people/premysl-pitter-2/. https://english.radio.cz/premysl-pitter-a-forgotten-czech-schindler-8630532 https://www.yadvashem.org/yv/pdf-drupal/czech-republic.pdf

7. Prague, Lidice, Terezín

1 Jonathan Smith, *Wilfred and Eileen* (London: Hutchinson, 1976).
2 https://encyclopedia.ushmm.org/content/en/article/wannsee-conference-and-the-final-solution
3 Callum MacDonald, *The Assassination of Reinhard Heydrich: The True Story Behind Operation Anthropoid* (Edinburgh: Birlinn, 2011), p. 204.
4 Ibid., pp. 222–3.
5 https://www.mo.gov.cz/images/id_7001_8000/7419/assassination-en.pdf
6 MacDonald, *The Assassination of Reinhard Heydrich*, pp. 249–50.
7 Ibid., pp. 247–9.
8 Ibid., p. 5.

9 https://encyclopedia.ushmm.org/content/en/article/reinhard-heydrich-in-depth
10 https://newspapers.ushmm.org/events/czech-town-of-lidice-destroyed-in-brutal-nazi-reprisal
11 https://www.mo.gov.cz/images/id_7001_8000/7419/assassination-en.pdf
12 MacDonald, *The Assassination of Reinhard Heydrich*, p. 281.
13 https://www.nytimes.com/1942/08/06/archives/british-repudiate-1938-munich-pact-say-fixing-of-czechoslovakias.html
14 https://www.europeum.org/en/events/invitation-debate-debat-d-idees-80-years-ago-general-de-gaulle-declared-the-munich-agreement-null-and-void/
15 https://www.lidice-memorial.cz/en/memorial/memorial-and-reverent-area/history-of-the-village-lidice/#c240
16 https://www.nytimes.com/1942/06/11/archives/nazis-blot-out-czech-village-kill-all-men-disperse-others-germans.html
17 https://www.stoke.gov.uk/Lidice
18 https://www.lidice-memorial.cz/en/memorial/memorial-and-reverent-area/history-of-the-village-lidice/
19 https://www.nytimes.com/2021/04/18/world/europe/marie-supikova-dead
20 Ibid.
21 https://www.bbc.co.uk/news/uk-england-stoke-staffordshire-19506080
22 https://www.nytimes.com/2021/04/18/world/europe/marie-supikova-dead
23 https://uprootedchildren.eu/en/materials/cards/marie-supikova/. https://encyclopedia.ushmm.org/content/en/article/subsequent-nuremberg-proceedings-case-8-the-rusha-case
24 https://english.radio.cz/memoriam-marie-supikova-one-last-survivors-lidice-massacre-8712796
25 https://arolsen-archives.org/en/news/marie-supikova-living-for-remembrance/
26 https://www.jewishvirtuallibrary.org/jewish-badge
27 https://www.worldjewishcongress.org/en/about/communities/CZ. https://www.jewishmuseum.cz/en/explore/permanent-exhibitions/history-of-the-jews-in-bohemia-and-moravia-in-the-19th-20th-century/
28 https://www.anumuseum.org.il/blog/prague-museum-2/
29 https://encyclopedia.ushmm.org/content/en/article/the-holocaust-in-bohemia-and-moravia
30 https://hmd.org.uk/resource/sir-nicholas-winton/
31 David James Smith, *One Morning in Sarajevo: 28 June 1914* (London: Weidenfeld & Nicolson, 2008), p. 232.
32 Ibid., pp. 268–9.
33 Ibid., p. 270.
34 Ludmila Chládková, *Jewish Cemetery in Terezín* (Terezín: Památník Terezín, 2004), pp. 51–4. https://encyclopedia.ushmm.org/content/en/article/reinhard-heydrich-in-depth
35 https://collections.ushmm.org/search/catalog/irn1004374. https://perspectives.ushmm.org/item/shoah-outtake-with-maurice-rossel
36 https://encyclopedia.ushmm.org/content/en/article/theresienstadt
37 https://encyclopedia.ushmm.org/content/en/article/theresienstadt-final-weeks-liberation-and-postwar-trials
38 https://encyclopedia.ushmm.org/content/en/article/theresienstadt
39 https://donne-uk.org/ilse-weber/

40 Milan Kuna, 'Music in the Terezín Ghetto' in Vojtěch Blodig et al., *Art Against Death: Permanent Exhibitions of the Terezín Memorial in the Former Magdeburg Barracks*, trans. Jan Valeška (Prague: Helena Osvaldová for the Terezín Museum, Terezín, 2002), p. 20.
41 https://www.defiantrequiem.org/concert-performances/defiant-requiem/acclaim/we-will-sing-to-the-nazis-what-we-cannot-say/
42 https://holocaustmusic.ort.org/places/theresienstadt/schachter-rafael/
43 Ibid.
44 https://www.defiantrequiem.org/concert-performances/defiant-requiem/description/
45 Albert Zoller, *Twelve Years with Hitler: Secretary to the Führer* (Barnsley: Pen & Sword, 2025), p. 43.
46 As detailed in Anne Sebba, *The Women's Orchestra of Auschwitz: A Story of Survival* (London: Weidenfeld & Nicolson, 2025).
47 https://www.ft.com/content/f67b6be4-96f2-4f1b-92a4-1212ca8967ff

8. Central and East Bohemia: Prague to Pardubice

1 The walk in this chapter in fact took place before the events in chapters 6 and 7, but for reasons of geographical coherence, it follows them in the book.
2 https://www.cheminsdememoire.gouv.fr/en/revue/liberating-france-0
3 https://www.britannica.com/event/Warsaw-Uprising. Chris Bellamy, *Absolute War: Soviet Russia in the Second World War* (London: Macmillan, 2007), pp. 616–19.
4 https://warfarehistorynetwork.com/article/prague-uprising-in-the-spring-of-1945/
5 https://english.radio.cz/petscheks-palace-once-headquarters-nazi-secret-police-8560321. https://www.prazskepovstani.cz/en/places-and-stories/pankrac-prison/
6 https://warfarehistorynetwork.com/article/prague-uprising-in-the-spring-of-1945/. Igor Lukes, *On the Edge of the Cold War: American Diplomats and Spies in Postwar Prague* (Oxford: Oxford University Press, 2012), p. 50.
7 Martin Gilbert, *Churchill and America* (London: Free Press, 2005), p. 349.
8 https://warfarehistorynetwork.com/article/prague-uprising-in-the-spring-of-1945/. Rona Mendelsohn, *Liberation: 65th Anniversary, 2010* (Prague: US Embassy, 2010), p. 14: https://www.aic.cz/osvobozeni/Liberation.pdf
9 Bryan Dickerson, *The Liberators of Pilsen: The US 16th Armored Division in World War II Czechoslovakia*, (Jefferson: McFarland, 2018), p. 133.
10 Eisenhower referred only to the requirement for 'careful coordination' in his memoir. Dwight D. Eisenhower, *Crusade in Europe* (London: William Heinemann, 1948), pp. 455–6.
11 https://www.historytoday.com/miscellanies/who-lost-czechoslovakia-communism
12 Lynne Olson, *Last Hope Island: Britain, Occupied Europe, and the Brotherhood That Helped Turn the Tide of War* (London: Random House Publishing Group, 2018), p. 429.
13 https://www.vevelke.cz/l/zapomenuta-marie-kuderikova/
14 https://ukar.ff.cuni.cz/en/about-us/history/ruzena-vackova/
15 Ibid.

16 https://victimsofcommunism.org/remembering-milada-horakova/. https://english.radio.cz/milada-horakova-politician-and-womens-rights-activist-executed-communists-8787151

17 https://www.pragueczechtravel.com/prague-tips/celakovice-small-town-day-trip.php. https://www.celmuz.cz/filemanager/files/file.php?file=278272

18 https://www.celmuz.cz/filemanager/files/file.php?file=278272. https://www.academia.edu/8854480/Time_to_Slay_Vampire_Burials_The_Archaeological_and_Historical_Evidence_for_Vampires_in_Europe

19 https://english.radio.cz/nymburk-back-first-republic-8214803

20 https://english.radio.cz/best-spas-czech-republic-8721557/9

21 https://www.bartolomejskenavrsi.cz/en/history-of-hillock/ossuary

22 https://www.jewishvirtuallibrary.org/kolin. https://topi.is.cuni.cz/bitstream/handle/20.500.14178/2213/Athens_23_eng.pdf?sequence=1&isAllowed=y

23 Laurence Rees, *The Nazi Mind: Twelve Warnings from History* (London: Viking, 2025), p. 312.

24 https://longreads.com/2016/08/23/the-secret-nazi-attempt-to-breed-the-perfect-horse/. https://militaryhistorynow.com/2018/11/25/operation-cowboy-how-american-gis-german-soldiers-joined-forces-to-save-the-legendary-lipizzaner-horses-in-the-final-hours-of-ww2/. https://web.archive.org/web/20090211212753/http://vault.sportsillustrated.cnn.com/vault/article/magazine/MAG1007241/index.htm. https://www.army.mil/article/149164/army_europe_czech_republic_celebrates_70th_anniversary_of_operation_cowboy

25 https://jewish-heritage-europe.eu/2021/11/30/cz-photographer-captures-invisible-synagogues/. https://kulturaktiv.org/en/events/stepan-bartos-unsichtbare-synagogen/

26 https://www.museumoftolerance.com/education/teacher-resources/holocaust-resources/what-is-holocaust-denial.html#19. https://www.auschwitz.org/en/history/auschwitz-and-shoah/the-number-of-victims/

27 https://www.jewishvirtuallibrary.org/aktion-1005

28 https://www.yadvashem.org/odot_pdf/Microsoft%20Word%20-%203576.pdf

29 https://digitalcommons.iwu.edu/cgi/viewcontent.cgi?article=1170&context=constructing

30 https://www.jewishvirtuallibrary.org/a-brief-history-of-holocaust-denial

31 https://www.france24.com/en/20181022-french-academic-convicted-holocaust-denier-faurisson-dies-vichy-89. https://www.adl.org/glossary/arthur-butz. https://www.jewishvirtuallibrary.org/irving-v-lipstadt

32 https://www.hdot.org/judge/#

33 https://www.historyextra.com/period/second-world-war/holocaust-denial-trial-who-david-irving-deborah-lipstadt-richard-j-evans/. https://www.jewishvirtuallibrary.org/irving-v-lipstadt

34 Richard Ovenden, *Burning the Books: A History of the Deliberate Destruction of Knowledge* (London: John Murray, 2022). Richard Ovenden, 'There is no political power without power over the archive', *The Observer*, 13.07.25.

9. Into Moravia: Pardubice to Ostrava

1 Steven Levitsky and Daniel Ziblatt, *How Democracies Die* (London: Viking, 2018).
2 https://ibccdigitalarchive.lincoln.ac.uk/omeka/collections/document/16397. https://www.lidovky.cz/ceska-pozice/wwii-era-bombs-under-czech-oil-refinery-to-spark-pardubice-mass-evacuation.A111202_145628_pozice_46909
3 https://www.zamecek-memorial.cz/en/
4 Michal Burian, Aleš Knížek, Jiří Rajlich and Eduard Stehlík, *Assassination: Operation Anthropoid, 1941–1942* (Prague: The Military History Institute, 2007), p. 82.
5 https://wno.org.uk/news/two-centuries-of-smetana
6 https://www.auschwitz.org/en/history/auschwitz-sub-camps/brnn/
7 https://english.radio.cz/svitavy-birthplace-oskar-schindler-8559604. http://www.muzeum.svitavy.cz/stale-exp/historical-circuit-of-town/oskar-schindler-memorial/172-2/
8 https://www.theguardian.com/world/2016/oct/11/former-schindlers-list-factory-plans-czech-museum-nazi-industralist
9 David M. Crowe, *Oskar Schindler* (New York: Perseus, 2004), p. 10.
10 Ibid., pp. 57–8.
11 In his film, Spielberg used Isaac Stern as a composite figure for Bankier, Mietek Pemper and Stern himself. In fact, Schindler's biographer David Crowe refers to Bankier as 'the financial genius who ran Schindler's factory in Krakow'. Crowe, *Schindler*, pp. 101–E2.
12 Ibid., p. 409. https://www.yadvashem.org/righteous/stories/schindler.html
13 Email to author.
14 https://www.yadvashem.org/righteous/stories/schindler.html
15 Ibid.
16 https://encyclopedia.ushmm.org/content/en/article/plaszow
17 https://encyclopedia.ushmm.org/content/en/article/oskar-schindler. https://www.yadvashem.org/righteous/stories/schindler.html
18 https://www.yadvashem.org/righteous/stories/schindler.html
19 https://english.radio.cz/schindlers-factory-holocaust-memorial-museum-survivors-officially-opens-brnenec-8850859
20 https://www.memoryofnations.eu/en/hermanova-louise-1916
21 Ibid.
22 https://encyklopedie.brna.cz/home-mmb/?acc=profil_osobnosti&load=2895
23 https://www.lidovky.cz/relax/lide/operace-anthropoid-jen-ciny-pro-vlast-prinesou-ovoce-rikal-kaplan-petrek.A170515_124521_lide_sij
24 https://english.radio.cz/17th-november-remembering-jan-opletal-martyr-occupied-nation-8625677 https://www.lowellmilkencenter.org/programs/projects/view/jan-opletal-martyr-of-an-occupied-nation/hero
25 MacDonald, *The Assassination of Reinhard Heydrich*, pp. 117–18.
26 https://www.nytimes.com/2025/04/17/us/politics/trump-harvard-international-students.html
27 https://www.prospectmagazine.co.uk/world/united-states/69642/is-trumps-america-a-new-reich
28 https://www.nytimes.com/2025/03/14/technology/elon-musk-x-post-hitler-stalin-mao.html

29 https://www.prospectmagazine.co.uk/world/united-states/69642/is-trumps-america-a-new-reich
30 https://www.telegraph.co.uk/us/politics/2025/05/25/fiona-hill-interview-trump-terrified-putin-seen-firsthand/
31 https://www.britannica.com/biography/John-Amos-Comenius. https://www.academia.edu/11462026/Was_Komensk%C3%BD_Offered_the_Presidency_of_Harvard
32 https://www.nm.cz/en/program/exhibitions/the-czech-national-uprising
33 https://spravy.pravda.sk/domace/clanok/162455-bedrich-smetana-malmenovca-masovy-vrah-terorizoval-nemcov/. https://www.faz.net/aktuell/politik/ausland/verbrechen-an-vertriebenen-das-massaker-in-prerau-13646843.html
34 https://www.industriemuseum.be/en/news/2023/3/the-story-of-the-ostrava-ironworks-and-steelworks
35 https://english.radio.cz/80-years-ago-moravia-ostrava-offensive-bloodiest-battles-czech-soil-8844927. https://english.radio.cz/liberating-ostrava-bloodiest-wwii-battle-czech-soil-8098548
36 https://english.radio.cz/liberating-ostrava-bloodiest-wwii-battle-czech-soil-8098548
37 https://www.vhu.cz/exhibit/tank-zizka-s-rakvi-stepana-vajdy-v-moravske-ostrave/
38 Vladimír Marek, 'A Too Proud Son of the Chodsko Region', pp. 64–5, *Czech Armed Forces Review*, 2/2011, https://web.archive.org/web/20130310125157/http://www.mocr.army.cz/assets/multimedia-a-knihovna/casopisy/czech-army/areview_2-2011.pdf
39 https://web.archive.org/web/20241221200528/https://vojenskerozhledy.cz/kategorie-clanku/bez-rozsudku
40 https://www.lidovky.cz/domov/komunisticky-cenzor-vymazal-bursika-hrdinu-od-kyjeva-razitkem-zavadne.A131104_220837_ln_domov_sm
41 https://www.warhistoryonline.com/instant-articles/czechoslovaks-battle-of-kiev.html
42 https://www.hrad.cz/en/president-of-the-cr/former-presidents/ludvik-svoboda
43 https://www.warhistoryonline.com/instant-articles/czechoslovaks-battle-of-kiev.html. ttps://www.edinburghnews.scotsman.com/sport/football/hibs/new-hibs-recruits-war-hero-grandfather-provides-constant-inspiration-4687960
44 https://www.stokesentinel.co.uk/sport/football/football-news/stoke-city-josef-bursik-grandad-4862408
45 https://www.memoryofnations.eu/en/vsterbova-jarmila-1931

10. Silesia, Poland, Auschwitz

1 Lewis Baston, *Borderlines: A History of Europe in 29 Borders* (Hachette, 2024).
2 https://encyclopedia.1914-1918-online.net/article/poland/
3 Angus Konstam, *Hunt the Bismarck* (Oxford: Osprey, 2019), p. 273.
4 Halik Kochanski, *The Eagle Unbowed: Poland and the Poles in the Second World War* (London: Penguin, 2013), p. 234.

5 Interview, Anna Clunes. https://www.gov.pl/web/unitedkingdom/ceremonies-in-newark-to-mark-repatriation-of-bodies-of-three-polish-presidents-in-exile2
6 https://www.bbc.co.uk/news/articles/cneej0r2n7go. For Zawacka's story, see Clare Mulley, *Agent Zo: The Untold Story of Courageous WW2 Resistance Fighter Elżbieta Zawacka* (London: Weidenfeld & Nicolson, 2024).
7 Clare Mulley, *The Spy Who Loved: The Secrets and Lives of One of Britain's Bravest Wartime Heroines* (London: Macmillan, 2012), pp. 102, 259. https://www.spectator.co.uk/article/the-bravest-of-the-brave-2/
8 Mulley, *The Spy Who Loved*, p. 333.
9 Ibid., pp. 244–51.
10 Ibid., p. 346.
11 https://encyclopedia.ushmm.org/content/en/article/the-kielce-pogrom-a-blood-libel-massacre-of-holocaust-survivors. https://web.archive.org/web/20250219055722/https://polin.pl/pl/rocznica-pogromu-zydow-w-kielcach
12 https://www.dw.com/en/polish-radical-right-wing-mp-disrupts-lecture-on-holocaust/a-65795483. https://www.bbc.co.uk/news/world-europe-68014535
13 Martin Gilbert, *The Boys: The Story of 732 Young Concentration Camp Survivors* (London: Henry Holt, 1996), pp. 261–6.
14 Interview, Michael Helfgott.
15 https://culture.pl/en/article/water-under-the-bridge-the-river-wisla-in-literature-music-art
16 Krzysztof Olszewski, 'The Rise and Decline of the Polish-Lithuanian Commonwealth due to Grain Trade', 2007, https://mpra.ub.uni-muenchen.de/68805/1/MPRA_paper_68805.pdf

17 Geoffrey P. Megargee (ed.) et al., *USHMM Encyclopedia of Camps and Ghettos, 1933–1945, Volume I, Part A* (Bloomington: Indiana University Press, 2009), pp. 274–5.
18 Robert Gellately, *The Gestapo and German Society: Enforcing Racial Policy 1933–1945* (Oxford: Oxford University Press, 1990), p. 219.
19 Philippe Sands, *East West Street: On the Origins of Genocide and Crimes Against Humanity* (London: Weidenfeld & Nicolson, 2016), p. 219.
20 https://www.holocausthistoricalsociety.org.uk/contents/germanbiographies/frankhans.html
21 Office of United States Chief of Counsel for Prosecution of Axis Criminality, *Nazi Conspiracy and Aggression, Volume II* (Washington: United States Government Printing Office., 1946), pp. 633–4. https://www.holocausthistoricalsociety.org.uk/contents/germanbiographies/frankhans.html
22 Ian Baxter, *The Ghettos of Nazi-Occupied Poland* (Barnsley: Pen & Sword, 2020), p. 19.
23 https://hmd.org.uk/resource/13-march-1943-krakow-ghetto-is-liquidated/
24 Judy Batalion, *The Light of Days: Women Fighters of the Jewish Resistance, Their Untold Story* (London: Virago Press, 2021), pp. 145–6. https://www.jewishgen.org/yizkor/Krakow2/kra030.html. https://www.yadvashem.org/articles/general/armed-resistance-in-krakow-and-bialystok.html
25 https://aihp.org/remembering-pharmacys-past-tadeusz-pankiewicz-a-biography-of-a-wwii-pharmacist/

26 https://collections.yadvashem.org/en/righteous/4016763. https://aihp.org/remembering-pharmacys-past-tadeusz-pankiewicz-a-biography-of-a-wwii-pharmacist/. https://wienerholocaustlibrary.org/2019/05/13/387/
27 https://collections.yadvashem.org/en/righteous/4016763
28 https://aihp.org/remembering-pharmacys-past-tadeusz-pankiewicz-a-biography-of-a-wwii-pharmacist/
29 https://www.britannica.com/biography/Saint-Maksymilian-Maria-Kolbe. https://web.archive.org/web/20140304201831/http://en.auschwitz.org/m/index.php?option=com_content&task=view&id=795&Itemid=8
30 https://www.nytimes.com/1972/10/16/archives/150000-at-auschwitz-pay-homage-to-polish-martyr.html
31 The story is told in a remarkable book, *The Birdman of Auschwitz: The Life of Günther Niethammer, the Ornithologist Seduced by the Nazis* by Nicholas Milton (Havertown: Pen & Sword, 2025).
32 The United States Holocaust Memorial Museum states 44,000 concentration camps, incarceration sites and ghettos, https://encyclopedia.ushmm.org/content/en/article/nazi-camps. The extermination camps were: Chełmno, Belzec, Sobibor, Treblinka, Majdanek, Auschwitz-Birkenau.
33 https://encyclopedia.ushmm.org/content/en/article/auschwitz
34 https://www.jewishvirtuallibrary.org/estimated-number-of-jews-killed-in-the-final-solution
35 https://encyclopedia.ushmm.org/content/en/article/auschwitz
36 Cesarani, *Final Solution*, pp. 454–9.
37 Ibid., p. 520.
38 https://encyclopedia.ushmm.org/content/en/article/auschwitz
39 Cesarani, *Final Solution*, pp. 718–21. https://encyclopedia.ushmm.org/content/en/article/auschwitz
40 https://encyclopedia.ushmm.org/content/en/article/auschwitz
41 Elie Wiesel, *Night* (New York: Hill & Wang, 2006), pp. 29–31.
42 Primo Levi, *If This Is a Man* (New York: The Onion Press, 1959), pp. 10–12.
43 Primo Levi, Introduction to Rudolf Höss, *Commandant of Auschwitz* (London: Phoenix Press, 2000).
44 Elie Wiesel, 'Con l'incubo che tutto sia accaduto invano', *La Stampa*, 14.04.87.
45 https://www.bbc.co.uk/news/articles/c5y98xyqew5o. https://www.nytimes.com/2025/02/25/world/europe/marian-turski-dead.html. https://polin.pl/en/marian-turskis-speech-80th-anniversary-liberation-auschwitz
46 https://www.washingtonexaminer.com/news/world/3301314/netanyahu-skips-auschwitz-ceremony-icc-arrest/
47 https://www.mp.pl/auschwitz/journal/english/261269,the-womens-hospital-at-auschwitz-birkenau
48 https://www.auschwitz.at/ella-lingens-en
49 https://www.auschwitz-prozess.de/zeugenaussagen/Lingens-Ella/
50 https://www.yadvashem.org/YV/en/exhibitions/righteous-auschwitz/index.asp
51 Ernst Klee, *Auschwitz: Täter, Gehilfen, Opfer und was aus ihnen wurde: ein Personenlexikon* (S. Fischer: Frankfurt, 2013), pp. 258–9.
52 https://hmd.org.uk/resource/witold-pilecki/

53 https://biogramy.ipn.gov.pl/bio/wszystkie-biogramy/106001,Rotmistrz-Witold-Pilecki.html
54 https://hmd.org.uk/resource/witold-pilecki/
55 Captain Witold Pilecki, *The Auschwitz Volunteer: Beyond Bravery* (Los Angeles: Aquila Polonica, 2012), p. xvii. https://www.bbc.co.uk/travel/article/20250113-the-man-who-volunteered-for-auschwitz. https://biogramy.ipn.gov.pl/bio/wszystkie-biogramy/106001,Rotmistrz-Witold-Pilecki.html
56 David G. Roskies (ed.), *The Literature of Destruction: Jewish Responses to Catastrophe* (London: The Jewish Publications Society, 1988), pp. 548–64.
57 https://www.auschwitz.org/en/museum/news/from-the-heart-of-hell-publication-with-manuscripts-of-zalmen-gradowski-a-member-of-sonderkommando-at-auschwitz-,1298.html
58 https://encyclopedia.ushmm.org/content/en/timeline-event/holocaust/1942-1945/auschwitz-revolt. https://www.gdw-berlin.de/en/recess/biographies/index_of_persons/biographie/view-bio/rosa-robota/?no_cache=1. https://jwa.org/encyclopedia/article/robota-roza
59 https://encyclopedia.ushmm.org/content/en/article/corrie-ten-boom. https://ca.thegospelcoalition.org/article/the-forgiveness-of-corrie-ten-boom/
60 https://encyclopedia.ushmm.org/content/en/article/westerbork
61 Etty Hillesum, *An Interrupted Life: The Diaries of Etty Hillesum 1941–1943* (New York: Pantheon, 1983), pp. 214–5.
62 Etty Hillesum, *Etty Hillesum: Letters from Westerbork* (New York: Pantheon, 1986), p. 56.
63 Hillesum, *An Interrupted Life*, p. 180.
64 Hillesum, *Letters from Westerbork*, p. xi.
65 Etty Hillesum, *Etty: The Letters and Diaries of Etty Hillesum* (Cambridge: William B. Eeerdmans Publishing Co., 1986), pp. 658–9.

Epilogue

1 Francis Fukuyama, *The End of History and the Last Man*, (New York: Free Press, 1992).
2 https://www.newstatesman.com/world/middle-east/2025/07/a-question-of-intent
3 Laurence Rees, *The Nazi Mind: 12 Warnings from History* (London: Viking, 2025).
4 https://www.ft.com/content/e5facc32-de48-42bf-9d2b-0402aa6402dd

Acknowledgements

This book was such a challenge to write that the acknowledgements are more than usually heartfelt. Some I cannot name because of the jobs they hold. Others who showed me kindness and friendship in the four countries through which I travelled have their names lost in the mists of time. I am immensely grateful to them all.

Jonathan Meakin was the chief researcher and chief historian, as he was on *The Path of Peace*. He prepared the ten chapter briefs, read over drafts meticulously, made numerous suggestions and helped research photographs. He is a master of the craft.

At Atlantic, Ed Faulkner proved as good an editor as I have experienced since Ion Trewin at Hodder & Stoughton for my first book. His team were outstanding, especially Tamsin Shelton on copy-editing, Kate Straker on publicity and Harry O'Sullivan on photographs and amendments. My agent Matt Cole at Northbank Talent Management was excellent as always.

Jess Macaulay is the brilliant artist who drew the maps in her inimitable style. She was a model of patience and empathy.

I would like to thank my walking companions for their company and enthusiasm on and off the trail: John Ashton, Maggi Morris, John James, Greg Hands and Mark Waldron. An additional thanks to John Ashton for generously allowing me to use his photographs in Chapter 6, and to Greg Hands for his photograph in Chapter 7.

Paul Antrobus deserves a paragraph to himself. He devoted an enormous amount of time to researching the best route across the Czech Republic, then revising it repeatedly when I became unable to walk as much each day, and drove his car as backup support for three separate weeks. His knowledge and love of the country is sans pareil.

In Prague I would like to thank British Ambassador Matt Field, his wife Martina, Kate Davenport, Jana Kerberos and Michael Zantovsky. In Poland I would like to thank Ambassadors Anna Clunes and her successor, Melinda Simmons, and in Kraków, Jonathan Ornstein.

Numerous historians and authorities opened themselves up to me, including John Coldstream, James Cowan, Steve Crawshaw, Naomi Gryn, Nicholas Milton and William Shawcross. Historians Jeremy Black, Joe Davies, John Jefferies and Edward Lucas very kindly read every chapter. Michael Helfgott provided invaluable information about his family. I am grateful to others who helped too, including Andy Bambridge, Zaki Cooper, Jim Dewes, Brian Donovan, Rory Forsyth, Louise James, James Jordan, Michael Laitner, Racheli Laitner, Michael Londesborough, Dave Macaulay, Georgina Paul, Wendy Robbins and William Rollo.

I would like to thank colleagues at Epsom College and now Wellington College for encouragement and support beyond any reasonable expectation. Sophie Lawrence and my team at the former helped more than they realized. Colleagues at the latter, especially Suzie Glynn, were extraordinary. Suzie showed skill, determination and perseverance as my personal assistant, ensuring that my proper job always came first and happened on time and to the very best of my ability.

I would like to thank the medical teams who helped me in the UK without whom I'd have been unable to complete the walk. My thanks to physios Chris Keevil and Rupert Molloy. Louise James was consistently helpful with sensible advice.

Sarah, my wife, was with me as I took my first step on the walk, and my last, and for many steps in between. She brought joy and companionship, never complaining about all the many absences and sacrifices that were involved in walking and in writing this book, and I'm deeply grateful to her. Thanks also as always to my three loving and delightful children Jessica, Susie and Adam, and their partners Jonny and Steph.

Index

Note: entries in *italics* indicate illustrations

Adlhoch, Hans, 97
AI (artificial intelligence), 359
aircraft technology, 275
Aislingen, Germany, 83
All Quiet on the Western Front (book, Remarque), 171
All Quiet on the Western Front (film), 83
Alsace, France, 16–17, 20, 30–31
   Grand Canal of Alsace, 30
Alternative für Deutschland (AfD), 60, 132, 165
Amsterdam, Netherlands, 344–5
Anne, Queen of Great Britain, 84
ANO party (Czech Republic), 291
anti-Slavism, 8, 54, 183, 356
antisemitism *see* Jews/Judaism
Antrobus, Paul, 186–9, 191, 193, 195–6, 201–3, *202*, 245, 257, 274–5, 282, 299, 311–12, 322
Arendt, Hannah, 70
Armoury Hotel, Prague, 201, *202*
Aryan master race (*Herrenvolk*), 104–5, 133, 140
Ashdown, Paddy, 225
Ashton, John, 186–7, 193, 196, 199–201, *202*
Asquith, Herbert Henry, 85
al-Assad, Bashar, 9
Atkins, Vera, 316
Attlee, Clement, 63, 151, 191

Augsburg, Germany, 52, 89–97, *92*, 106, 114
   1942 bombing raids, 90–92
   Peace of Augsburg (1555), 90
Auschwitz-Birkenau concentration camp, Poland, 237, 278, 286, 331–41, 349
   atrocities in, 328
   Auschwitz I, 322, 335–6
   Auschwitz III (Monowitz), 336
   Birkenau, 322, 335
   camp commandant's house, 333
   children and, 336
   crematoria, 3, 268, 335–6, 343
   deaths in, 267, 334
   destruction of evidence, 268
   extermination methods, 334
   'female penal colony', 332
   Frankfurt trial (1963–5), 71, 340
   gas chambers, 124–5, 335–6
   liberation of, 338
   medical experiments, 80, 339
   Oświęcim station, 330, 333
   political prisoners, 341
   railway tracks, 335
   Roma prisoners, 341
   Sonderkommando rebellion, 343–4
   Vistula river and, 322
   Witold Report, 342

Auschwitz-Birkenau concentration camp, Poland (*cont.*)
   Women's Orchestra of Auschwitz, 239
   Zyklon B gas, 335
Austerlitz, Battle of (1805), 86, 207
Austria, 138, 269, 314, 339
   Anschluss, 134, 136, 339
Austro-Hungarian Empire, 193, 196, 232, 275, 312

Baader-Meinhof Gang, 57–9
Babiš, Andrej, 291
Babyn Yar massacre, Ukraine, 70, 268
Bad Bellingen, Germany, 19–20, 33
Bankier, Abraham, 285
Barenboim, Daniel, 240, *240*
Barmen Declaration (1934), 110–11
Bärnau, Germany, 187
Bartered Bride, The (Smetana), 238, 280
Bartoň, Eliška, 277
Bartoň, Ivan, 277
Bartoň, Josef, 276–7, *277*
Bartoš, Alfréd, 276
Bartoš, Štěpán, 266, 267
Basel, Switzerland, 22–3, 25, 28–30
Bassett, Richard, 169
Baston, Lewis, 313
Bavaria, Germany, 75–9, 82–5, 98, 104
BBC (British Broadcasting Corporation), 159, 359
Będzin, Poland, 169–70
Beer Hall Putsch (1923), 75, 134
Belarus, 184, 309, 357
Belgium, 199–200
Belgrade, Serbia, 41
Belzec extermination camp, Poland, 268, 334
Beneš, Edvard, 183, 191–2, 205, 212
   Beneš decrees, 192, 205
   government-in-exile (London), 183, 205, 212, 220, 276

Berchtesgaden, Bavaria, 76
Berehovo, Czechoslovakia (now Ukraine), 124
Bergen-Belsen concentration camp, Germany, 157–60, 268, 334
   liberation of, 157–60
Berlin, Germany, 79, 133
   Battle of Berlin (1945), 249
   Berlin Wall, 96
Bern, Switzerland, 23–5
Beroun, Czech Republic, 205–6
Białystok, Poland, 325
Biden, Joe, 61–2, 89
Bielenberg, Christabel, 49–50, *50*
Bielenberg, Peter, 49–50, *50*
Bismarck, Otto von, 116, 133
   'Bismarck Towers', 116
Bismarck (German battleship), 315
Black Death, 34, 79, 291
Black Forest, Germany, 41, 48, 52–3, 55, 60
Blenheim Palace, Oxfordshire, 84
Blenheim, Battle of (1704), 84–5
Bleriot, Louis, 275
Blindheim, Germany, 84, 87
Bocchetta, Vittore, 154
Bogarde, Dirk, 157–8
Bohemia, 180–83, 193–4, 207, 244–5, 281
   'Golden Road', 193–4
   Jews in, 228
Bomber War (Neillands), 91
Bonhoeffer, Dietrich, 35, 111, 167–8, 171–3, *172*, 328, 349, 361
Bonhoeffer, Klaus, 173
Bonn, Germany, 156
Borderlines (Baston), 313
Bormann, Martin, 146, 324
Boutique 005 hotel, Ulm, 65, 87
Bradley, Omar Nelson, 252
Braun, Eva, 76–7

Braun, Grzegorz, 318–19
Bray, Berkshire, 43
Breisach, Germany, 30, 33–5
Breivik, Anders, 60
Bremen (German steamship), 139
Breslau, Germany, 79
Brest Litovsk, Treaty of (1918), 104
Brněnec, Czech Republic, 286–8
Buber, Martin, 26
Buchenwald concentration camp, Germany, 121, 168, 268, 334
Budapest, Hungary, 41, 248
Buerk, Michael, 128, 360
Buršík, Josef (Czech war hero), 302–3, *303*
Bursik, Josef (footballer), 304–5
Butcher, The Baker, The (Smith), 212
Butz, Arthur, 268–9

Cabaret (musical), 133
Cajetan, Thomas, 106
Canaris, Wilhelm, 168–72, *170*
Canterbury, Kent, 35
Catherine, Princess of Wales, 105
Catholic Church, 87, 90, 106–7, 112–14, 181, 274
Čelákovice, Czech Republic, 247, 257
Cesarani, David, 138
Český Těšín, Czech Republic, 312
Chalampé, France, 31
Chamberlain, Neville, 76, 180, 185–6, *186*, 189, 207, 217, 222, 355–6, 314
Charlemagne, Holy Roman Emperor, 108, 116, 118, 193
Charles III, King of the United Kingdom, 105
Charles IV, Holy Roman Emperor, 181, 193, 206
Charles V, Holy Roman Emperor, 90, 107

Charles the Bold, Duke of Burgundy, 34–5
Chełmno extermination camp, Poland, 216, 220, 278, 334
Cheshire, Leonard, 158
Christabel (TV drama), 49–50
Christianity, 110–14, 117, 172
Christianstadt concentration camp, Poland, 289
Churchill, Clementine, 85
Churchill, John, 1st Duke of Marlborough, 84–5
Churchill, Randolph, 85
Churchill, Winston, 61, 84–5, 86, 87, 94, 131, 144–5, 170, 191, 220, 252–3, 256, 304, 316
Clages, Gerhard, 276
Clapton, Eric, 309–10
Clunes, Anna, 315
Cold War, 70, 166, 168, 180, 291, 294
Coldstream, John, 158
Comenius, Jan, 298
Communism, 133, 171, 188, 193, 195, 199, 224, 247, 318–19
concentration camps, 121, 268, 334
 death marches, 121–2, 124–5, 154, 268
 extermination methods, 334
 mass murder, 132
 Sonderkommando units, 343–4
 see also names of individual camps; Holocaust
Confessing Church, 26, 110, 172
Cooper, Artemis, 94
Counter-Reformation, 83, 87, 90
Cowan, James, 95–6
Crawshaw, Steve, 143
cuckoo clocks, 53
Cunning Little Vixen, The (Janáček), 281
Čurda, Karel, 215

Curzon, George, 1st Marquess Curzon of Kedleston, 144
Czech Republic, 178–207, 211–40, 243–68, 274–305, 309–12, 319
  chaty (huts), 247
  Church and, 193, 195
  Communist era, 183, 188–9, 193, 195, 199, 224, 247
  deportation of Jews, 233–5
  German-Czech Declaration of Reconciliation (1997), 192
  golden era (1880s–1930s), 258
  government-in-exile, London, 183, 205, 212, 220, 276
  Jews in, 225–35, 262, 291
  music, 280–81
  Nazi oppression, 254–5
  post-war expulsion of Germans, 193–4, 197, 205
  Prague Spring (1968), 183, *184*, 257
  railway system, 256–7
  Sokol ('falcon') organization, 196
  student protests (1939), 294–6
  synagogues, 266
  Ukrainians and, 299
  Velvet Divorce (1992), 184
  Velvet Revolution (1989), 184, 224, 296
  World War II, 191–2, 199, 203, 212–22
  Youth Union, 254
  see also Lidice; Prague; Sudetenland; Theresienstadt
Czech Silesia, 181, 312
'Czechoslovakia', 180, 182–3, 189, 226, 312, 334
Czechowice-Dziedzice, Poland, 323, 327

Dachau concentration camp, Germany, 76, 79, 97, 103, 121, 168, 334
Daluege, Kurt, 217
Danube river, 41, 61–2, 62, 82–3, 85–7, 322, 348
de Gaulle, Charles, 31, 217
de Lattre de Tassigny, Jean, 31
Dedek, Bedřich, 197
Defiant Requiem: Verdi at Terezín (Sidlin), 239
democracy, 273, 296, 359
Desbois, Patrick, 70
Desert Fox, The: The Story of Rommel (film), 69
Diet of Worms (1521), 107
Dillingen, Germany, 83
Dimbleby, Richard, 158–60, *159*, 168, 268
Doležalová, Marie, 220–22, *222*
Donau Main canal, 118
Donauwörth, Germany, 85, 87–8, 94, 101–2
Douglas-Hamilton, Douglas, 14th Duke of Hamilton, 94
Dresden, Germany, 92
Dreyfus, Alfred, 23
Droździkowska, Irena, 326
Dubček, Alexander, 183
Dubno, Ukraine, 151
Dvořák, Antonín, 281

Eberhard I, Duke of Württemberg, 57
Eden, Anthony, 144, 217
Edict of Tolerance (1782), 226
Edward VII, King of the United Kingdom, 181, 260
Edward VIII, King of the United Kingdom (later Duke of Windsor), 148–9
Eichmann, Adolf, 41, 81, 236
Einstein, Albert, 64, *64*, 256
Eisenhower, Dwight D., 30–31, 249, 252–3
El Alamein, Battle of (1942), 70

Elbe river, 203, 244–7, 246, 260, 266, 275, 348
Elizabeth I, Queen of England, 197
Elizabeth II, Queen of the United Kingdom, 131
Elizabeth Stuart, Queen of Bohemia, 181, 197, 207
Elizabeth, Empress of Russia, 263
Ensslin, Gudrun, 57–9, 58, 68, 71
Epsom College, Surrey, 5, 13, 42, 117
Erasmus, 22
Escape Artist, The (Freedland), 13
Estonia, 358
ethnic cleansing, 16, 191, 193
Eugene, Prince of Savoy, 84
Europe, 9, 60, 63, 84, 223, 231, 334–5, 355, 360
   Council of Europe, 188
   European Union (EU), 188, 312–13, 319
Evans, Richard J., 296
extermination camps, 334

Faktor, František, 189
Faulkner, William, 180
Faurisson, Robert, 268
Ferdinand I, Holy Roman Emperor, 292
Field, Martina, 222
Field, Matt, 222, 223
'Final Solution', 212, 228, 268, 334–5
Finkelstein, Daniel, 26, 35
First Czech Tank Brigade monument, Ostrava, 300–303
Flemming, Liselotte, 162
Floss, Germany, 166–7
Flossenbürg, Germany, 132–3
Flossenbürg concentration camp, Germany, 41, 79, 121, 132, 154, 167–9, 171–2, 334
Forwood, Anthony, 158
Fosse Carolina canal, Germany, 116–17

France, 23, 84, 146, 229, 269
   fall of, 16, 31
   Maginot Line, 20–21
Francis, Pope, 270, 274
Frank, Anne, 26, 157, 345
Frank, Hans, 148, 153, 239, 323–5, 324, 354
Frank, Karl, 296
Frank, Margot, 157, 345
Frank, Niklas, 153
Frank, Otto, 345
Frankfurt, Germany, 79
Frankl, Viktor, 255
František, Josef, 180
Franz Ferdinand, Archduke of Austria, 232
Franz Joseph I, Emperor of Austria, 292
Frederick II (the Great), King of Prussia, 51, 263
Frederick V, King of Bohemia, 207,
Freedland, Jonathan, 13
Freedom and Direct Democracy party (Czech Republic), 291
Freiburg im Breisgau, Germany, 35–6, 45
Freisler, Roland, 68
Freud, Sigmund, 226
Freund, Arnošt, 288
Freundová, Louise, 288–9, 289
Frick, Wilhelm, 139, 217
Fryštát, Czech Republic, 312
Fügner, Jindřich, 196
Furtwangen im Schwarzwald, Germany, 48–9

Gabčík, Jozef, 180, 213–16, 276, 292
Gajowniczek, Franciszek, 328–30
von Galen, Clemens, 112–13, 113
Gareis, Heinrich, 133
Gaza Strip, Palestine, 54, 89, 109, 193, 240, 279–80, 330, 358, 361–2

Geneva Convention, 143
George V, King of the United Kingdom, 144
George VI, King of the United Kingdom, 131
German-Czech Declaration of Reconciliation (1997), 192
Germany, 21–2, 24–5, 77–8, 131–2, 165–6, 269
   Abwehr (military intelligence), 168, 171–2
   AfD party, 60, 132, 165
   'American Zone', 62–3
   Counter-Reformation, 83, 88, 90
   'First Reich', 133
   Generalplan Ost, 183
   'German Christians' movement, 26
   immigrant violence, 59–60
   industrial sector, 77–8
   Jews in, 78–9, 107–9, 168
   Kristallnacht (1938), 26, 34, 57, 107–8, 167
   Lebensraum, 104, 183
   Poland and, 283, 314, 323
   Protestant Reformation, 90, 105–7
   racism, 78, 169
   railway system, 65, 118–19, 164
   Reichsbahn, 333
   Reunification (1990), 169
   'Second Reich', 133
   Sudetenland and, 182–3, *182*, 189–92
   Teutonic Order, 314
   Third Reich, 111, 133, 153, 323
   Völkisch movement, 104–5, 132
   Wirtschaftswunder ('economic miracle'), 77–8
   see also Nazi Party/Nazism; World War I; World War II
Gettysburg address (1863), 112
Gillespie, Douglas, 4, 35, 200

Gladiator (film), 299
'Gleiwitz incident' (1939), 283
Gnadl, Anna, 122–3, *123*
Goebbels, Joseph, 81, 146, 264, 296, 348, 354
Goertz, Jürgen, 64
'Golden Road', 167, 193–4, 197, 205–6
Gonin, Mervyn, 160
Goodbye to Berlin (Isherwood), 133
Göring, Albert, 31–3, *32*
Göring, Hermann, 26, 31, 33, *32*, 148, *149*, 212
Göth, Amon, 286, 322
Gradowski, Sonia, 344
Gradowski, Zalman, 342–4, *344*, 347, 360
Graebe, Hermann, 151–3, *152*, 168
Granville, Christine, *see* Skarbek, Maria Krystyna
Greece, 334
Groos, Walter, 96–7, *97*
Gross-Rosen concentration camp, Poland, 286
Grunwald, Battle of (1410), 313–14, 332
Grunwald Commemoration Badge, 332
Gryn, Bella, *126*, 127
Gryn, Gabi, 124
Gryn, Geza, 124–5, *126*
Gryn, Hugo, 9–10, 124–7, *126*, 141, 320, 360
Guernica (Picasso), 220
Gundelfingen, Germany, 45
Günzburg, Germany, 79–80
Gurs concentration camp, France, 34
Gutach im Breisgau, Germany, 45–6
Gütenbach, Germany, 47–8
Guterres, António, 280

Haarlem, Netherlands, 345
Habsburg Empire, 33–4, 181–2, 292
von Hagenbach, Peter, 34–5

Hague Conventions, 144
Hahnbach, Germany, 162
HALO Trust, 96
Hamas, 269, 358
    attack on Israel (7 October 2023), 8, 9, 48, 153
Hamilton, Elsbeth, 223
Hammond, Martin, 157
Hands, Greg, 223, 290–91, 293, 297–8
Hanfstaengl, Ernst, 85
Harris, Arthur 'Bomber', 91
Harris, Kamala, 61, 89. 160
Harrison Report (1945), 63
Harvard University, 296, 298
Havel, Václav, 184, 192, 224, 259, 299
Healey, Denis, 225
Heath, Edward, 225
Heidelberg, Germany, 92
Helfgott, Ben, 319–21, *321*, 337, 347
Helfgott, Michael, 321
Hermann, Alexander, 289
Herrlingen, Germany, 68
Hersbruck, Germany, 154–5, *155*, 169
Herzl, Theodor, 22–3
Hess, Rudolf, 94–6, 147, *149*
Heydrich, Reinhard, 81, 183, 205, 212, 228, 233, 334–5
    assassination, 180, 212–15, *214*, 249, 276–7, 292, 354
    assassination reprisals, 216–20
    funeral, 216
Hiding Place, The (Corrie ten Boom), 345
Hill, Fiona, 296
Hillesum, Etty, 344–7, *347*, 349, 361
Hilsner, Leopold, 226
Himmler, Heinrich, 81, 104–5, 107, 146, 150, 171, 183, 212, 216, 265, 348
Hiroshima, Japan, 145–6
Hirt, August, 17

Hirzel, Susanne, 68
Hitler, Adolf, 17, 24, 41, 67, 75–6, 85, 94, 147, *186*, 269, 296, 356
    assassination attempt (July 1944), 49–51, 69, 97, 171–2
    assassination attempt (March 1943), 170
    Beer Hall Putsch (1923), 75, 134
    Berlin and, 133
    Christianity and, 110, 117, 216
    death, 76–7, 146
    Frederick II and, 263–4
    Heydrich assassination and, 215–20
    ideology of, 104–5, 110
    Jews and, 137–9, 268
    Mein Kampf, 24, 80, 94
    Nazi rallies, 134–7, *135*
    Nuremberg and, 134–5
    Poland and, 323–4
    Regensburg and, 119
Hitler Youth, 66
Hitler, Stalin, Mum and Dad (Finkelstein), 26
Hitler's War (Irving), 269
Hoax of the Twentieth Century, The (Butz), 269
Höchstädt an der Donau, Germany, 83–5, 87
Hoesch, Leopold von, 49
Hohenlohe, Count, 260
Hohenstadt, Germany, 155
Holbein the Elder, Hans, 93
Holbein the Younger, Hans, 93
Holocaust, 8, 34, 121–2, 152, 158, 228, 267–9, 320–21, 330, 336–8
    deportation of Jews, 17–18, 233–5
    extermination methods, 334
    Final Solution, 212, 228, 335
    Holocaust denial, 23, 267, 269, 338, 358
    mass transportations, 333

Holocaust (*cont.*)
  Nazi mass murder, 132, 151
  see also Auschwitz-Birkenau;
    concentration camps
'Holocaust by Bullets', 70
Holy Roman Empire, 33, 59, 75, 102, 119, 133–4, 180–81, 206
Horáková, Milada, 255–6, 270, *270*
Horne, Alistair, 316
Höss, Hedwig, 333
Höss, Klaus, 331, 333
Höss, Rudolf, 331, 333, 335–6
von Hösslin, Roland, 97
Hostouň, Czech Republic, 265
Hotel Hirschen, , 55urg, 36, 45, 52
Hotel La Casa, Tübingen, 56
How Democracies Die (Levitsky & Ziblatt), 273
Hradištko, Czech Republic, 257
Huber, Kurt, 67
Hungary, 14, 41
  deportation of Jews, 17–18
  Jewish population, 138, 286, 335
Hurley, Elizabeth, 50
Hus, Jan, 181
Hussite Wars (1419–34), 181, 198, 206

If This Is a Man (Levi), 336
IG Farben, Buna complex, 336
International Military Tribunal, 145, 150–51
Iran, 9
Iron Curtain, 166, 168, 188–9, *190*, 211, 291
Irving, David, 269
Isar river, 150
Isherwood, Christopher, 133
Israel, 8, 22, 267, 269, 279, 287, 358
  attacks on Gaza, 89, 109
  creation of, 22–3, 26, 167
  October 7 attack (2023), 8–9, 48, 153, 269, 358
  'Righteous Among the Nations' designation, 123–4, 162, 205, 318, 326
  Yad Vashem Holocaust Museum, 27, 32, 123, 162, 287, 326
Italy, 154, 220

J'accuse (Zola), 23
Jackson, Robert H., 146–7
Jagiellonian dynasty, 181
James, John, 135–6, 140–41, 154–7, 162–7, *163*, 274, 280–81, *282*, 290, 293, 331
James, Louise, 140–41, 280
James I and VI, King of England and Ireland and King of Scotland, 181
Janáček, Leoš, 281
Japan, 78, 145–6, 355
Jesenská, Milena, 231
Jews/Judaism, 8–10, 107
  antisemitism, 22–6, 31–2, 57, 141, 226, 229, 338, 356, 358
  in Czech Republic, 225–6, 233
  displaced persons, 62–3
  Final Solution, 212, 228, 335
  in Germany, 78–9, 107–9, 137–40
  Landjudentum, 79
  persecution of, 34, 41, 57, 78–9, 107–9, 140
  Yom Kippur, 112
  see also Holocaust; Nazi Party/Nazism; Nuremberg Race Laws
Jodl, Alfred, 294
Johnson, Boris, 42, 165–6
Joseph II, Austrian Emperor, 226, 231–2
'Judaeo Bolshevism', 137
Judt, Tony, 70
Jung, Carl, 22

Kafka, Franz, 226, 231
Kafka, Jiří, 223
Kaisheim, Germany, 102
Kalderon, Hadas, 153
Kaltenbrunner, Ernst, 148, 150
Karlsbad, Czech Republic, 181, 260
Karlštejn, Czech Republic, 206
Kašpar, Jan, 275
Katyn Massacre (1940), 146, 315
Keitel, Wilhelm, 148, 150, 171, 294
Keller, Tim, 202
Keneally, Margaret, 288
Keneally, Thomas, 287–9
Kernerova, Jana, 285
Kielce pogrom (1946), 318
Kimmerling, Josef, 122–3, *123*
Kindertransport programme, 229
KKP party (Poland), 318–19
Kladruby nad Labem, Czech Republic, 264–5
Klein, Gienek, 319–20
Kodin, Andrey, 158
Kolbe, Maximilian, 111–12, 328–30, *329*, 337, 347, 349
Kolín, Czech Republic, 262–4, *263*
Kolín, Battle of (1757), 263
Kraków, Poland, 283, 285–6, 309, 313, 323–7, 353–4
  Apteka pod Orłem ('The Eagle Pharmacy'), 326
  Jewish ghetto, 325–6
  Wawel Castle, 313, 323, 354
Kristallnacht (1938), 26, 34, 57, 107–8, 167
Krone Hotel, Lauffen, 54
Kruse, Käthe, 88–9, *88*
Kubiš, Jan, 180, 213–16, 276, 292
Kudeřiková, Marie, 254–5
Kurhotel Markushof, Bad Bellingen, 33
Kyiv, Ukraine, 70, 357

La Roche-Guyon, France, 69
landmines, 96
Landsberg prison, Germany, 17, 94
Latvia, 358
Lauffen, Germany, 54–5
Lauffen-am-Neckar, Germany, 55
Le Pen, Jean-Marie, 23
League of German Girls, 66
League of Nations, 359–60
Leclerc de Hauteclocque, Philippe, 249
Leigh Fermor, Patrick, 47, 90, 93–4, 101–2, 132, 348, 356
Leipheim, Germany, 62–3
'Let It Grow' (Clapton), 310
Levi, Emilia, 336
Levi, Primo, 336–7, *336*
Ley, Robert, 146
Ležáky massacre, Czech Republic, 216, 277–8, 334
Lhota Nad Moravou, Czech Republic, 294
Lidice massacre, Czech Republic, 216–22, *218*, *219*, 334
Lieberose concentration camp, 124–5
Linck, Wenzel, 106
Lincoln, Abraham, 112
Lingens, Ella 339–41, *340*, 347, 360
Lingens, Kurt, 339
Lingens, Peter, 341
Linz, Austria, 41
Lipstadt, Deborah, 269
Lithuania, 334, 358
Litomyšl, Czech Republic, 280–81
Lloyd George, David, 144
Łódź, Poland, 221, 337
London, England, 22, 229
  Blitz, 145
London Charter (1945), 145
Loos, Battle of (1915), 200
Loučná River, 280
Louis XIV, King of France, 84, 86

Lucas, Edward, 319
Luckner, Gertrud, 36–7, *37*, 167, 360
Ludwig I, King of Bavaria, 117–18
Ludwig Canal, Germany, 117
Lueger, Karl, 22
Luppe, Hermann, 161–2, *161*, 167
Lustig, Joshua, 122
Luther, Martin, 52, 90, 105–8, 110, 114, 122
    Jews and, 107–8
Lutheranism, 90
Lynn, Vera, 158

Maas, Hermann, 26–8, *27*, 113
Macleod, Iain, 225
Macron, Emmanuel, 339
Maduro, Nicolás, 82
Maginot, André, 20
Maginot Line, 20–21
Mahler, Gustav, 226, 281
Mahler, Horst, 58
Maier, Johann, 119–20
Majdanek extermination camp, Poland, 334
Man's Search for Meaning (Frankl), 255
Marcomannic Wars (AD 166–180), 299
Marcus Aurelius, Roman Emperor, 299
Maria Theresa, Holy Roman Empress, 226, 231
Marienbad, Czech Republic, 181, 260
Maritim Hotel, Ulm, 61
Marshall, John, 278–9
Marshall, Susan, 278–9
Masaryk, Jan, 183, 226
Masaryk, Tomáš Garrigue, 226
Mason, James, 69
Maté, Gabor, 33
Maurer, Max, 122–3, *123*
Mauthausen concentration camp, Austria, 125, 334
Meakin, Jonathan, 180

Mein Kampf (Hitler), 24, 80, 94
Memorial to the Children Victims of the War, Lidice, 218
Mengele, Josef, 80–81, *81*, 339
Mengele, Rolf, 80
Merkel, Angela, 78
Město Touškov, Czech Republic, 198–9
Metamorphosis, The (Kafka), 231
Meyer, Albert, 108
Miller, Lee, 76, 77
Mit brennender Sorge ('With Burning Concern') (Pius XI), 112
Molotov-Ribbentrop Pact, 314
monarchy, 105
Monheim, Germany, 105
Montgomery, Bernard Law, 293
Moral Maze (radio programme), 127
Morava river, 291
Moravia, 180–81, 183, 228, 281–2, 286, 289, 291–2, 300
Moravská Třebová, Czech Republic, 290–91
Morris, Maggi, 186–7, 193, 195–6, 199
Moscow Declaration on Human Atrocities (1943), 144
Movement for International Peace, 205
Mucha, Alphonse, 181, 225
Müller, Franz, 68, 71
Muller, Ludwig, 110
Munich, Germany, 23, 60, 79, 133–4
    Nazism and, 75–6
    Prinzregentenplatz apartment, 76
Munich Agreement (1938), 189–91, 212–13, 217, 224, 253
Munich University, 67
Musk, Elon, 296
Mussolini, Benito, 75
Muth, Carl, 67
Mýto, Czech Republic, 205
Mže river, 197–8

Nacht und Nebel (resistance prisoners), 102
Nagasaki, Japan, 146
Napoleon Bonaparte, 85–7, 119
Napoleonic Wars (1803–15), 85–8
National Front (France), 23
NATO (North Atlantic Treaty Organisation), 166
Natzweiler concentration camp, Alsace, 17
Nawrocki, Karol, 319
Nazi Party/Nazism, 3, 24–8, 51, 66–8, 75–9, 89, 107, 359
  animal breeding, 264–5
  architecture, 132, 134, 136
  carbon monoxide gas, 220, 334
  Christianity and, 110–14, 117, 216
  death marches, 121–2, 124–5, 154, 268
  destruction of evidence, 268
  Einsatzgruppen, 69–71
  'Final Solution', 212, 228, 268, 334–5
  Gestapo, 231–2, 292–3
  ideology, 104, 110, 134, 136–7, 216, 220
  Jews and, 107–9, 137–8, 233–4
  Kristallnacht (1938), 26, 34, 57, 107–8, 167
  mass murder, 132, 151, 169–70, 268, 334–5
  'Mother's Cross' medal, 123
  murder of children, 336
  'Museum of the Extinct Race', 227–8
  music and, 239
  Nazi rallies, 134–7, *135*
  Nuremberg Laws (1935), 94
  Race Laws, 76, 94, 137–41
  racial purity, 133, 140, 264–5
  SA (*Sturmabeilung*), 31–2, 138–9, *139*

Sonderaktion 1005 ('Special Action 1005'), 268
  Soviet Union and, 54
  SS (*Schutzstaffel*), 70, 233, 268, 335, 339, 343
  swastikas, 117, 136
  Wannsee Conference (January 1942), 212, 228, 334–5
  women's rights, 254
  see also concentration camps; Germany
Neave, Airey, 147, 150
Neillands, Robin, 91
Némirovsky, Irène, 332
Netanyahu, Benjamin, 89, 240, 279–80, 330, 339, 348, 358–9
Netherlands, 26, 144, 170, 334, 344–6
Neuenburg am Rhein, Germany, 30–33
Neurath, Konstantin von, 183
Neuve Chapelle, France, 200
New Caledonia, 262
New World Symphony (Dvořák), 281
New York Times, 219
New Yorker magazine, 148
Newsnight (TV series), 296
Nicholas II, Russian Tsar, 24, 144
Niemöller, Martin, 26, 110–12, *111*
Niethammer, Günther, 331–2
Nietzsche, Friedrich, 22
Nieuwpoort, Belgium, 4
Nott, David, 361–2
Nový Jičín, Czech Republic, 299
Nuremberg, Germany, 76, 78, 101, 114, *115*, 133–7, 142–3, 148, 161–2
  allied bombing of, 148
  Kongresshalle, 136
  Nuremberg Race Laws (1935), 94, 137–41
  Nuremberg Rallies, 134–7, *135*

Nuremberg, Germany (*cont.*)
　Nuremberg Trials (1945–46), 34,
　　95, 141–54, *149*, 218, 222
　Palace of Justice, 142–3, *143*
　Zeppelinfeld, 134, 136, *137*
Nymburk, Czech Republic, 257–9,
　258

Oberlindhart, Germany, 122
Oberottmarshausen building plant,
　Augsburg, 96
'Observations on the Birdlife of
　Auschwitz' (Niethammer), 331
Oder river, 299, 311, 348
'Office for Religious War Relief', 36
Ohne Namen ('Without a Name')
　(sculpture, Bocchetta), 154
Okamura, Tomio, 291
Okhrana (Russian secret police), 24
Olomouc, Czech Republic, 291–2
Olše river, 312, *313*
　Friendship Bridge, 312–13, *313*
Olympic Games
　Berlin (1936), 138
　Paris (2024), 102, 109
On the Jews and Their Lies (Luther), 107
Opava and Ostrava, Battles of (1945),
　300–302
Operation Anthropoid, 212–17
Operation Barbarossa, 170–71
Operation Border Stone, 188
Operation Clarion, 109
Operation Cowboy, 265
Operation Nordwind, 30
Operation Sealion, 170
Operation Seven, 172–3
Operation Silver A, 276–7
Operation Torch, 70
Operation Valkyrie (July 1944), 49–51,
　69, 97, 171–2
Opletal, Jan, 294–6, *295*
Oradour-sur-Glane, France, 217

Ostrava, Czech Republic, 273,
　300–305, *302*, 311
Ostravice river, 300–301
Ottmarsheim, France, 29
Otto I, Holy Roman Emperor, 133
Ottokar II, King of Bohemia, 258
Ovenden, Richard, 269

Palestine, 26, 167, 193
　British Mandate of Palestine, 69
　Mandatory Palestine, 63, 228
Pankiewicz, Tadeusz, 326–8, *327*
Pardubice, Czech Republic, 266, *267*,
　274–6
Paris, France, 227, 248–9
Parker, Geoffrey, 55
Parler, Peter, 262
Passerelle des Trois Pays (Three
　Countries Bridge), Basel, 28
Pattison, Emma, 5, 117
Patton, George S., 120, 199, 203,
　252–3
Pavlův Studenec, Czech Republic, 193,
　194
Pegnitz river, 114, *115*, 141–2, 155,
　348
Peierls, Rudolf, 158
Pence, Mike, 167
'Perpetual Diet of Regensburg', 119
Peter III, Emperor of Russia, 263
Petřek, Vladimír, 292–3, *293*
Pfaffenweiler, Germany, 52, 55
Pfarrernotbund, 26
Picasso, Pablo, 220
Píka, Heliodor, 199
Pilecki, Witold, 341–2, *342*, 347
Pilsen, Czech Republic, 185–7, 195,
　199–200, *200*, 213, 252
Piorun (Polish destroyer), 315
Pitt the Younger, William, 86, 87
Pitter, Přemysl, 205, *206*
Pius XI, Pope, 112–13

Pius XII, Pope, 112
Płaszów labour camp, Poland, 286
Poděbrady, Czech Republic, 259–60, 260, 262
Podgórze, Kraków, 325
Poland, 24, 136, 171, 179, 181, 249, 309–10, 312–34
    antisemitism, 318–20
    Communist era, 316–19
    deportation of Jews, 286
    government-in-exile, London, 315–16, 318
    Jewish population, 138, 285–6, 321, 325, 334
    Kielce pogrom (1946), 318
    KKP party, 318–19
    World War II 283, 314–16, 323
Polanski, Roman, 326
Polish-Czech War (1919), 312
Pollack, Susan, 160
populism, 9, 60
Potsdam Conference (1945), 192
Potuňček, Jiří, 278
Power of the Powerless, The (Havel), 224
Prague Spring International Music Festival, 240
Prague, Czech Republic, 167, 180–85, 191, 199, 206, 211, 222, 225–30, 245, 247–8, 256, 261
    Charles Bridge, 181, 240, 257
    Charles Square, 261
    Church of Saints Cyril and Methodius, 212, 215
    Czech Radio Building, 250
    Jewish Museum, 228
    Jewish quarter, 225–8, 227
    Prague Castle, 181, 213, 216
    Prague Spring (1968), 183, *184*, 257
    Prague Uprising (1945), 247–56, 251, 253, 298
    Strahov Stadium, 196

student protests (1939), 294–6
Wenceslas Square, 257
Winton Children Farewell Memorial, 230
women under Nazi occupation, 254–5
Zbraslav district, 206–7
Přelouč, Czech Republic, 266
Přerov, Czech Republic, 297–8
Princip, Gavrilo, 232
Prisoners of Fear (Lingens), 339
Probst, Christoph, 67
Prosecuting the Powerful (Crawshaw), 143
Protestant Church, 90, 105–6, 111, 114, 181
Protocols of the Elders of Zion, The, 24–5
'Proud Boys', 358
Putin, Vladimir, 9, 105, 184–5, 224, 261, 273–4, 296–7, 305, 319, 339, 348, 355, 357–9

racism, 110
RAF (Royal Air Force), 90–92
Ramillies, Battle of (1706), 84
Rassinier, Paul, 268
Rauff, Walter, 69
Ravensbrück concentration camp, Germany, 36, 49, 168, 216, 221
Reagan, Ronald, 359
Red Cross, 143, 233–4
Rees, Laurence, 264, 359
Reformation, 90, 105–7
Regensburg, Germany, 41, 119–22, *120*
Reichsparteitag des Friedens ('Rally of Peace'), Nuremberg, 136
Reims, France, 14
religion, 48, 90, 110–14, 239
Remarque, Erich, 171
Requiem (Verdi), 238
'Rest is History, The' podcast, 13, 52

Reutlingen, Germany, 59–60
Revolutionary Socialists, 97
RFE (Radio Free Europe), 359
Rhine river, 21, 28–30, 348
Rhine Valley, 48
von Ribbentrop, Joachim, 49, 148–50
Riefenstahl, Leni, 134
Riespach, Alsace, 19
'Righteous Among the Nations' designation, 123–4, 162, 205, 318, 326
Ringhotel Alpenhof, Augsburg, 89, 114
Robota, Shoshana, 344
Rocek, Eva, 239
Rohrbach, Germany, 49
Rokycany, Czech Republic, 201, 203, 204, 205, 214
Roma, 168, 182, 291, 299, 334, 341
Roman Empire, 299
Rommel, Erwin, 68–70
Roosevelt, Franklin D., 62, 144–5, 180, 252, 264, 310, 356
Rossel, Maurice, 233–5
Rote Armee Fraktion (RAF) *see* Baader-Meinhof Gang
Ruckdeschel, Ludwig, 119–20
Rüegsegge, Eduard, 24
Ruff, Ludwig, 136
Rumbula massacre, Latvia, 70
Russia, 24, 70, 78, 85–6, 104–5, 180, 183–5, 224, 305, 309
  dachas, 247
  'Pale of Settlement', 24
  Russian Liberation Army (ROA), 250
  Russian Revolution (1917), 24, 137
  see also Soviet Union
Russo-Ukrainian War (2014–), 9, 191, 299, 357–8
Ruthenia, 182

SA (*Sturmabteilung*, storm troopers), 31–2, 138–9, *139*
Saarland, 138
Sachsenhausen concentration camp, Germany, 125, 334
Sacks, Jonathan, 330
Said, Edward, 240, *240*
Saint-Jean-de-Côle, France, 103
São Paulo, Brazil, 80
Sarajevo, Bosnia and Herzegovina, 232
Sargent, Orme, 253
Sasse, Martin, 107
Sauckel, Fritz, 150
Sayer, Jeremy, 35
Schächter, Rafael, 237–9, *238*
Schiller, Alfred and Isla, 221
Schindler, Emilie, 283, 285–6
Schindler, Oskar, 7, 119, 153, 282–8, *284*
  Schindler museum, Kraków, 325
Schindler's Ark (Keneally), 287
Schindler's List (film), 7, 283, 285–6
Scholl, Hans and Sophie, 66–8, *67*, 71, *71*, 113
Scholl, Inge, 71
Scholl Foundation, 71
Scholz, Olaf, 78, 339
Schwarz, Franz, 80
Schwarz, Joseph, 167
Schwenningen, Germany, 53
Seldon, Anthony, *15*, 223, 244
  Churchill's Indian Summer, 61
  Epsom College and, 5, 13, 42, 56, 117–18
  ill health, 45–6, 56–7, 59, 177–8, 187–8, 195, 201–3, 245, 259, 261, 290, 310–11, 361
  mental health, 56–7
  Path of Peace, The, 4, 29, 354
  religion and, 43
  Sarah and, 43–4, 103–4, 290, 331–2

Tonbridge School and, 140, 157–8
Truss at 10, 42, 165
Wellington College and, 240
Western Front Way and, 4–7, 47
Seldon, Arthur (father), 9, 156–7
Seldon (née Pappworth), Joanna (first wife), 5, 9, 43–4, 103, 127, 140–41, 167, 321
Seldon (née Sayer), Sarah (wife), 5, 13–15, 35, 43–6, *44*, 103–4, 135–6, 166–7, *244*, 266
   Anthony's illness and, 179, 260–61, 311
   death of mother, 278–9
   honeymoon, 243
   Path of Light walk, 18–19, 33, 36, 46–7, 52, 63–6, 79, 83, 102–3, 215, 243–7, 327, 330–33
   Prague and, 257, 261
Seven Years War (1756–63), 263
Shakespeare, William, 207
Shawcross, Hartley, 151–2
Shawcross, William, 152–3
Shirer, William L., 134–5
Sidlin, Murry, 239
Silesia, 181–2
Simferopol massacre, Ukraine, 70
Simmons, Melinda, 357
Simpson, Wallis, 149
Simultankirche St Margareta church, Illschwang, 155
Skarbek, Maria Krystyna, 316–18, *317*
Sky News, 274
Slavonic Dances (Dvořák), 281
Slavs, 8, 54, 183, 196, 356
Slovakia, 14, 182, 281
Smetana, Bedřich, 280–81
Smith, Jonathan, 211–13, 215
'Smolensk conspiracy' (1943), 170
Sobibor extermination camp, Poland, 268, 334

social media, 359
Sola river, 322, 333
Solingen, Germany, 160
Southport knife attacks, 109–10
Soviet Union, 54, 70, 145–6, 156, 171, 180, 199, 249–52, 293–4, 300–301, 323
   atrocities, 311–12
   Poland and, 314
   Red Army, 77, 145, 236, 249, 251–2, 286–7, 300–301, *302*, 311, 322
   World War II, 199, 203
   see also Russia
Spa Conference (1920), 312
Spain, 140, 220
Spandau prison, Germany, 95, 150
Special Operations Executive (SOE), 213, 316–18
Spectator magazine, 43
Speer, Albert, 95, 133–4, 136, *149*, 150
Spielberg, Steven, 7, 283
St George's Church, Gutach im Breisgau, 46
St Jean de Côle, France, 136
St Lorenz Church, Nuremberg, 114
St Petersburg, Russia, 24
Stalag V-B' POW camp, Villingen, Germany, 54
Stalin, Joseph, 142, 144–5, 192, 249, 252, 269, 274, 294, 296, 314, 356
Starmer, Keir, 87, 115, 297
von Stauffenberg, Claus, 50–51, 69, 97
Stehlík, Václav, *204*, 205, 214
Štěrbová, Jarmila, *304*, 305
Strasbourg, France, 16–17, 30
Strasser, Gerhard, 123
Streicher, Julius, 107, 147, 150, 161
Střeň, Czech Republic, 293–4
Stříbro, Czech Republic, 196–7
Šťulíková, Růžena, 278, *279*
Stürmer, Der, newspaper, 107, 161

Stuttgart Declaration (1945), 111
Sudeten German Party, 283
Sudetenland, 182–3, *182*, 185, 189–92, 197, 199, 205
Suite Française (Némirovsky), 332
Sulzbach-Rosenberg, Germany, 156
Sumption, Jonathan, 358
Sunak, Rishi, 297
Sunday Times, 330
Švédské Šance massacre (1945), 298–9
Svitavy, Czech Republic, 281–3, *288*
  Schindler memorial, *284*, *285*
Svoboda, Ludvík, 304
Syria, 9

Tachov, Czech Republic, 194–5, 197, *198*
Taiwan, 273
Taylor, Telford, 146
Tehran Conference (1943), 274
Tempest, The (Shakespeare), 207
ten Boom, Betsie, 345
ten Boom, Casper, 345
ten Boom, Corrie, 345
Terezín (Theresienstadt) concentration camp, Czech Republic, 121, 231–9, *234*, 334
  cultural life, 236–9, *236*
  ghetto, 233–7, *235*
  Red Cross inspection, 233–5, 239
Thames river, 29
That's Life (TV programme), 230
Thatcher, Margaret, 150
Theresienstadt *see* Terezín
Thirty Years War (1618–48), 33, 55–6, 90, 181, 198, 207, 292, 322
Thirty-Four (Burke), 32
Time magazine, 148
Time of Gifts, A (Leigh Fermor), 93
Time of My Life, The (Healey), 225
Times, The, 165
Tonbridge School, Kent, 140, 157–8

Train of Powder, A (West), 148
Treblinka concentration camp, Poland, 167, 268, 320, 334
von Tresckow, Henning, 51
Treuchtlingen, Germany, 108–9, *109*
Trial, The (Kafka), 231
Triumph of the Will (Nazi propaganda film), 134
von Trott zu Solz, Adam, 50
Truman, Harry S.,
Truman, Harry S., 63, 252
Trump, Donald, 9, 83, 160, 167, 191, 223–5, 240, 261, 269, 339, 348, 358–9
  assassination attempt, 47–8
  comparisons with Hitler, 296–7
  Gaza and, 193
  Harvard University and, 296
  Putin and, 185, 224, 296–7
Truss, Liz, 42–3, 165–6
Tübingen, Germany, 52, 56–7
Tübingen University, 57, 59
Turski, Marian, 337–9, *338*, 347, 355–6
Tyrš, Miroslav, 196

Uffheim, France, 20, 28
Ukraine, 96, 105, 185, 261, 299, 357–8
  Russo-Ukrainian War (2014–), 9, 191
Ulm, Germany, 41, 60–61, *62*, 64–6, *64*, 68–71, 83, 87
  Battle of Ulm (1805), 66
  Einsatzgruppe trial (1958), 70–71
United Nations (UN), 356, 358, 360, 280
United Nations Relief and Rehabilitation Administration, 63
United States, 9, 63, 104, 139, 220, 224, 358–60
  Czechoslovakia and, 180

Holocaust Memorial Museum, Washington, DC, 114
Prague Uprising and, 252–3
presidential election (2024), 61, 89, 160
storming of Congress (6 January 2021), 358
World War II, 76, 120–21, 145, 168, 199, 203, 225, 252, 256, 258, 275
Urválek, Josef, 256

Vacková, Růžena, 255, 261
Valčík, Josef, 276
Vance, J. D., 180, 185, 223–4, 339, 348
Vane-Tempest-Stewart, Charles, 7th Marquess of Londonderry, 148
Venezuela, 82–3
Versailles, Treaty of (1919), 138, 144, 189, 356
Via Claudia Augusta, Germany, 116
Vichy France, 31
Vienna, Austria, 41, 86, 134, 138, 181, 248
Vilnius ghetto, Lithuania, 152
Vistula river, 249, 322, 325, 348, 354
Vltava river, 246–7, 348
Vltava (Smetana), 280–81
Vöhrenbach, Germany, 52
Volkswagen group, 78
Vosges mountains, 20
Vrba, Rudolf, 13–14, 16–18, *18*, 25, 360
Vrba-Wetzler Report, 14, 268
Vysoké Mýto, Czech Republic, 279–80, 282

Wager, Bebo, 97
Wagner, Richard, 239
Wagner, Robert, 16–17, *18*
Wałęsa, Lech, 315
Wankheim, Germany, 59, 60

Wannsee Conference (January 1942), 212, 228, 334–5
War of the Spanish Succession (1701–14), 88
Warsaw, Poland, 315–16, 325
Warsaw Uprising (1944), 249, 315–16, 322
Wawel Castle, Kraków, 313, 323, 354
Weber, Ilse, 237, *238*
Weil, Simone, 105
Weiner, Alfred, 268
Weissenburg in Bayern, Germany, 116–17
Wellington College, Berkshire, 240
Wells, Alastair, 5, 117–18, 166
Welzová, Emilie, 277, *277*
Wenceslas II, King of Bohemia, 195, 206
Werner, Alfred, 51
West Ukrainian People's Republic, 312
West-Eastern Divan Orchestra, 240
West, Rebecca, 148
Westerbork transit camp, Netherlands, 345–6
Western Front Way, 4–7, 35, 199–200
Westminster Hour (radio programme), 87
Westphalia, Peace of (1648), 33, 55, 90
Wetzler, Alfred, 14
White Mountain, Battle of (1620), 181, 206–7
'White Rose' anti-Nazi movement, 67–8, 113
White Rose Foundation, 71
Wiener, Alfred, 25–8, *25*, 344
Wiesel, Elie, 336–7
Wildt, Michael, 108–9
Wilfred and Eileen (Smith), 211
Wilhelm II, German Kaiser, 85, *86*, 144, 170, *170*
Willett, Marjorie, 9

Windermere, Lake District, 320
Winter's Tale, The (Shakespeare), 207
Winton, Nicholas, 229–30, *230*
Witkoff, Steve, 224, 261
Wittenberg, Germany, 108
Wolf's Lair, Rastenburg, Poland, 215
Woods, John C., 149
World at War, The (TV series), 49–50, 150
World Jewish Relief, 320
World War I (1914–18), 4, 15–16, 20–21, 30, 104, 232
   Armistice (11 November 1918), 16
   Czechoslovak Legion, 182
   German Spring Offensive, 15–16
   Kilometre Zero, 4, 14–15, *15*
   Maginot Line, 20–21
   Poland and, 314
   Schlieffen Plan, 87
   Treaty of Versailles (1919), 138, 144, 189, 356
   war crimes, 143–4
World War II (1939–45), 16–17, 30–31, 131, 199, 203, 273, 353–6
   80th anniversary, 7, 273, 288, 353–5
   allied bombing raids, 66, 90–92, 109, *109*, 145, 148, 162, 275
   allied invasion of Germany, 31
   appeasement, 185–6
   atomic bombs, 146
   Battle of Britain (1940), 180, 315
   'Colmar Pocket' offensive, 30–31
   D-Day (6 June 1944), 68–9
   eightieth anniversary of, 7
   German POW camps, 54
   German repatriation, 192
   German surrender, 293–4
   Italian surrender, 294
   liberation, 248–9
   London Blitz, 145
   murder of Jews, 69–70
   Nuremberg Trials (1945–46), 34, 95, 141–54, *149*
   Poland and, 283, 314–16, 332
   post-war displaced persons, 62–4
   post-war rebuilding project, 93
   war crimes, 144–5
   see also Holocaust; Nazism
Wörnitz river, 87

Xi Jinping, 9, 273

Yad Vashem Holocaust Museum, Jerusalem, 27, 32, 123, 162, 287, 326
Yalta Conference (1945), 145, 180, 203, 310, 319
Yushchenko, Viktor, 169

Záměček Memorial, Pardubice, 276
Zander, Alfred, 24–5
Žantovský, Michael, 223–5
Zawacka, Elżbieta, 316–18, *317*
Zelensky, Volodymyr, 240
Zemmour, Éric, 23
Zhukov, Georgy, 294
Zimmermann, Samuel, 96
Zionist Congress (Basel, 1897), 22–2
Zola, Émile, 23
Zuckerberg, Mark, 338
Zyklon B gas, 263, 335